A LIFE IN ART:

Harry Wilcox and the
Woman with Dreamy Eyes

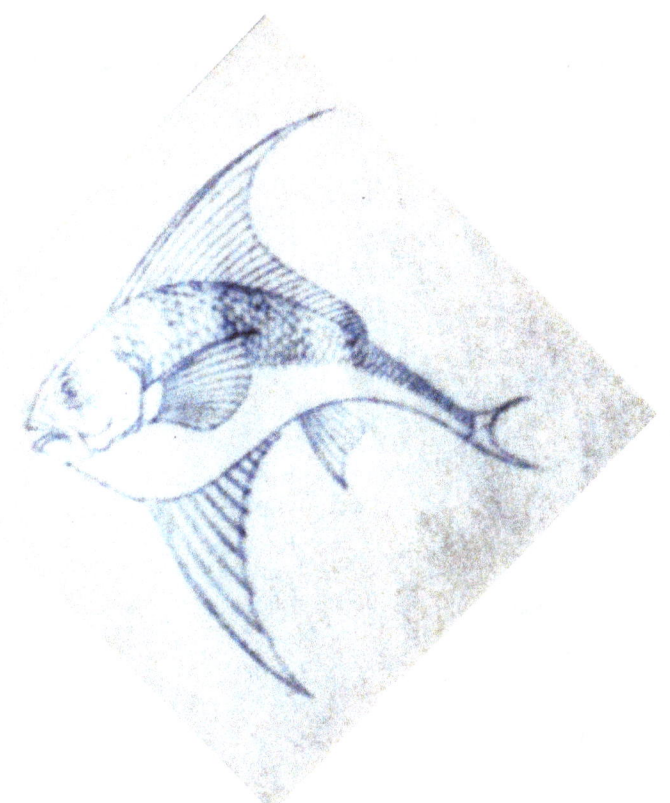

by
Joyce Wilcox Graff
and
James Hammond Wilcox

Cover art: Fish, by Harry Wilcox. Water color and air brush, 10.5 x 26.5 inches

Frontispiece: Fish Study by Harry Wilcox. Pencil, 3.75 x 3.75 inches.

ISBN: 978-0-9882579-0-0 (paperback)
ISBN: 978-0-9882579-5-5 (hardcover)
ISBN: 978-0-9882579-3-1 (deluxe hardcover)
ISBN: 978-0-9882579-4-8 (electronic book)
ISBN: 978-0-9882579-3-1 (e-html fixed format)

Library of Congress Control Number: 2012949714

 Registered Trademark

Garnet Star Publishing, Boston, Massachusetts

Printed in the United States of America

Praise for A Life in Art

A LIFE IN ART is a fascinating picture of the life and times of an American commercial artist in the years before, during and after the Great Depression. It is masterfully brought to life with a comprehensive collection of illustrations — not only of Harry Wilcox's works of art — but also with photos of people, places and artifacts from his and his ancestors' lives... [includes] genealogical information about the families that make up the direct line of Wilcox descent beginning in 1565 in England.
— *Ann Hege Hughes, Genealogical Publishing*

Inspiring ... stories of the Wilcox clan and its allied families, many lines of which converge and flourish in Williamsport, Lycoming County. I thoroughly enjoyed reading this work. It allowed me entry into the life of an interesting and dynamic individual ... I am all the richer for having met Harry Wilcox, artist.
— *Gary Parks, Executive Director, Lycoming County Historical Society, Pennsylvania*

Well written and a delight to read. Joyce and Jim have told Harry Wilcox's story in the context of his family, his location and his times. The use of family photos and Harry's art work throughout hold the attention of readers of all ages and enrich the story. End notes allow the story to unfold without interruption while providing supporting documentation.
— *Lou-Jean Rehn, Certified Genealogist, Colorado*

DEDICATED

to our mother,
June Freed Wilcox

and to the memory of our father
Harry Hammond Wilcox Jr.

and to all our children

We entrust you with all our love and our memories
of all our forebears who have made us what we are.

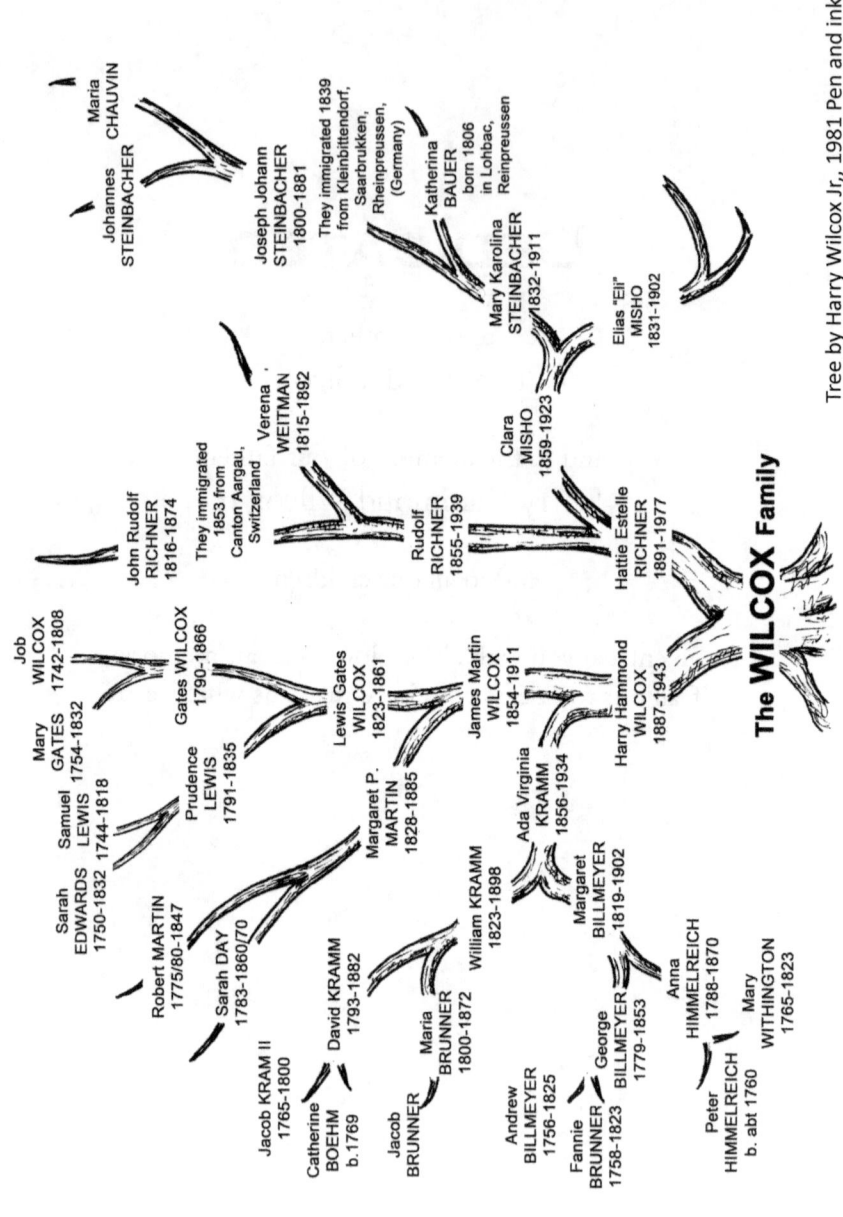

The WILCOX Family

Tree by Harry Wilcox Jr., 1981 Pen and ink.

Johannes STEINBACHER
Maria CHAUVIN

Joseph Johann STEINBACHER
1800-1881

They immigrated 1839 from Kleinbittendorf, Saarbrukken, Rheinpreussen, (Germany)

Katherina BAUER
born 1806 in Lohbac, Reinpreussen

Mary Karolina STEINBACHER
1832-1911

Elias "Eli" MISHO
1831-1902

Clara MISHO
1859-1923

John Rudolf RICHNER
1816-1874

They immigrated 1853 from Canton Aargau, Switzerland

Verena WEITMAN
1815-1892

Rudolf RICHNER
1855-1939

Hattie Estelle RICHNER
1891-1977

Job WILCOX
1742-1808

Mary GATES
1754-1832

Samuel LEWIS
1744-1818

Gates WILCOX
1790-1866

Prudence LEWIS
1791-1835

Lewis Gates WILCOX
1823-1861

Sarah EDWARDS
1750-1832

Margaret P. MARTIN
1828-1885

James Martin WILCOX
1854-1911

Robert MARTIN
1775/80-1847

Sarah DAY
1783-1860/70

Ada Virginia KRAMM
1856-1934

Harry Hammond WILCOX
1887-1943

Jacob KRAM II
1765-1800

Catherine BOEHM
b.1769

David KRAMM
1793-1882

William KRAMM
1823-1898

Margaret BILLMEYER
1819-1902

Jacob BRUNNER

Maria BRUNNER
1800-1872

Andrew BILLMEYER
1756-1825

George BILLMEYER
1779-1853

Anna HIMMELREICH
1788-1870

Fannie BRUNNER
1758-1823

Peter HIMMELREICH
b. abt 1760

Mary WITHINGTON
1765-1823

iv

CONTENTS

CATALOG OF PORTFOLIO

The following works of Harry Wilcox Sr. appear in this book.

Works by Verna Wilcox Alair

Works by Harry Wilcox Jr "Bud"

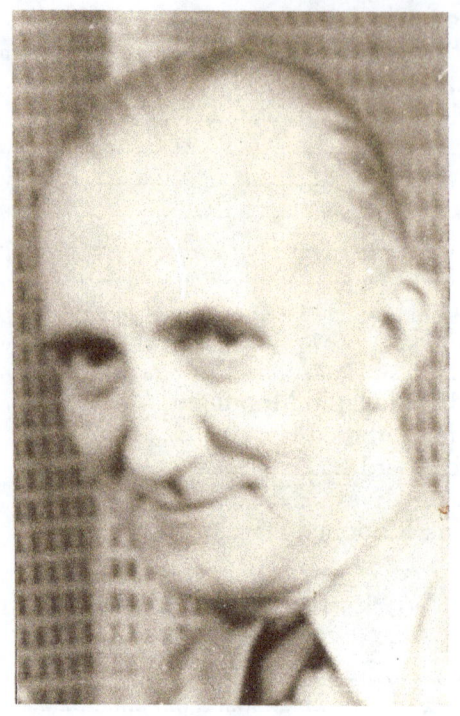

Harry H. Wilcox

Acknowledgements

We never knew our grandfather. Of the four of us who are his grandchildren, Meredith was four when he died, and the rest of us were born after his death in 1943. Yet we were surrounded by his spirit, his art, and the fond memories recounted to us by our father, his son.

As ever, when there is a body of art to be divided among two children and four grandchildren, there were disagreements about who should get what. We realized early that there would never be enough originals to go around, but perhaps there could be copies. In the 1980's Joyce traveled to visit our Aunt Verna in Detroit and her son Meredith, also in Michigan, and photographed the paintings by our grandfather in their possession.

In the 1990's, Aunt Verna's house was destroyed by fire, taking with it the largest number of our grandfather's paintings. Joyce's photographs now comprise the bulk of his extant work. Through the photographs and this book, we pass his work along to our children and our children's children.

Harry Wilcox was a quiet man with a sly sense of humor who loved his feisty wife and their children. The profession he embraced no longer exists in the same form it did for him in 1910-1943. Much of what he did then by hand for illustration, animation, advertising, and mapmaking is done today with photography, clip art, and computer graphics. He retouched photographs, created flattering representations of articles for sale, added charming illustrations to the Story Section of the Williamsport *Grit*, and drew maps for the War Department. He was one of the pioneers of the advancement of air brushing techniques for photo retouching and commercial art. The fish picture on the cover of this book demonstrates his mastery of the air brush.

Jim is the genealogist who has spent many years tromping through cemeteries with our Dad and poring through deeds and census records and piles of original documents, scanning mountains of old photos, gathering thousands of relations back to Europe, including many who fought in the American Revolution and other conflicts throughout the history of this nation.

Joyce is the more academic researcher and writer who has glued this all together. We could not have done this without the kind assistance of our mother June Freed Wilcox, our sister Margaret Wilcox Smith, our cousin Meredith Alair, and cousins George A. "Jim" Richner Jr., Ed Richner, and Norman Cole. Many thanks to all of you for the stories and photographs you have shared.

It has been a wonderful partnership. Researching this work and these times has revealed much about a struggle to make a living doing piece work during the Depression. We hope that you will enjoy these insights into our grandfather's life and art.

And special thanks to our father, Harry Hammond Wilcox Jr., who is called "Bud" in this book as he was in his family growing up, whose memory we cherish and who inspired us with the love and honor he always expressed for his own father, our grandfather, Harry Wilcox the artist.

Joyce Wilcox Graff
James Hammond Wilcox
2012

Chapter 1: Roots

Harry Hammond Wilcox was born in 1887, the son of James Martin Wilcox and Ada Virginia Kramm Wilcox in the village of Limestoneville, Pennsylvania, a crossroads in a farming community that had been created by his great-grandfather David Kramm, in 1835, just north of the Chillisquaque Creek.[1]

Harry's father James was a butcher in Williamsport, and the family lived at 1100 Isabella Street, Williamsport. The family spent most weekends "in the country" in Limestoneville, while James stayed "in town" in Williamsport working as a butcher in a grocery store. During the summer, when school was not in session, the children stayed mostly in the country.

Harry grew up surrounded by the beauty of Montour County, nestled among the rolling foothills of the Allegheny Mountains, on the farm of his grandfather, William Kramm, in a house William had built for his daughter, Ada Virginia, Harry's mother.[2]

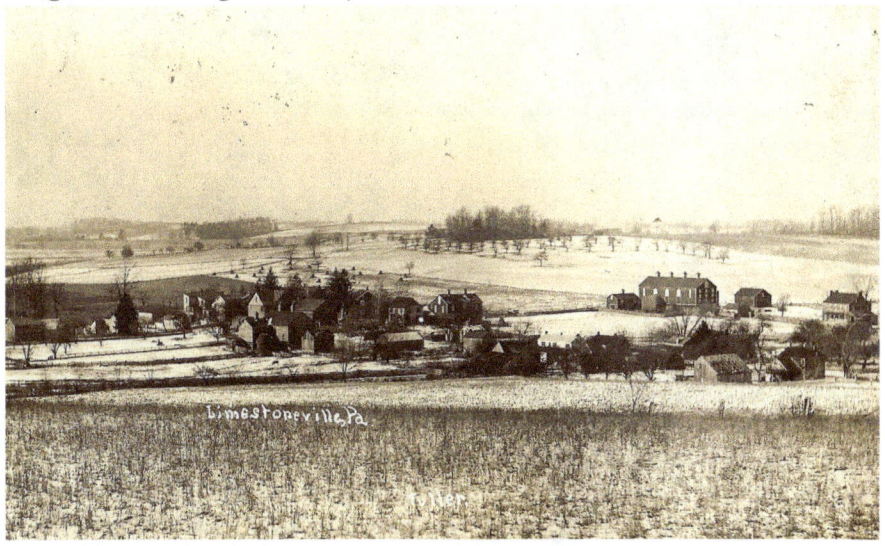

Kramm farm, Limestoneville, Pennsylvania, 1900.
Postcard from Aunt Til to Ada Virginia.

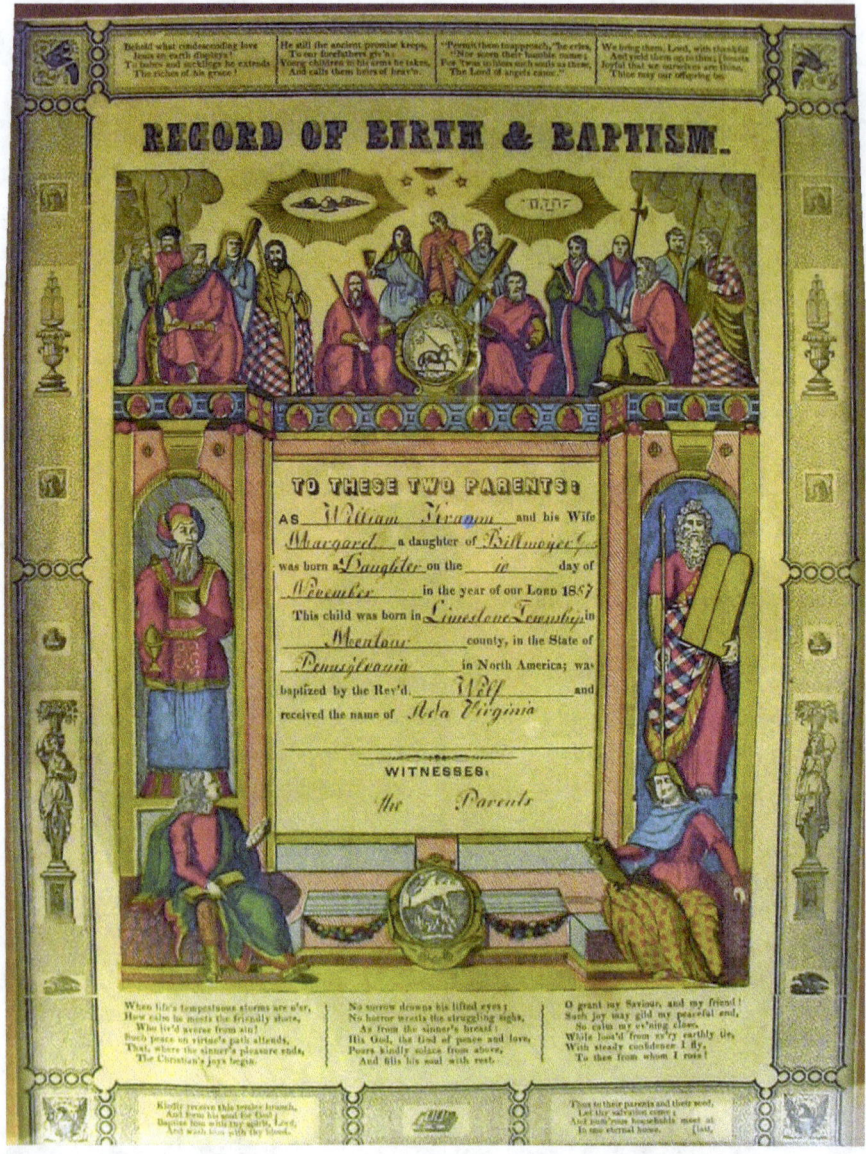

Birth record of Ada Virginia Kramm, Harry's mother. "To these two parents, as William Kramm and his wife Margaret, a daughter of George Billmeyer, was born a daughter on the 10th day of November in the year of our Lord 1857. This child was born in Limestone Township in Montour County, in the State of Pennsylvania in North America; was baptized by the Reverend Wolf, and received the name of Ada Virginia. Witnesses: the parents."

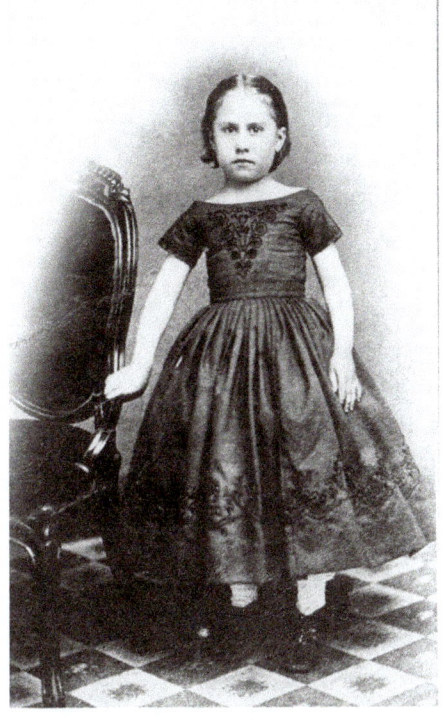

Ada Virginia Kramm

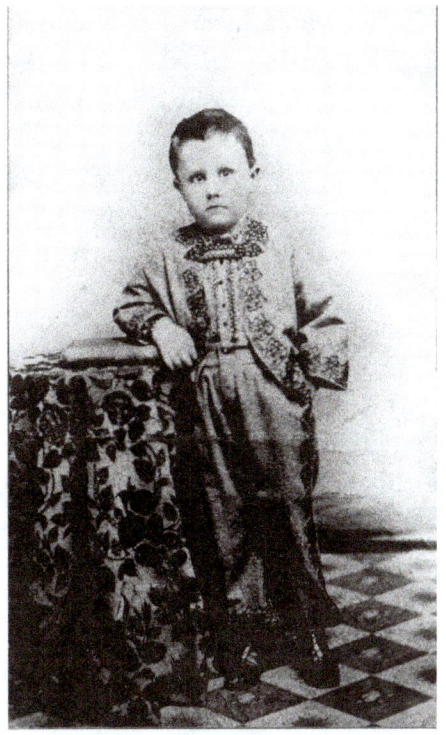

Ada's brother,
William Hammond (Ham) Kramm

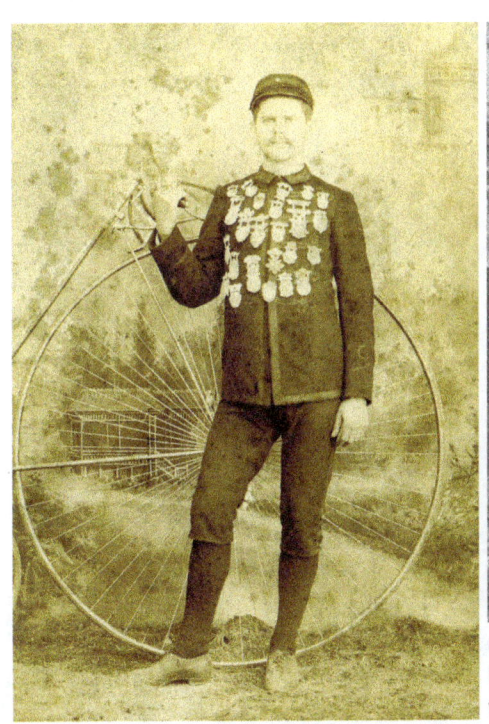

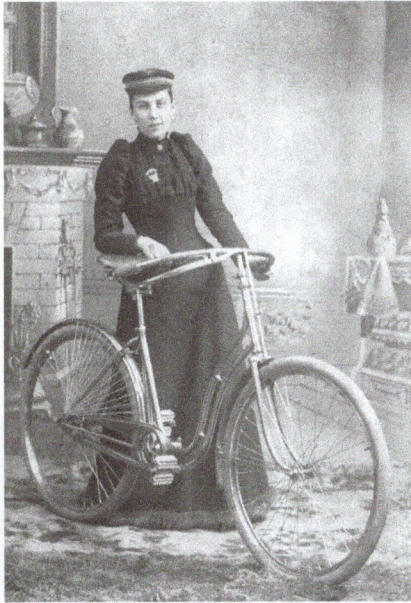

Uncle Harry Hammond Kramm, champion bicyclist, and his wife Carrie Geise Kramm who also rode in competition. See p. 219.

The Kramm farm spanned hundreds of acres, a family farm that raised food for the growing family as well as for sale. There was corn, barley, wheat, hay for livestock, and a variety of vegetables for the family. The barn was built with an overhang on the sides to minimize the amount of rain and water runoff from the roof that might get blown into the dairy barn.

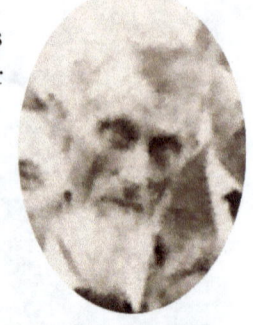

David Kramm, 1881

About 1835, David Kramm left his home in the Saucon Valley of central eastern Pennsylvania and settled on a large tract of rich farming land in Limestone township, Montour County, Pennsylvania. David and Maria Brunner Kramm had fourteen children. Over the years he built houses on the land for several of his children, and subdivided the property.

The only known picture of David Kramm was taken at the wedding celebration of his grandson William Hammond "Ham" Kramm, to Huldah Fisher in 1881.

William Kramm is found in the 1870 Census with real estate valued at $29,200 — quite a sizable farm for the day. William Kramm was born in 1823 in Lehigh Co., Pennsylvania, and died in 1898. His wife Margaret Billmeyer, a daughter of George and Anna Himmelreich Billmeyer, was born 1819 and died in 1902. With Billmeyer families all over the area, there was no shortage of cousins.

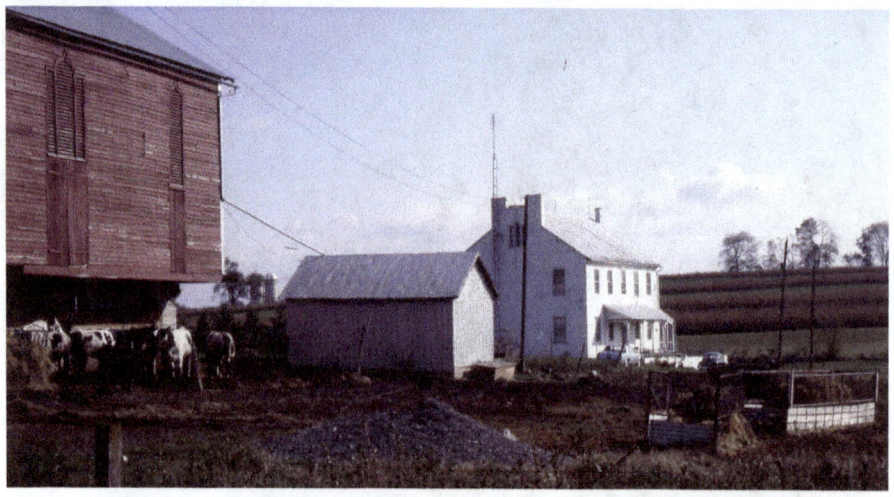

William Kramm's farmhouse and barn in Limestoneville. Photo taken 2009.

6

The house built for Ada Virginia was on the southeast corner of the crossroads that is Limestoneville. It was in this house that Harry Wilcox was born. Ada's brother, Ham Kramm, lived with his wife on the northwest corner, and ran the mercantile store on the southeast corner, the right-hand side of Ada's double house.

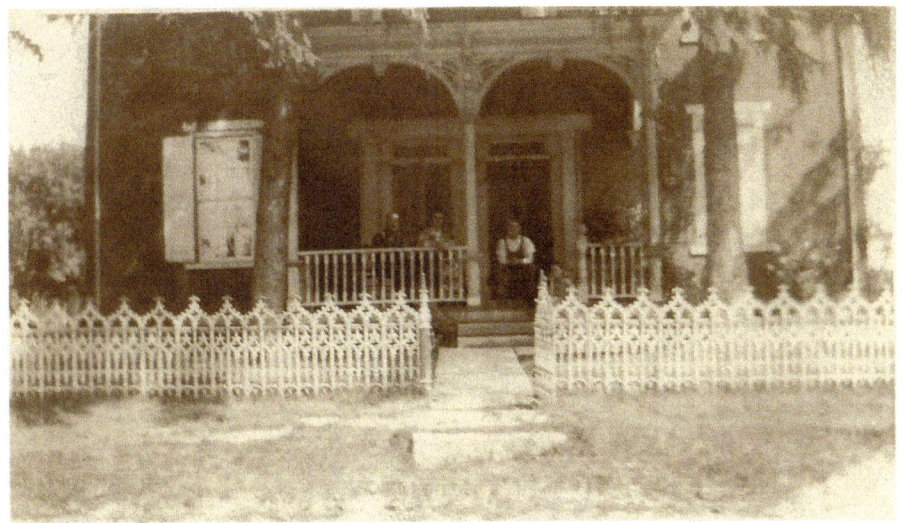

Aunt Til's house, Anna Matilda Kramm Kaufman, Mrs. Oliver Kaufman.

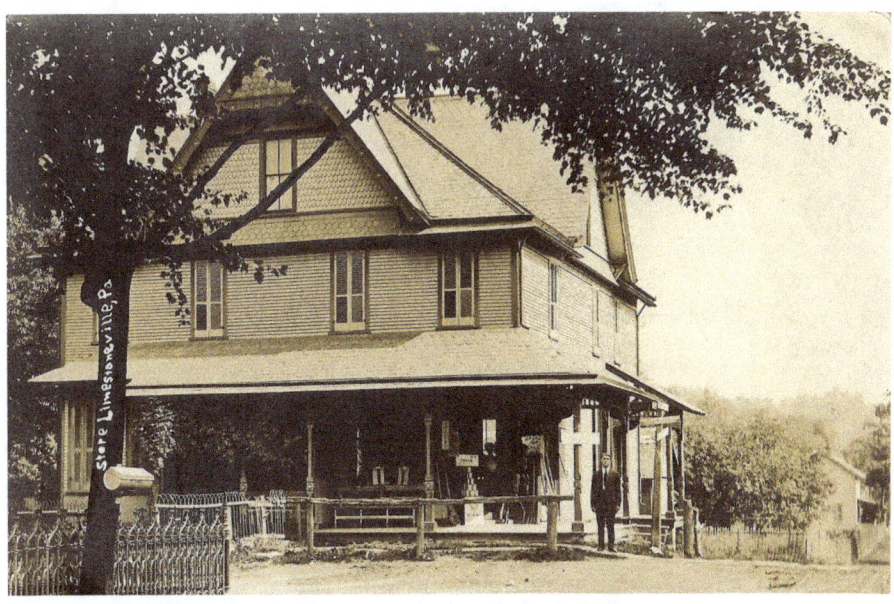

Ham Kramm's general store at Limestoneville. Ada Virginia lived in the left-hand side of this double house, and Harry was born in this house.

Ham and Huldah are found in the 1900 census for Liberty, Montour County, Pennsylvania, with her parents living with them in Limestoneville. In that census we learn that Huldah was the mother of eight children with none living. They lost all their children before the age of three. His family plot in the Harmony Cemetery in Milton, Pennsylvania, tells part of the story. We know two of the children by name:

- Homer Fisher Kramm, born 29 June 1884 and died 23 March 1887
- Hermon Billmeyer Kramm, born 12 September 1888 and died 7 December 1889

and there are several small markers with no inscriptions for babies who died in early infancy.

After Ham died in 1905, Huldah Fisher Kramm sold their house to Ada Virginia and went to Anglesea, New Jersey. The 1910 census for Bloomsburg, Columbia County, Pennsylvania, finds the widow Huldah Fisher, age 47, living with her brother, William H. Fisher, his wife Mary, and their widowed father Daniel Fisher, age 87. Huldah died in 1916 in Milton, Pennsylvania, at the home of her niece.

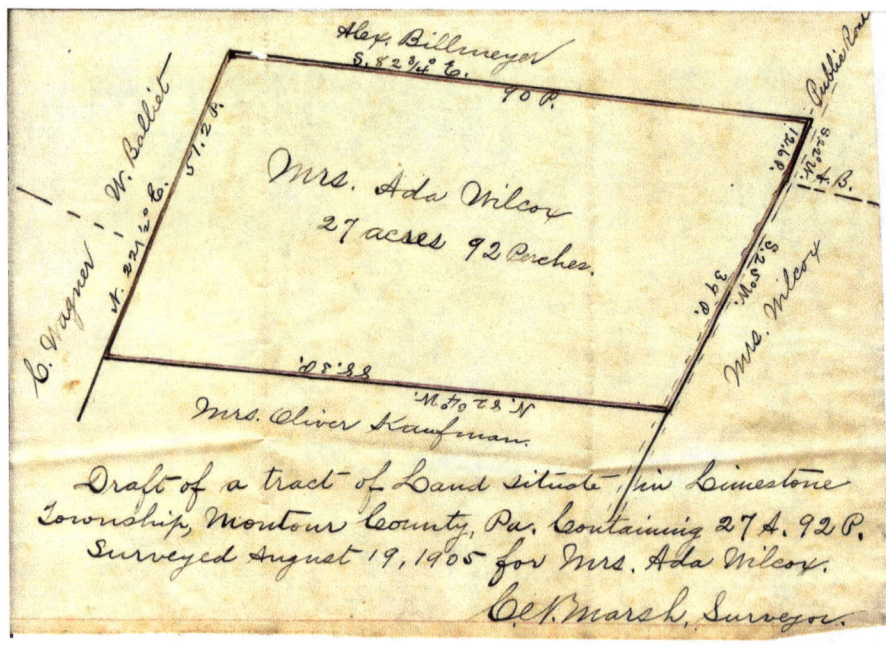

Survey done for Ada Virginia Kramm Wilcox in 1905, showing the adjacent plots owned by her siblings.

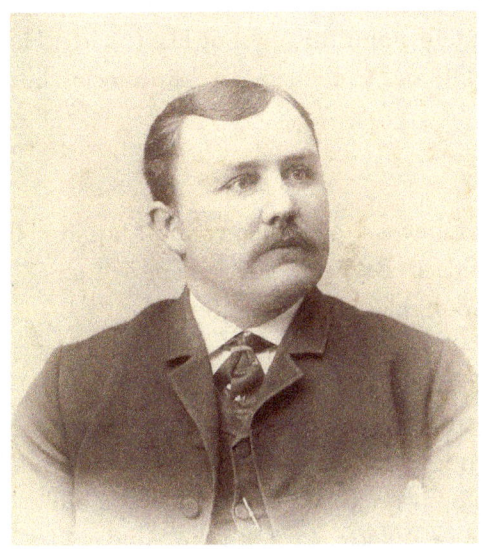
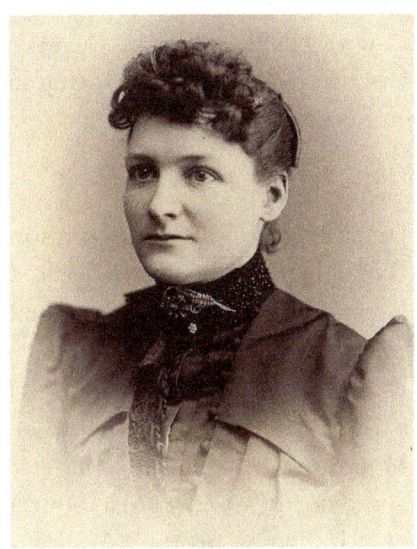

William Hammond Kramm,
his wife Huldah Fisher Kramm

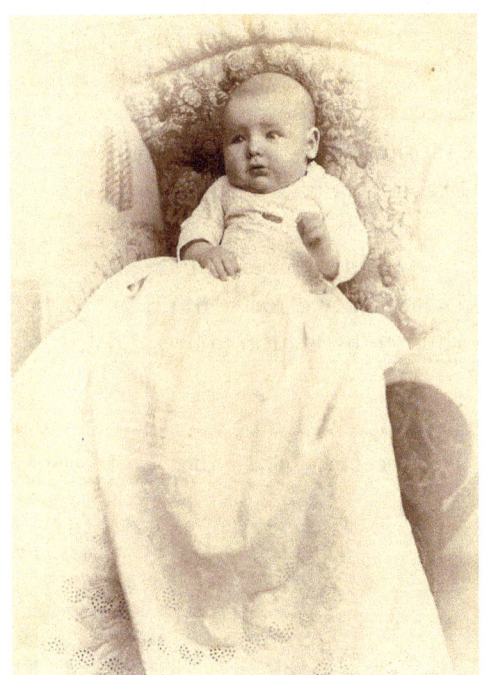
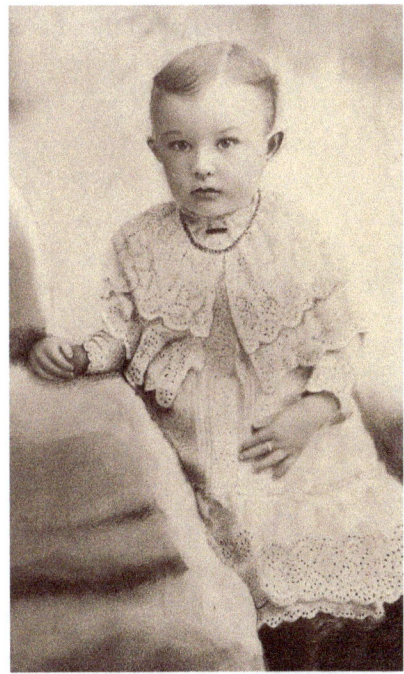

Hermon Kramm, 1888-1889
died age 14 months

Homer Kramm, 1884-1887
died age 2 years 9 months

Ada Virginia moved into Ham's house on the northwest corner. Limestoneville would be the grounding-point throughout Harry's life. He was tied to his large and loving family, and to the land of Limestoneville and Pennsylvania.

James Martin Wilcox was the son of Lewis Gates Wilcox and Margaret P. Martin. He was one of seven children: Bruce, Sadie, Adolphus Lee, James, Daniel, William (who died young), and Lewis Gates Jr.[3]

James had also been reared on a farm. His boyhood days were spent in a neat two story log house on the site now occupied by a frame house in Montoursville, near the concrete bridge built across Turkey Run creek, at the northeast corner of Four Mile Drive. When that bridge was built in 1913, James' brother, Adolphus Lee Wilcox, wrote to the Sunday *Grit*, sharing an account of the "Good Old Time" when pigeons, wolves, and game were plentiful in Montoursville.

> "This log house was the home of [my] grandfather, Robert Martin, and in it Mr. and Mrs. Martin, who had been Sarah Day, reared a family of five boys and six girls. When Mr. Martin died, he left his land to his children, having set aside for each one a parcel of ten acres. Margaret Martin became Mrs. Lewis Gates Wilcox, [my mother] and the Wilcox' family of six boys and one girl were brought up on the ten acre tract that had fallen to Mrs. Wilcox.
>
> "In those days … deer and wild turkey came right up to human habitation in broad day,

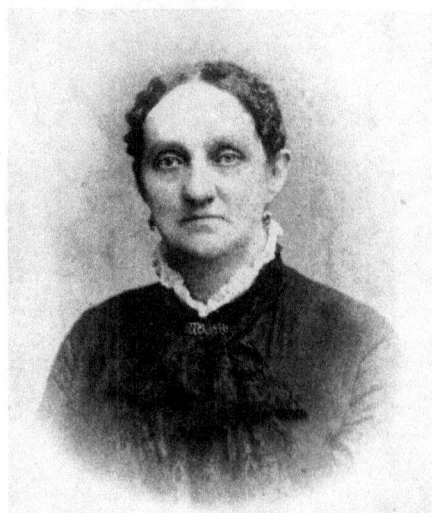

Left:
Margaret P. Martin Wilcox,
mother of those pictured on the next page.

Next page:
James Martin Wilcox and his siblings
Top row:
Lewis Gates Wilcox Jr
James Martin Wilcox
Center:
Bruce, Adolphus, and Dan Wilcox
Bottom row:
Sarah "Sadie" Wilcox Follmer
and her husband Pete Follmer

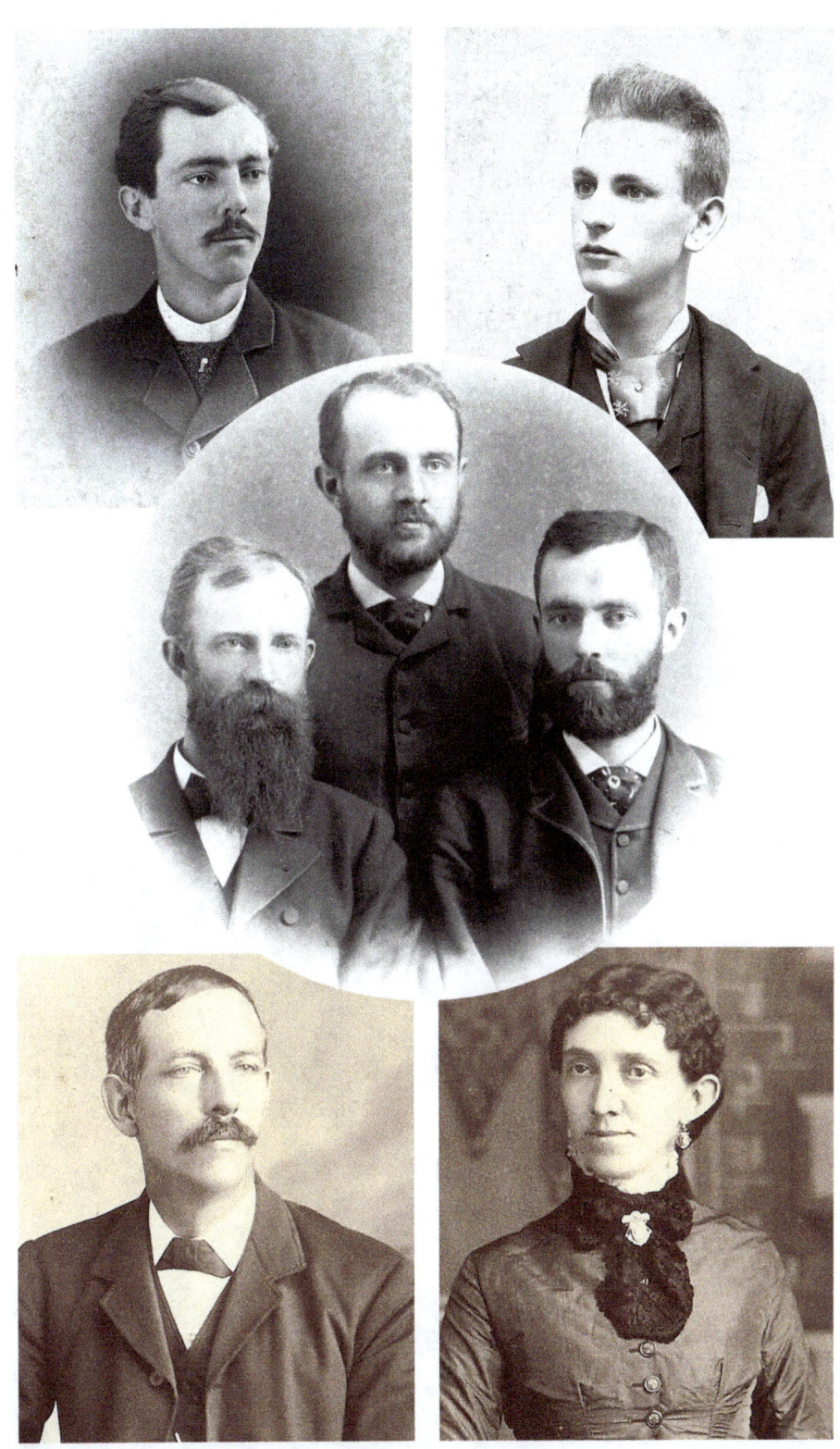

and in fall and spring farmers often made more money from the sale of wild pigeons they killed as the flocks passed north in spring and south in fall, than they did from some of their crops, shipping the birds by the barrel to the larger cities. The howling of wolves was a familiar sound during the nights, especially in winter, and wild animals — game and beasts of prey — abounded."[4]

James worked with Fred Houck, who ran a grocery, "Meat, Vegetables, and Provisions" on West 4th Street in Williamsport, east of Campbell Street, on the south side of the street. Fred was married to his cousin, Ida May Shearer. James is usually listed as a butcher in city directories and census records. He did not own his own store, but it is more correct to say that he ran the butcher department of the store.[5]

Nonetheless, James had a sensitive and artistic side, as shown in his handwriting. They married in 1880.

James M. Wlcox, butcher at F. J. Houck's grocery, "Meat, Vegetables, and Provisions" on West 4th Street, Williamsport.

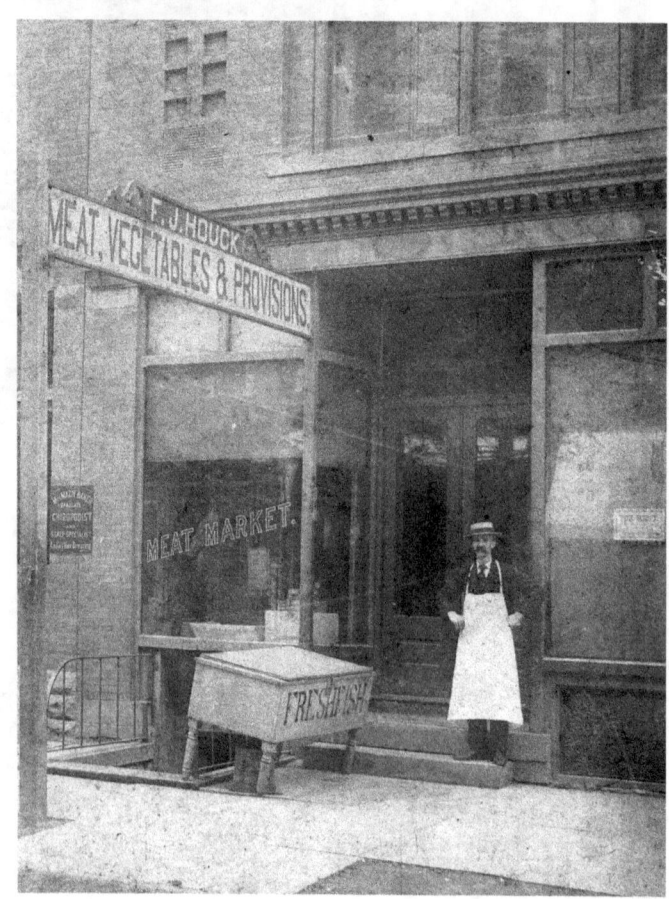

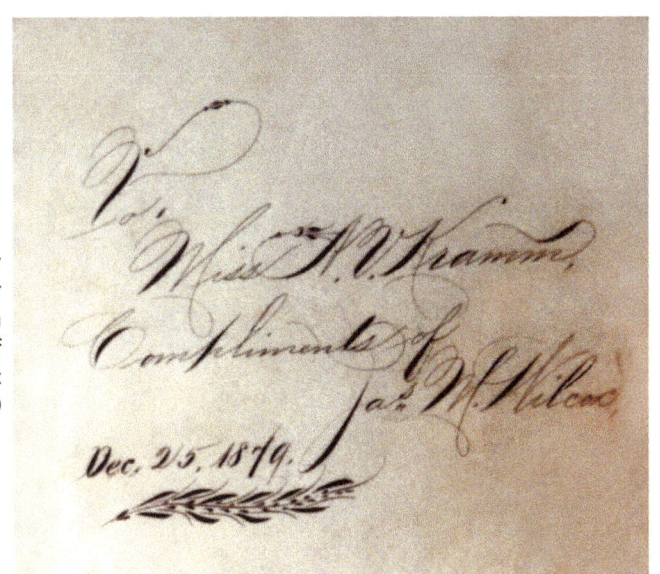

Inscription in a book:
For
Miss A. V. Kramm
Compliments of
James M. Wilcox
Dec. 25, 1879

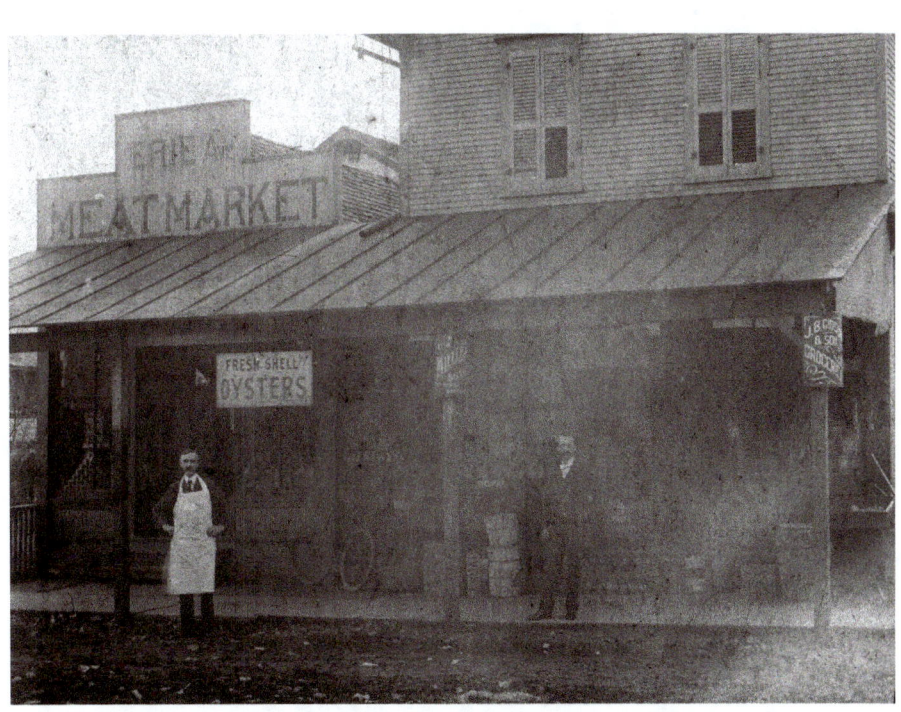

James M. Wilcox standing outside the Meat Market in his butcher apron.
The Meat Market was part of J. B. Gibson & Sons, Grocers
at 1061 Erie Avenue, Williamsport.

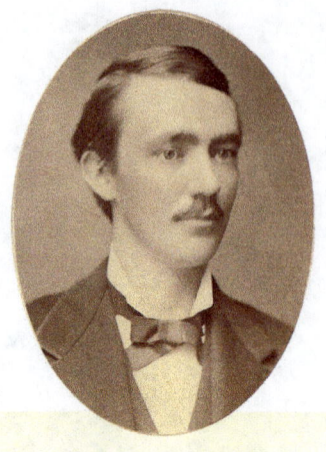

James M. Wilcox

Mr. & Mrs. Wm. Kramm

Request the pleasure of your company

at the marriage of their daughter,

Ada,

— TO —

James M. Wilcox,

Tuesday Afternoon, Dec. 14, 1880.

CEREMONY AT 2 O'CLOCK.

LIMESTONEVILLE, PA.

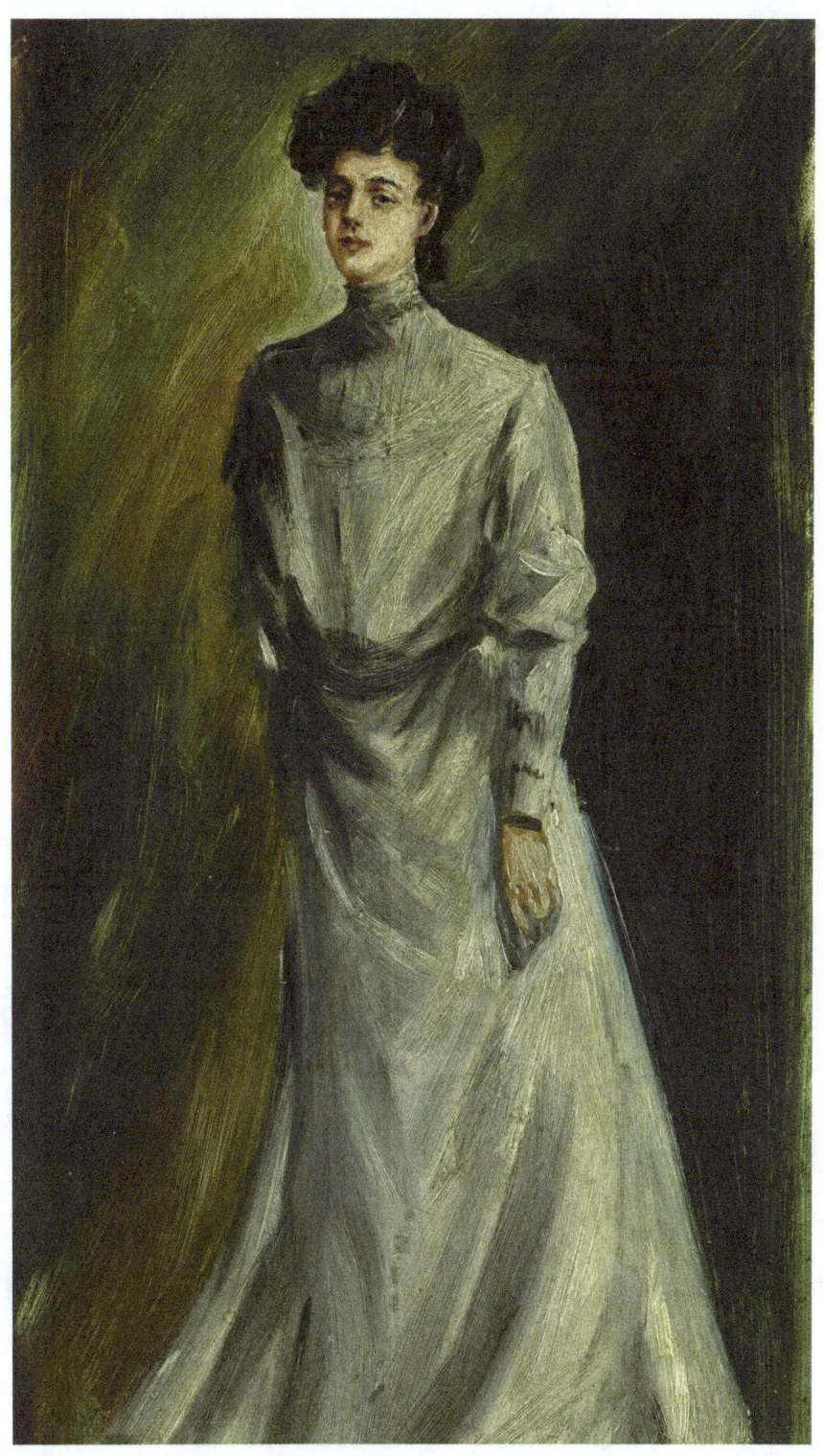

Ada Virginia Kramm Wilcox, portrait in oil, signed "A. Pelz"

Ada and James set up housekeeping in Limestoneville among Ada's large extended family, with James' family nearby in Williamsport and Montoursville. They were deeply rooted in the land and history of Pennsylvania.

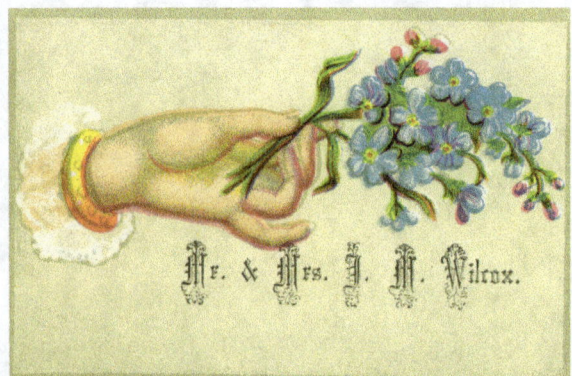

Printed calling card:
Mr. & Mrs. J. M. Wilcox

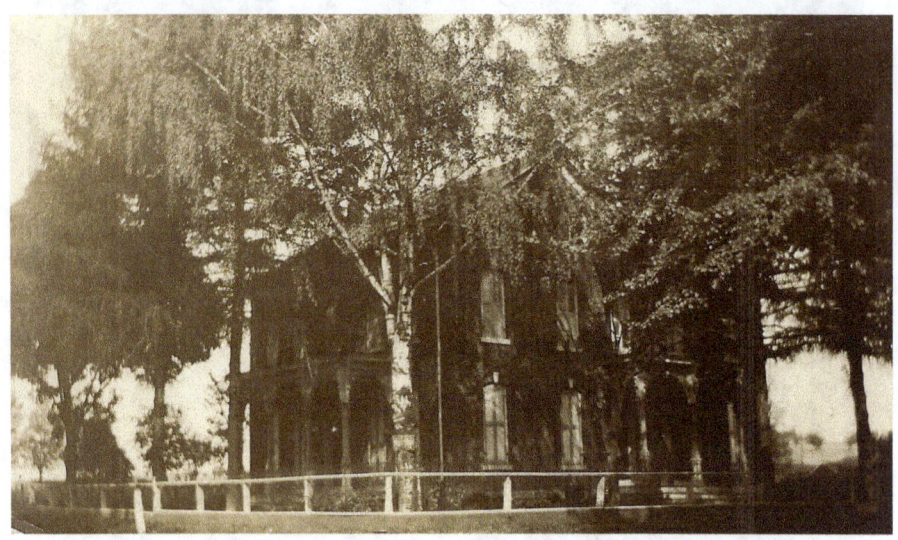

Ham Kramm's home in Limestoneville. After Ham's death Ada bought the house from his widow Huldah, and moved into this house.
This is the house built by David Kramm for his son, William Kramm, where the Golden Wedding pctures on the following pages were taken.

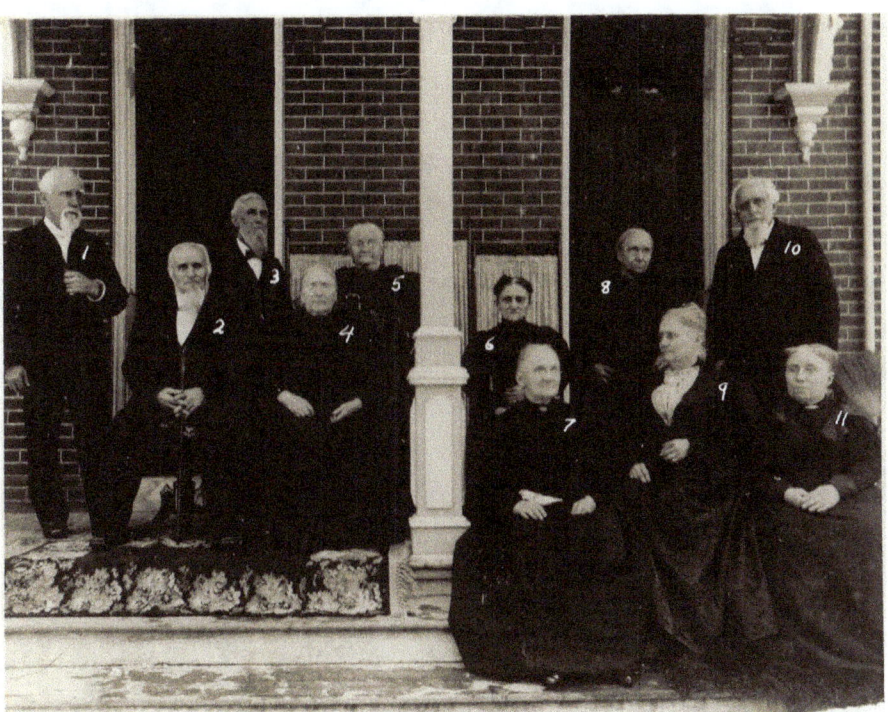

Photograph of the children of David and Mary Brunner Kramm
on the occasion of the Golden Wedding Celebration for William and Margaret Billmeyer Kramm. This photo that on the following pages were taken on the east side porch of the home of their son William Hammond "Ham" Kramm on the northwest corner of the crossroad at Limestoneville, Montour Co. Pennsylvania. The date was 5 Feb 1896 and the photographer was H.B. Montgomery of Milton, Pennsylvania. Some time after 1936, this house had its porches completely removed, and the house was covered with clapboard siding.

Numbered Left to Right:
1. Edward Kramm
2. William Kramm
3. Reuben Kramm
4. Margaret Billmeyer Kramm, wife of William Kramm
5. Maria Kramm Billmeyer, wife of Martin Billmeyer Jr.
6. Susanna Kramm Hunsinger, wife of William Hunsinger
7. Matilda Kramm Billmeyer, wife of Charles Billmeyer
8. Sarah Ann Kramm Ravert, wife of Charles Ravert
9. Christianna Kramm Bird, wife of Joseph Bird
10. Ephraim Kramm
11. Tavilla Kramm Koch, wife of Daniel Koch

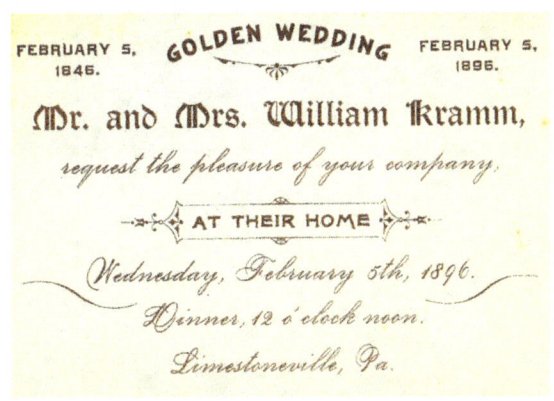

FEBRUARY 5, 1846.   GOLDEN WEDDING   FEBRUARY 5, 1896.

Mr. and Mrs. William Kramm,

request the pleasure of your company,

⟶⟶ AT THEIR HOME ⟵⟵

Wednesday, February 5th, 1896.

Dinner, 12 o'clock noon.

Limestoneville, Pa.

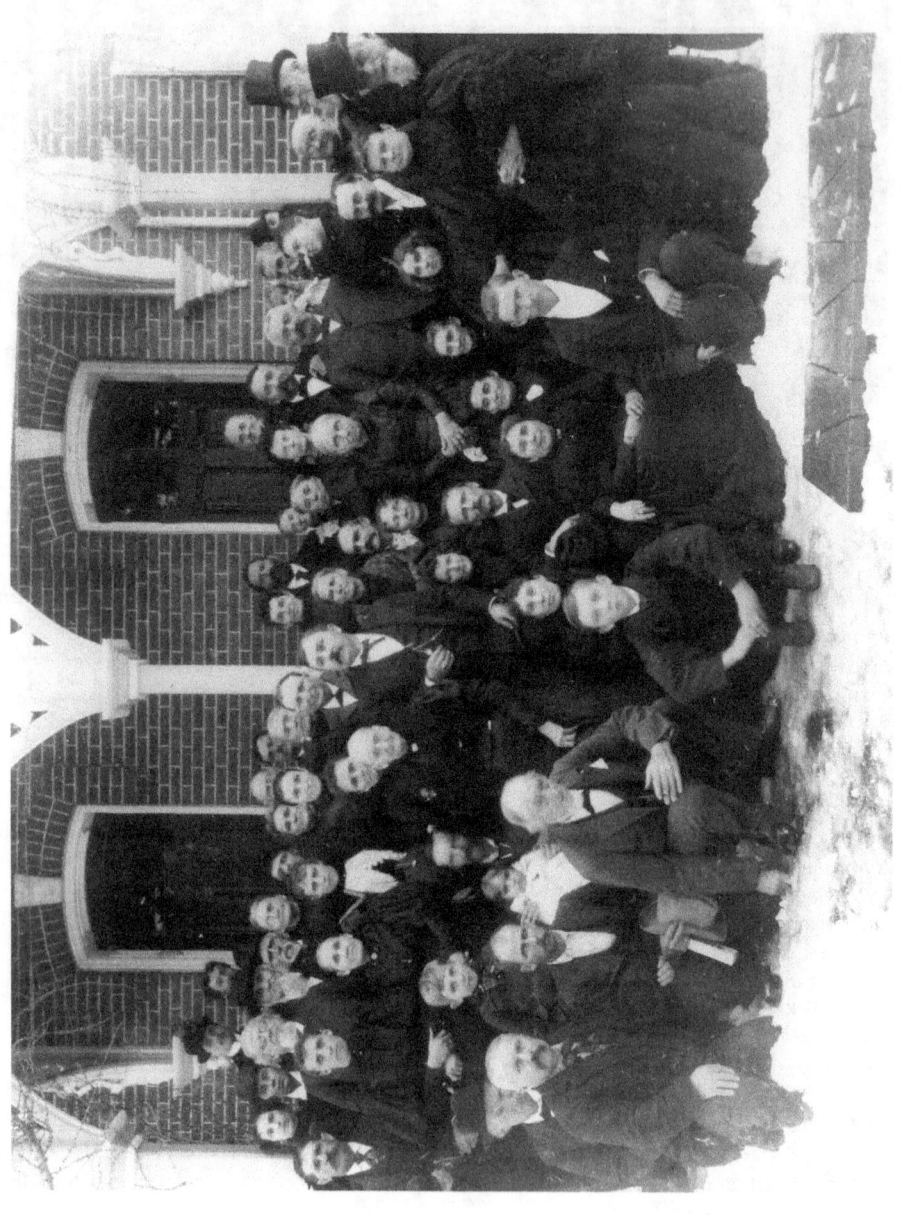

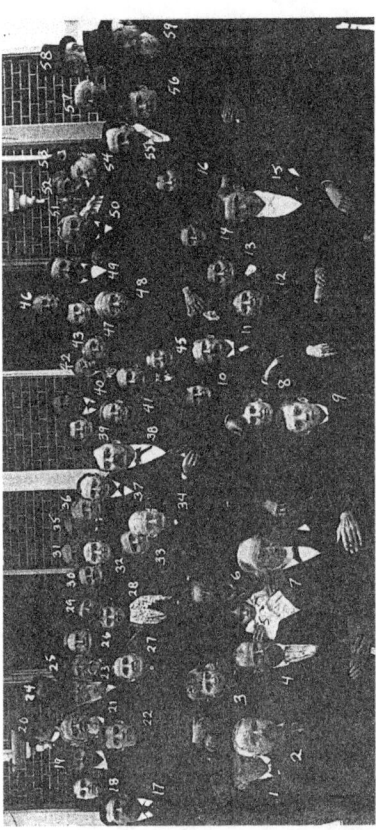

Photograph of relatives and friends at the Golden Wedding Celebration for William and Margaret Billmeyer Kramm on 5 Feb 1896. This photo was taken on the east side porch of the home of their son, William Hammond Kramm, on the northwest corner of the crossroads at Limestoneville, Montour Co. Pennsylvania. The photographer was H.B. Montgomery of Milton, Pennslyvania.

1. William Davis, a neighbor; 2. Reuben Billmeyer, son of Maria Kramm Billmeyer; 3. Harry Hammond Wilcox, son of James Martin and Ada V. Kramm Wilcox; 4. James Murray, a neighbor; 5. Verna Margaret Wilcox, daughter of James Martin and Ada V. Kramm Wilcox; 6. James Martin Wilcox, husband of Ada Virginia Kramm; 7. Daniel Fisher, father of Huldah E. Fisher Kramm; 8. Ada Virginia Kramm Wilcox (Mrs. James Martin Wilcox); 9. Warren Kramm Wilcox, son of James Martin and Ada V. Kramm Wilcox; 10. Huldah E. Fisher Kramm (Mrs. William H. Kramm); 11. William D. Steinbach; 12. Anna Matilda Kramm Kaufman (Mrs. Oliver I. Kaufman); 13. Adah M. Steinbach (Mrs. William D. Steinbach), daughter of Matilda Billmeyer Kramm; 14. Emma Billmeyer (Mrs. William Billmeyer); 15. Wilbur Steinbach, son of Adah and W. D. Steinbach, and future husband of Grace Billmeyer; 16. Grace Billmeyer, daughter of Emma J. Ryan and William Billmeyer; 17. Oliver I. Kaufman, husband of Anna Matilda Kramm Kaufman; 18. Hattie Martin, future wife of Clyde B. Kaufman; 19. Clyde Benton Kaufman, son of Anna Matilda Kramm and Oliver Kaufman; 20. Myron Francis Kaufman, son of Anna Matilda Kramm and Oliver Kaufman; 21. George Billmeyer Jr, brother of Margaret Billmeyer Kramm; 22. William Kramm; 24. Sarah "Sadie" Reed, future wife of Myron F. Kaufman; 25. Edward Kramm; 28. Sarah Ann Billmeyer Montgomery (Mrs. H. B. Montgomery), the wife of the photographer and daughter of Hannah "Flora" and Henry Billmeyer; 32. Hannah "Flora" Billmeyer (Mrs. Henry Billmeyer); 33. Frances Billmeyer Fisher Kramm; 34. Mary Creasy Fisher, mother of Huldah Fisher Kramm; 35. Andrew Billmeyer (b. 1856), son of George Billmeyer Jr. and Abigail Boudeman; 36. Margaret Billmeyer Kramm (Mrs. William Kramm); 37. Henry Billmeyer (b.1842), son of Elizabeth Hower and Jacob Billmeyer, grandson of Margaret Himmelreich and Martin Martin; 38. William Hammond "Ham" Kramm, son of William and Margaret Billmeyer Kramm; 39. Ella Dietrich Billmeyer; 40. Daniel Koch; 41. Elizabeth Billmeyer Ryan (Mrs. Franklin Ryan), sister of Margaret Billmeyer Kramm; 42. Elizabeth Woolever Kramm (Mrs. Edward Kramm); 43. Tavilla Kramm Koch (Mrs. Daniel Koch); 44. Harry N. Billmeyer, son of Alexander and Angela Blue Billmeyer; 45. Adah M. Billmeyer Steinbach (Mrs. William D. Steinbach), daughter of Charles and Matilda Kramm Billmeyer; 46. Matilda Kramm Billmeyer (Mrs. Charles Billmeyer); 47. Alice Kramm Millspaugh (Mrs. John Millspaugh), daughter of Edward and Elizabeth Woolever Kramm; 48. Sarah Ann Kramm Ravert (Mrs. Charles Ravert); 49. Clarence Hedding; 50. William Billmeyer, son of Maria Kramm and Martin Billmeyer; 52. Peter Billmeyer, son of George and Anna Himmelreich Billmeyer; 54. Carrie Ellen Billmeyer Swanger (Mrs. J. D. Swanger), daughter of Hannah "Flora" and Henry Billmeyer; 55. J. D. Swanger, husband of Carrie Ellen Billmeyer Swanger; 56. Emma J. Billmeyer Gauger (Mrs. Horace Gauger, daughter of Maria Kramm and Martin Billmeyer Jr.; 57. Maria Kramm Billmeyer (Mrs. Martin Billmeyer, Jr.); 58. Reuben Kramm; 59. Ephraim Kramm .

19

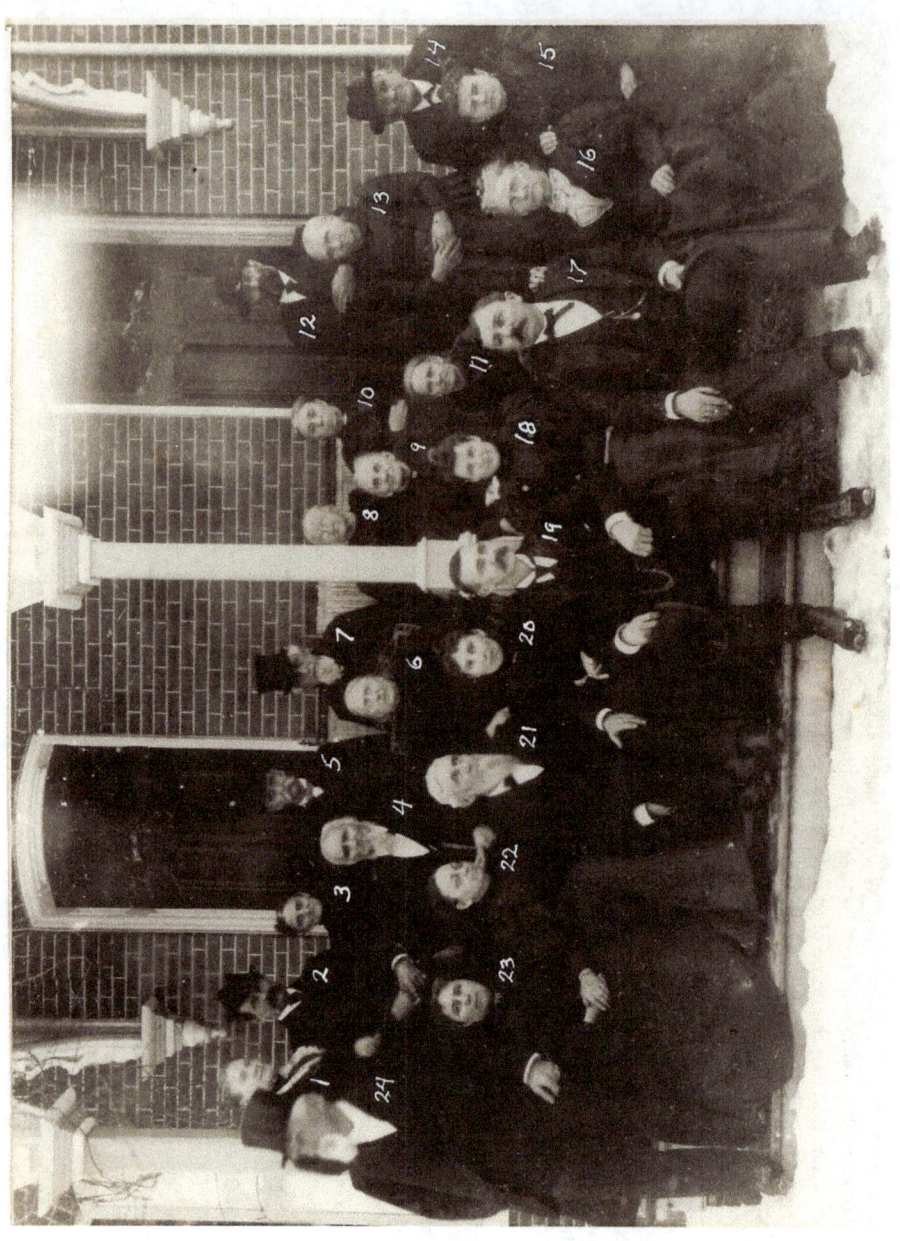

Photograph of the children of David and Mary Brunner Kramm and their spouses, together with the children of William and Margaret Billmeyer Kramm and their spouses, on the occasion of the Golden Wedding Celebration for William and Margaret Billmeyer Kramm on 5 Feb 1896. Photo by H.B. Montgomery of Milton, Pennsylvania.

See also "The Kramm Family" on page 219.

Numbered back to front, left to right:

1. Elizabeth Woolever Kramm (Mrs. Edward Kramm)
2. Oliver Kaufman
3. Susanna Kramm Hunsinger (Mrs. William Hunsinger)
4. William Kramm
5. William Hunsinger
6. Margaret Billmeyer Kramm (Mrs. William Kramm)
7. Ephraim Kramm
8. Maria Kramm Billmeyer (Mrs. Martin Billmeyer, Jr.)
9. Matilda Kramm Billmeyer (Mrs. Charles Billmeyer)
10. Tavilla Kramm Koch (Mrs. Daniel Koch)
11. Elizabeth Billmeyer Ryan (Mrs. Franklin Ryan, sister of Margaret Billmeyer Kramm. Elizabeth may have been remarried and be listed as Elizabeth B. Johnson in an article in the Danville paper.
12. Daniel Koch
13. Sarah Ann Kramm Ravert (Mrs. Charles Ravert)
14. Alex Billmeyer (son of Jacob Billmeyer, cousin of Margaret Billmeyer Kramm)
15. Emma J. Billmeyer Gauger (Mrs. Horace Gauger, daughter of Maria Kramm Billmeyer)
16. Christianna Kramm Bird (Mrs Joseph Bird)
17. William Hammond Kramm
18. Huldah Fisher Kramm (wife of William Hammond Kramm)
19. James Martin Wilcox
20. Ada Virginia Kramm Wilcox (Mrs James M. Wilcox)
21. Reuben Kramm
22. Anna Maria Kemmerer Kramm (Mrs Reuben Kramm)
23. Anna Matilda Kramm Kaufman "Aunt Til" (Mrs Oliver I. Kaufman)
24. Edward Kramm

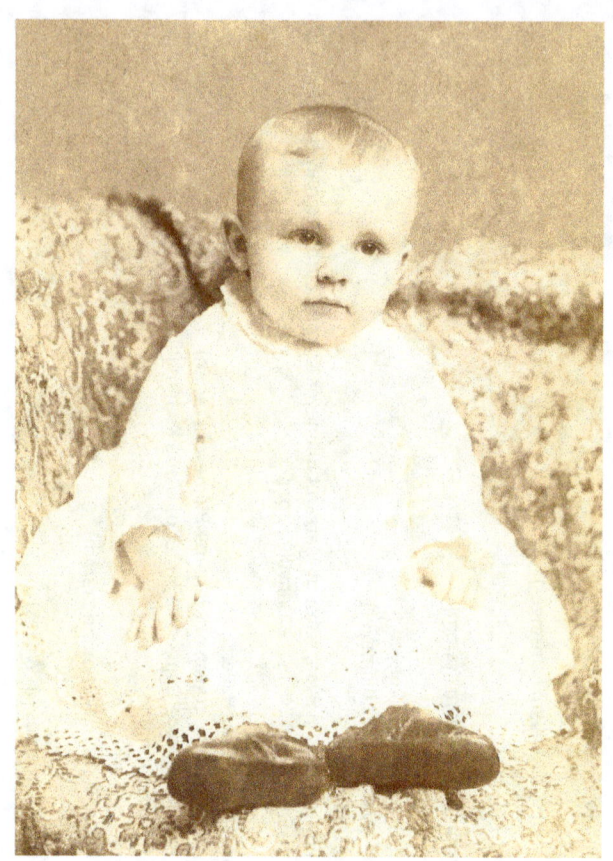

Harry Hammond Wilcox, 1887

Chapter 2: Early Years

Ada Virginia Kramm and James M. Wilcox had four children: Warren, Lee, Harry, and Verna. Lee died unexpectedly at age seven of inflammation of the bowel, a blow to his parents.

All three of the surviving children learned music and art from early ages. Harry's older brother Warren played the piano and harmonica. His sister Verna played piano and organ, and Harry was also a fine piano player and an aspiring artist — all professions uncommon in a working class family.

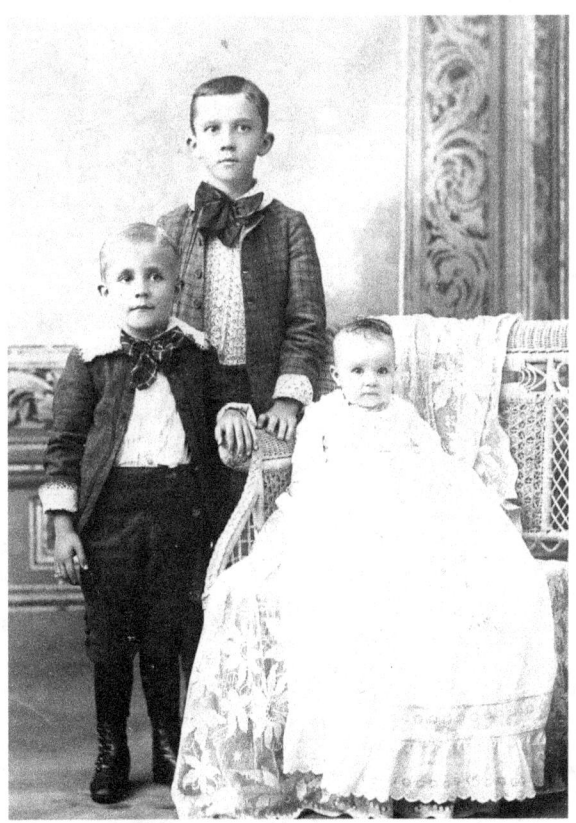

Left to right: Harry, Warren, Verna Wilcox, 1892,
after the death of their brother Lee.

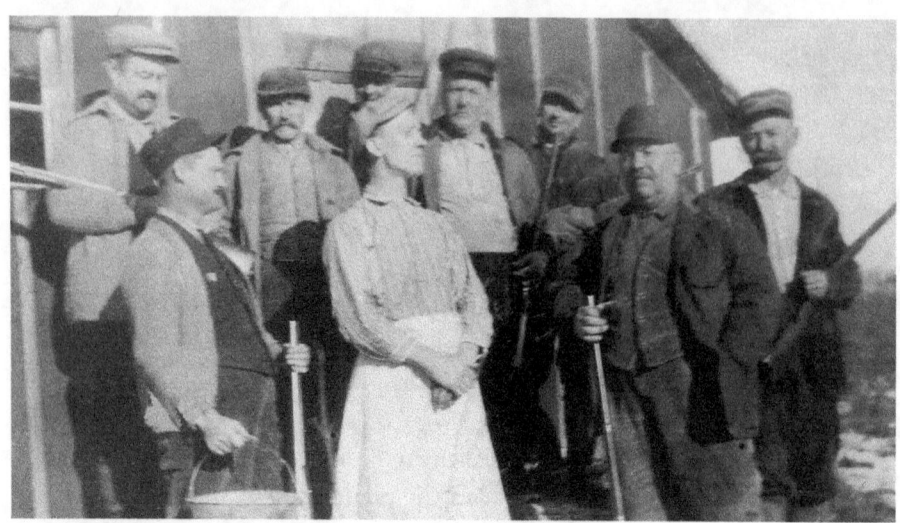

At the Hunting Club. Warren is in the middle, wearing an apron.

Ada's recipes
(original size, her writing)

Tea Cake [Cookies]
2 cups of sugar
1 cup of butter
3 eggs
1 c. of sweet milk
1 tsp [baking] soda*
1 tsp cream of tartar*
* or 2 tsp baking powder
[Add 7-8 c. flour to] mix a stiff dough to roll out. Cut in shapes and decorate. Bake at 375° F. for 10-12 min. Make 3-4 dozen cookies.

Variety [Spice] Cake
1 1/2 c, sugar
4 eggs
1/2 c. butter
1 tsp cream of tartar*
1 tsp [baking] soda*
2 c. flour
1 tsp cloves [ground]
1/2 tsp cinnamon
1/2 c. raisins
1/2 c. sweet milk.
* or 2 tsp baking powder
Bake at 375° for 25 min.

Warren worked most of his life as a waiter and bar clerk at a local hotel. He enjoyed music, played piano, and sang. He always had a harmonica in his pocket. Among his papers were mountains of sheet music of popular songs.

He worked for a time as a cook for a local hunting club. His mother wrote out a series of recipes for him to take along in a small notebook. All the recipes are brief, and assume a basic knowledge of cooking— cream the butter and sugar, add the eggs one at a time, beat well. Separately mix together the dry ingredients. Add the butter mixture, the dry ingredients, and any other liquids. Add raisins last. Notice that she does not specify how much flour for the Tea Cakes. We have modernized the recipes in the captions.

Modern baking powder was patented in 1898 and was not mass produced and sold as a product until 1903. Before that time, in order to achieve the same effect one used a combination of baking soda and cream of tartar, a by-product of wine-making. To substitute baking powder (which is more reliable in baked goods), use as much baking powder as the sum of the two: 1 tsp soda plus 1 tsp cream of tartar equals 2 tsp baking powder.

A "teaspoon" (abbreviated tsp) was the spoon used to stir your coffee. A "tablespoon" (Tbsp) was the spoon used to serve at table. When we were testing and modernizing her recipes for you, we realized that her spoon must have been bigger. We have three silver tablespoons from that era— all three measured 2 Tablespoons or more!

Fannie Farmer is credited for standardizing these measures in her *Boston Cooking School Cookbook*, first published in 1896. She went to the manufacturers and asked them to standardize, which they did, producing tin cups with measuring lines, and sets of spoons to measure Tablespoon, teaspoon, and fractions of a teaspoon.

Cakes and cookies were baked in a medium oven which when you were cooking with wood or gas was not measured with a thermometer but rather with your hand. If you open the oven, you immediately know if it's high, medium, or low. Bake the cake until a until a knife comes out clean when stuck into the center of a cake, or until the cake springs back when lightly touched. Cookies were baked until they were slightly brown around the edges. To make sure they bake evenly, bake them on the

Corn Starch Pudding

1 quart of milk, 3 [med**] eggs, 2 scant tablespoons full of corn starch [=6 tbsp]. Vanilla to flavor, sweeten to taste.

[*Modern cooks, start here:* Separate the eggs. Beat the whites to soft peak, add 1/4 c. sugar, and set aside. In a small bowl put 1/4 c. cold milk, 1/2 c. sugar, 6 Tbsp corn starch, the egg yolks, 1/8 tsp salt. Mix with a fork until smooth and set aside.] Let the [rest of the] milk [3 3/4 c.] come to a boil, and then add your other things [the corn starch mixture, stirring constantly. Cook for another 1-2 minutes until thickened. Remove from heat.] After it is done you stir in your [vanilla and] whites of eggs lightly. Sit it out to get cold [then chill in fridge. Delicious with fresh fruit.]

Fruit Cake*

1 lb of sugar [2 1/4 c.]
1 lb of butter
1 lb of flour [3 1/4 c.]
10 eggs [1 lb eggs**]
2 lb raisins [4 cups]
2 lb currants [4 cups]

*Ada's Fruit Cake is a classic pound cake recipe with too much fruit for modern tastes. Try this instead:

** Ada is using medium eggs. If yours are larger, use fewer.
1 lb eggs = 10 medium, 8 large, or 6 X-large eggs

Ada's Classic Pound Cake
Makes one 9 x 5 inch loaf cake

1/2 pound butter	1 c. sugar
5 medium eggs (or 4 large)	2 c. cake flour
1/2 tsp. salt	1 tsp. vanilla

Cream the butter and sugar until smooth. Add the eggs one at a time and mix smooth. Mix the salt into the flour, and add to the butter and egg mixture. Note that this cake has no leavening. It is pretty dense and wonderfully moist. You can add 1/2 to 1 cup of raisins, chocolate bits, or nuts to make it special—be creative. Bake at 325° F. for 75 minutes, or until a knife or toothpick comes out clean. Do not overbake. It should be golden, not brown.

bottom shelf for half the time, turn them 180 degrees, and bake on the top shelf for the remaining time or until done.

The recipes she wrote out for Warren assumed his good basic knowledge of cooking, and were not intended to be complete. For example, roll the Tea Cakes out about 1/8 to 1/4 inch thick, and cut into shapes. For diamonds, cut 2" strips of dough, and then cut that strip diagonally to make diamond shapes. For rounds, use a water glass to cut the dough. Put them on the pans with space between as they will swell in the baking. Decorate them with cinnamon sugar, or a sprinkle of nutmeg, or a nut half, and then bake.

Warren was employed also at the Lycoming Rubber Company as a "stocker," packing the merchandise into boxes for shipping.[16] The Rubber Company, located at the end of Isabella Street, was one of the larger employers in Williamsport. They made rubber boots and coats, and later sneakers. The sign on the display in the photograph (circa 1900) shows that between 1896 and 1898 the total wages paid out for day labor rose 67%, and the gross production (in dollars) rose 127%, more than doubling in two years.

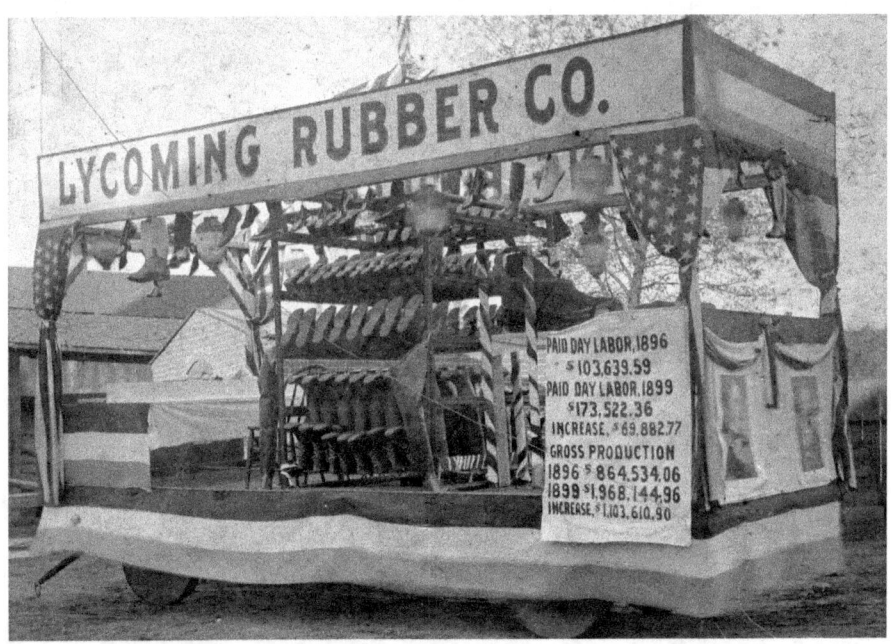

A display of the rubber boots and coats manufactured by the Lycoming Rubber Company, about 1900. The sign heralds the rapid growth of their business, with gross production up 127% in three years.

Verna was a particularly talented musician, accomplished on piano, organ, and violin. She was a pianist and organist for Erie Avenue Baptist Church (now called Central Avenue Baptist Church) in Williamsport at the northwest corner of Seventh Avenue and Memorial Avenue. She gave private lessons, and held recitals with her students. Through the church and a shared interest in music she met a tall, handsome and athletic young man, John Emminger, who played cornet and probably also sang in the choir at her church.

John was the youngest son of Letitia and Daniel Emminger, a veteran of the Civil War.[6] Following his parents' death, at the age of seven, John was sent to the Soldiers' Orphans School, and later finished high school at the Scotland School where he learned the telegrapher's trade and studied stenography and bookkeeping. Following graduation he went to Williamsport to live with his sister, Mrs. A. E. Shook, and to work as an operator for the Postal Telegraph and Western Union. John and Verna would marry in 1916.

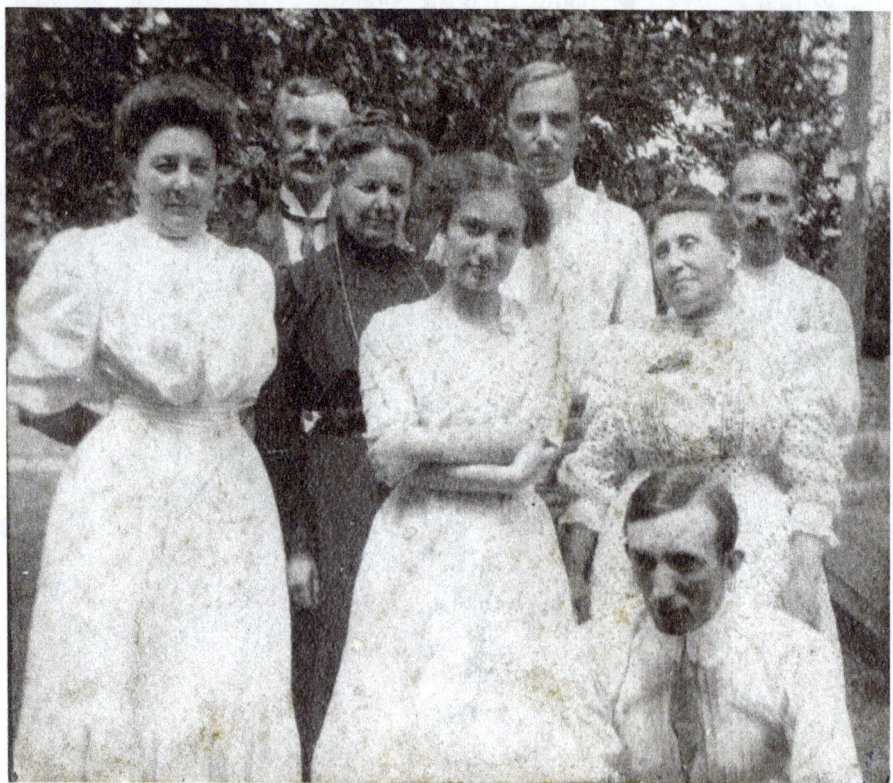

A musicale with friends. Left to right: Mrs. Catherine Cotner, James M. Wilcox, possibly Mrs. A. E. Shook (John's sister), Verna Wilcox, John Emminger, Ada Virginia Kramm Wilcox, Phillip Cotner. Harry Wilcox is crouching in front at right.

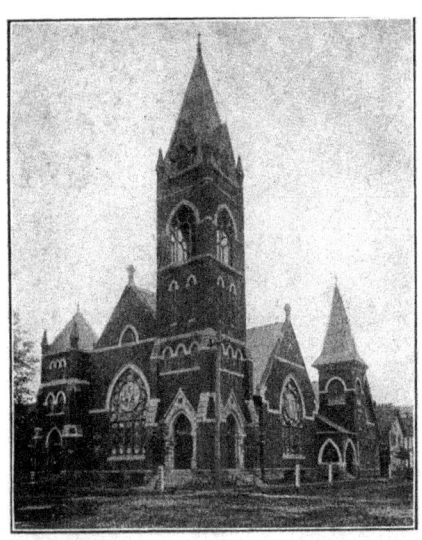

Erie Avenue Baptist Church
Williamsport, Pa.

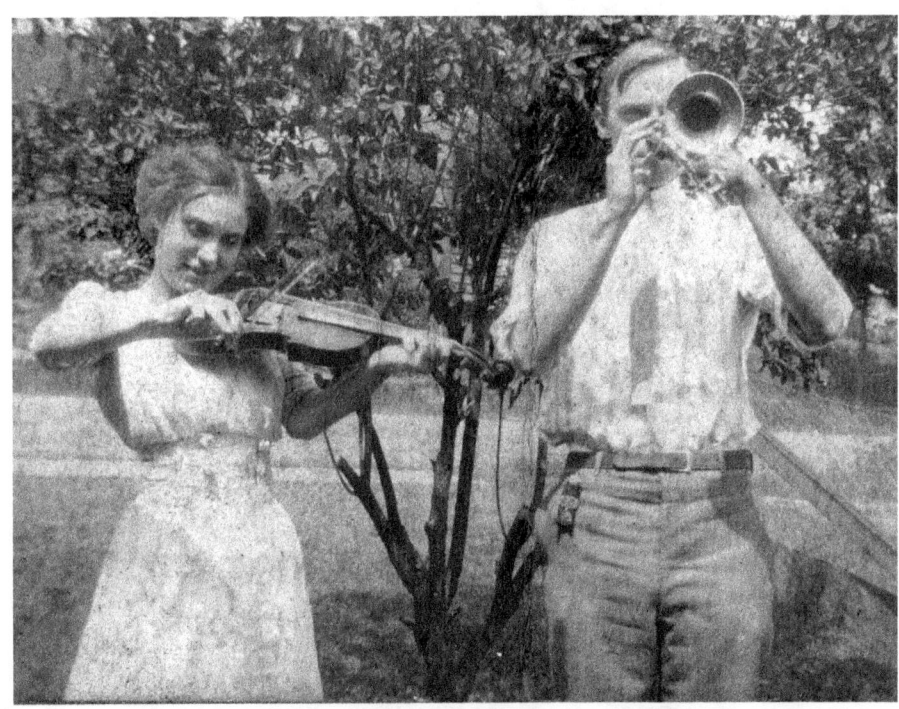

Verna Margaret playing the violin, with her future husband, John Emminger, on cornet.

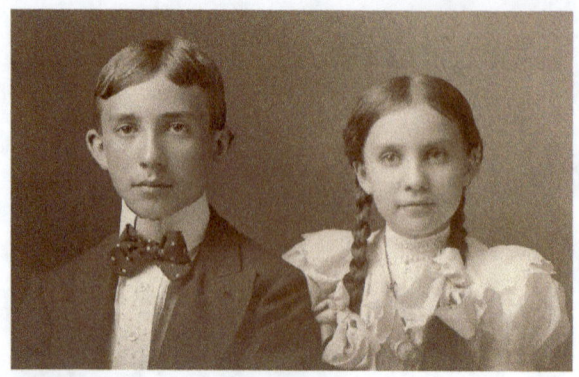

Harry and Verna, 1898

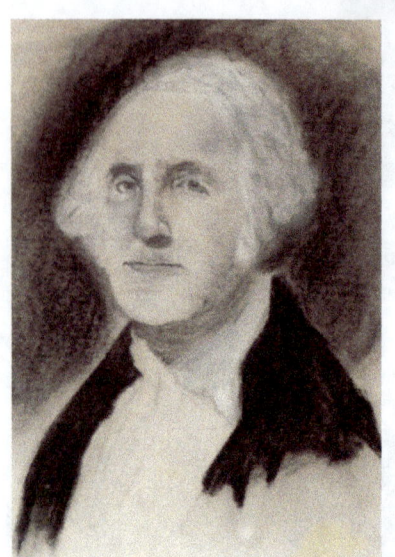

Left:
George Washington, drawn by Harry Wilcox. Ink and charcoal, before 1897 (before age 10)

Below:
Still Life, by Harry Wilcox.
Water color, before age 14, while he was attending Transeau School on Park Avenue, Williamsport.

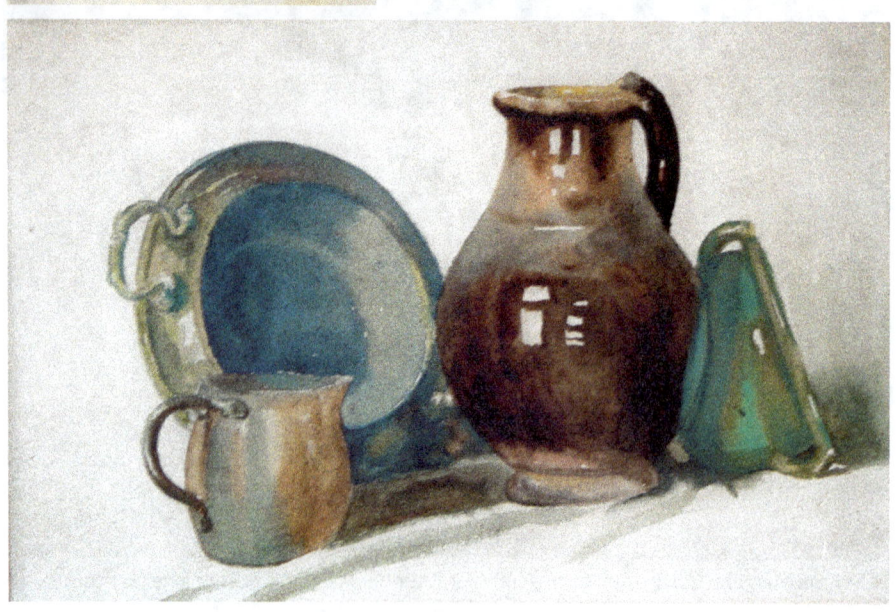

Harry began painting at an early age, encouraged by his father, James, whose beautiful handwriting also shows artistic talent. During his 14th summer, Harry wrote to his father from Limestoneville, "Wish you were here. We could have done some painting."

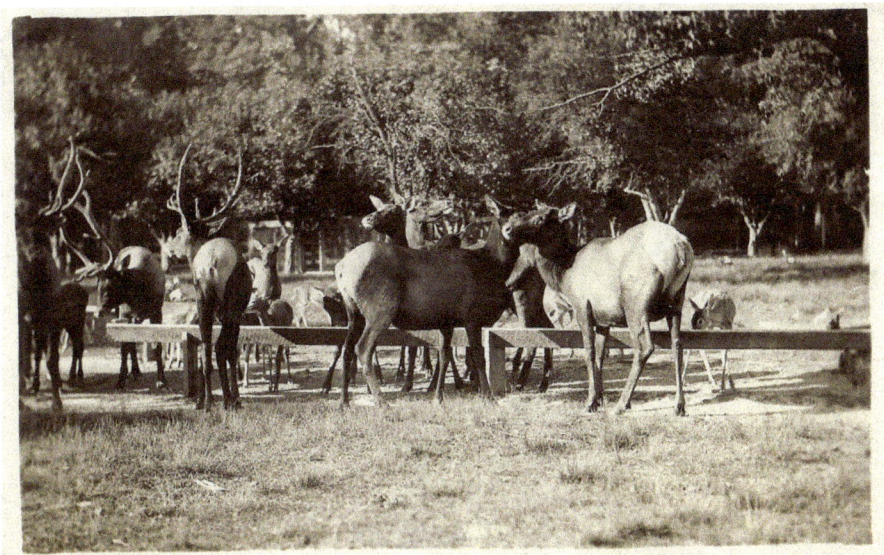

Postcard from Harry Wilcox in Limestoneville to his father, James Wilcox, in Williamsport, July 22, 1909. Picture shows the Elk and Deer Ranch of Alexander Billmeyer in Washingtonville, a picnic destination. See below for the other side of the postcard.

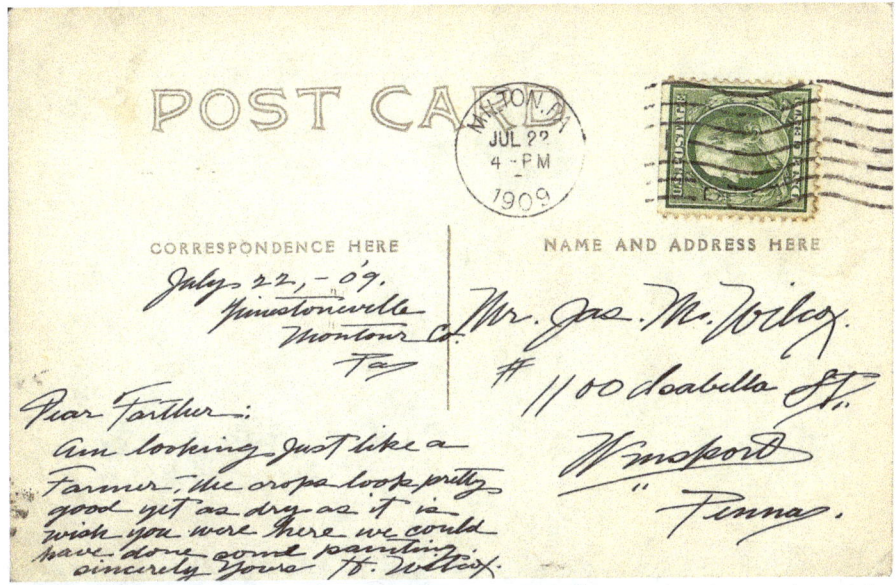

"Dear Father. Am looking just like a farmer. The crops look pretty good yet as dry as it is. Wish you were here. We could have done some painting. Sincerely yours, H. Wilcox"

31

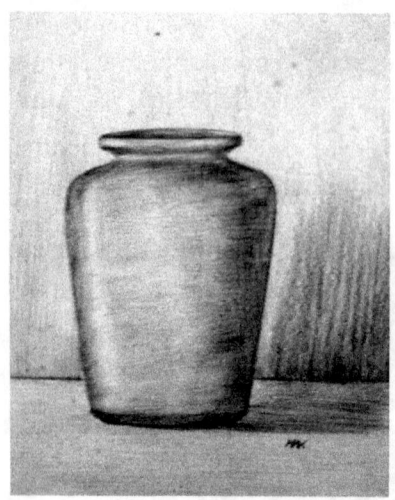

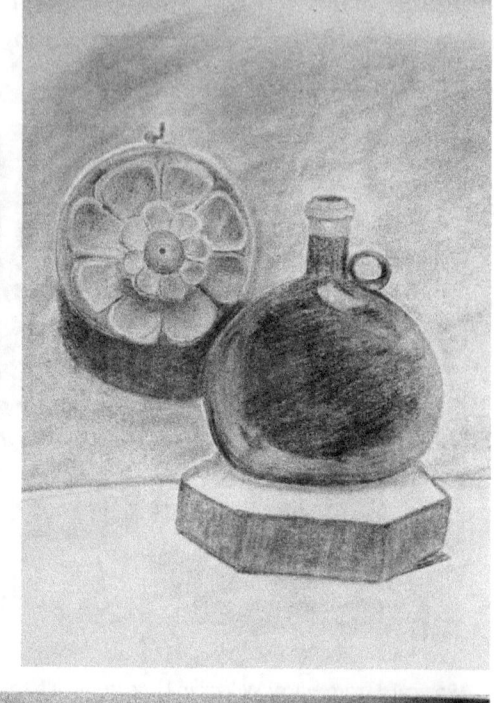

Vase and two jugs.
Studies for school
by Harry Wilcox
Pencil on paper
before age 14

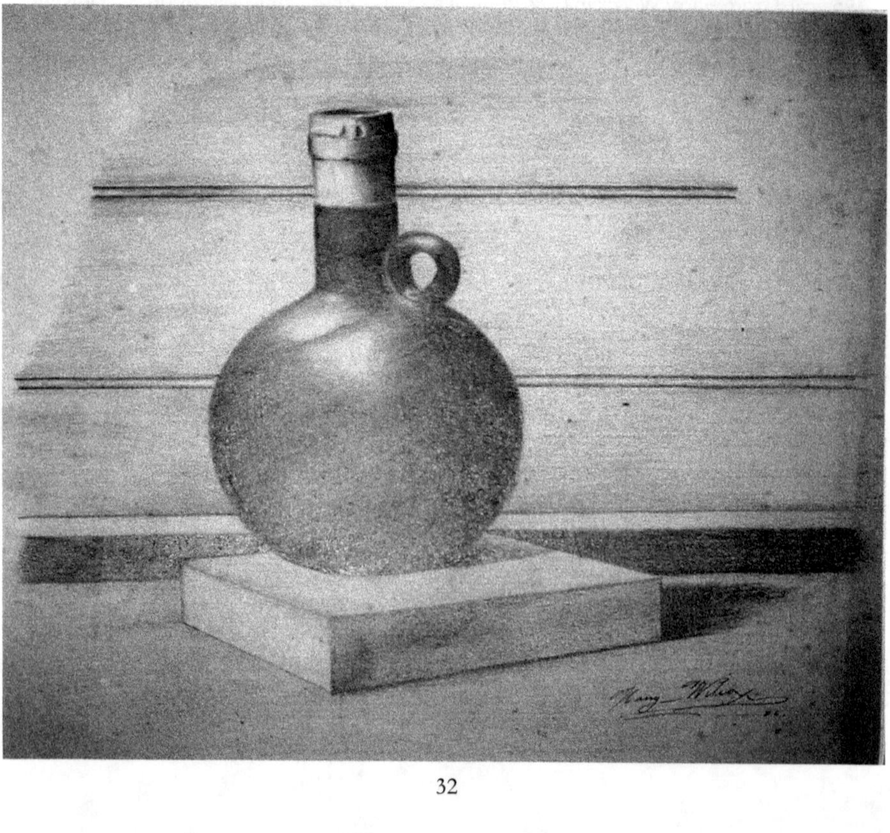

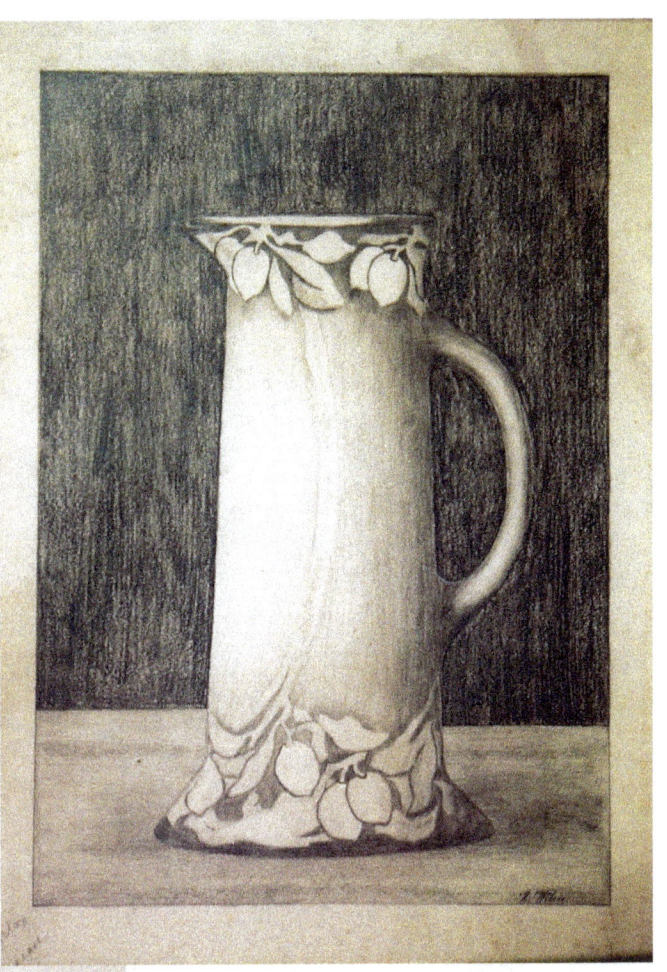

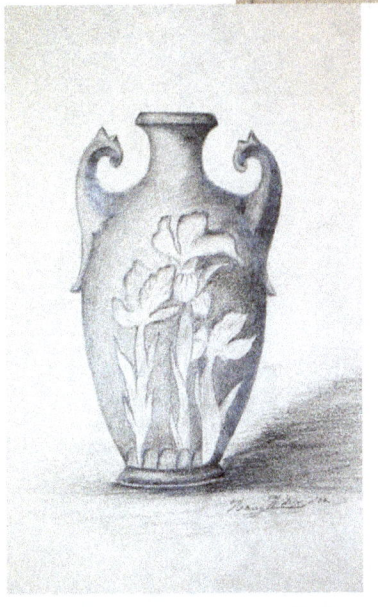

Silver penny pitcher
Iris vase.

Studies for school
by Harry Wilcox
Pencil on paper.
before age 18

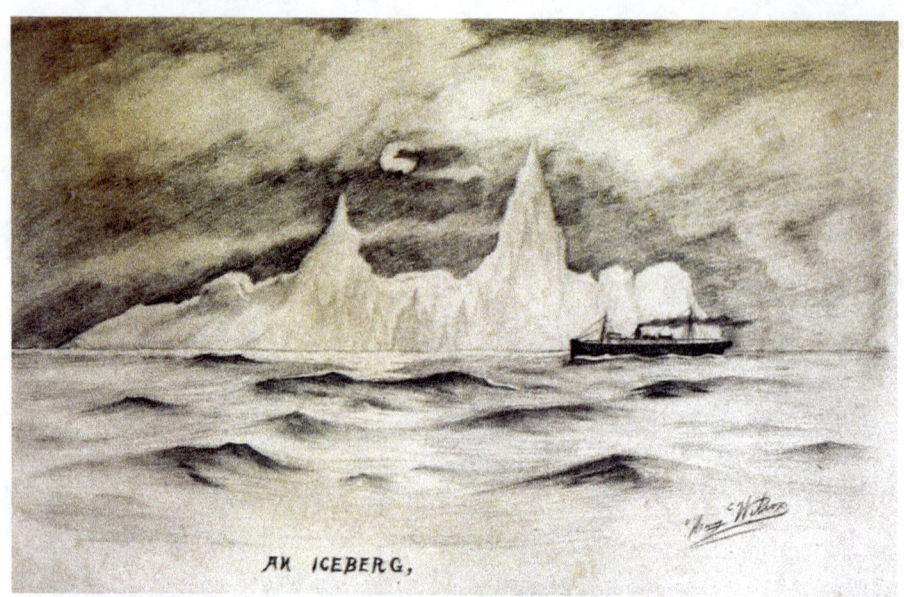

An Iceberg, by Harry Wilcox. Pencil on paper. Before age 18.

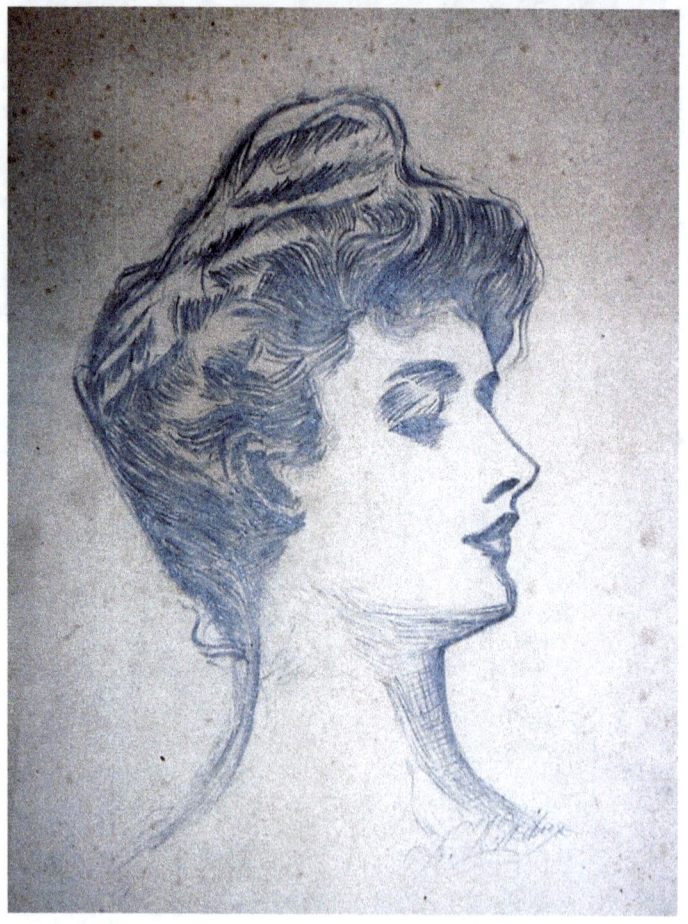

Woman dozing, by
Harry Wilcox.
Pencil on paper.
Before age 18.

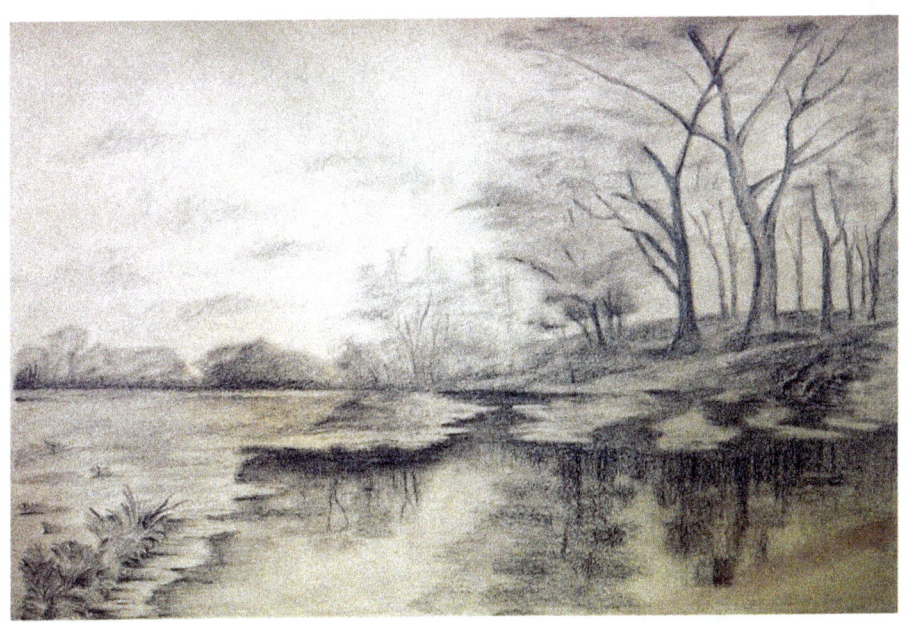

Lake scene, by Harry Wilcox. Pencil on paper. Before age 18.

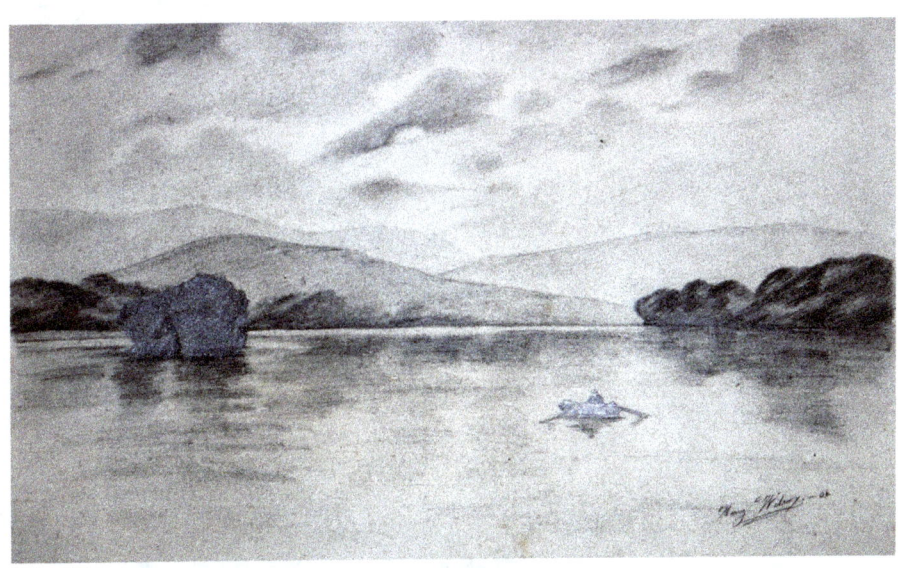

On the lake, by Harry Wilcox. Pencil on paper. Before age 18.

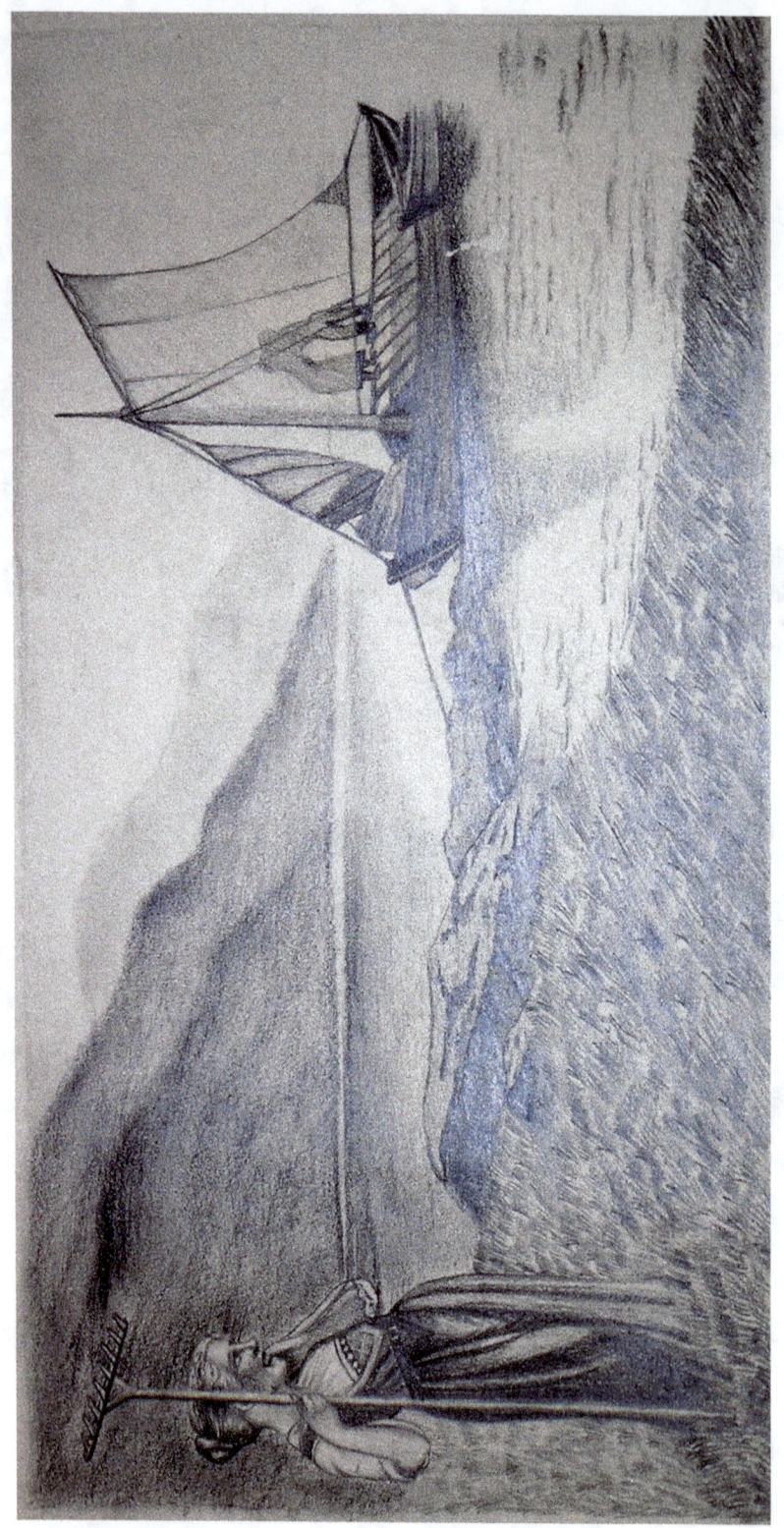

Caught Them Kissing! by Harry Wilcox
Pencil on paper. Before age 18.

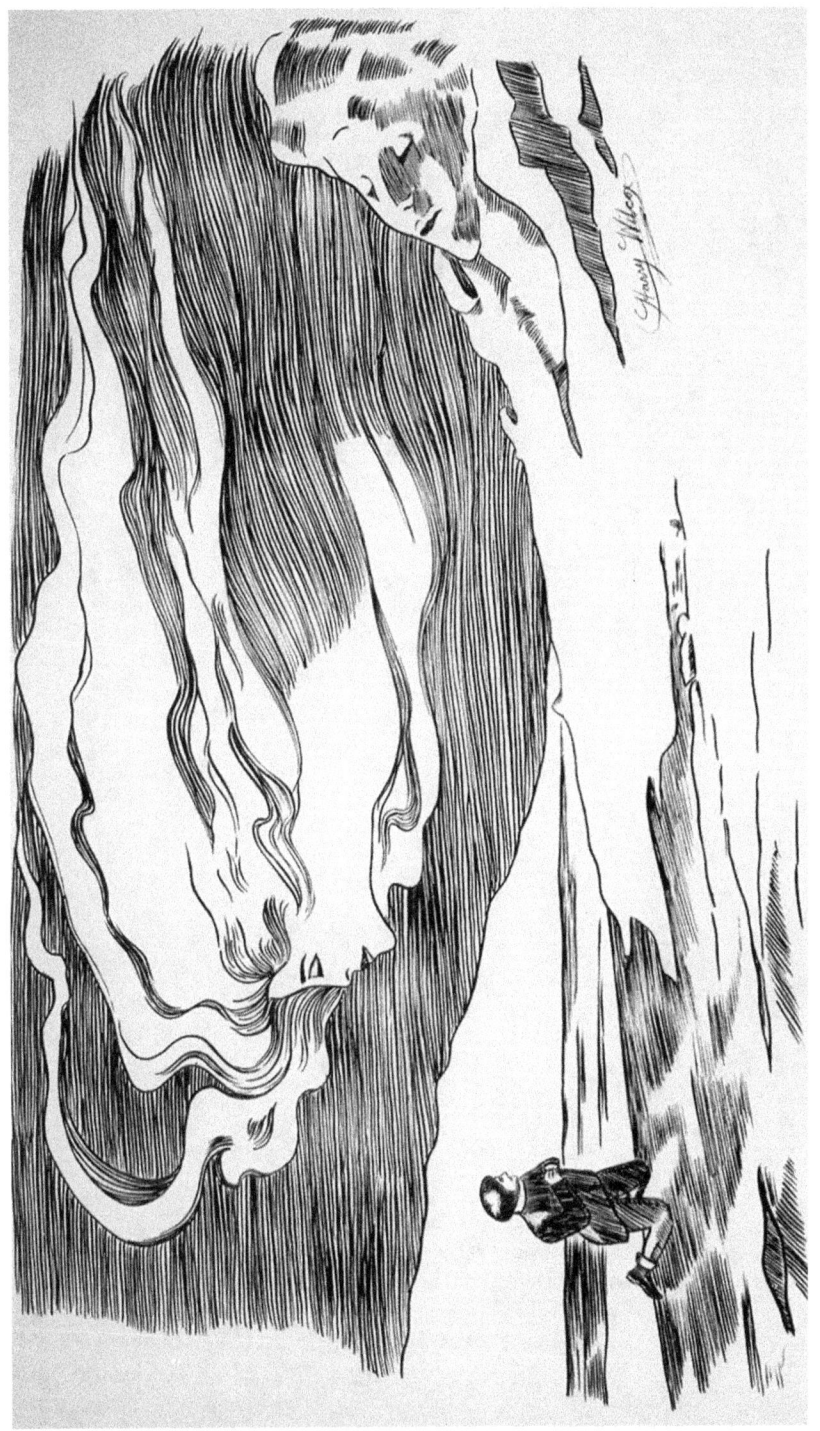

When a Man's in Love, by Harry Wilcox. Pen and Ink on paper. Before age 18.

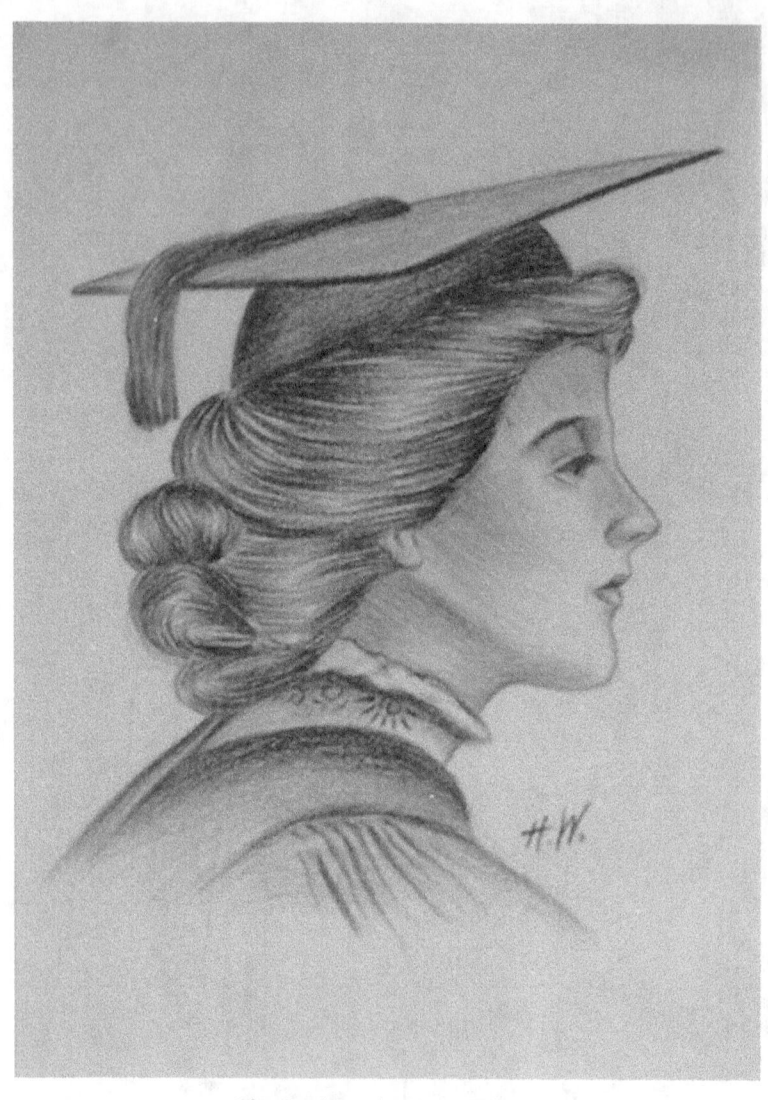

The Graduate, by Harry Wilcox,
Pencil on brown paper, about 1911.
This was likely inspired by the
graduation from high school of his sister Verna Margaret.

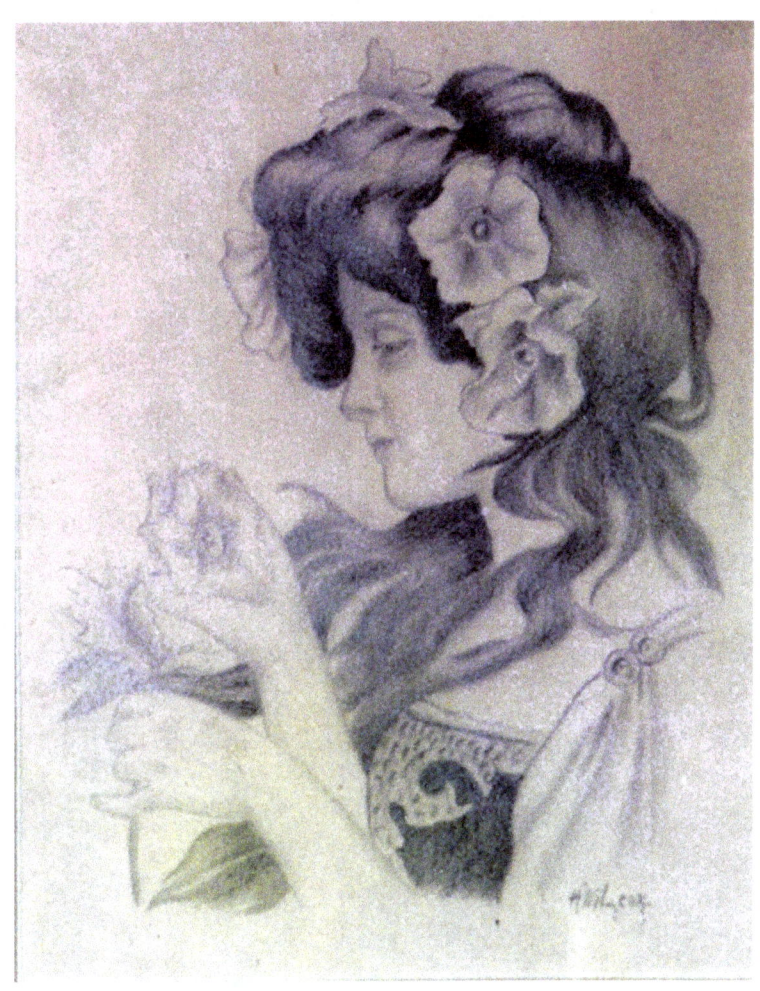

Girl with Morning Glories, by Harry Wilcox,
Pen and ink on brown paper, about 1911.

Harry attended Transeau School (say "TRAN-zoo"), a public school building with grades 1-12. In 1904, in the 11th grade, he was inspired by the Russo-Japanese War to draw a political cartoon. His teacher must have seen great potential, and sent it off to the new magazine of political satire, *Judge*. It was accepted by *Judge*, and published a year later, on the second Easter of the conflict, April 22, 1905.

The Russo-Japanese War (February 1904 - September 1905 grew out of Russia's desire to secure a warm-water port on the Pacific Ocean for their navy as well as for commerce. Vladivostock could only be used in the summer, but Port Arthur, leased to Russia by China, would be usable year round, and would put them in a good position to control Korea as well. Japan considered this an intrusion into their domain. After negotiations broke down in 1904, Japan attacked Port Arthur. The Japanese were strong, and the Russians blundered. In late April, Japanese forces

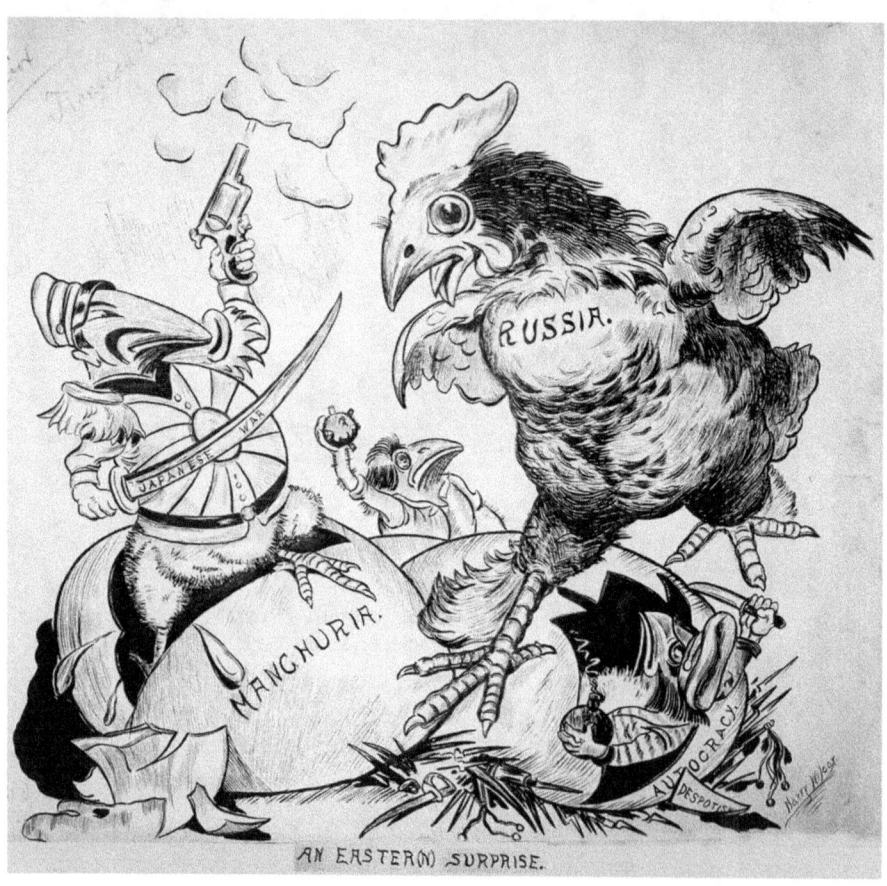

An Easter(n) Surprise. Political cartoon by Harry Wilcox, about 1904 (age 18).
Pen and ink on paper.

defeated Russia in the Battle of the Yalu and pushed into Manchuria from Korea. As depicted in the cartoon, there was also unrest at home. In fact the seeds of the Russian Revolution were sown in 1904. The leading Marxist Plekhanov wrote that the war "promises to shatter to its foundations the regime of Nicholas II." But the Czar would not actually be deposed for another ten years.

In the accompanying article, *Judge* says "The big Russian hen begins to see what a mistake she made when she hatched out that Manchurian egg. The fabled mare's nest was not more charged with evil. Besides a more than equal competitor, a brood of domestic ills sprang to life out of that fateful shell which threatens the czar's throne as never before. It is another of those ironies of history that the monarch whose greatest bid for fame was a proposition of universal peace should see that fame melting away in the miseries of an unprecedented war."[7]

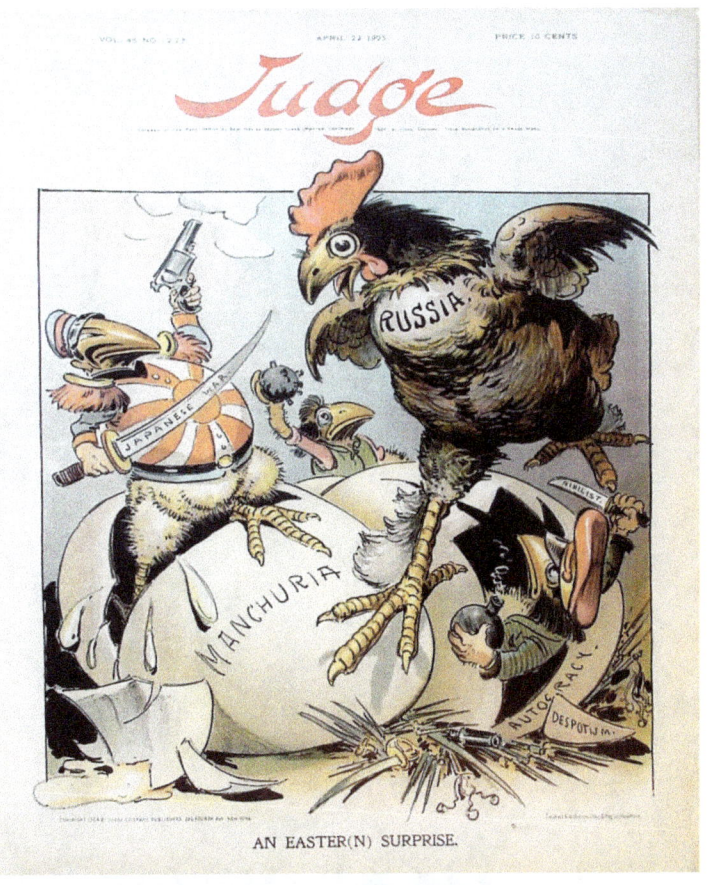

Cover of the political commentary magazine *Judge*, April 22, 1905.
Courtesy of graphicwitness.com

41

In his senior year of High School, there appeared on the chalkboard one day a very unflattering caricature of Mr. Gilmore, the somewhat autocratic principal, complete with horns and pitchfork. Given the masterful chalk work, there was no doubt as to the identity of the artist. Harry was "asked out of school," ending his formal schooling.

Beginning in 1907, Harry Wilcox went to work for the Williamsport *Grit* newspaper company as a commercial artist and illustrator. In those days advertising required a commercial artist to prepare attractive pictures of the goods on offer, cartoon whimsy to capture the imagination, or photo retouching to add sparkle and perfection.

The Williamsport *Grit* was a weekly newspaper founded in 1882. In its first year, it had a circulation of 4,000 readers, and by 1900 it had already expanded to 100,000 readers. The paper included news and features aimed at rural America, and followed an editorial policy which owner

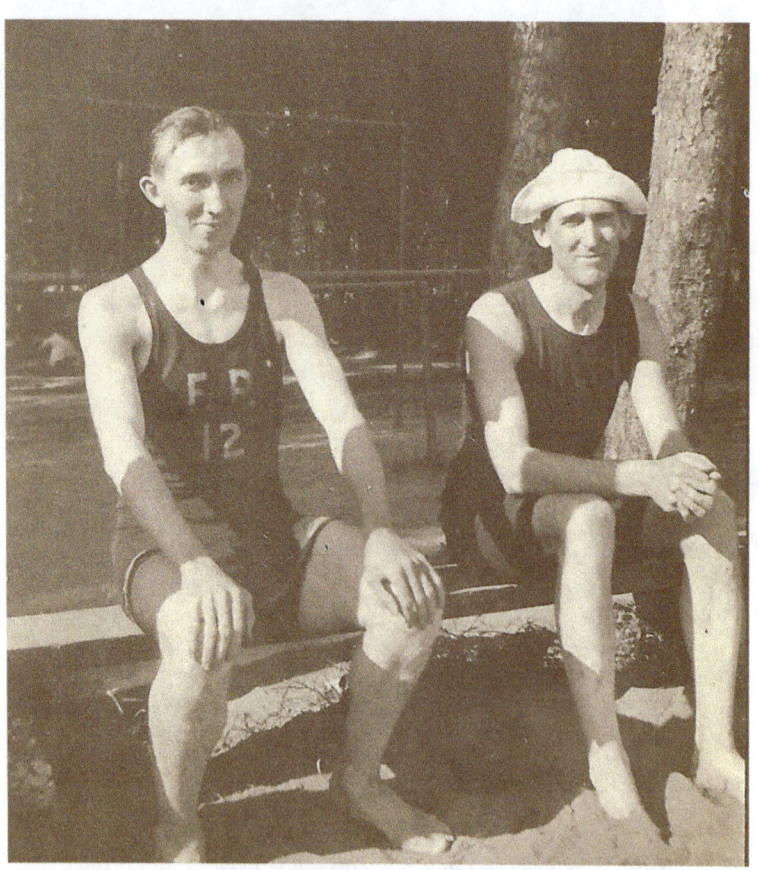

Harry and Warren swimming, about 1906.

Dietrick Lamade (say LAH-mah-dee) outlined during a banquet for *Grit*'s employees in 1900:

> "Always keep *Grit* from being pessimistic. Avoid printing those things which distort the minds of readers or make them feel at odds with the world. Avoid showing the wrong side of things, or making people feel discontented. Do nothing that will encourage fear, worry, or temptation . . . Wherever possible, suggest peace and good will toward men. Give our readers courage and strength for their daily tasks. Put happy thoughts, cheer, and contentment into their hearts."[8]

Lamade introduced such innovations as national newsboy delivery and direct mail, and eventually parlayed his weekly into one of America's biggest and most

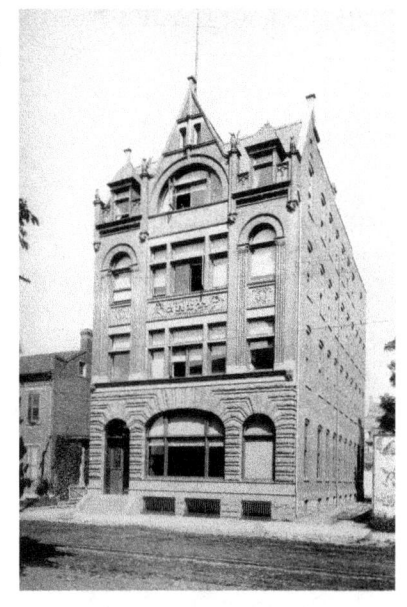

Above:
Grit's headquarters anchored the corner of William and West 3rd Streets in Williamsport. Photo from Van Auken, *Sunday Grit: A Newspaper Legacy,* p. 11.

Left:
Dietrick Lamade pressured the circulation department to reach 250,000 circulation by 1905. Cartoon reprinted in Van Auken, *Sunday Grit: A Newspaper Legacy,* p. 18.

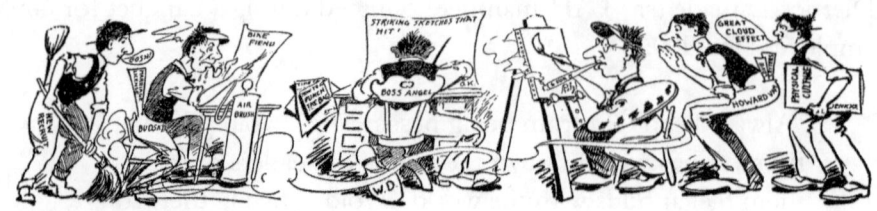

Bird's Eye View of the Art Department

Cartoon of activities in the Art Room. Van Auken, *Sunday Grit: A Newspaper Legacy,* page 20.

enduring national publications, featuring news, human interest articles, comic strips that sometimes filled ten pages, puzzles, and serials in fiction supplements. Harry illustrated the *"Grit* Story Section." Circulation reached 300,000 in 1916.

Grit management referred to members of the Art Department as "knights of the pencil." One manager quipped: "Every effort to establish a genuine Bohemia has been fruitless. The artists insist on having their hair cut regularly, and have wholly eschewed the pipe."[9]

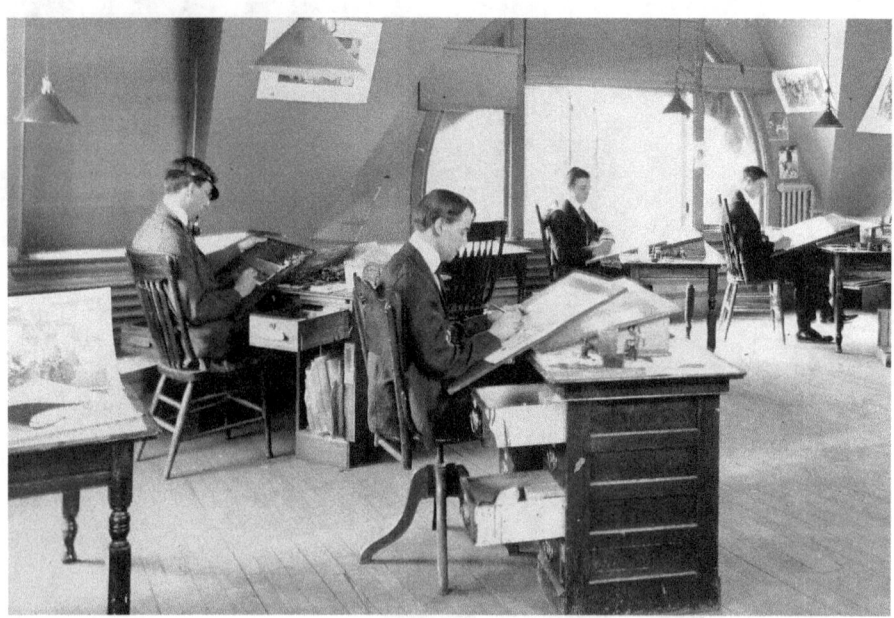

"The Artists Room occupied the fourth floor of the *Grit.* Now highly collectible, the prints created by *Grit* were often included as inserts, and decorated the pages of the national newspaper. Photo and caption from Van Auken, *Sunday Grit: A Newspaper Legacy,* page 20.

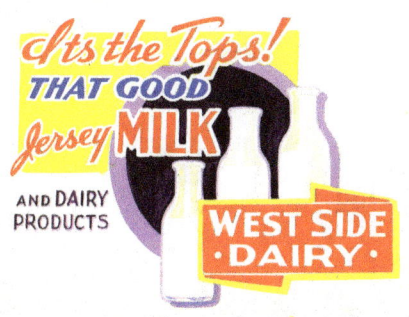

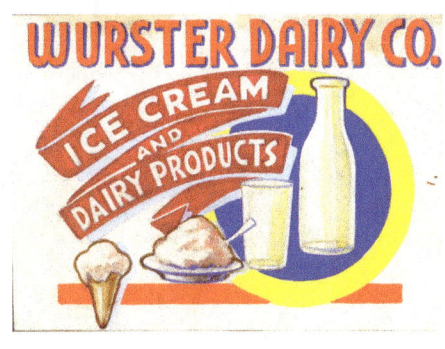

Advertising drawn by Harry Wilcox. Water color.

Harry enjoyed working with the men and women at the *Grit*, including going with them on various outings. "So many women worked for *Grit* that a young woman jokingly suggested the company create a Marriage Bureau."[10]

Between 1910 and 1913 Harry received several postcards from Dietrick Lamade from travel destinations such as Panama, Cuba, and Switzerland.

With a respected position in a booming newspaper, Harry was firmly launched in his career.

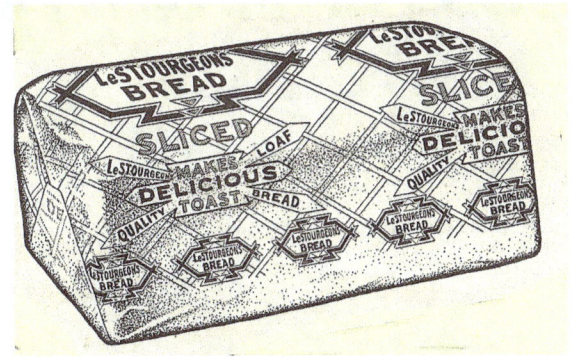

Advertising drawn by Harry Wilcox.
LeStourgeon's Bread
"LeStourgeon's quality loaf bread makes delicious toast."

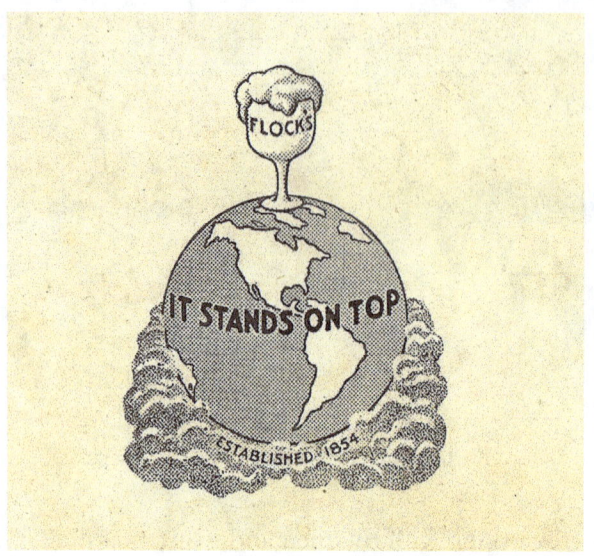

Advertising drawn by Harry Wilcox.
Pen and ink.
Flock's beer, established 1854, Williamsport
"It stands on top"

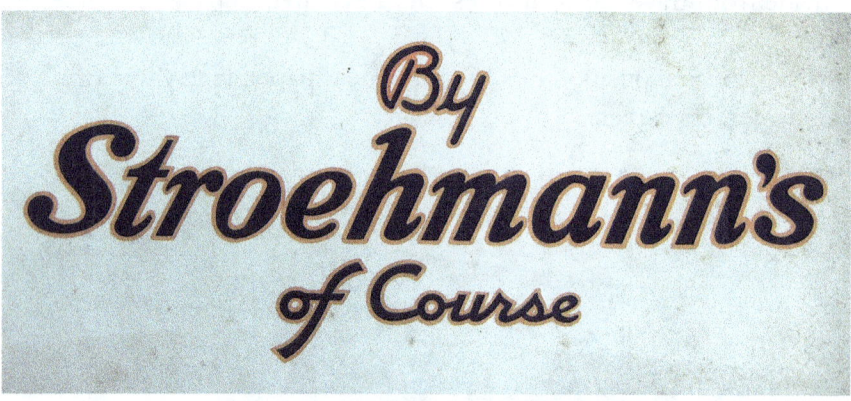

Tagline for the Stroehmann Brothers' bakery
which sold its original sliced bread to WonderBread.

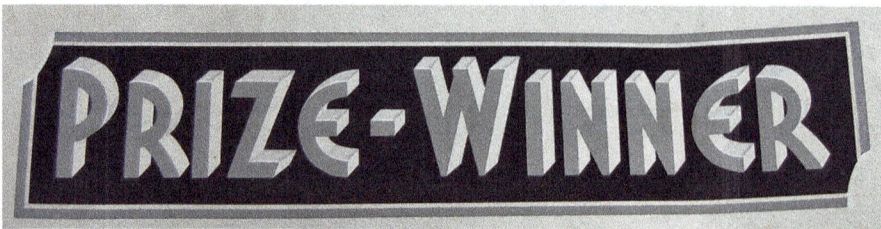

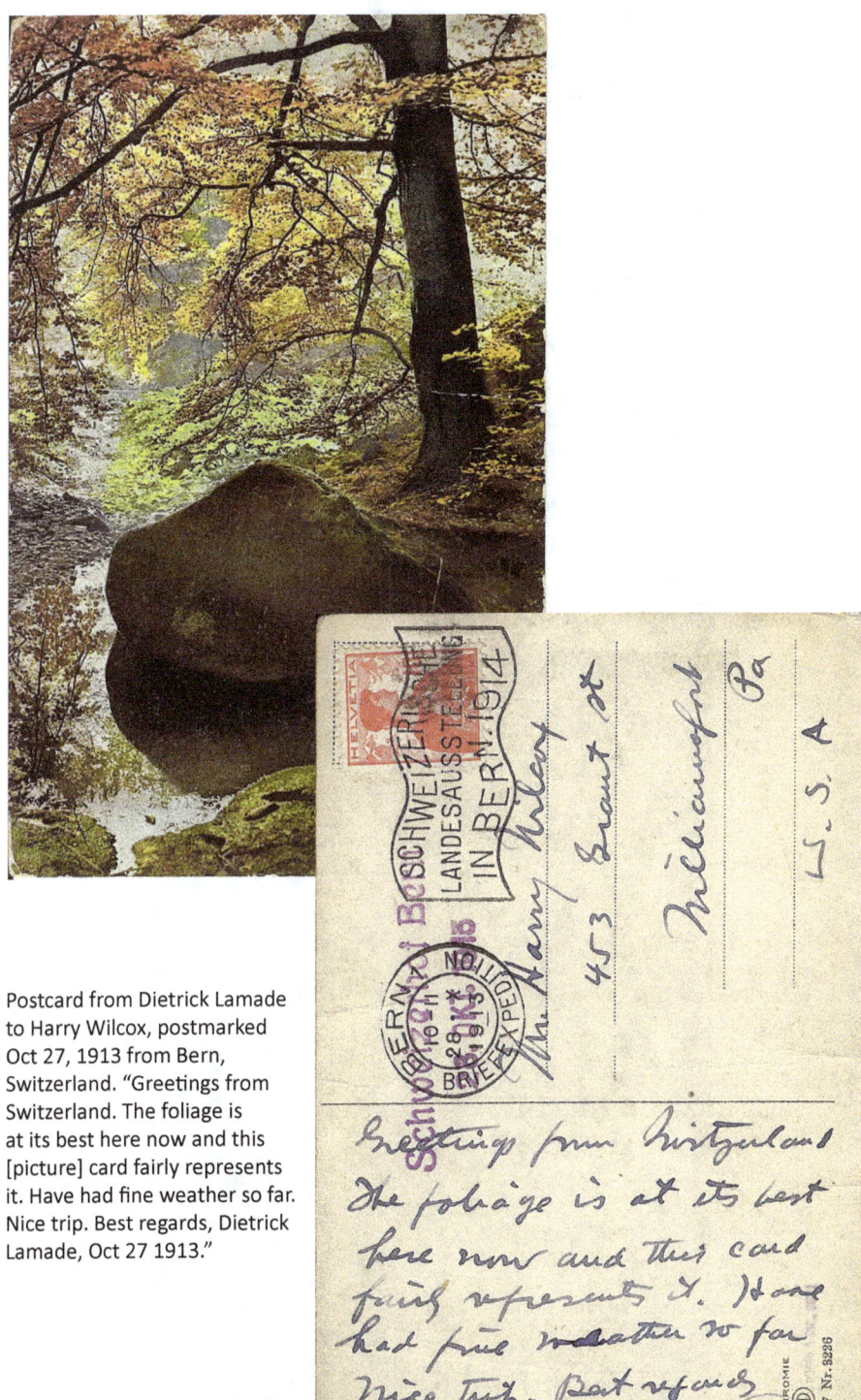

Postcard from Dietrick Lamade to Harry Wilcox, postmarked Oct 27, 1913 from Bern, Switzerland. "Greetings from Switzerland. The foliage is at its best here now and this [picture] card fairly represents it. Have had fine weather so far. Nice trip. Best regards, Dietrick Lamade, Oct 27 1913."

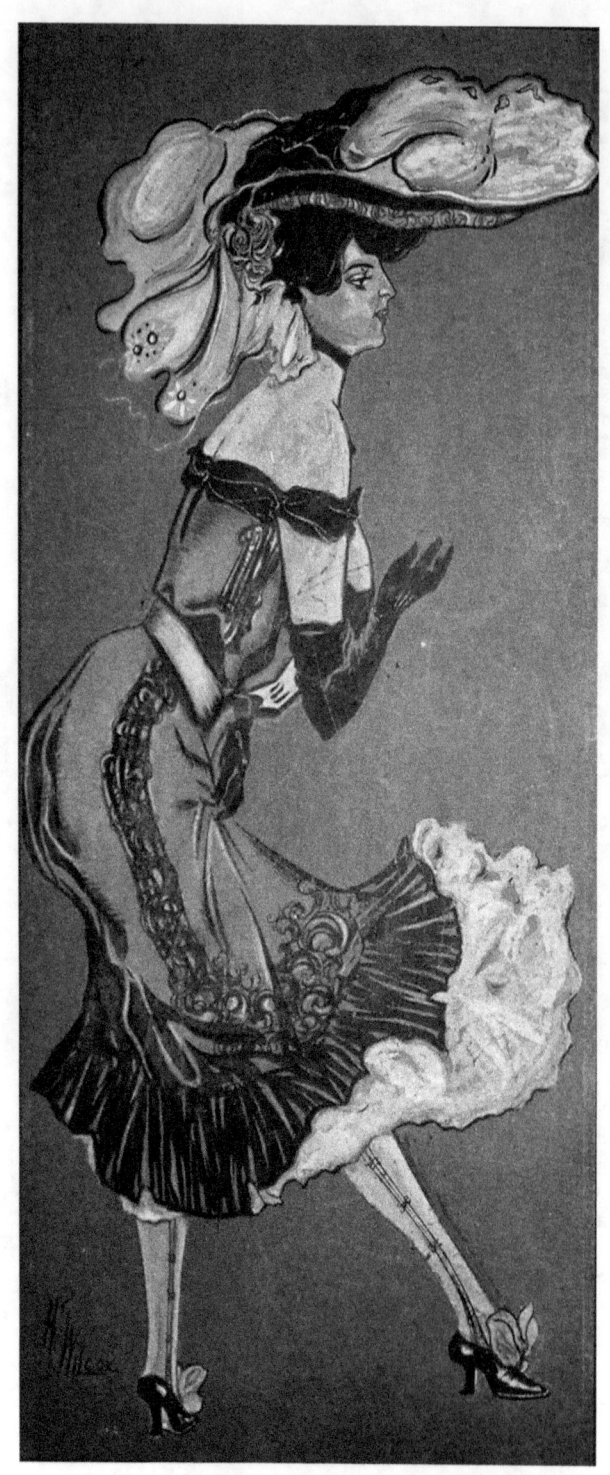

Can-Can. by Harry Wilcox.
Watercolor on paper.

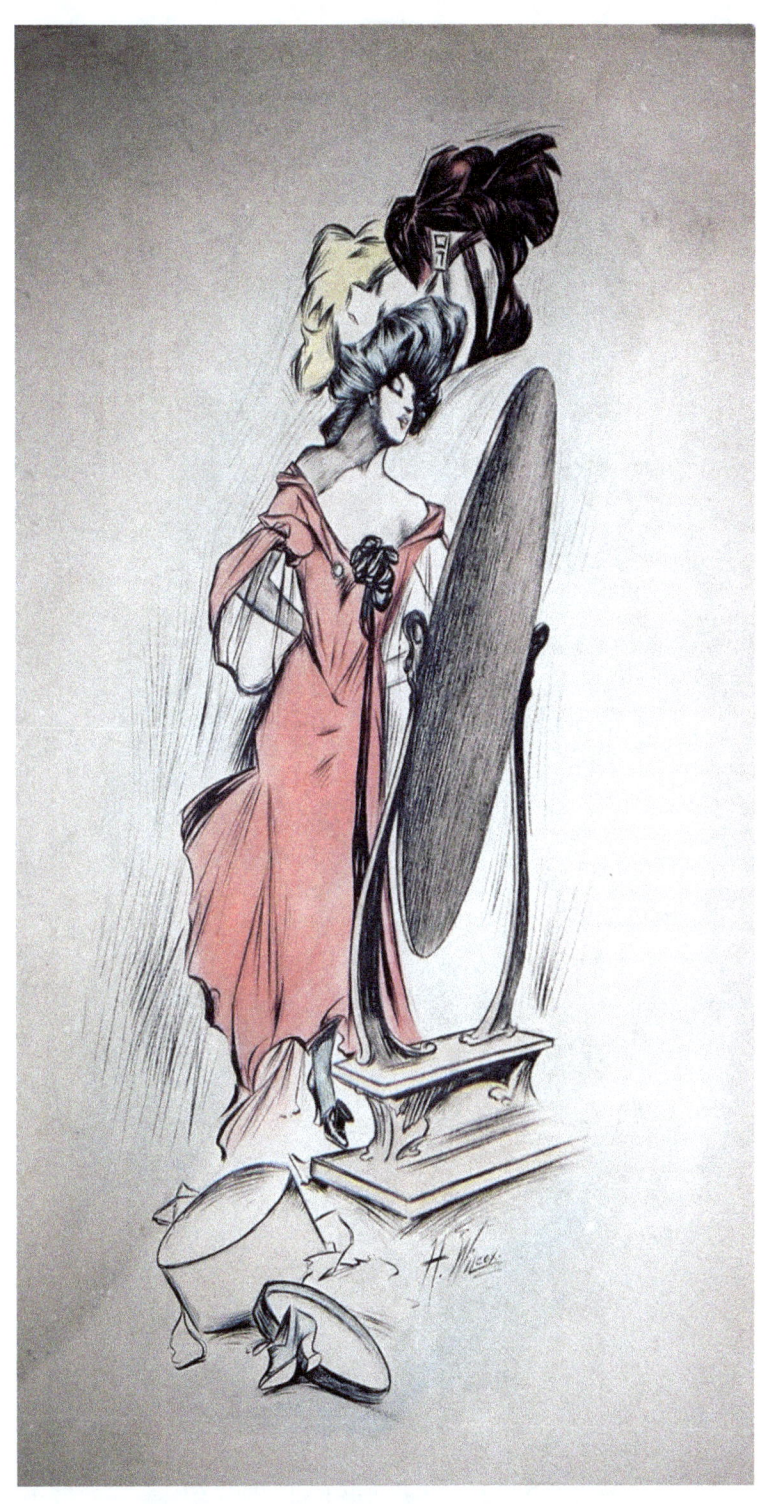

A New Hat, by Harry Wilcox. Watercolor on paper.

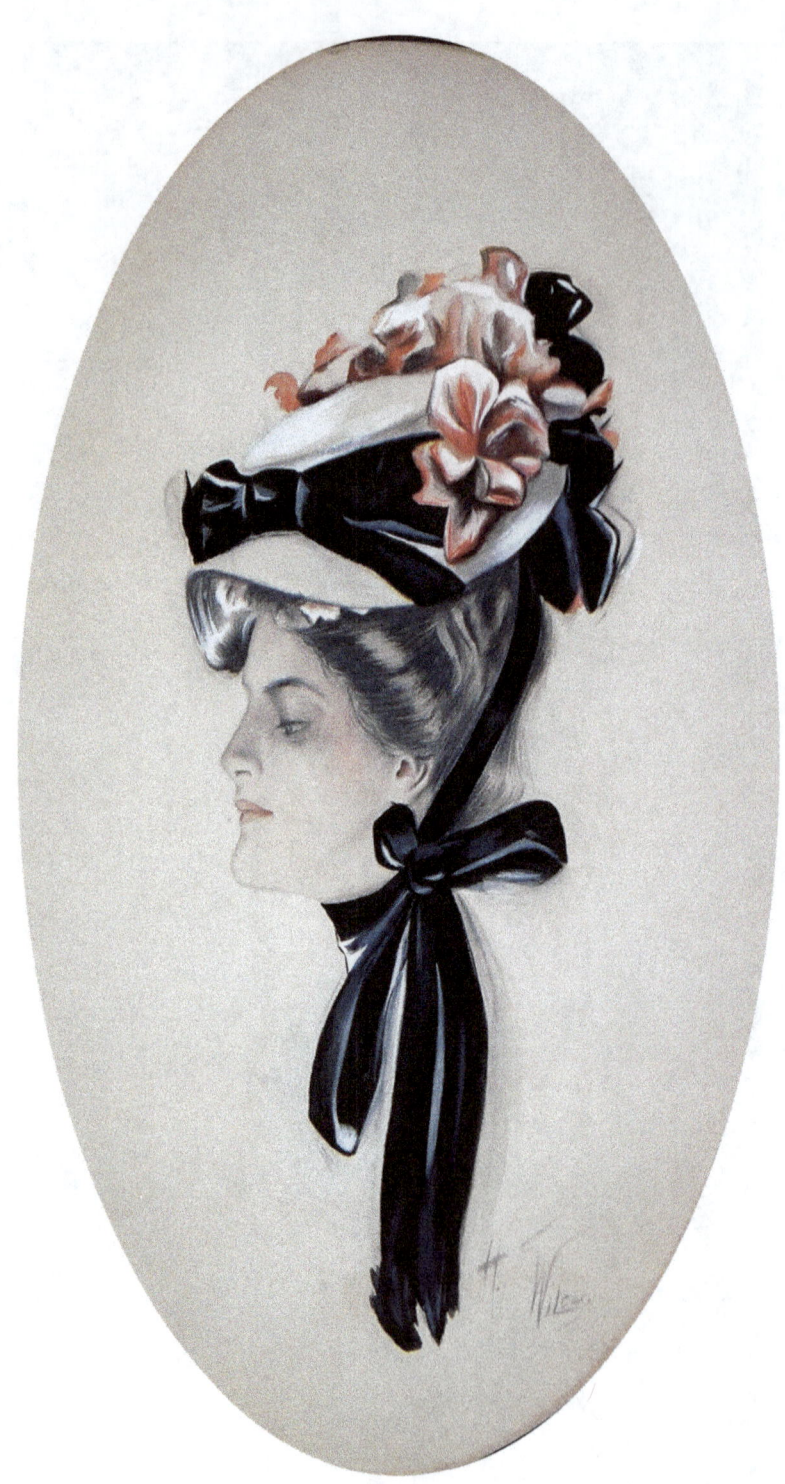

Woman with a pink ribboned hat, by Harry Wilcox.
Watercolor on paper.

CHAPTER 3:
THE WOMAN WITH DREAMY EYES

For Labor Day in 1908, there were many festive events:

> "Williamsport has no regular Labor day celebration this year
> but there are side attractions enough for a city twice this size,
> and from present indications no one need die of [boredom]
> in this vicinity to morrow [sic]. Every park, and almost
> every surrounding town has planned a celebration, and
> local pleasure seekers have a long list from which to choose.
> Probably the most important events are the Jersey Shore Odd
> Fellows picnic and the river carnival at Nippono park, and the
> annual picnic of the local lodge of Elks at Emory's Park, near
> Montoursville."[11]

Harry went with friends from the *Grit* to a church Festival. There he met
a young woman who lived at the other end of town, about six miles from
his home. He was fascinated by her "dreamy eyes."

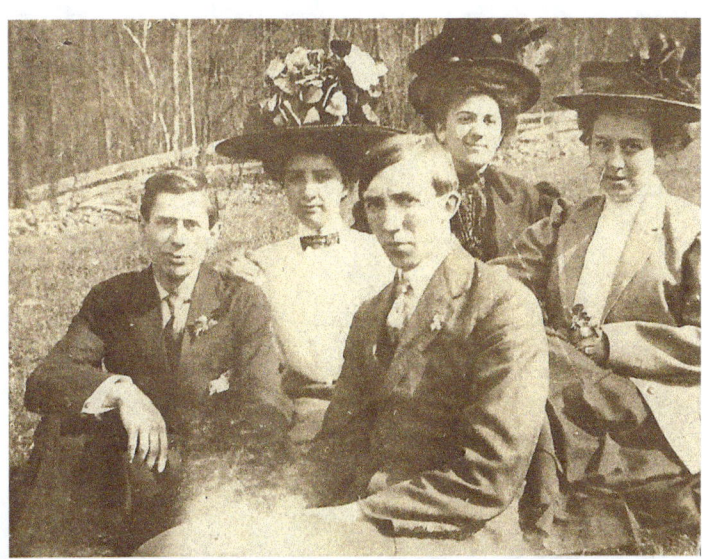

An outing with
friends. Harry
Wilcox is in the
front center of
the group.

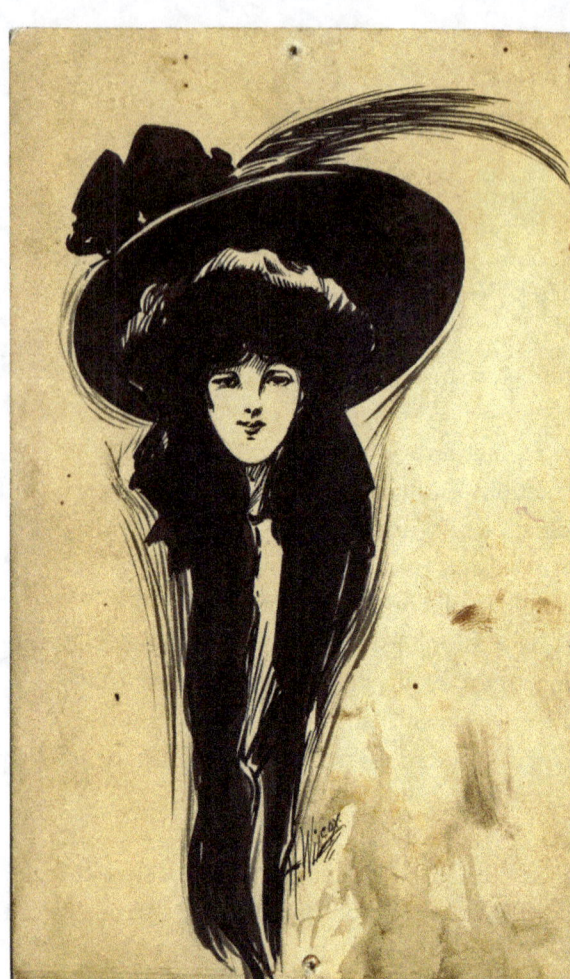

Woman with a long collar. Signed Postcard, front and back, pen and ink, by Harry Wilcox.

> "Williamsport
> Sept 7, 1908
> Dear Harriet,
> Suppose you have forgotten me by this time. Well I have not forgotten you since I met you at the festival. Hope this card will find you as well as usual. Have not seen you since the night of the festival. Write some time.
> My address is: Grit Publishing Company, Art Department.
> Sincerely yours,
> H. Wilcox"

Since Hattie is normally a nickname for Harriet, he called her Harriet in the beginning, but her given name was Hattie.

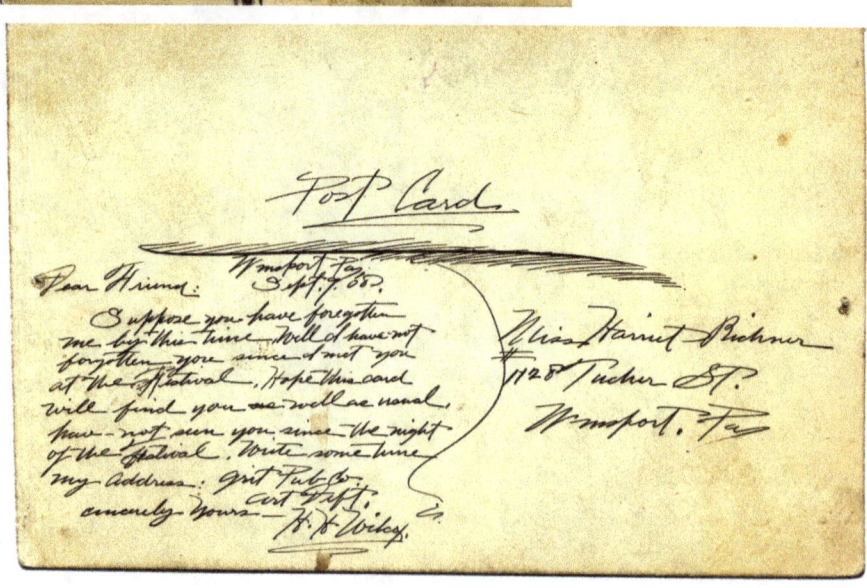

Woman with a locket.
Postcard, front and back,
pen and ink, by Harry
Wilcox.

"Williamsport
        Sept 25, 1908
Dear Harriet,
 Received your card. Was
glad to hear from you.
Will see you at Church
Sunday eve.
 Write soon.
 Sincerely yours,
 H. Wilcox"

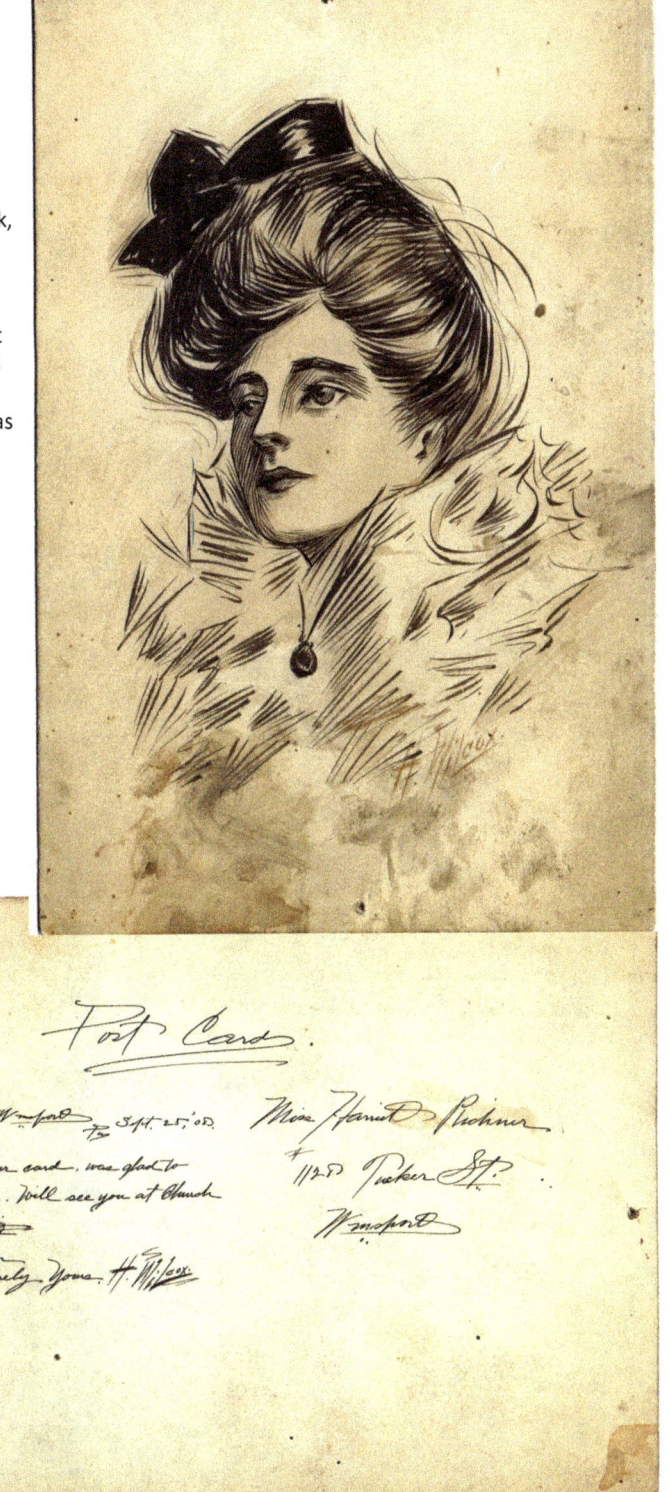

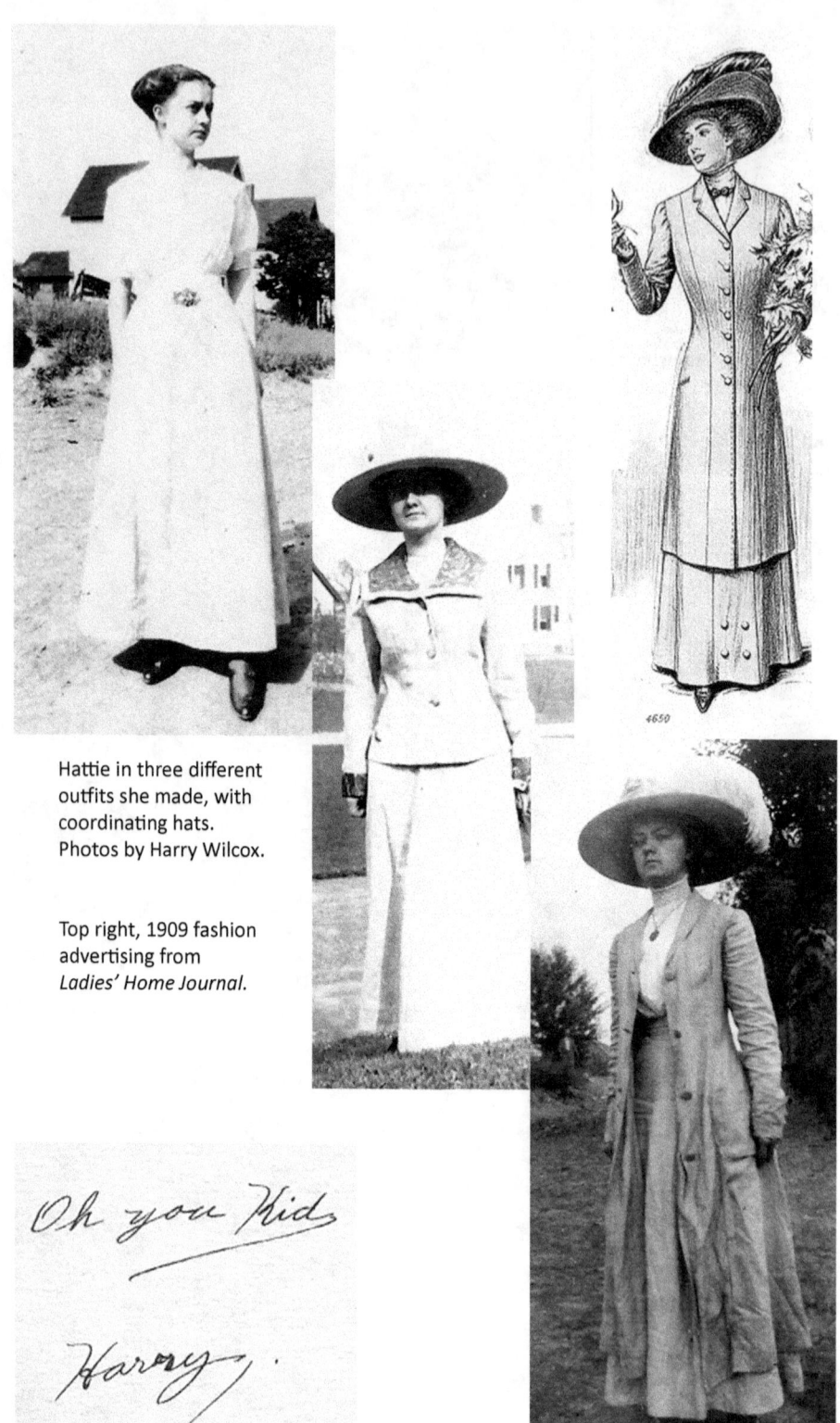

Hattie in three different
outfits she made, with
coordinating hats.
Photos by Harry Wilcox.

Top right, 1909 fashion
advertising from
Ladies' Home Journal.

4650

Oh you Kids

Harry.

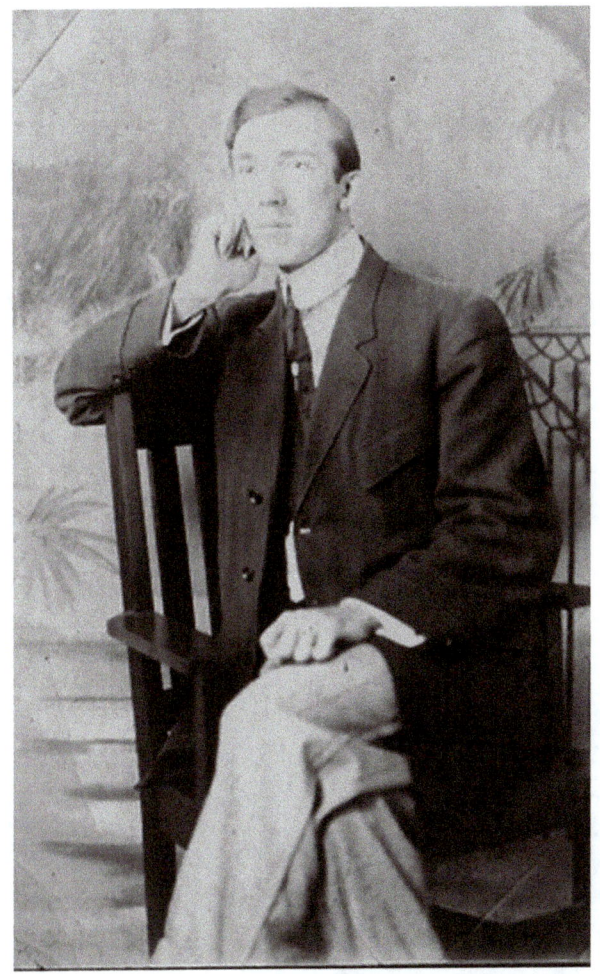

Harry Wilcox, 1911

BELL TELEPHONE

HARRY H. WILCOX

Commercial Artist

PHOTO RETOUCHING

143 WEST FOURTH STREET • WILLIAMSPORT, PA.

THIRD FLOOR HOUSEL BUILDING

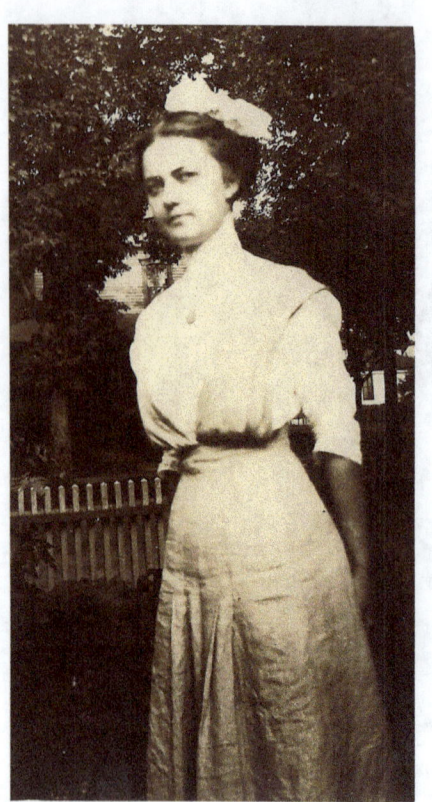

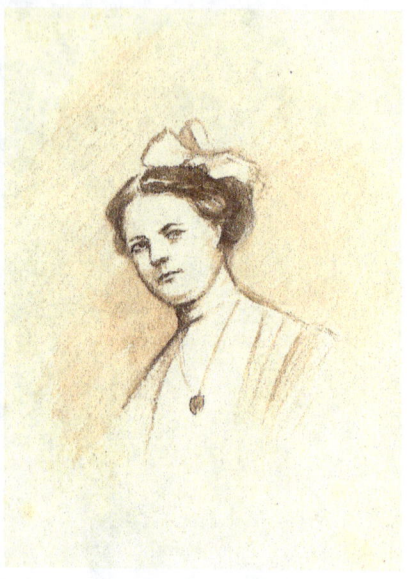

Hattie in a ribbon hat, watercolor.
Photo and drawing by Harry Wilcox

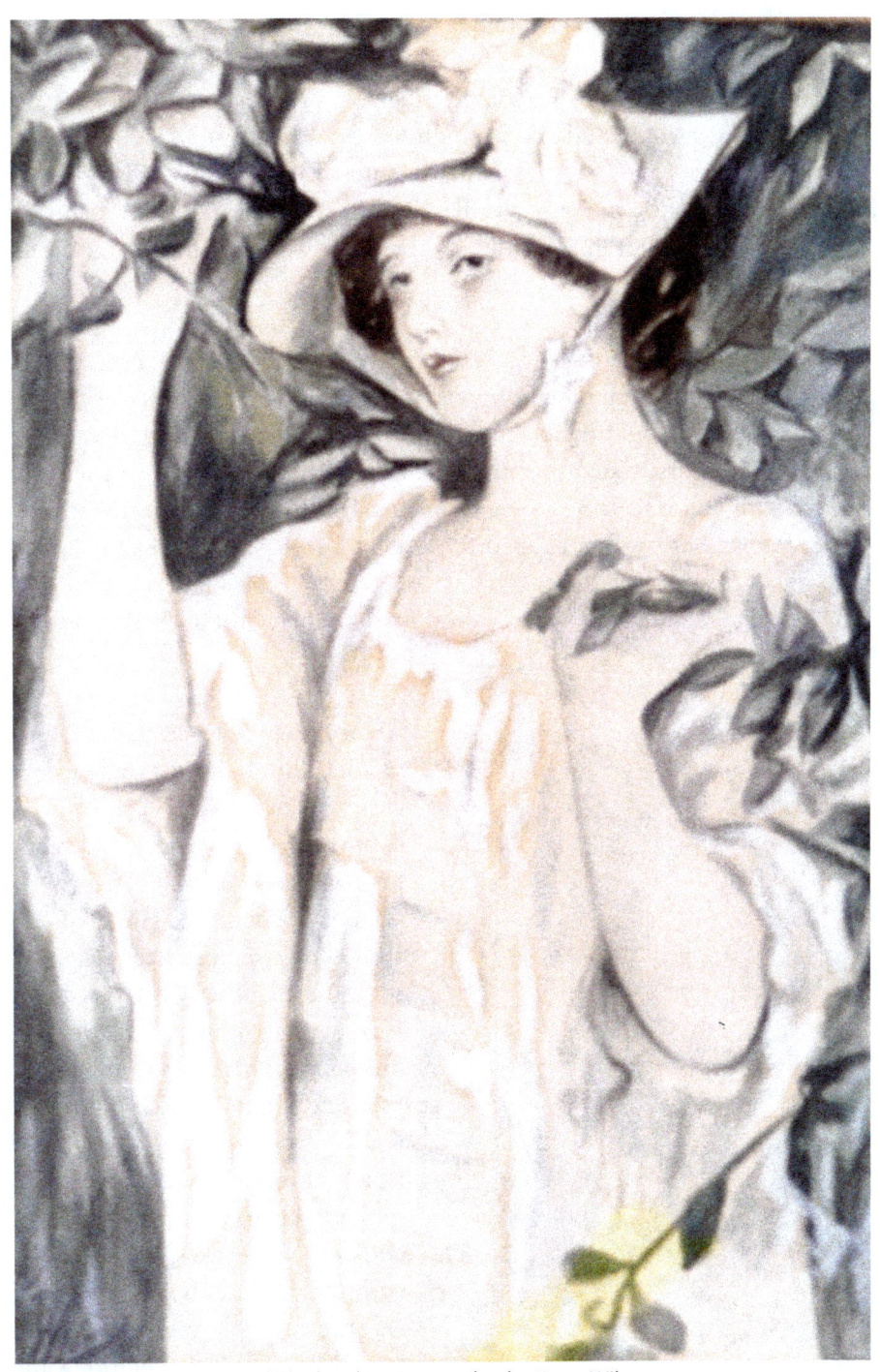

Lady in the Elms, watercolor, by Harry Wilcox

Hattie Estelle Richner was the fifth of six children of a second-generation Swiss immigrant family.

Hattie's grandfather, John Rudolf Richner, a stone mason, was born about 1816 in Switzerland and immigrated to America in 1854.[12] His son, Rudolf Richner, called "Dickie," the seventh of eight children, was born in 1859 in Norristown, Pennsylvania. Rudolf and his wife Clara Misho Richner had six children.[13] Hattie was the lucky woman who caught the artist's eye.

Rudolf Richner, a fine cabinet maker, built the house at 1128 Tucker Street for his family, all of whom were short in stature. In order not to squander heat, he built the ceilings short. One particularly remarkable feature was a spiral staircase with short treads, that were difficult for people with larger feet. At 4 feet 10 inches, Hattie was the tallest woman in her family; her brother topped them all at 5 feet 5 inches tall.[14]

The four girls had lived in one bedroom while their brother had another bedroom to himself.

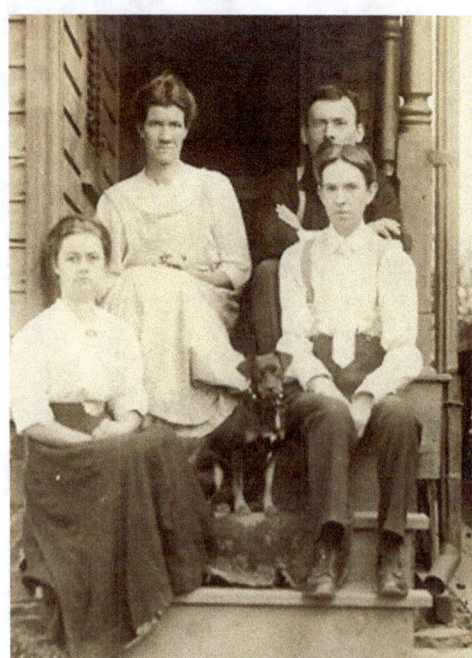

Hattie Richner (front left) working as a tailor for the Driscoll family in Williamsport. Eliza and James Driscoll and their son Thomas.

Their father believed that young women should have a trade in case they needed to be able to support themselves. He had seen his own father crippled in an accident, leaving the family in straitened circumstances. Each of Rudolf's daughters had a trade. Emmy was a seamstress and dressmaker; Mary was a milliner; Julia and Hattie were both tailors.

In addition, each had a specialty in the kitchen. Emmy baked cookies, Mary cakes, Julie helped with the general cooking. Hattie was the expert in yeast bread. She would stand at the dough tree and knead bread.

On one occasion Hattie proudly served a pie to her family, which her stern Swiss-German father was to cut and allocate around the table. He got out his hefty hand-made knife and worked hard. "Hattie!" he exclaimed, "This is the toughest pie crust you have ever made!" With that, the pie plate fell in half – he had cut through the metal pie plate. No one dared to laugh.

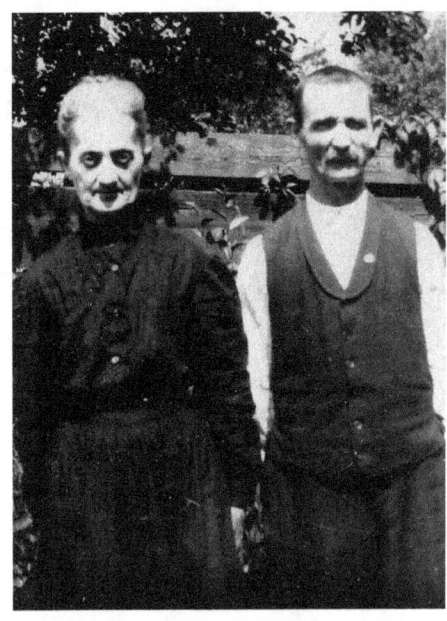

Clara and Rudolf "Dickie" Richner, about 1920

In the early part of the 20th Century, the postal service delivered mail twice a day to residences and three times a day to businesses. A postal card mailed in the morning would be delivered in the afternoon. Hattie and Harry exchanged hundreds of postal cards, frequently spelling out the arrangements for that very evening. When you had your camera film developed, you could ask that they be printed on postcard stock. Harry's photographs were often made up as postcards.

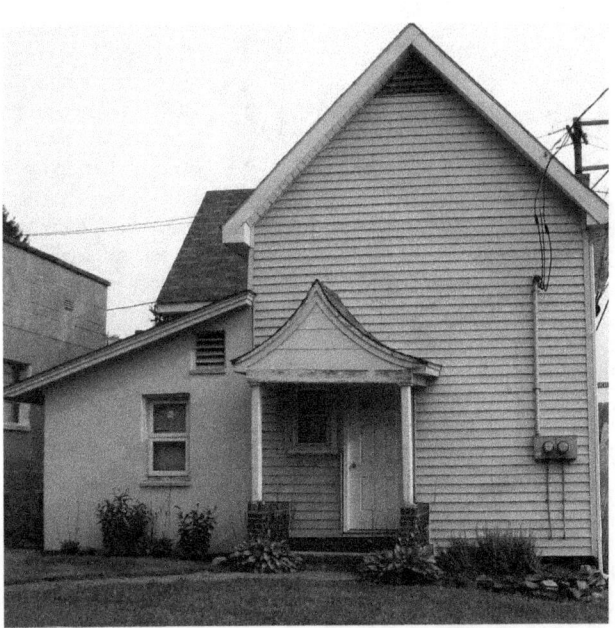

1128 Tucker Street, Williamsport, built by Rudolf "Dickie" Richner. "This is the back (south) side of the house toward Washington Blvd. The street (or alley) is on the east side of the house. Both sides of the house originally had porches that were removed by later owners. On the Tucker Street side was a sitting porch and the other was a back porch. The privy was under where there is now a building next door." Interview with June Wilcox, 2012. Photo taken 2009.

Julia and Hattie took pride in dressing fashionably, showing off their talents and those of their sisters — beautifully tailored clothes, and the dramatic hats so fashionable at the time.

Large hats required large hat pins — to keep them in place perched on an elegant coiffure, and to keep the hat from blowing away. Most hat pins were about eight inches in length, but the larger the hat, the longer the hat pin required. Laws were passed in 1908 in America which limited the length of hatpins, as there was a concern they might be used by suffragettes as weapons. Also by the 1910s, ordinances were passed requiring hatpin tips to be covered so as not to injure people accidentally.

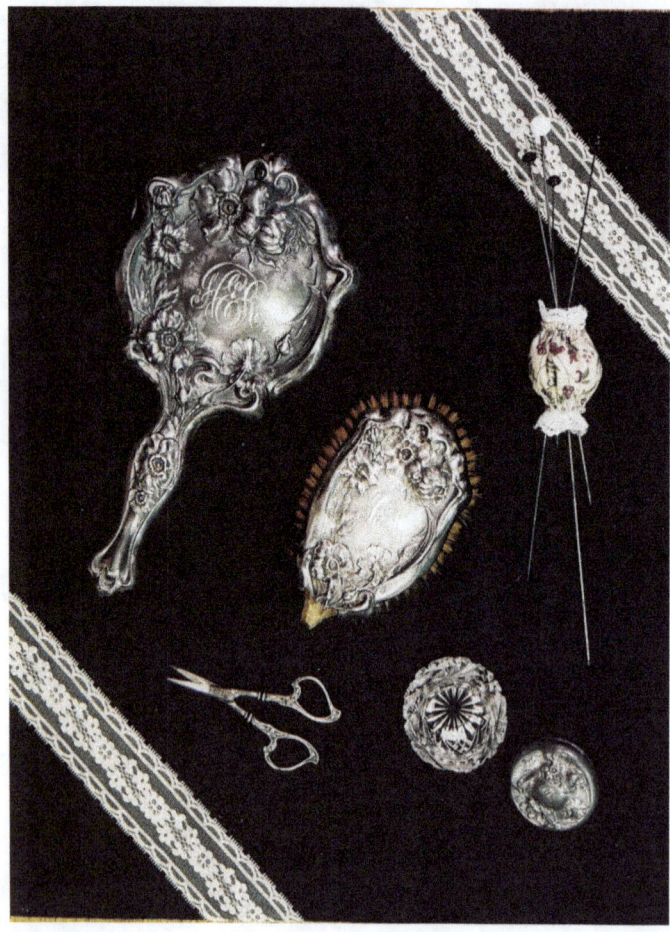

Silver vanity set given by Harry Wilcox to Hattie Estelle Richner, monogrammed "HER": mirror, brush, scissors, and a cut glass dish for pins with a silver lid. The two longest hatpins in this set are ten inches long.

Their fashionable dress provided great inspiration for the young artist. He loved to paint Hattie, the object of his affections, especially focusing on her eyes. She was parsimonious with her smiles throughout her life. This policy clearly stemmed from early days, as he teased her about catching her smiling in one photograph – a rare occurrence.

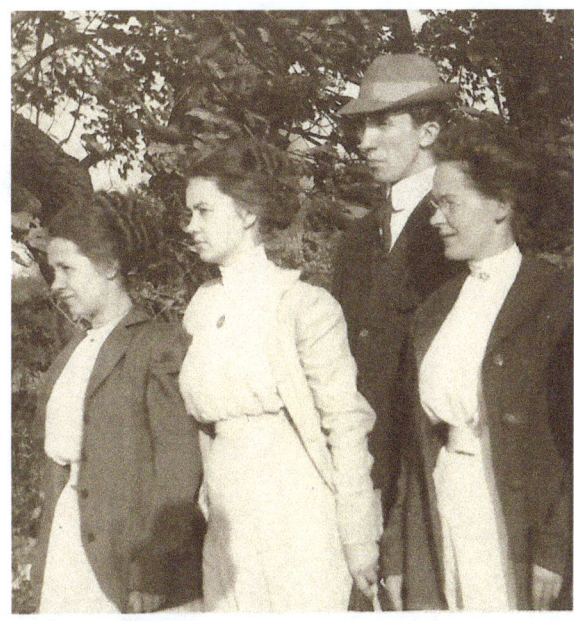

Julia and Hattie Richner, Harry Wilcox, and Emmy Winder.

At this point, the older two girls were married: Emmy to James Mahlon "Doc" Winder, and Mary to Charles Winder. Charlie was the nephew of Doc Winder. Both of them worked for the Williamsport Wholesale Grocery. Julia and Hattie were still living at home on Tucker Street with their parents. Doc was not a doctor, though he had once driven a car for a doctor.[14]

Julia made uniforms for postal workers and policemen. Hattie worked for a time as a tailor for the Driscoll family in Williamsport. Weekends were spent with her sisters, her handsome beau Harry Wilcox, and other friends. One favorite outing was to take a paddle boat or a canoe to Sylvan Dell, a scenic spot along the Susquehanna River where the young people often went for picnics.

Harry was fascinated with Hattie, photographing her face and form from every angle and using these as inspiration for many wonderful paintings of beautiful women in elegant clothes and hats. But most of all, he strove to capture that elusive quality in what he called her "dreamy eyes." At the end of 1910 he asked her to be his wife.

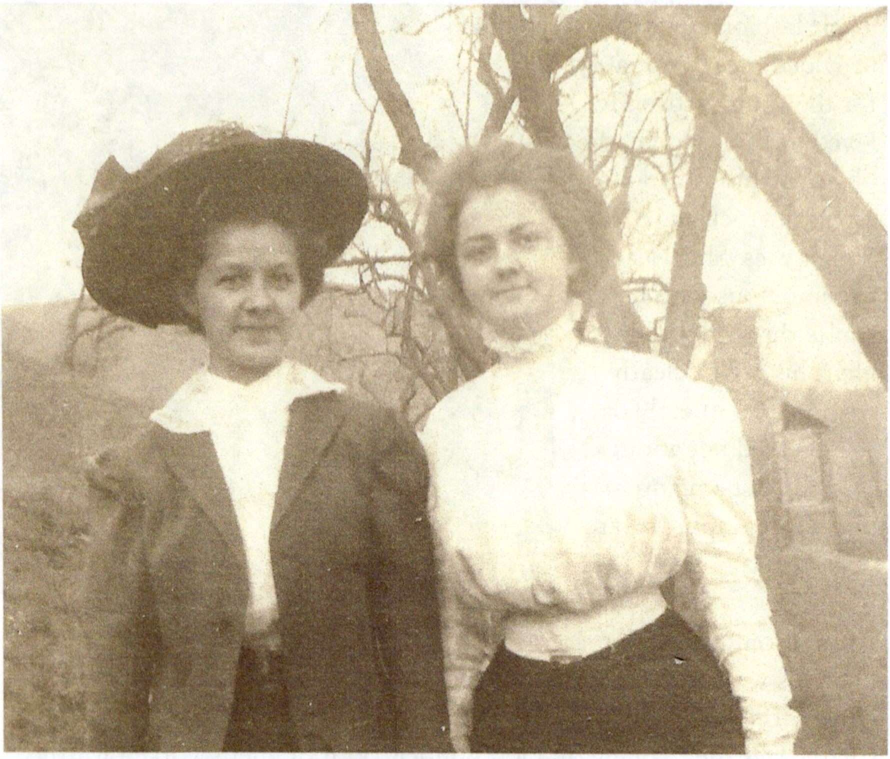

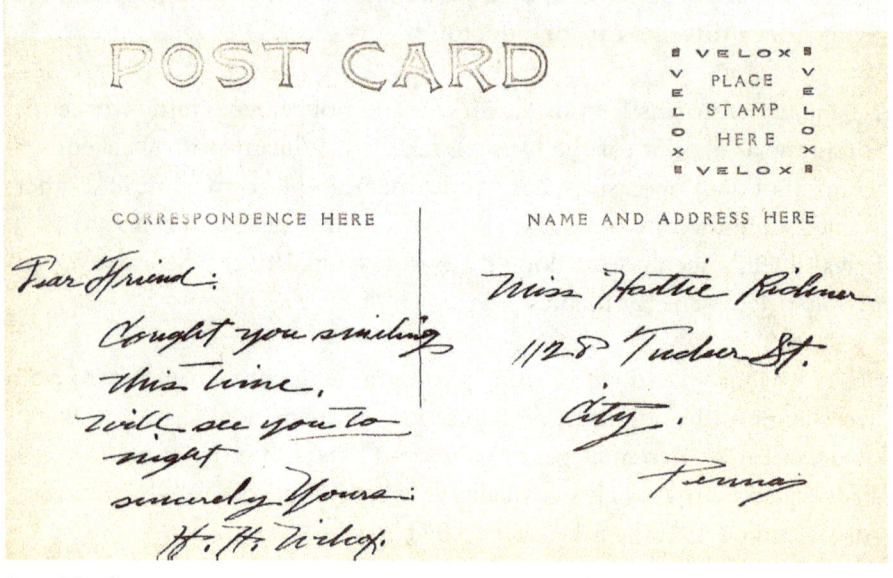

Julia Richner and Hattie Richner, behind their father's house on Tucker Street.
Photo by Harry Wilcox

Dear Friend,
Caught you smiling this time.
Will see you to-night.
Sincerely Yours, H. H. Wilcox

Miss Hattie Richner
1128 Tucker Street
City
Penna.

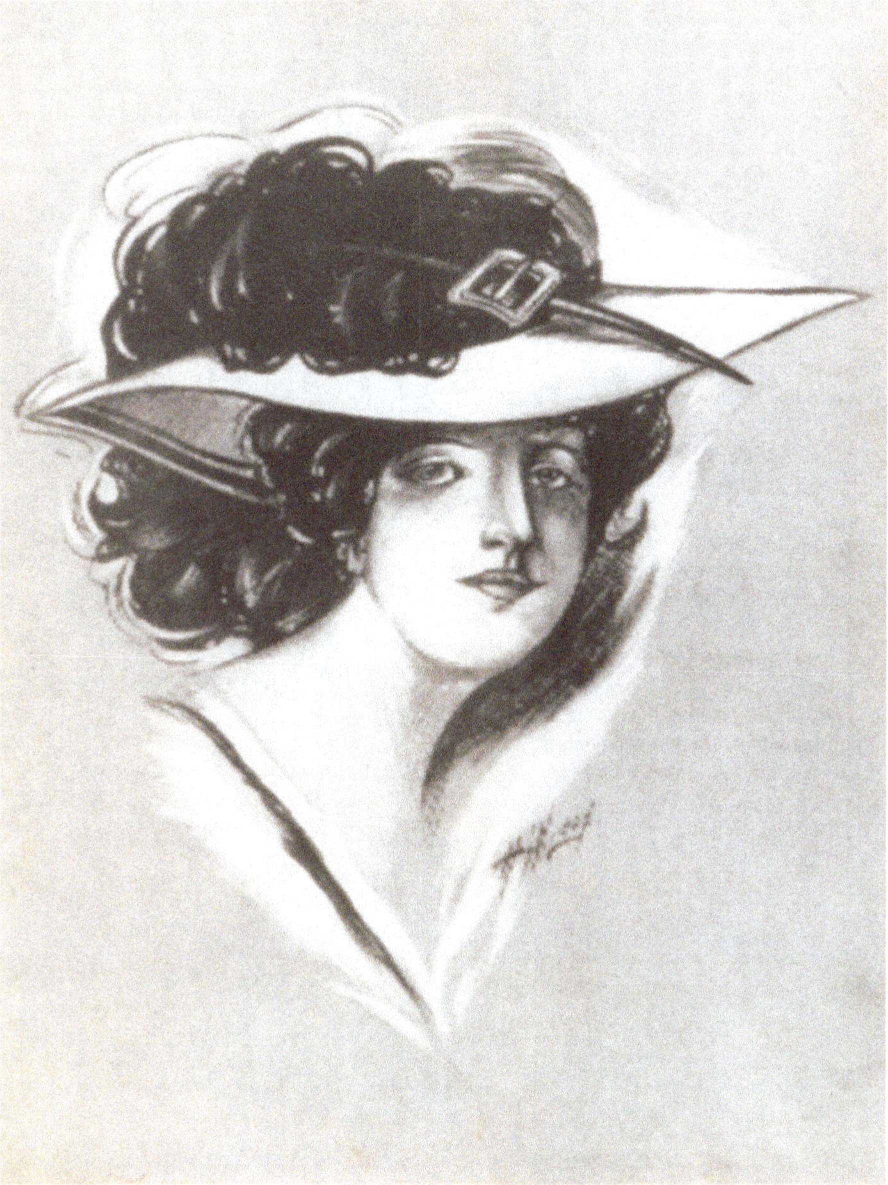

Fashionable Lady, by Harry Wilcox
Chalk and charcoal.

Right:
Label from
Arnold's Art Stores, Williamsport,
where Harry took his paintings
to be framed.

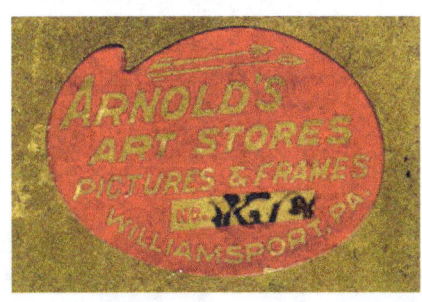

63

Just had a pipe dream . . .

Postcard, front and back
Pen and ink, by Harry Wilcox

"Williamsport, Pa.
Oct 2, '08

Arrived home safe.
Will see you Sunday evening at
church. Hoping that cold is better.
Yours sincerely,
H. Wilcox"

Notice in the pipe smoke what he is
dreaming about. This drawing echos
the concept in "When a Young Man
is in Love," page 37.

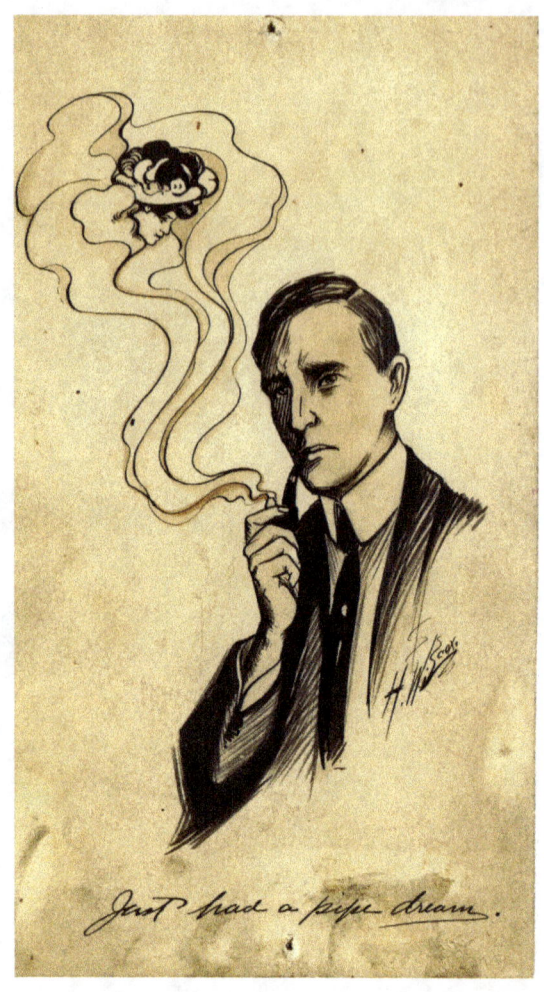

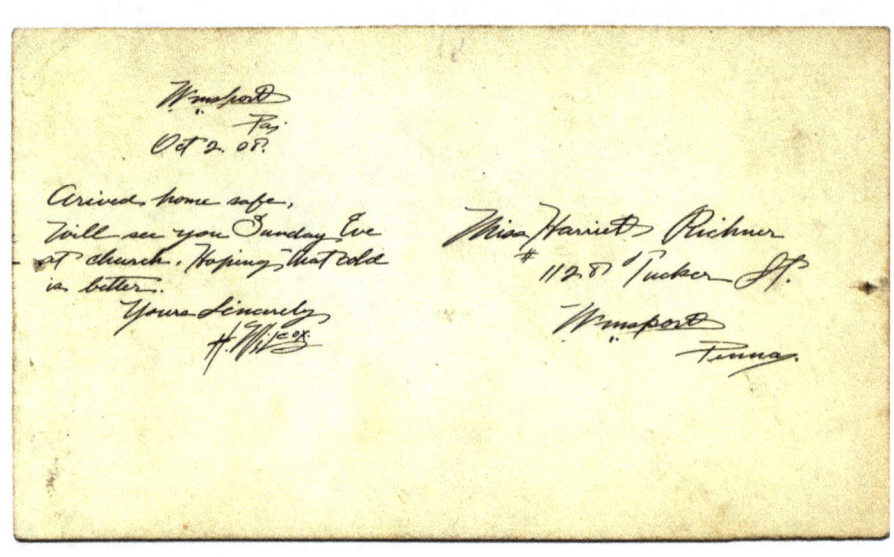

Wondrous hat

Postcard, front and back,
pen and ink by Harry
Wilcox

"Will see you tonight,
H. Wilcox"

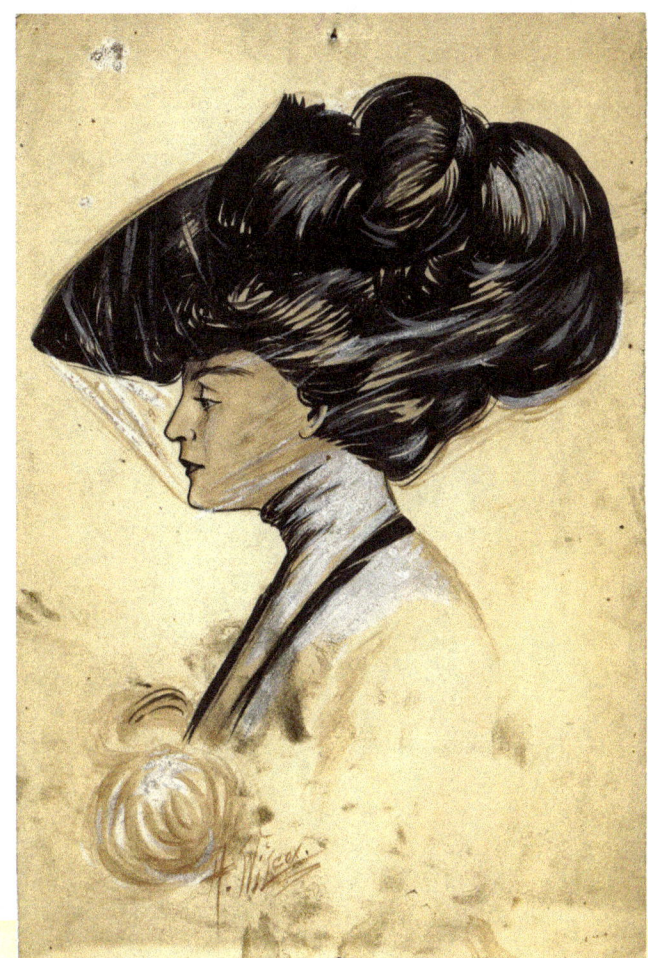

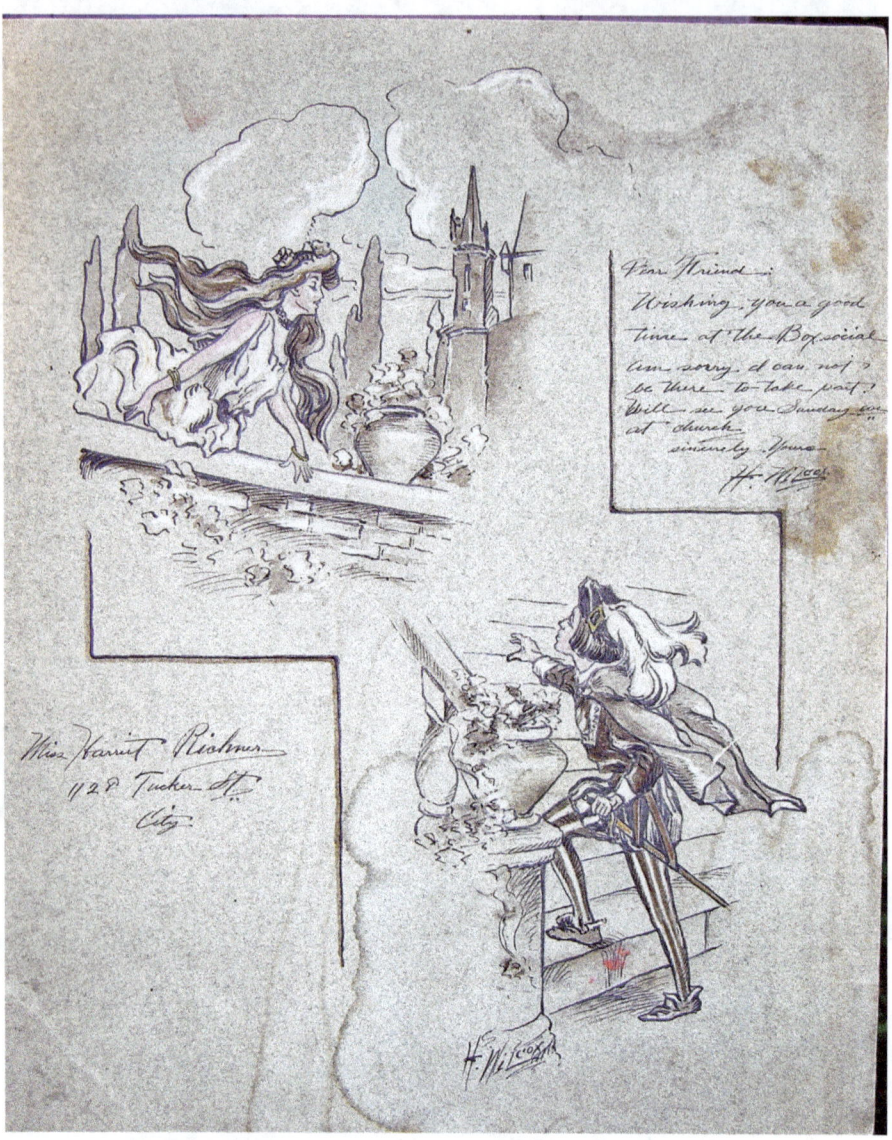

Romeo and Juliet revisited
Greeting card by Harry Wilcox. Pen and ink and colored pencil

"Dear Friend,
Wishing you a good time at the Box Social. I am sorry I cannot be there to take part. Will see you Sunday eve at church.
Sincerely yours,
H. Wilcox"

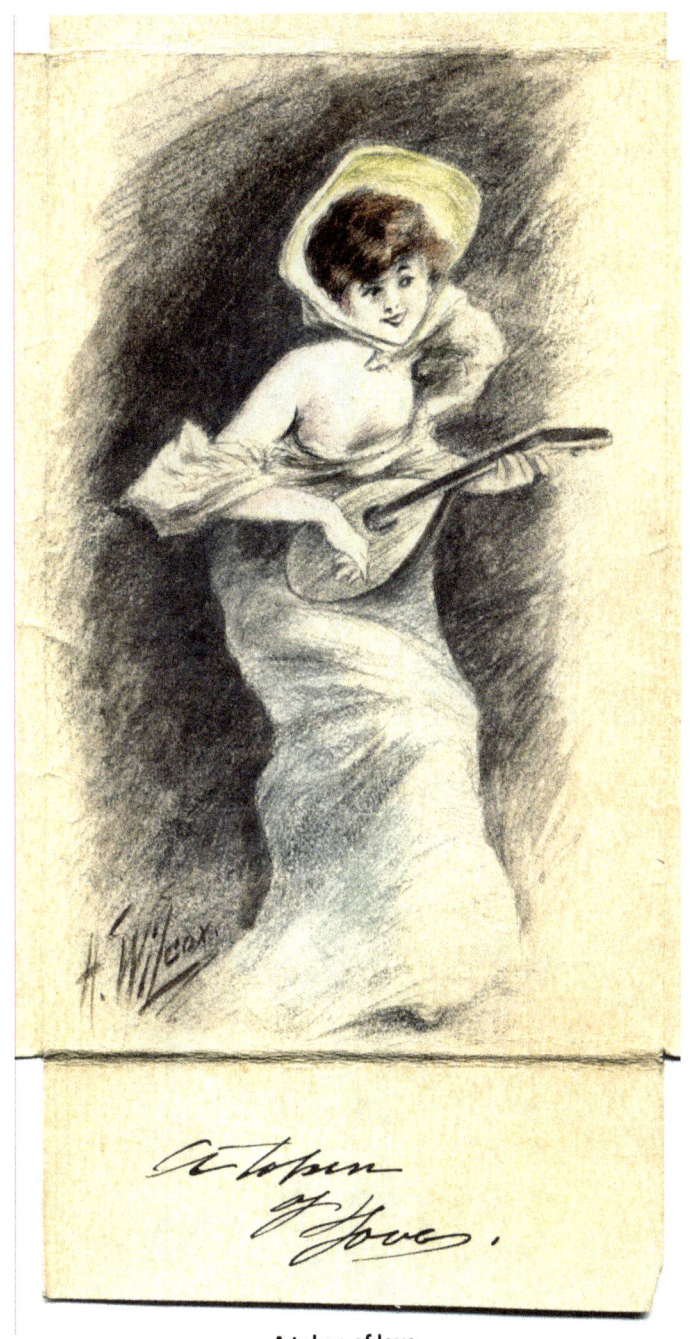

A token of love.

Drawn on the inside of the envelope by Harry Wilcox.
Colored pencil.

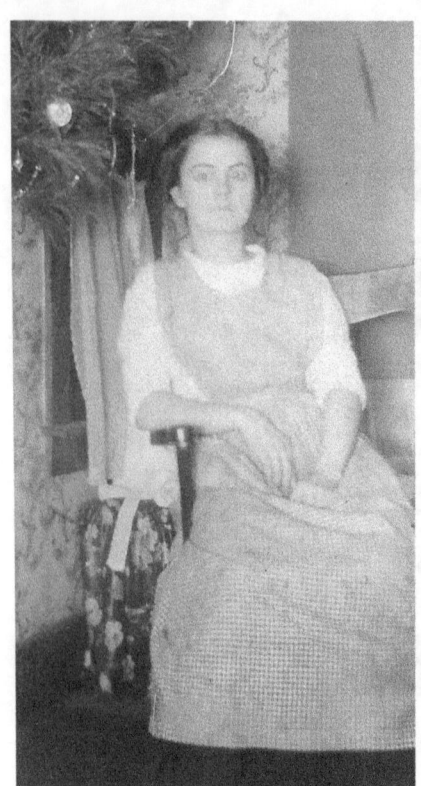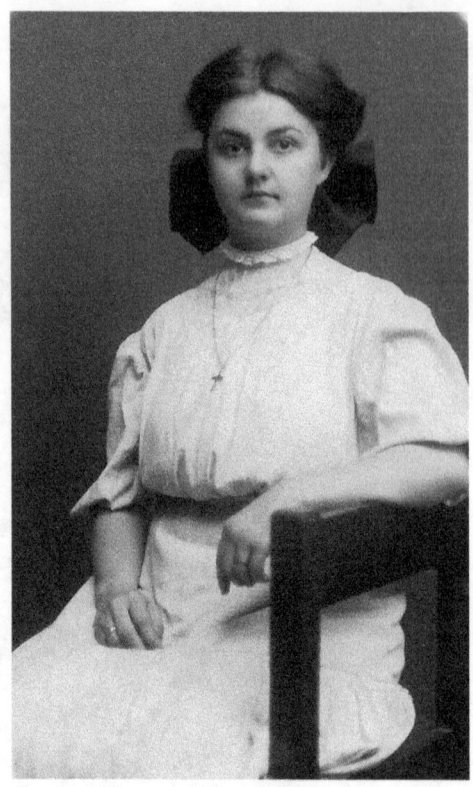

Hattie 1911

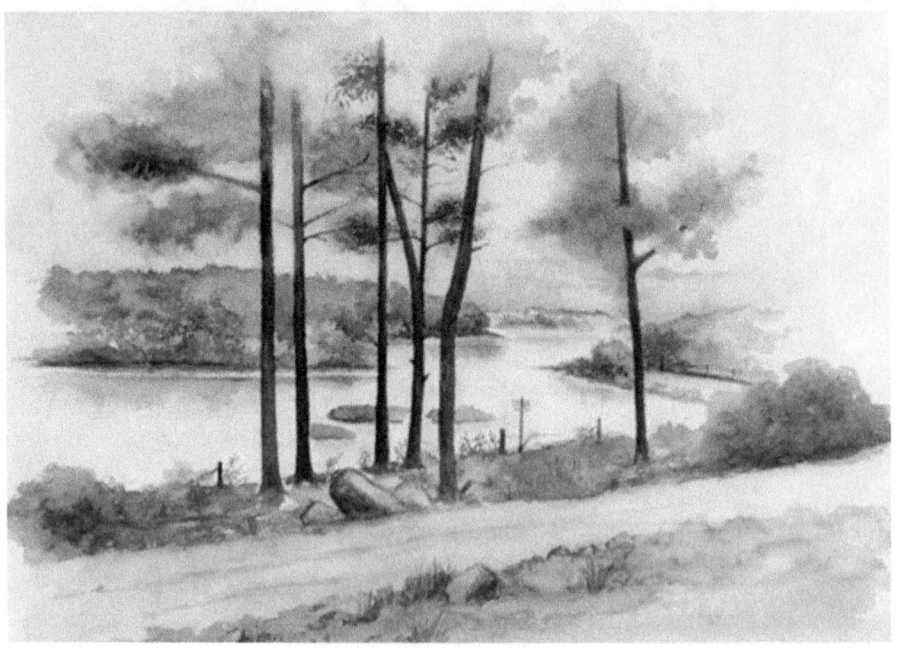

Sylvan Dell, along the Susquehanna River, a favorite picnic spot,
by Harry Wilcox, watercolor

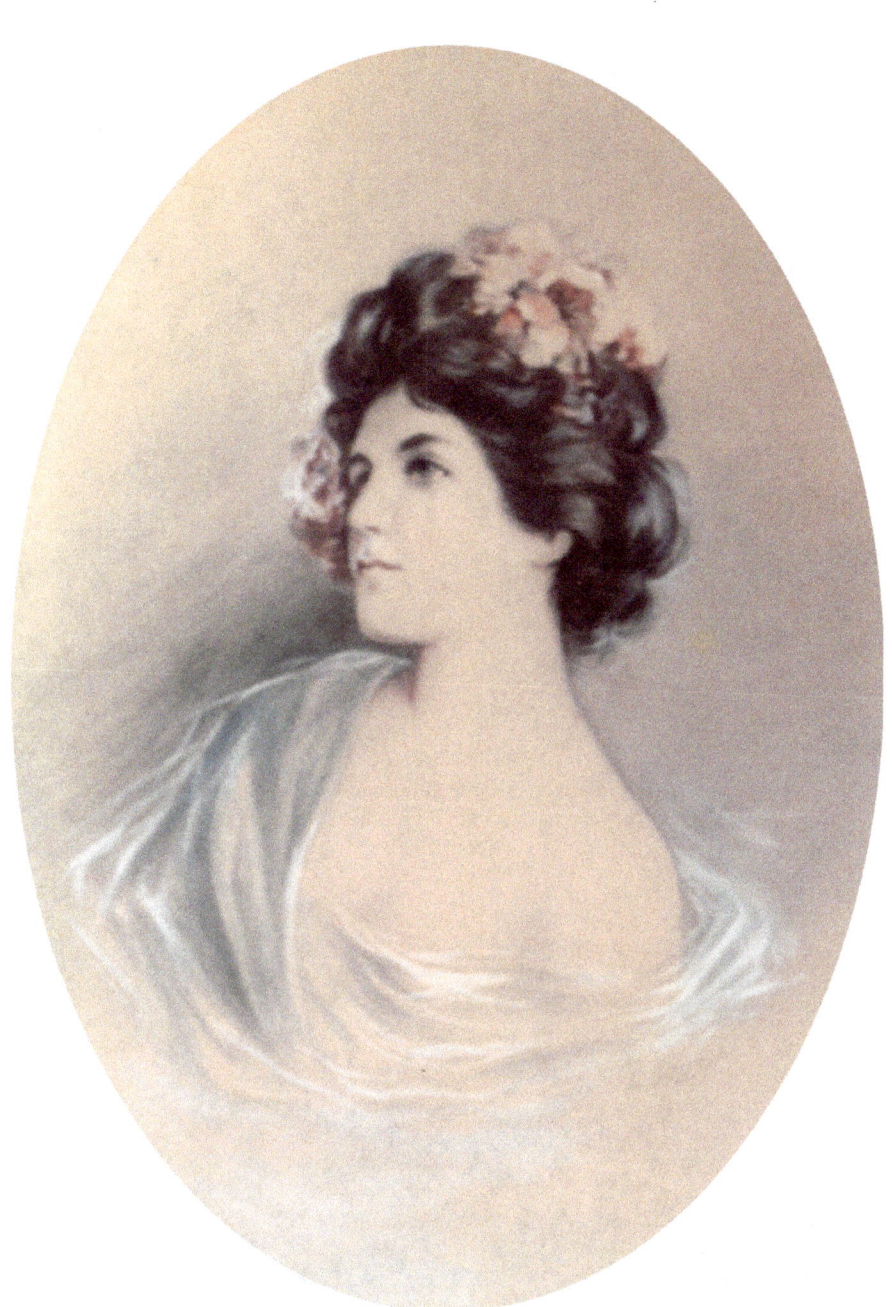

Woman with Dreamy Eyes, by Harry Wilcox. Watercolor on paper.

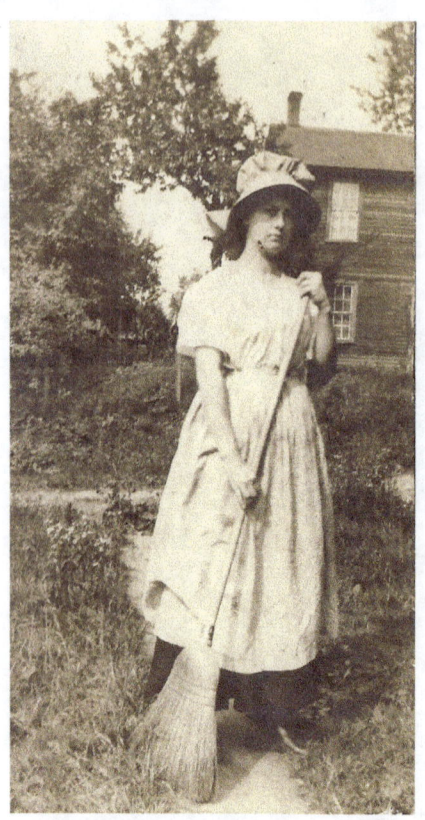
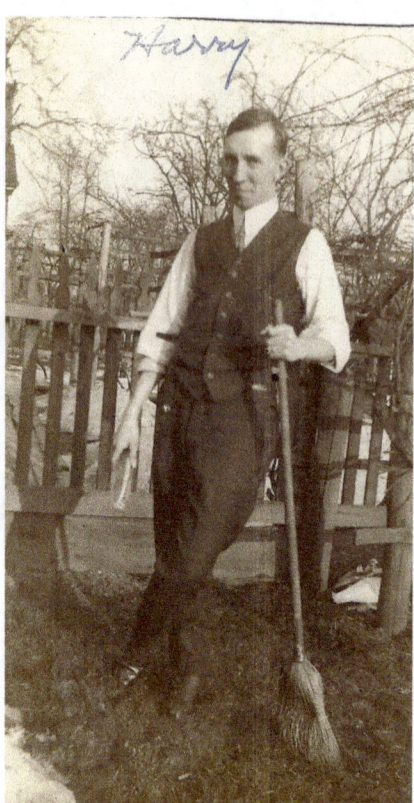

Hattie and Harry gardening — Hattie in the back yard at her father's house
on Tucker Street, Harry in the back yard of his mother's house at 1100 Isabella Street,
about 1909.

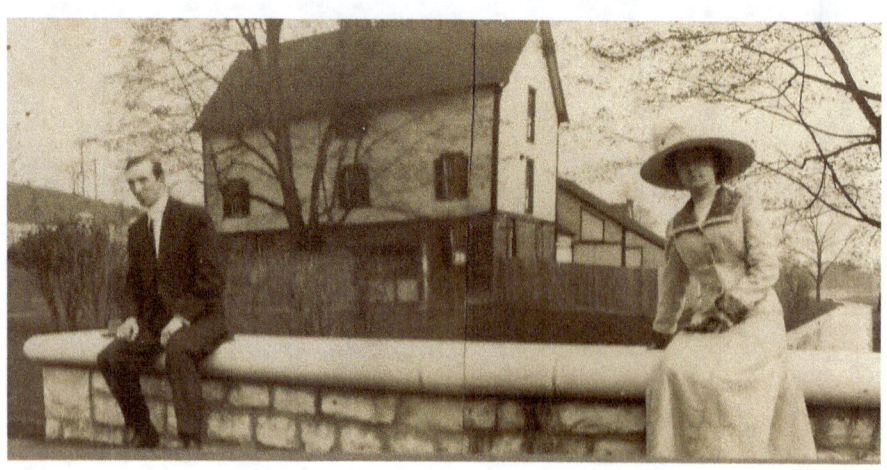

Harry and Hattie, dreaming of their own house.

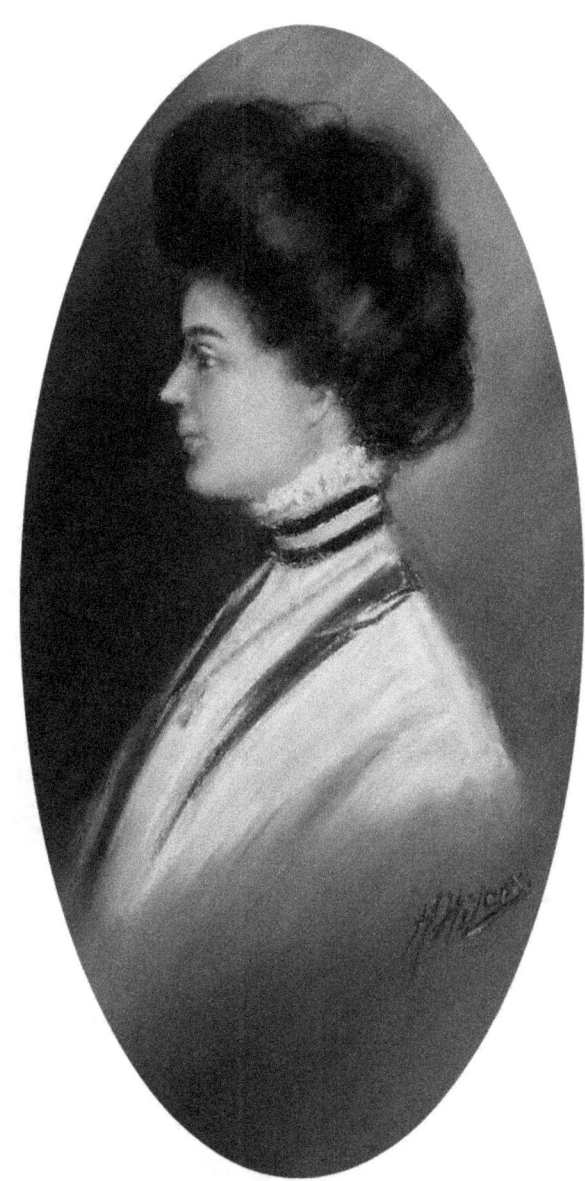

Hattie Richner, by Harry Wilcox

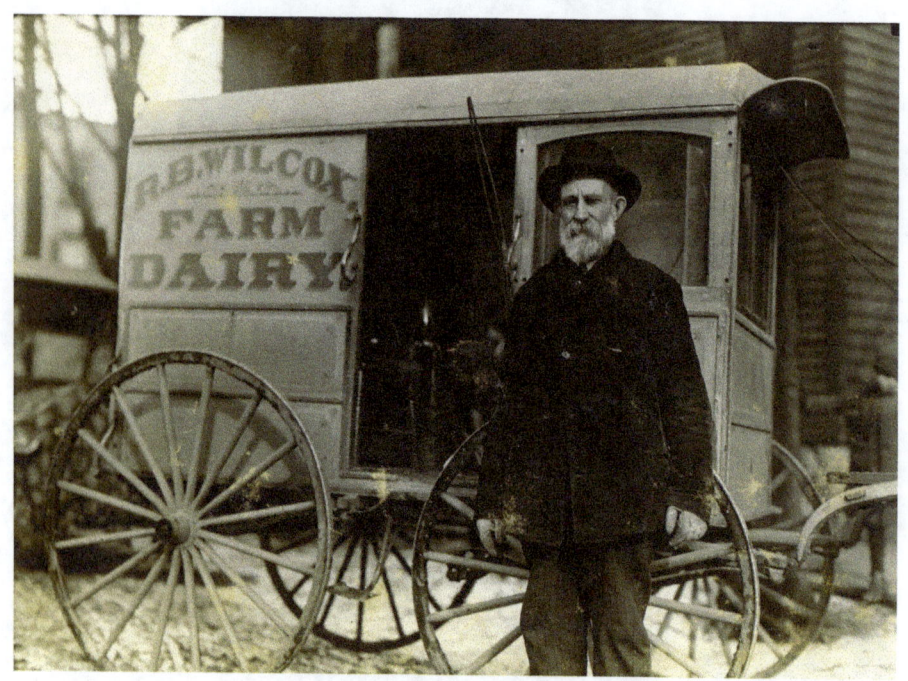

Robert Bruce Wilcox, James' eldest brother, delivering products from his Dairy Farm. His delivery wagon would have been similar to James'.

CHAPTER 4: TRAGEDY AND JOY

On January 28, 1911, the *Williamsport Gazette & Bulletin* reported:
> "Driver's Collar Bone Broken In Accident. James M. Wilcox, about 50 years old who was injured Thursday evening when a delivery wagon he was driving collided with an East End Trolley in Pine Street, sustained a broken collar bone and was taken to his home at 1100 Isabella Street, where he probably will be confined for several weeks."

Eight days later, on February 5, 1911, the Sunday Edition reported his obituary:
> "WILCOX - James M. Wilcox died at his home 1100 Isabella at 6 o'clock last evening following a short illness. About a week ago he was injured when a trolley struck his wagon in the East End and threw him to the street. Pneumonia developed and was the primary cause of death. … He was widely known throughout the city and vicinity through his connection with various tea companies."

Harry, his brother Warren, and sister Verna were all deeply affected by the death of their father. Not only did it have an emotional impact, it severely affected the economics of the family.

Verna was living at home on Isabella Street and was teaching music and

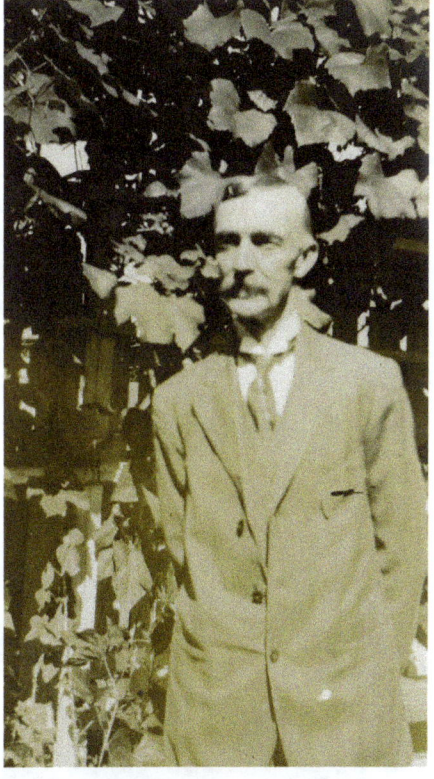

James M. Wilcox, butcher

73

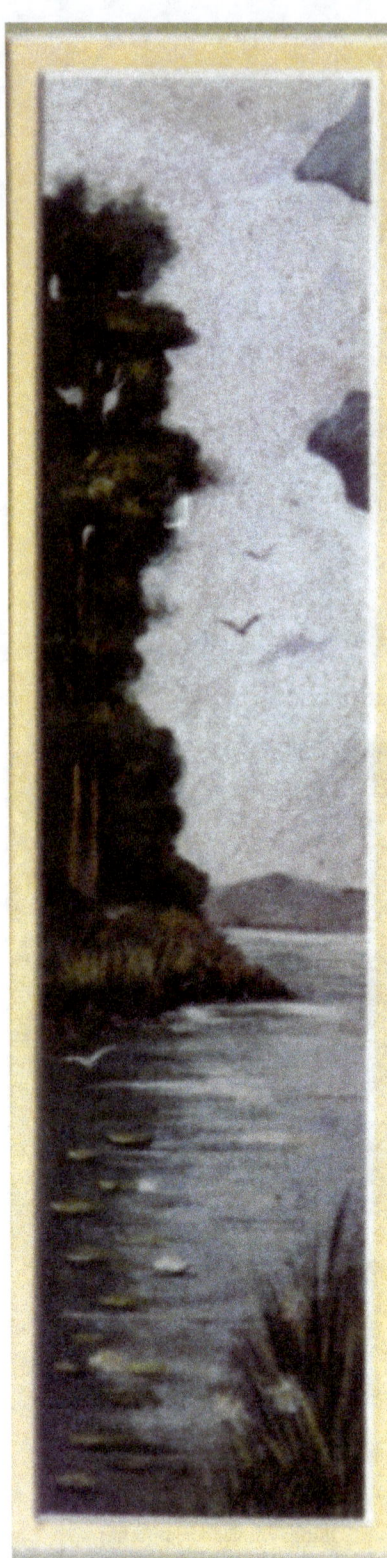

playing the organ in the Erie Avenue Baptist Church. In June 1911, she earned a Teachers' Certificate, with highest marks in Reading, Writing, Mental Arithmetic, and Music. In 1912, Verna was considering a teaching position at Pott's Shorthand College in Williamsport.[15]

Warren was also living at home. In 1910, Warren was working as a waiter in a restaurant.[16] Later he tended bar at the Occidental Hotel, across from the Market House in Williamsport.[17]

Harry and Hattie went forward with their wedding plans, marrying August 24, 1911, at St. Mary's Episcopal Church on Almond Street in Williamsport.[18] The *Grit* reported on September 3, 1911:

"Wilcox-Richner. *Grit* Artist married to Miss Hattie E. Richner. Mr. Harry Wilcox and Miss Hattie E. Richner, both of this city, were united in marriage in St. Mary's Episcopal Church, Thursday morning Aug 28 at 5 o'clock by the Rev. F. W. B. Dorset. They left immediately for a wedding trip which included a visit to Philadelphia, Atlantic City, New York, and other Eastern cities. Last week they spent several days near

Along the Susquehanna, by Harry Wilcox, watercolor.

Milton [in Limestoneville], visiting relatives. Mr. Wilcox has been employed a number of years as an artist by *Grit* and is regarded as a young man of ability in his line. Mr. and Mrs. Wilcox will reside in this city."

Five o'clock in the morning was not an unusual time for a wedding in those days – they needed to get from the East End to the Park Hotel to catch the train for their wedding trip. Married on Thursday, they were able to take advantage of the long Labor Day weekend.

They set up housekeeping at 1108 Washington Street, Williamsport, not far from Hattie's family home on Tucker Street.

A year later, on August 21, 1912, their daughter Verna Kathryn was born in Williamsport. Thrilled with his new daughter, Harry added a new favorite theme to his painting: mother and child.

In 1915, Hattie and Harry moved to 1058 E. Third Street.

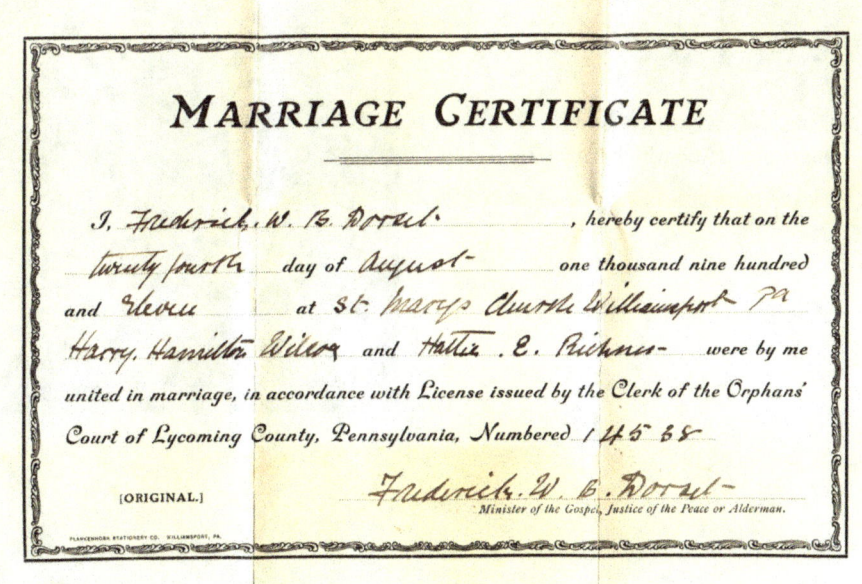

Marriage certificate, signed by Rev. Frederick W. B. Dorset. Rev. Dorset misspelled Harry's middle name, which should be Hammond, not Hamilton.

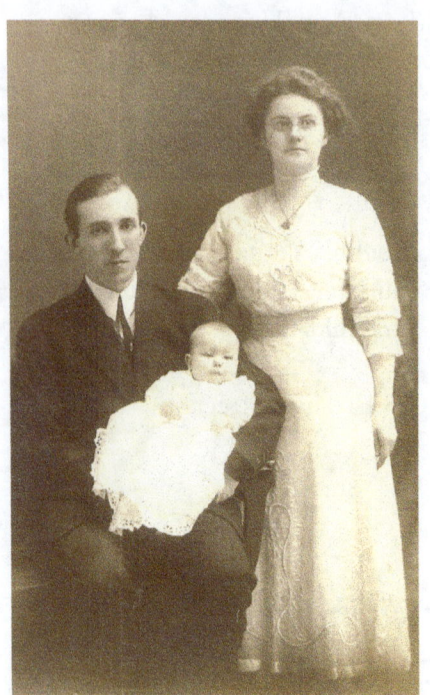

Harry and Hattie with baby Verna.

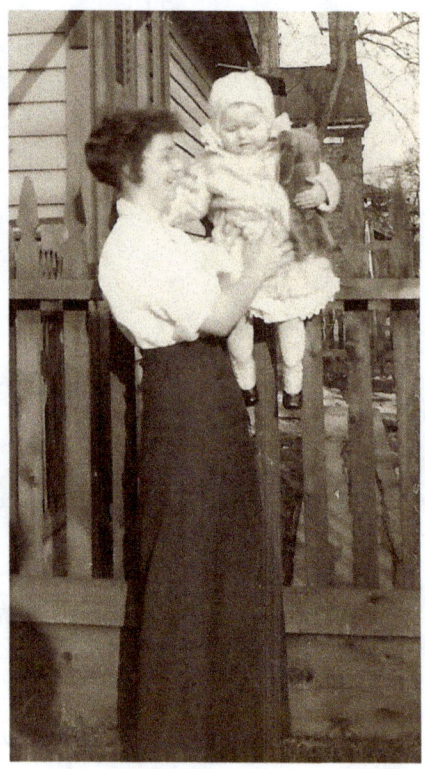

Hattie and Verna

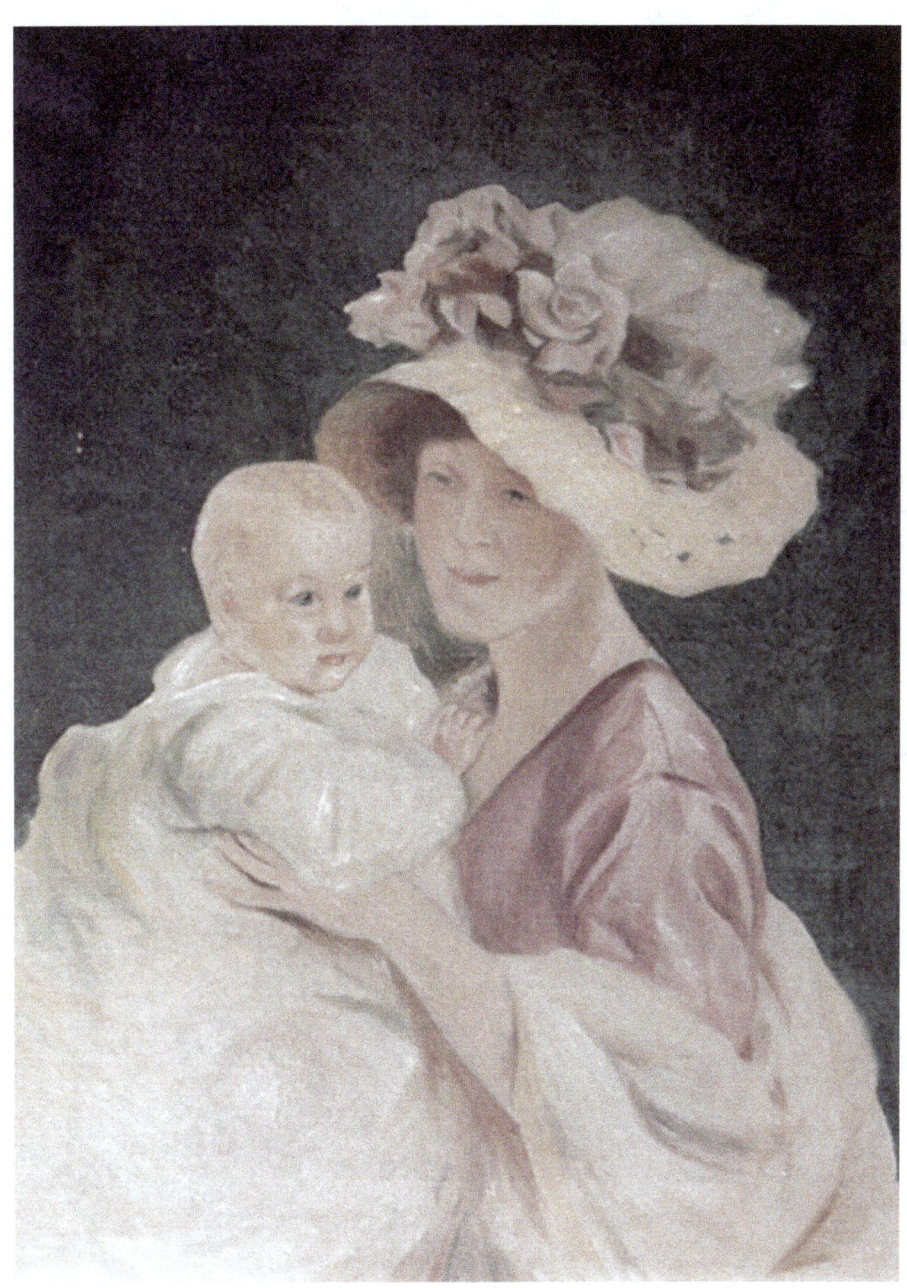

Mother and child, by Harry Wilcox. Oil on canvas

Harry's sister, Verna Margaret, married John Grenfall Emminger in 1916 at the Erie Avenue Baptist Church in Williamsport, PA. A year later they too welcomed a daughter, Jane Ann Emminger.

Less than a year later, on October 20, 1918, Verna Margaret Emminger gave birth to a son, Daniel J. Emminger.

On October 29, 1918, Warren wrote to Harry and Hattie:

"Dear Brother and Sister and family. Read your Cartoon. Will say very clever. We are all well except Verna has been sick lately together with her giving birth, it's a boy, and influenza too. Give regards to Hattie, Verna, and Baby. — Warren." The following day, Verna Margaret died.

The Spanish influenza pandemic of 1918 took a heavy toll worldwide, and no less in Williamsport. Eleven days after the birth of her son Daniel, exhausted from childbirth and the Spanish flu, Verna Margaret Wilcox Emminger died. Jane was a few days short of her first birthday when her mother died at age 26 years 6 months 17 days. John moved to Sharon, Pennsylvania, some 200 miles away, with his two very small children.[19]

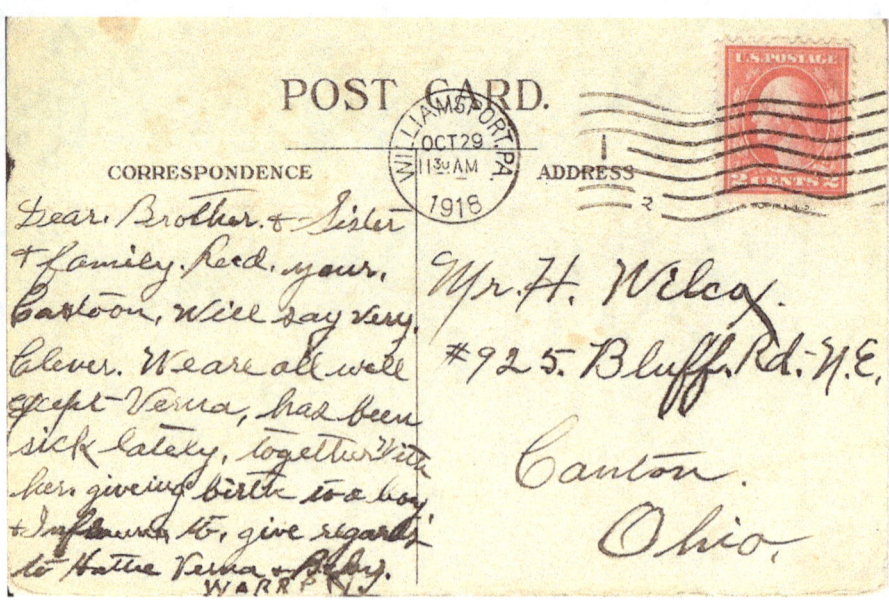

Warren in Williamsport to Harry in Canton, Ohio, October 29, 1918

John took a job with American Steel and Wire Company as a bookkeeper and as the company telegrapher. He was a member of the basketball and baseball teams, and was a leader of the plant orchestra, playing the cornet. He continued to sing in the choir of his church.[20]

December of 1917 found Harry, Hattie, and daughter Verna Kathryn in Canton, Ohio, working in the industrial inner city of Canton, and continuing to do piece work for the *Grit*. Exactly what job drew him to Canton is not known. Republic Steel was in Canton, along with a wide range of opportunities in advertising, illustration, and photo retouching. The fact that this move coincided with the involvement of the United States in World War I may be significant. Certainly the War Department required a great many artists for advertising campaigns, map-making, and the new field of animation.

Like many young artists of his time, Harry was fascinated with animation.

John Randolph Bray and Earl Hurd had patented a new method of automating the production of the thousands of drawings needed to produce a moving cartoon. The simple line drawings that had comprised most of automation up to this point took on new character, as backgrounds could be drawn on celluloid ("cels") which would then be stacked together and moved independent of one another to cause motion in successive photographs. As Hurd said, speaking of his patent, "One of the objects of my invention is to enable such animated cartoons to be made with the minimum of effort and expense and to facilitate the rapid execution of any series of poses relating to or constituting a single scene."[21]

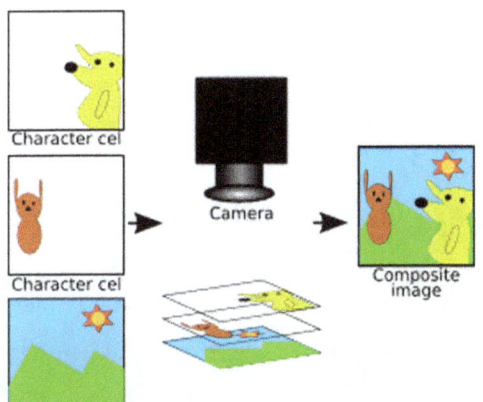

This image shows how two transparent cels, each with a different character drawn on them, and an opaque background are photographed together to form the composite image. Leybourne, *The Animation Book,* 1979.

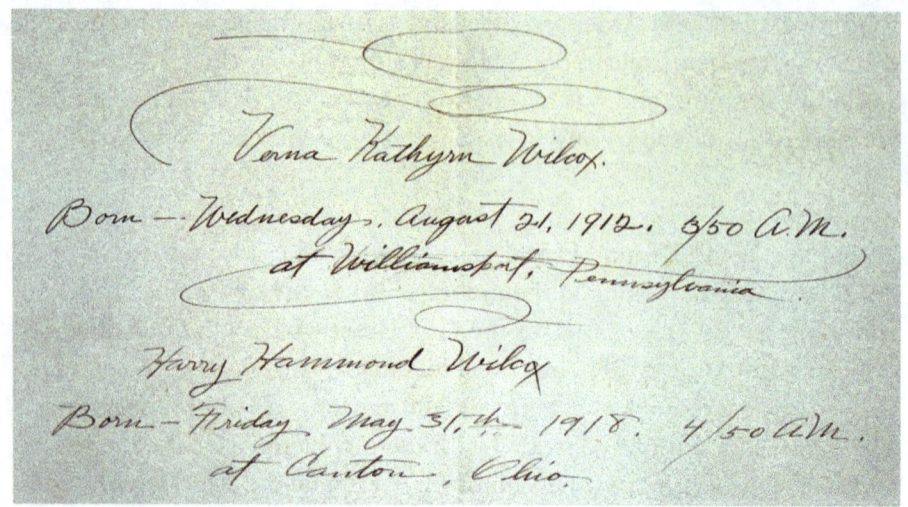

Harry Wilcox records the births of his two children. In his handwriting.

Harry continued to do work periodically for the *Grit* while pursuing new opportunities in Ohio. He bought a house in Canton, which Hattie would always say was her favorite house ever.

Baby Harry Jr. (called "Baby" and later "Brother" or "Bud") was born in Canton, Ohio, on May 31, 1918. Hattie quickly went back to Williamsport to be near her sisters while recovering from the birth. They would certainly have helped a great deal caring for 5-year-old Verna. Whether it was discontent with the job in Canton or Hattie's discontent at being so far from her sisters, by November the house was sold, and Harry was living in the YMCA in Canton to finish up his job there, while his wife and children were back in Williamsport.

In April 1919, Max Fleischer released his first "Out of the Inkwell" cartoon starring Ko-Ko the Clown. Harry's interest in animation was

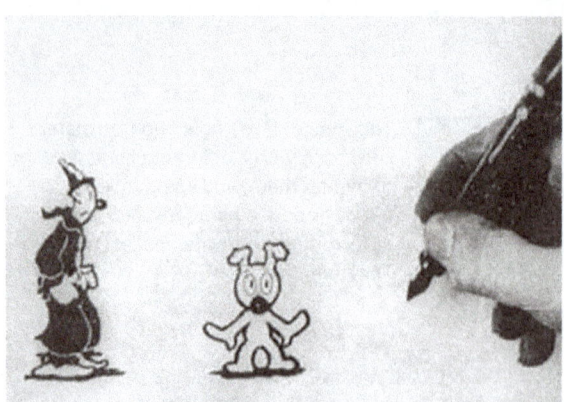

Film still from the "Ko-Ko Chops Suey" (1927) Inkwell Imps cartoon starring Ko-Ko the Clown and Fitz the Dog, by Max Fleischer.

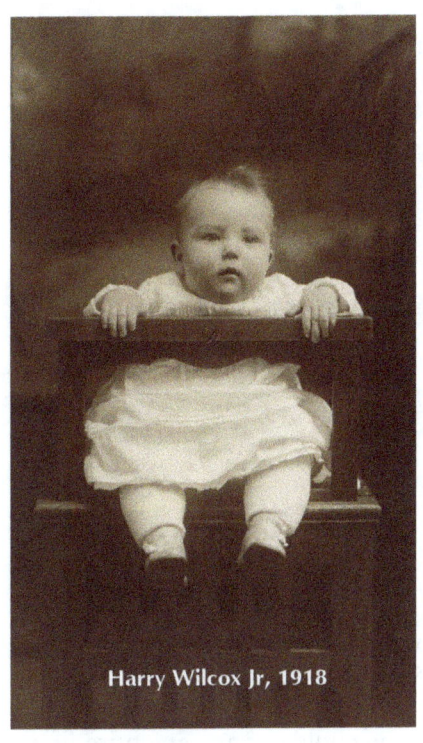

Harry Wilcox Jr, 1918

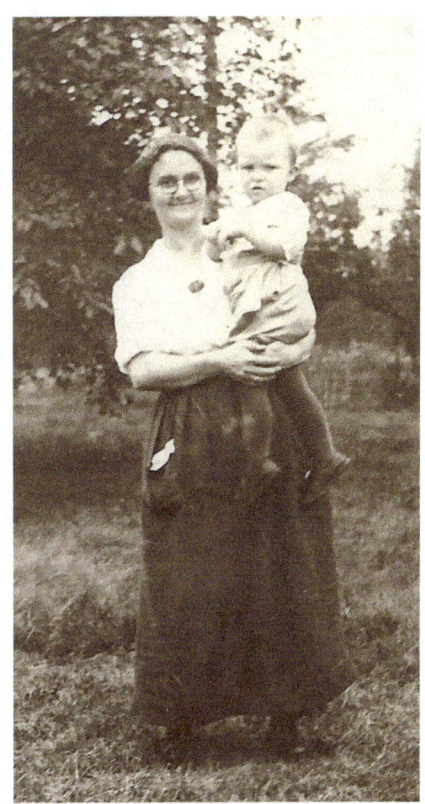

Hattie and Bud, 1919.

"Canton, Ohio, August 1918
Dear Wife,
Received the picture of Verna and Baby. It is fine. Gee he is fat and bright looking. Am glad you had them taken. With love, Harry."

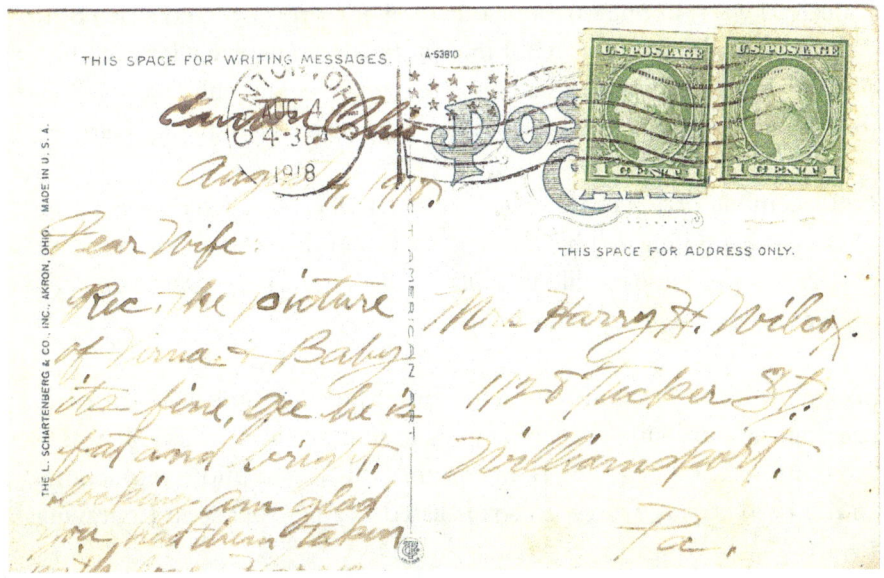

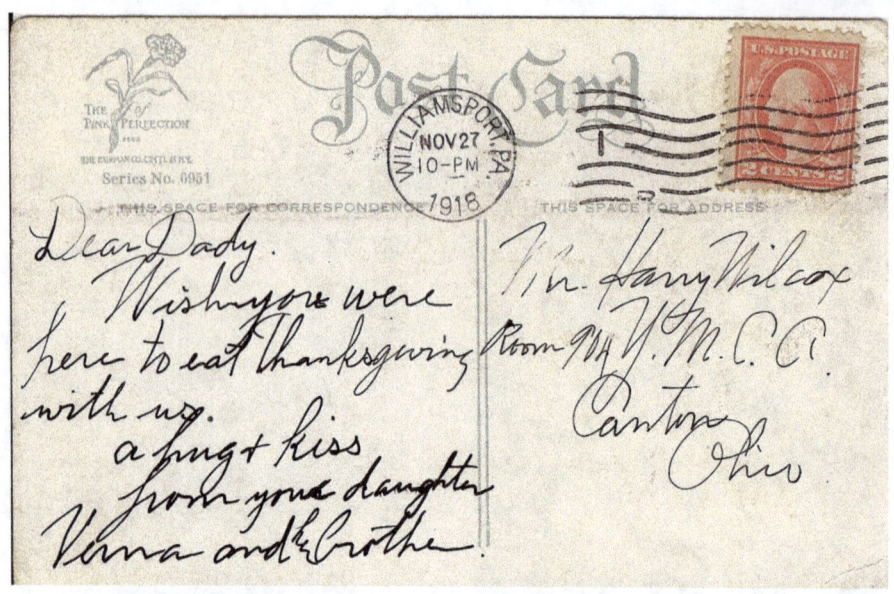

"November 22, 1918
Mr. Harry Wilcox, Room 904, Y.M.C.A., Canton, Ohio
Dear Daddy,
Wishing you were here to eat Thanksgiving with us. A hug and kiss from your daughter, Verna and her brother." In Hattie's handwriting.

rising. Always expert with line drawings, he could execute an entire figure without lifting his pen. Fleischer's pen-and-ink comedies excited him. "The cartoons were marvels of invention, imagination and charm and were also hilariously funny. No two cartoons ever started the same way. Ko-Ko makes his entrance in an almost infinite variety of brilliantly conceived ways: in one cartoon, a drop of ink drips off Max's pen onto a sheet of paper, the blot that it makes transforming itself into the figure of the clown; in another, a half-finished Ko-Ko grabs the pen and draws the rest of himself after Max is called away from the drawing board."[22]

By December 1919, Harry was in Merchantville, New Jersey, across the Delaware from Philadelphia, seeking work in Philadelphia. He commuted by ferry from Merchantville to Philadelphia because the Delaware River bridge was not built until the 1920's.

Seeking work as a commercial artist meant putting some work into a portfolio, and walking into companies to inquire about work. He was hired quickly, and began work in commercial art and photo retouching. In the 1920 census, Harry Wilcox is listed as an "Artist at an Engraving

Merchantville, N.J., December 7, 1919
to Mrs. Harry H. Wilcox 1128 Tucker Street, Williamsport (her parents' home)
Dear Hattie, Verna, and Baby,
Hope you got my letter, as I am anxious to hear from you all. It stormed all day Saturday so I did not get around much. So start out Monday to look for work. Hope you and children are well. With love, Harry

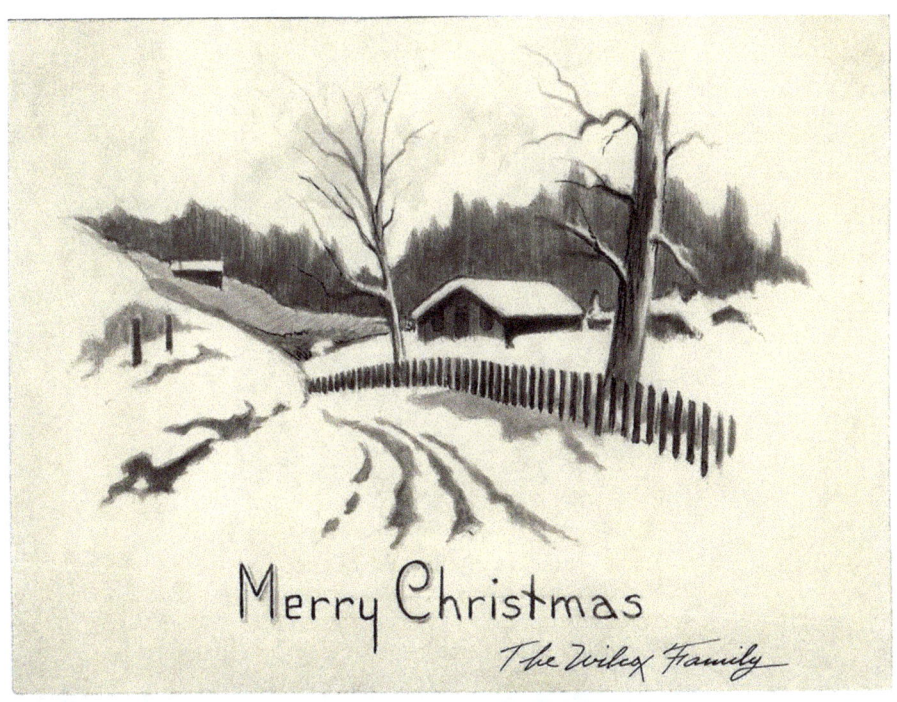

Hand-drawn card by Harry Wilcox, sent to Julia and Ross Conn. Courtesy of Fred Barrett.

House," living in Camden, New Jersey, boarding with Arthur Emerson in Merchantville.

On February 21, 1921, another baby was born, Lewis Richner Wilcox. He died after only a few days,[23] leaving Hattie weak and despondent. She reached out to her sisters again for support during her recovery. Her sister Mary went to Merchantville to care for Hattie, Verna and Bud, while Harry continued working in Philadelphia. Mary took her daughter Verena with her to Merchantville, and Verena attended school there for a time.[24] Hattie must have had a serious bout with post-partum depression which impacted her for several years.[25] Her sisters described it as a "breakdown."

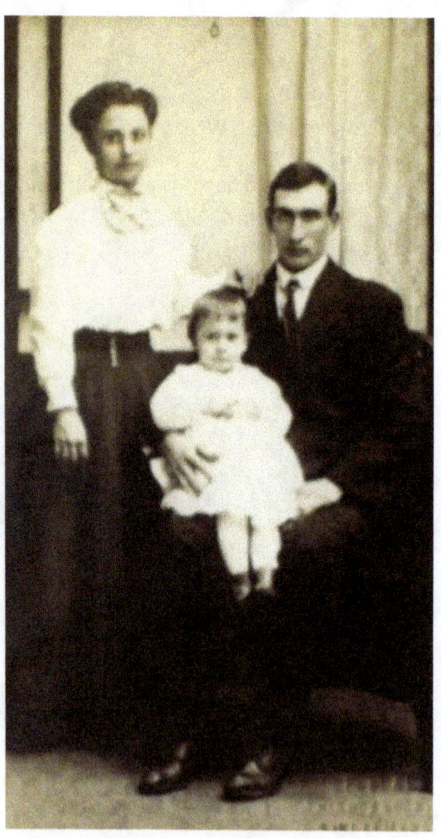

Hattie's sister Mary Richner Winder, her husband Charles Winder, and their daughter Verena (born October 1909), about 1911. Verena is a family name in the Richner family, just as Verna is a family name in the Wilcox-Kramm family.

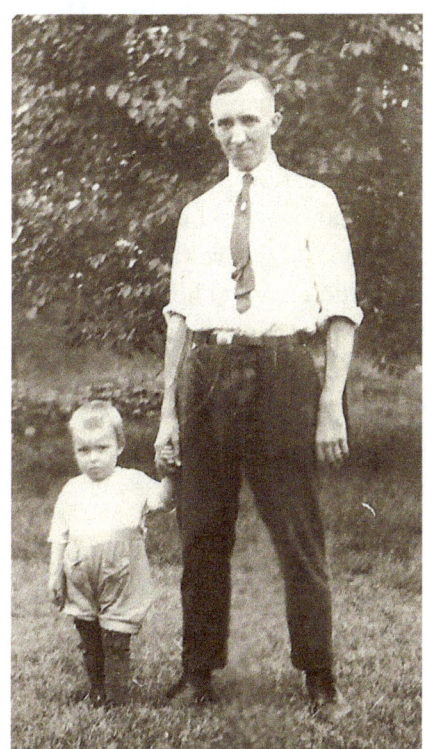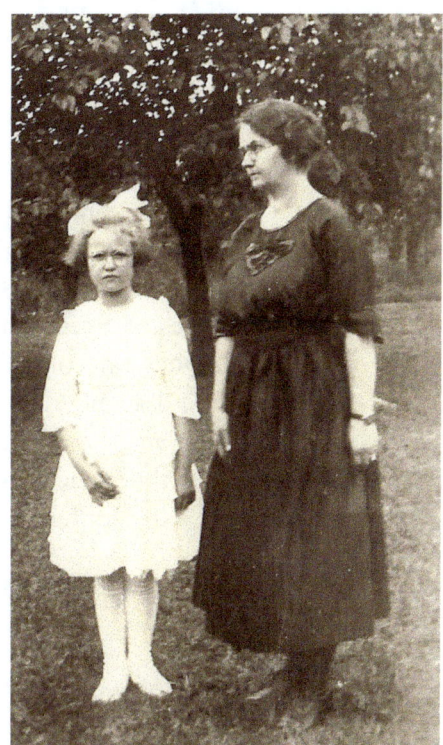

Harry with Bud, and Hattie with Verna, 1920 in New Jersey

During this time, Harry worked multiple jobs to support his growing family, even working for at least a year as a "ship worker" in Camden. This may all have been an effort to supplement the precarious work of animation.

As artist Les Clark recalls,

"I remember the New York cartoons, The Barnyard Fables and Felix the Cat. I must have wanted to be an animator, because when I was a kid, I'd stay through two or three features just to see the cartoons over and over again, not knowing I'd be involved in animation in my later life."[26]

The animation industry was taking off, and Harry wanted to be part of it. At the end of 1920, Max Fleischer had invented the Rotograph which allowed an animated figure to be superimposed not only over a static background, but now over a moving background as well. The results were more graceful, and more exciting to a young artist. The heart of the animation business was in New York. Many artists who would become famous in the Disney company worked at this time in New York, including Ben Sharpsteen and Dick Huemer.

Dick Huemer recalls the ups and downs of the animation business:

> "In those days, [animation] was a very precarious business. At contract time in the spring, when the studios signed up for another series, there was a frightening period where you didn't know whether it was going to be renewed or not. There were sometimes lapses of a few months at which you would do other things. Once I decorated parchment lamp shades with scenes. Fashion drawing I did at one time for *Pictorial Review*. Finally the thing really exploded in 1921; no more Mutt and Jeff. So I went to Fleischer's, who were only doing the clown back then. He [Ko-Ko the Clown] didn't even have a name then."[27]

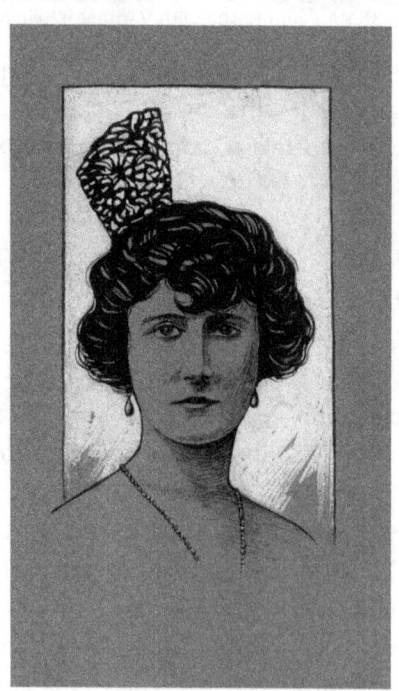

Spanish lady, by Harry Wilcox. Pen and ink on greyboard.

In 1923, Harry moved his family to Irvington, New Jersey, from which he commuted to New York. During this time he was offered a job by a young animation company headed by a young entrepreneur from Kansas named Walt Disney, who was setting up a new animation studio in California. Disney made several trips to New York to recruit artists from the animation studios there.

Disney used California as an enticement to join his new company. "Boy, you will never regret it," he wrote to artist Ub Iwerks. "This is the place for you – a real country to work and play in."[28] But California was too far away from Williamsport to suit Hattie. She did not want to be so far from her sisters. Her mother had recently died, and she wanted to be nearer to her aging father. So Harry declined.

Looking back on the Disney offer, my parents always said that it was good he turned it down – if Harry had gone to California in the 1920's, our parents would never have met, and we would never have been.

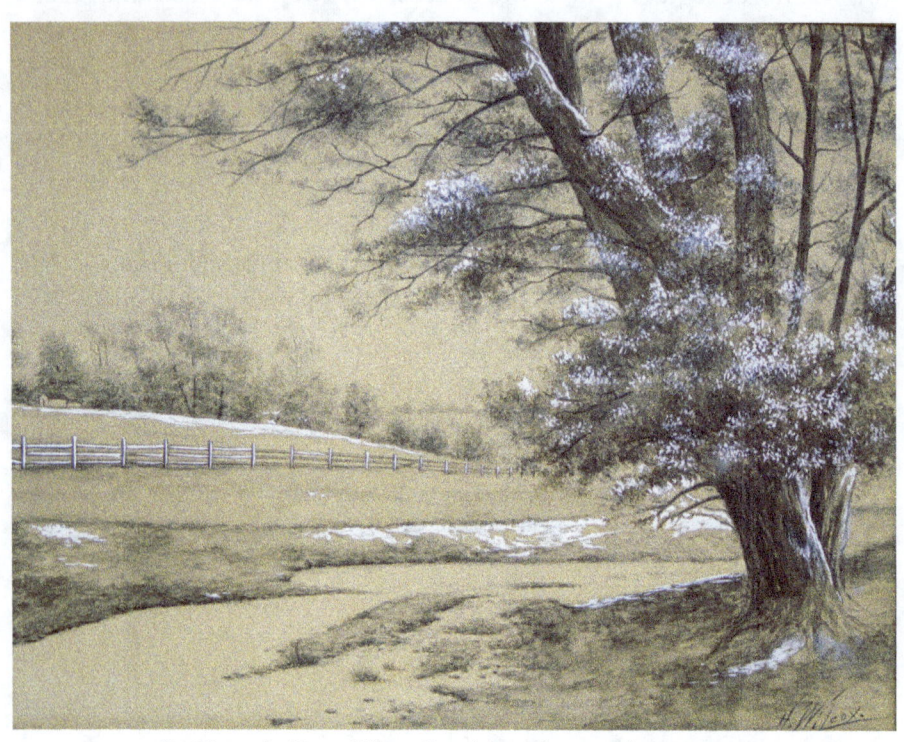

First Snow, by Harry Wilcox. Pen, ink, and watercolor on paper.
Presented as a gift to Julia and Ross Conn, about 1912.

CHAPTER 5:
PEREGRINATIONS AND DEPRESSION

In 1923 the family moved to 238 Lincoln Place, Irvington, New Jersey, near New York, where young Bud started going to school. In 1924 they moved to another house in Irvington, 137 Ball Street. Harry was working long hours in New York City and commuting home to New Jersey.

Ben Sharpsteen provides some insights into the world that Harry would have encountered in New York.

"I first entered the animation business in New York City following my service in the Marine Corps in World War I. I started as an apprentice in an animation studio that was owned by Hearst Enterprises [Hearst International Film Service]. They had a license to handle all of the characters in the Hearst comic sections. When I first went there, I did menial things such as erasing pencil marks off of drawings after they had been inked, filling in places that should be black, and then doing the actual inking of the drawings after the animators had penciled them. As the weeks went by, I was gradually given more important work and it was probably at the end of about six months that I gained the status of full animator, although I was by no means efficient.

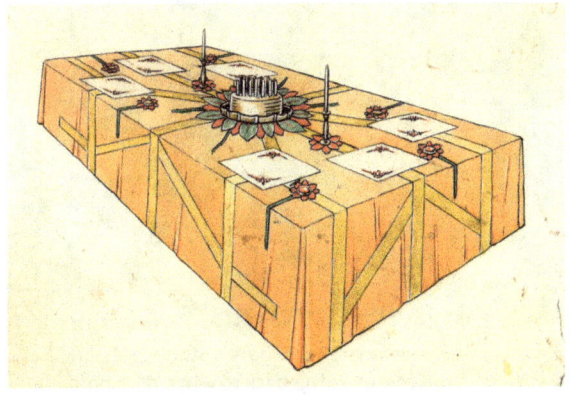

Holiday Table design by Harry Wilcox for an advertising campaign. Watercolor and ink.

As time went on, I moved from one studio to another in
New York City … I was discouraged by what I thought to
be the low standards of the animation field. The attitude in
the business was that it did not matter so much, that the kids
would laugh at this, and so forth. It did not seem to me to be
a safe thing with which to cast my future …"[29]

In fact, the field of animation began to put the artist in the background,
as the facilitator of tales about animals. "The films with human
characters and then the films with animal stars represent the progressive
retreat of the animator behind the screen."[30]

As much as they loved animation, it was important to make a living and
support the family. In 1924, Harry was working for Moore's Studio,
Newark, where he did commercial art, illustrations, advertising, and
photograph retouching.

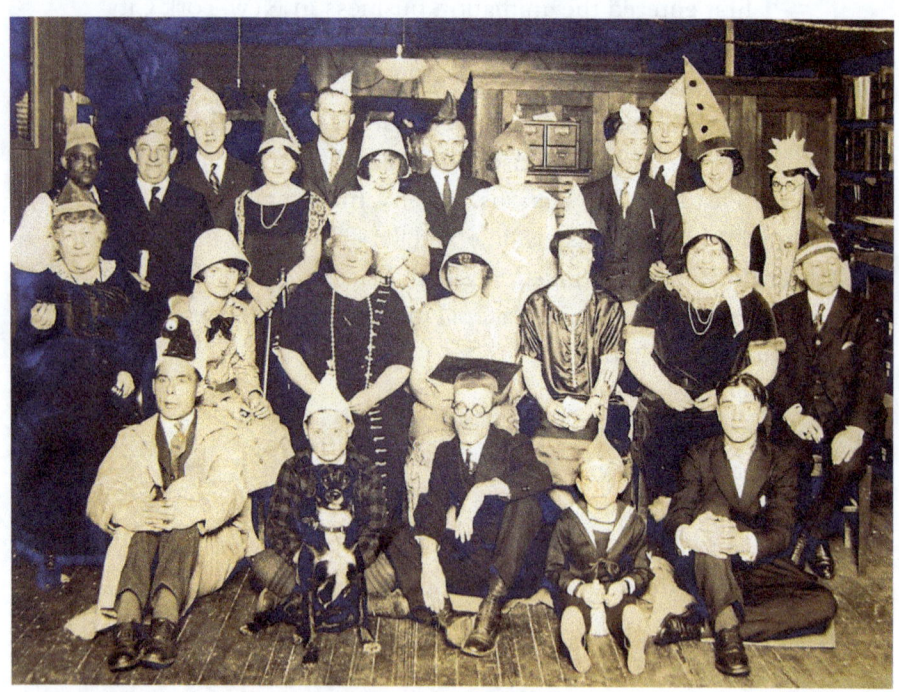

New Year's Eve staff party at Moore's Studio, Newark, New Jersey, January 1, 1925. Harry
Wilcox is in the center of the back row in a dark party hat. Hattie is the last person standing
on the right. Verna is seated in the second row, second from left in the light colored cloche
hat. Bud is seated on the floor in the front row, second from the right, in a sailor suit with
glasses.

For his own pleasure, however, he drew beautiful, fashionable and spirited women, and scenes along lakes, rivers, and the Atlantic Ocean.

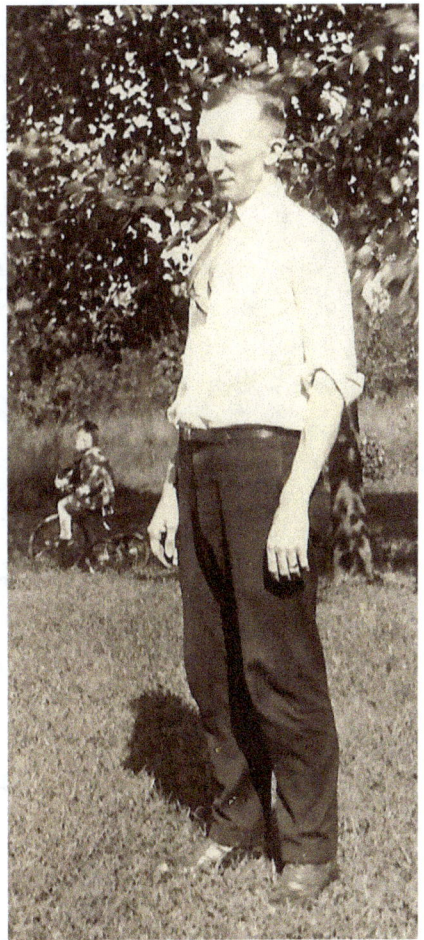

Right:
Harry in Irvington, New Jersey.
That's Bud biking
in the background.

Below:
Verna and Bud,
about 1920.

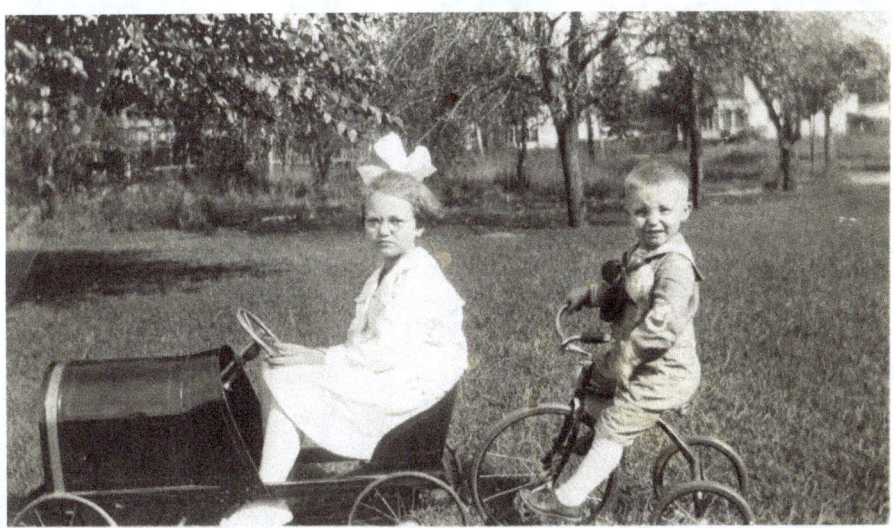

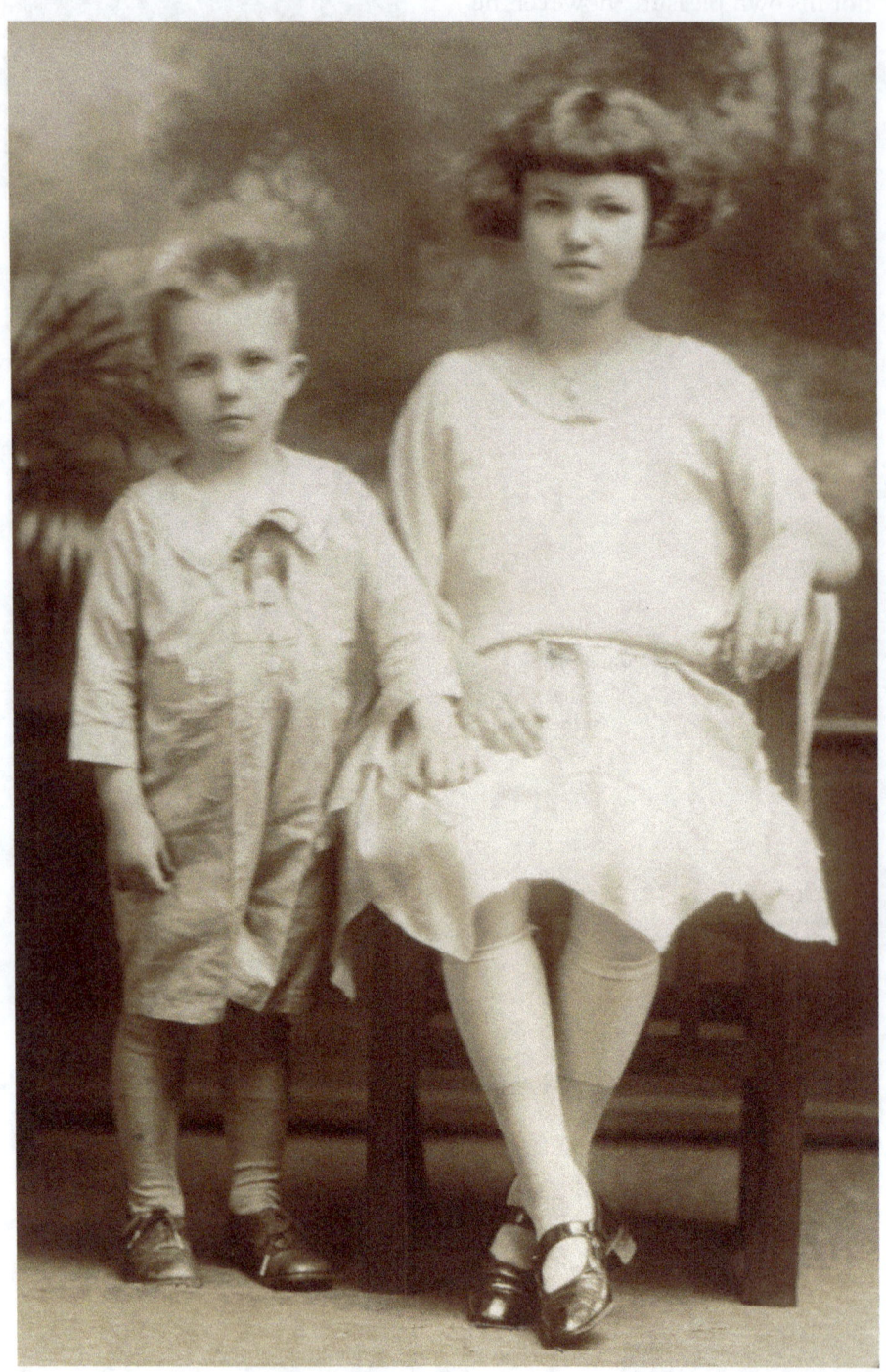

Bud and Sis, 1921, Merchantville, New Jersey.

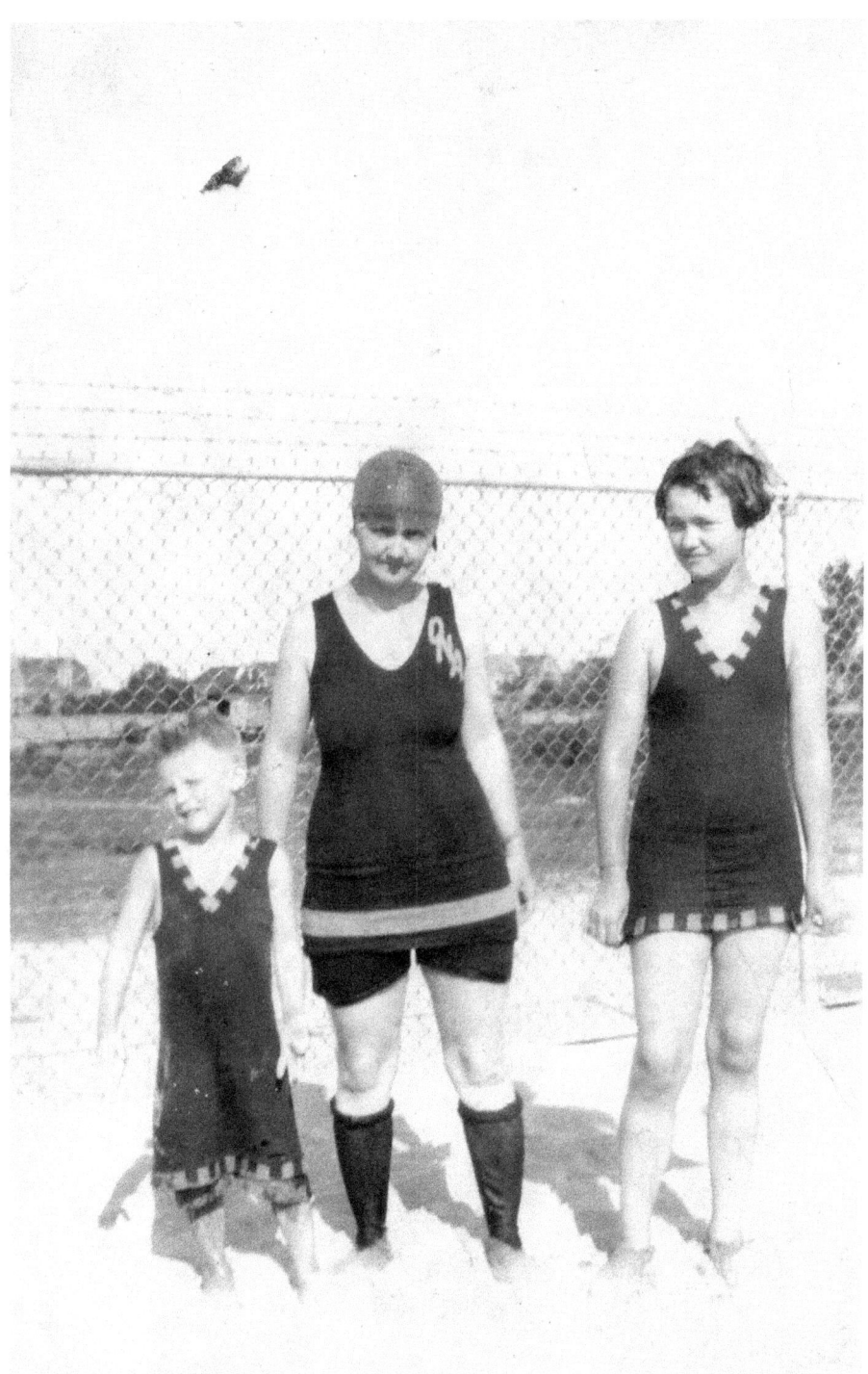

At the beach in New Jersey, 1921, Bud, Hattie, and Verna. Hattie made all the bathing costumes, with matching outfits for Verna and Bud. Notice the biplane flying overhead.

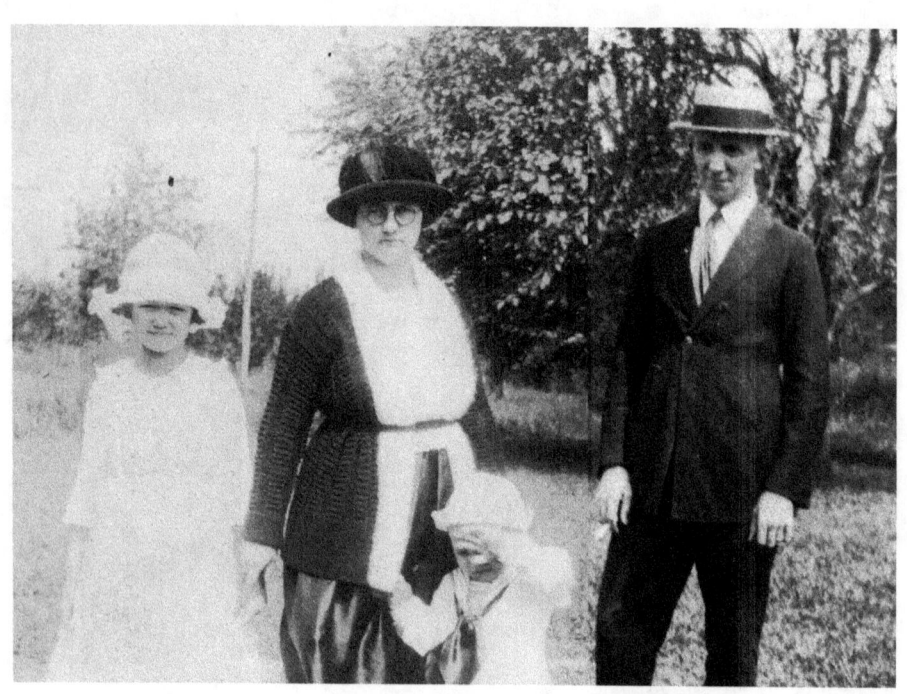

Verna, Hattie, Bud, and Harry, 1922 in Merchantville, New Jersey.

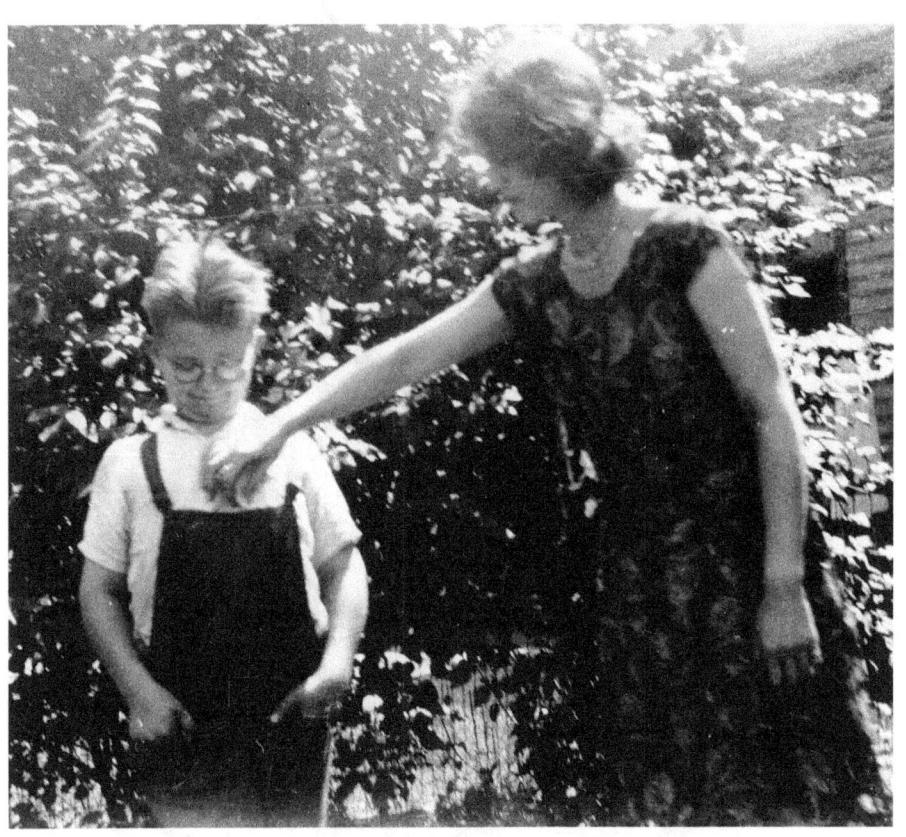

Bud and Sis, 1925 in New Jersey. "It's a bug!"

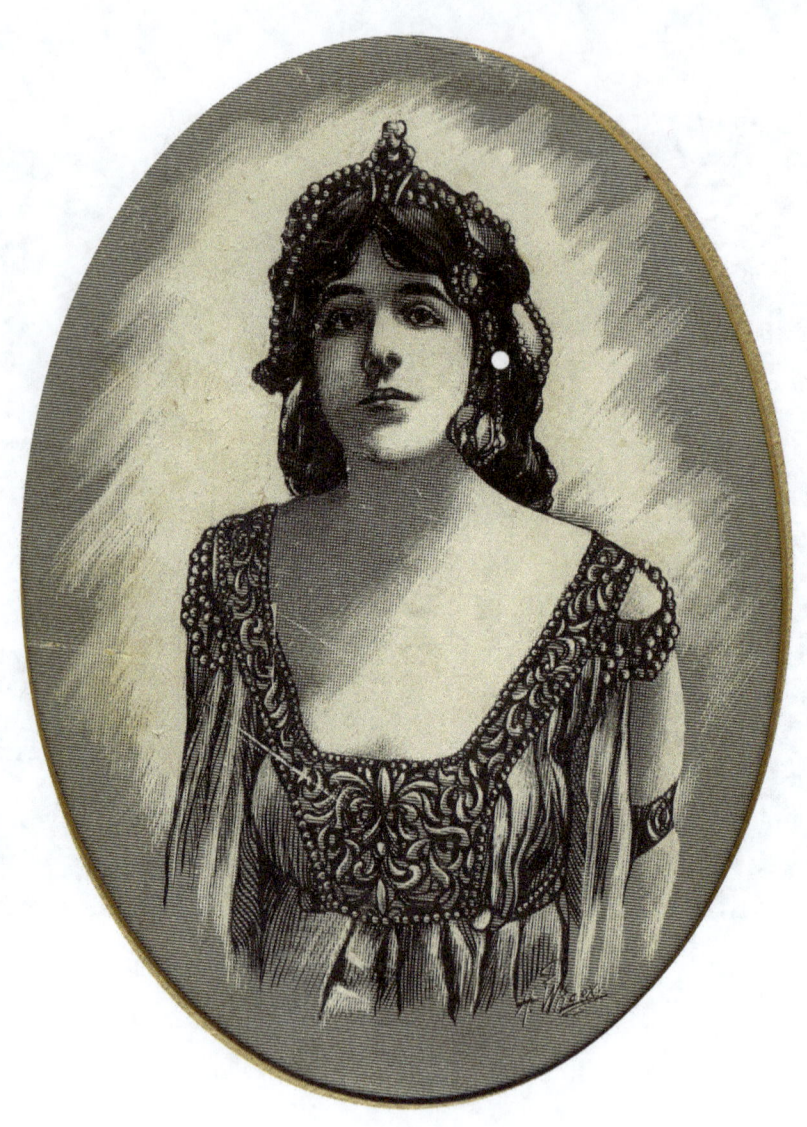

Woman on scratchboard, by Harry Wilcox.

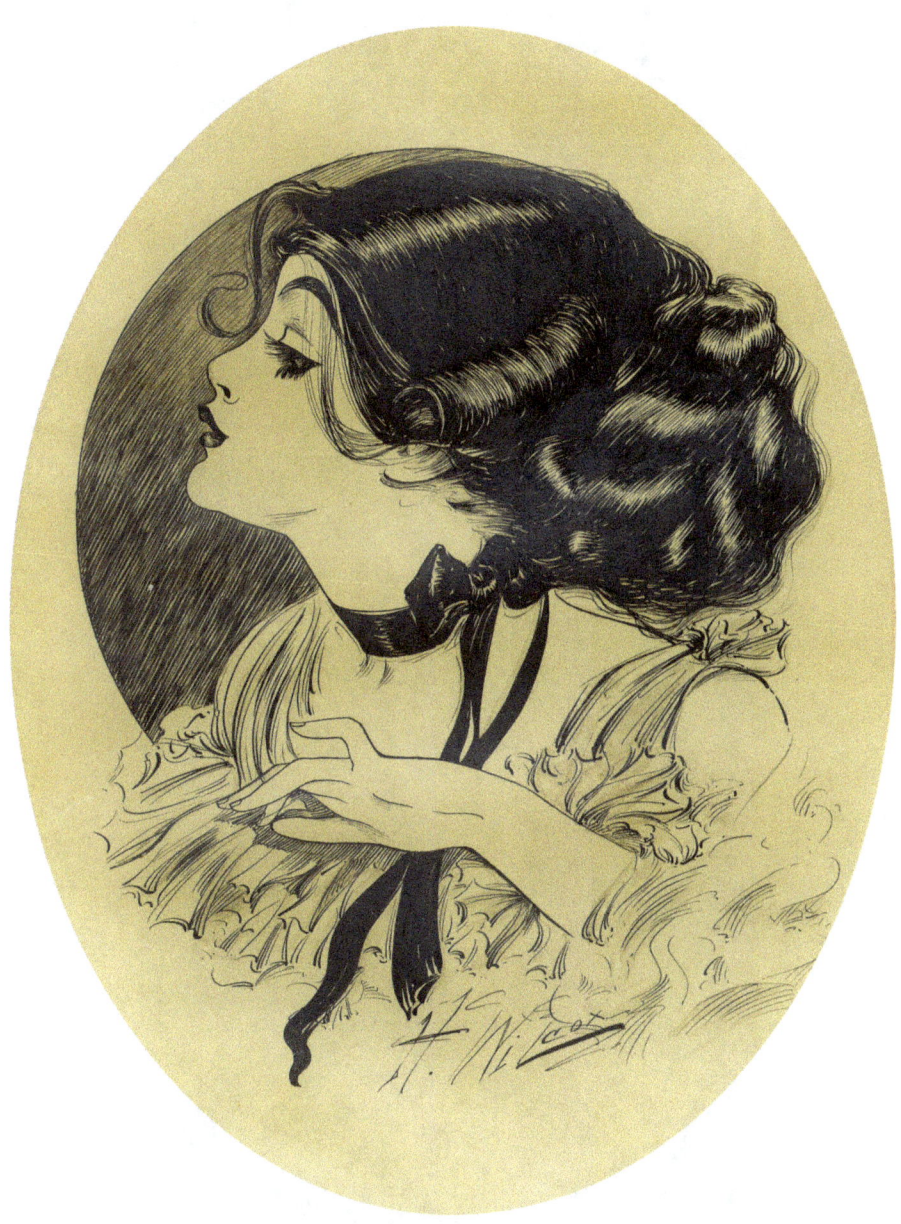

Girl with a ribbon, by Harry Wilcox. Pen and ink on brown paper.

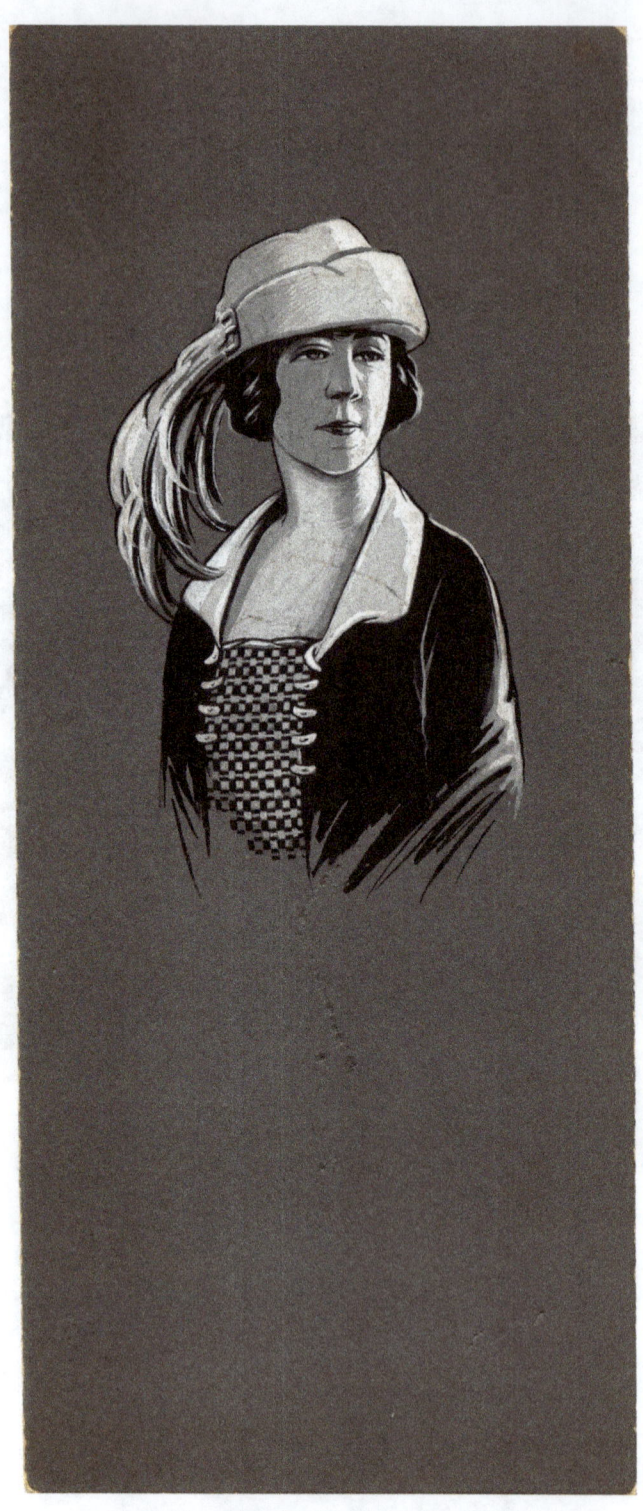

Woman in a white feathered hat, by Harry Wilcox
Pen and ink on greyboard.

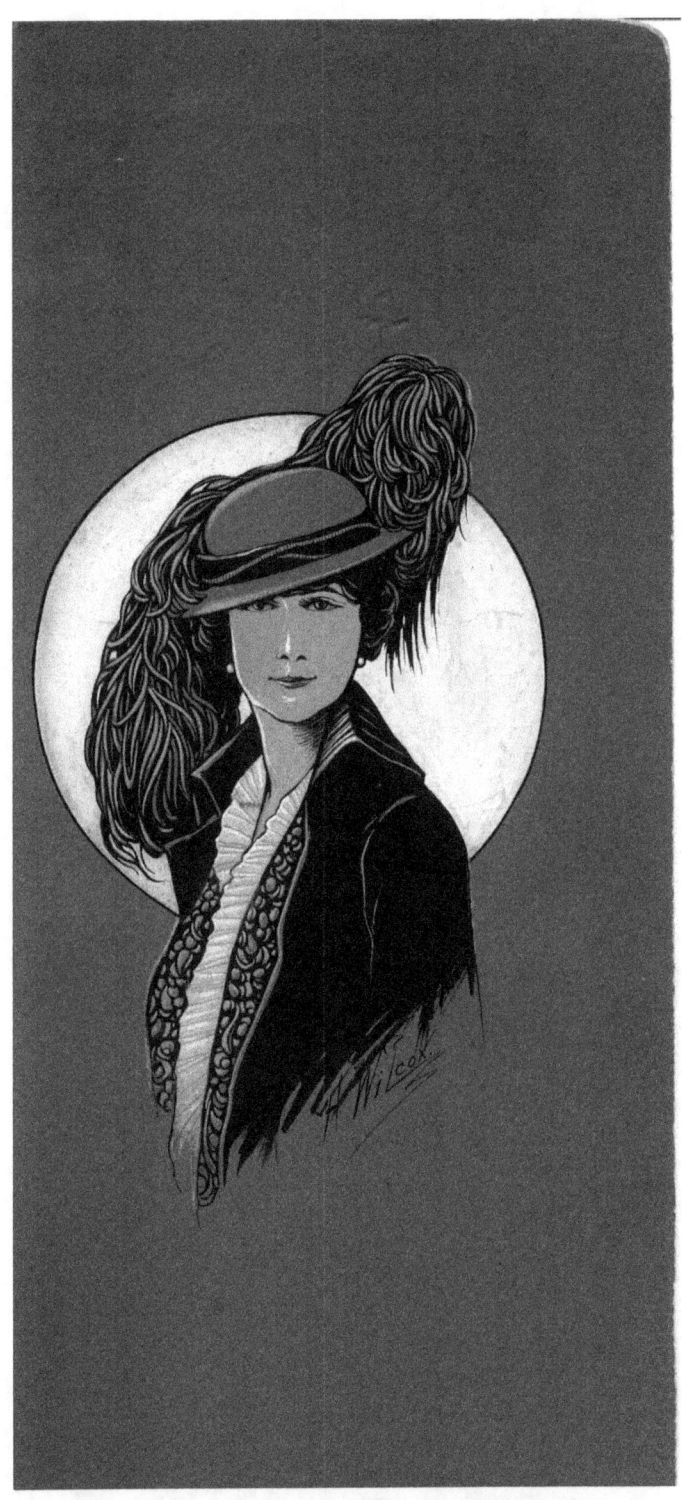

Woman in a feathered hat in moonlight, by Harry Wilcox
Pen and ink on greyboard.

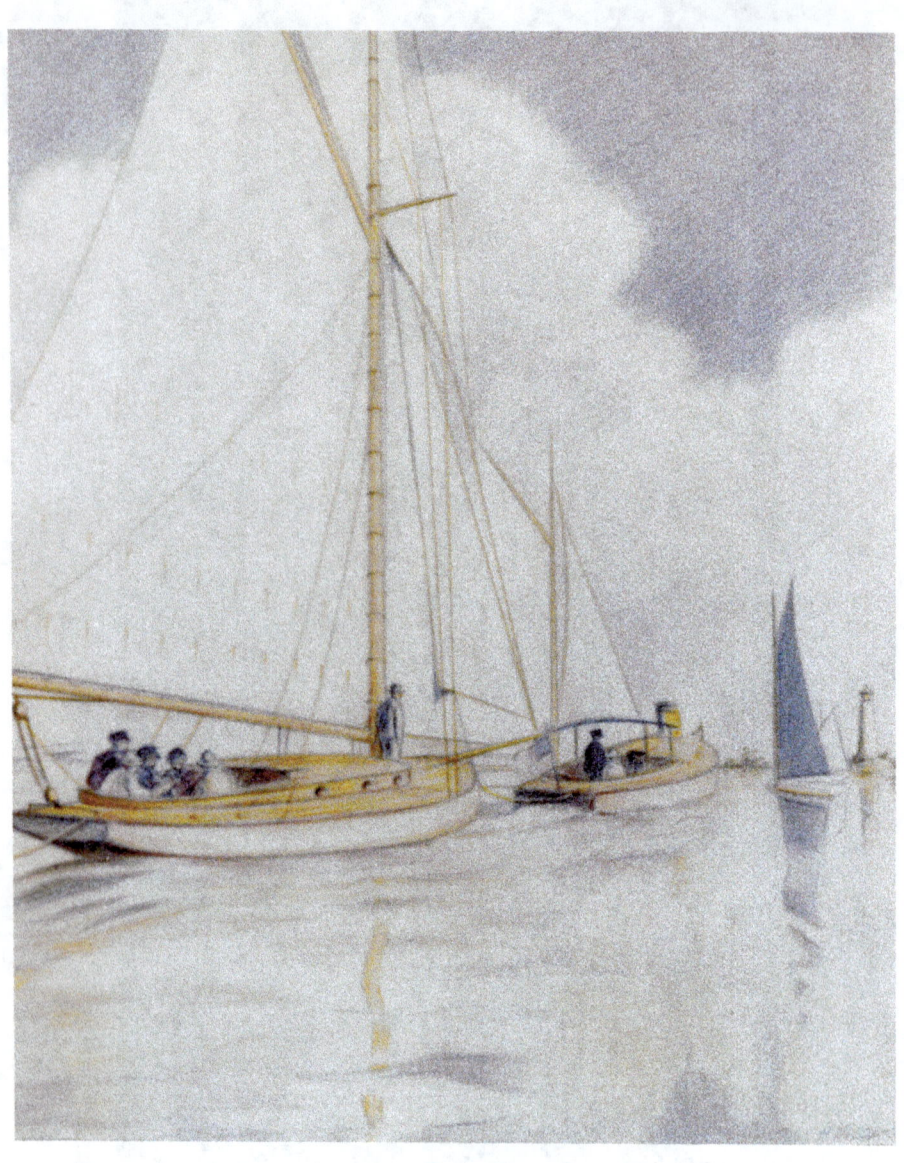

Boating, by Harry Wilcox.
Pastels and pencil.

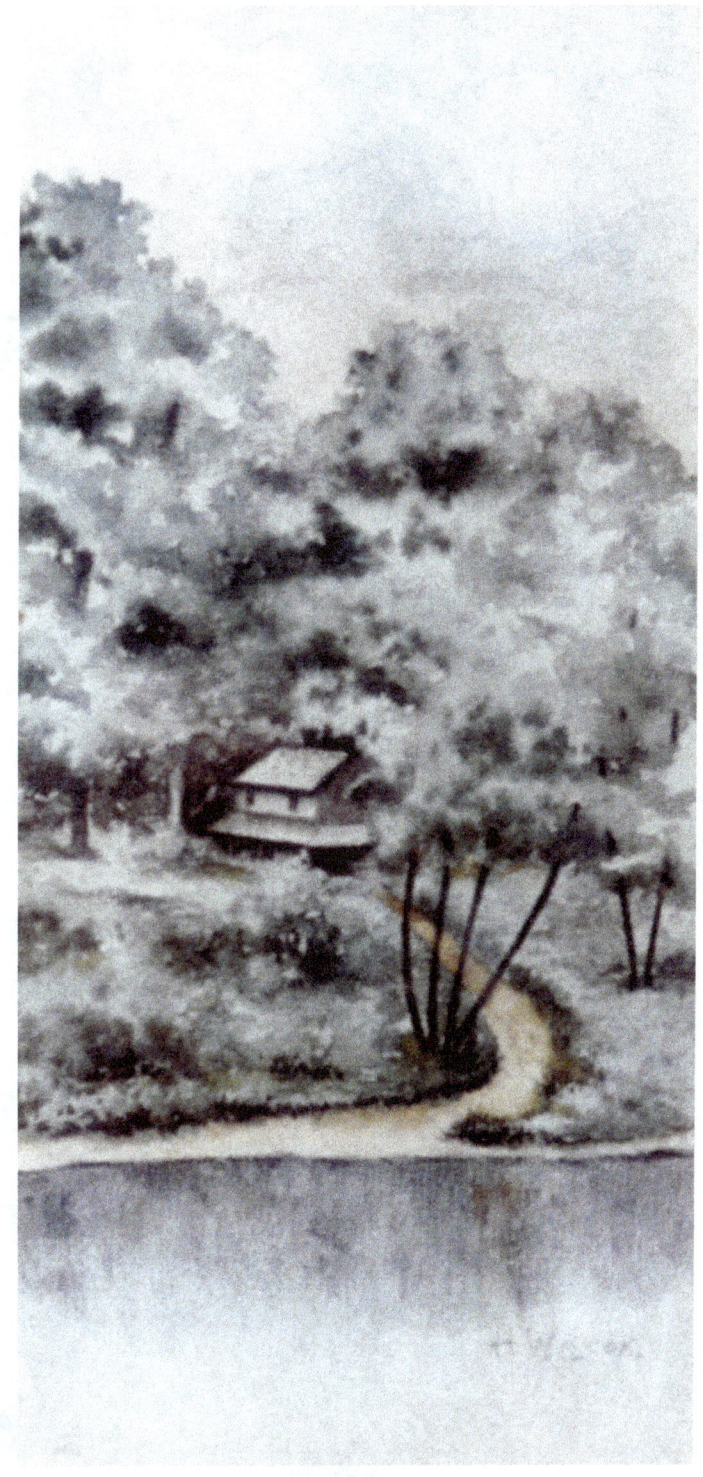

Along the Loyalsock, by Harry Wilcox
watercolor.

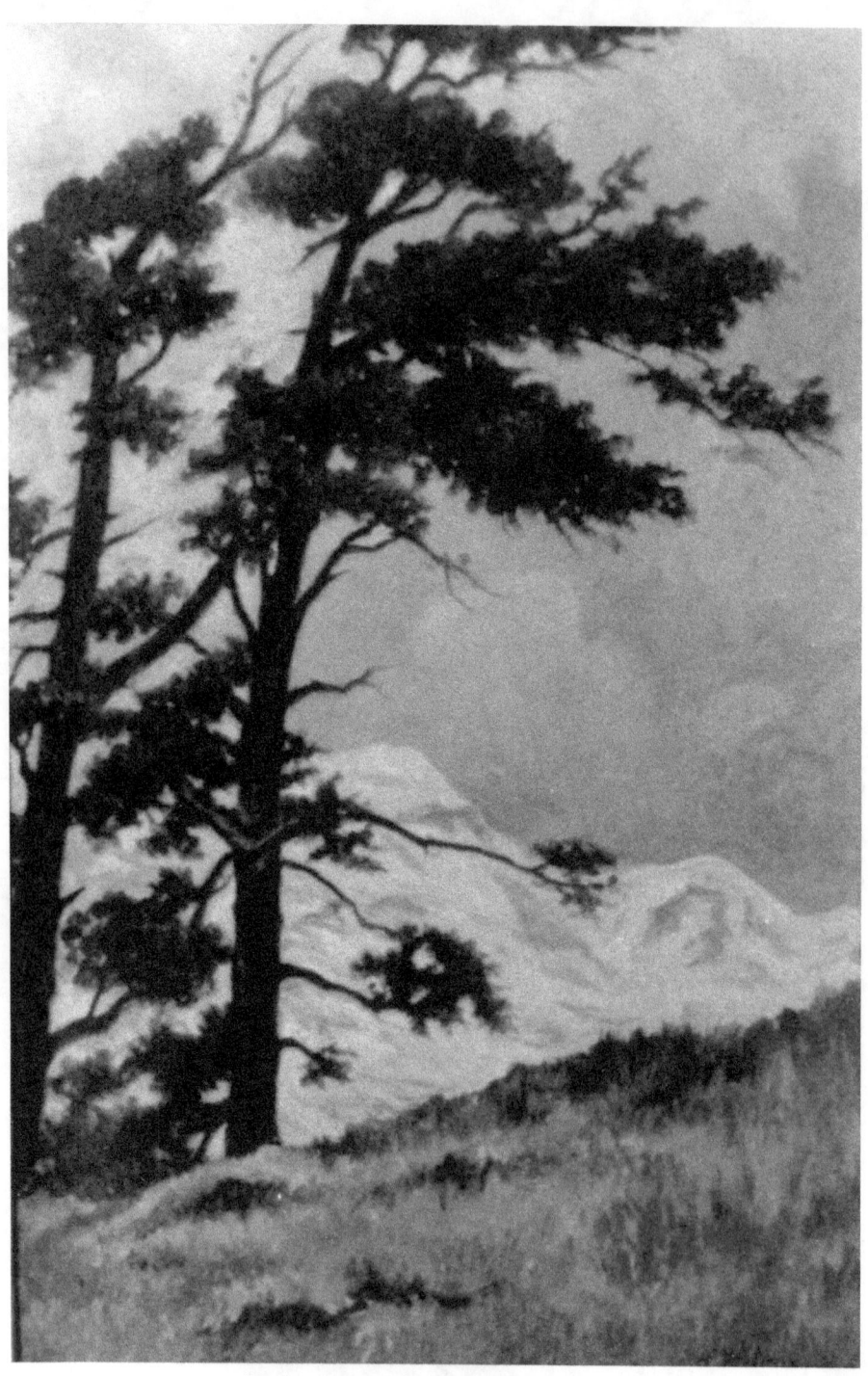

Mountain scene, by Harry Wilcox
Pen and ink on scratchboard.

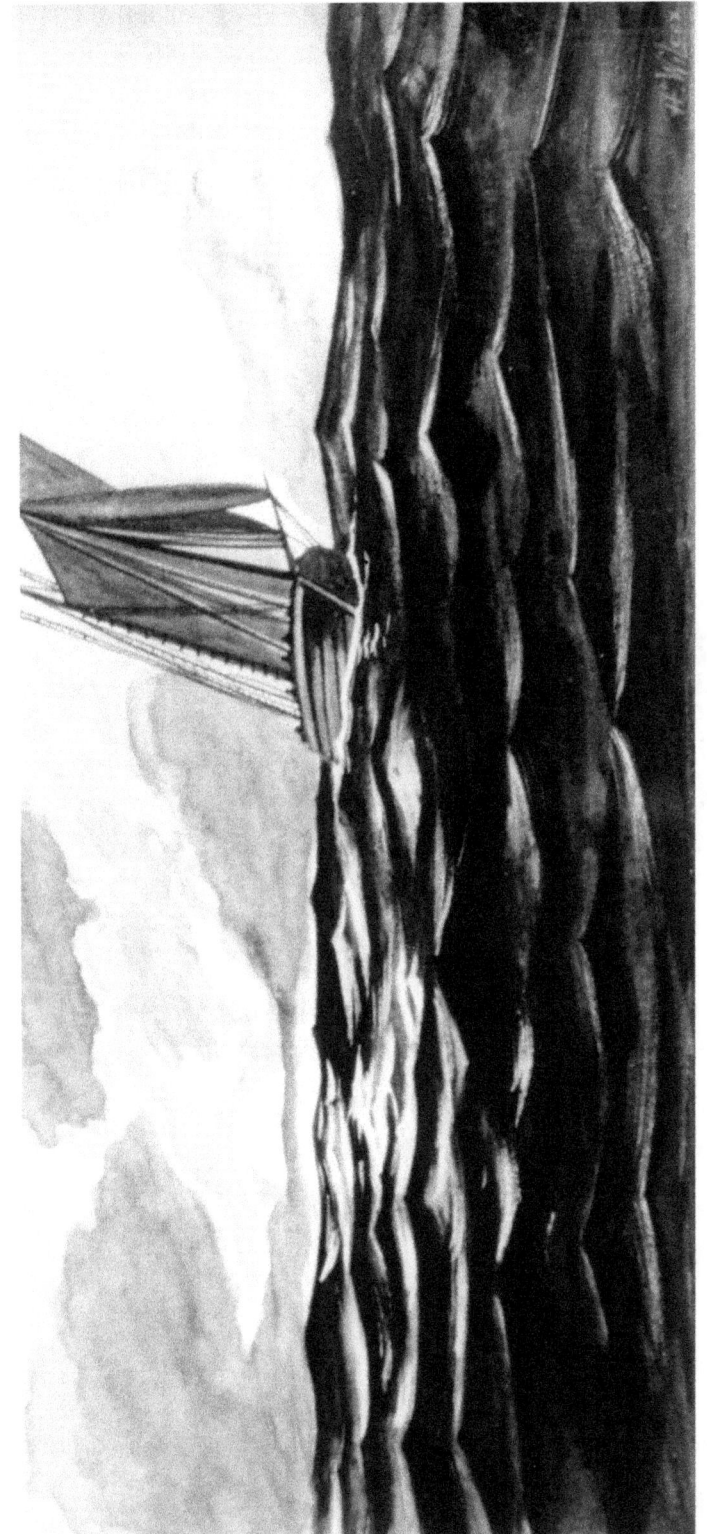

Night Sail, by Harry Wilcox.
Pen and Ink.

In 1925, Harry contracted pneumonia and was very ill indeed. Hattie wrote on a postcard of the ambulance that took him to the hospital that she feared for his life. Pneumonia before penicillin was a seriously life-threatening illness for which there was no treatment other than tea and honey (and sometimes whiskey), good food, tender loving care, sunshine, and crisp country air. Once he was released from the hospital, Harry and Hattie decided to go home to Limestoneville, "to the country," to recuperate and regain his strength.

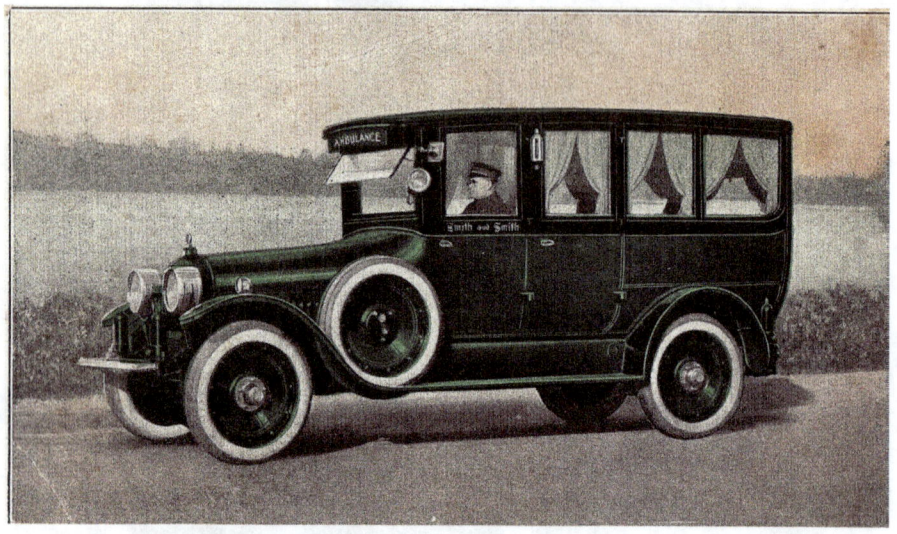

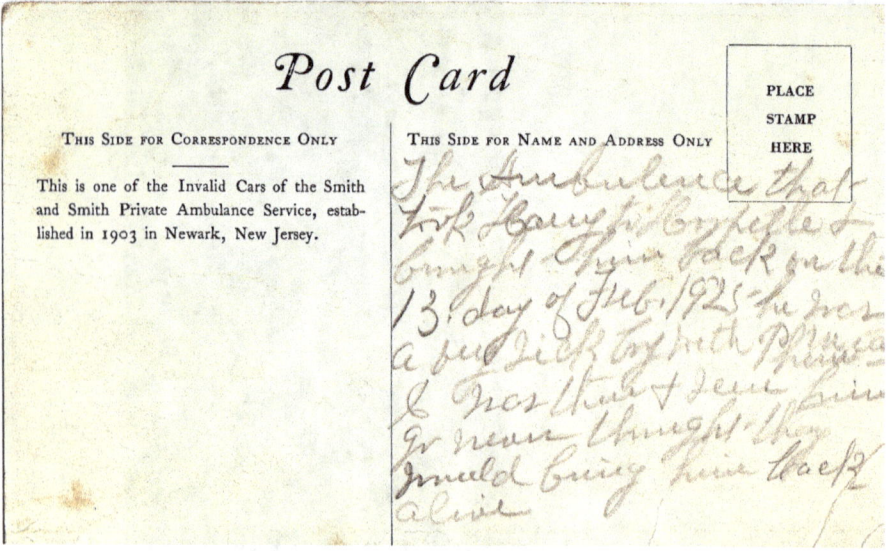

Front and back of a commercial postcard, in Hattie's writing: "The Ambulance that took Harry to hospital and brought him back on the 13th day of February 1925. He was a very sick boy. I was there and seen [sic] him. I never thought they would bring him back alive."

On the farm, it was an easy walk from the main house to the spring house, a small brick structure built over a small fresh water spring, used to store milk and other perishables — the equivalent in its day of a modern refrigerator. It was a pleasant and reassuring walk, with a lovely view of the fertile fields, the sweet smell of the waving crops, and the reward of milk and other good things to eat.

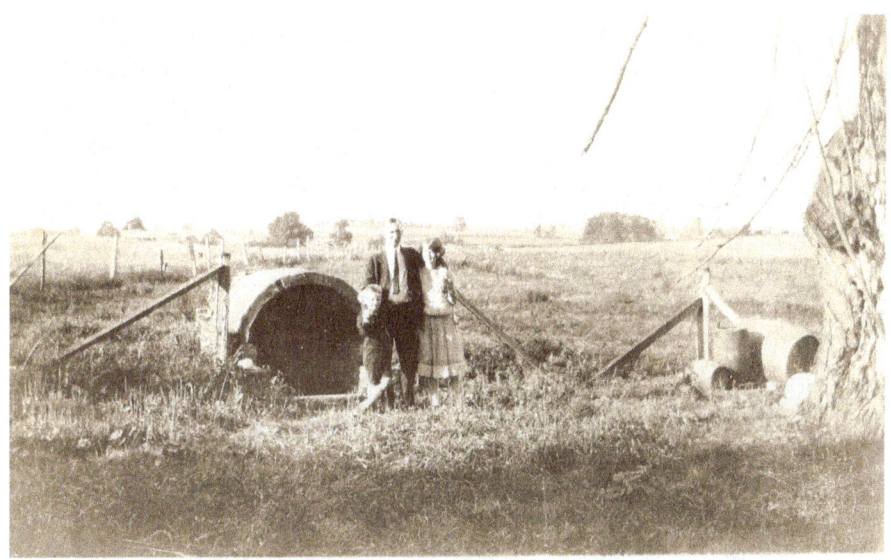

The spring house. Left to right: Bud, Harry, and Verna Wilcox.

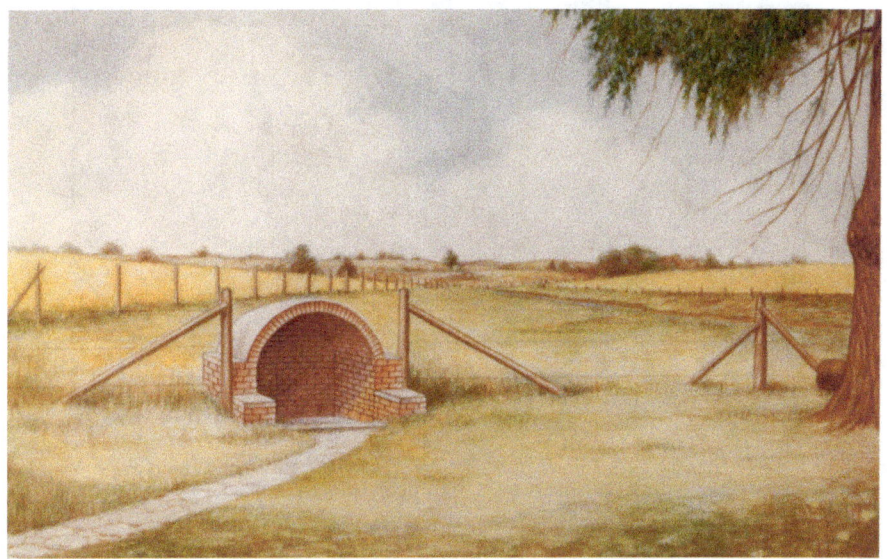

The spring house, by Harry Wilcox. Watercolor.

In 1926 they set out once again, this time to Detroit, where Harry had been offered a job at General Motors, doing illustrations of the interiors of automobiles for advertising. Harry was happy at work, but Hattie was not happy at home. In fact she moved them eight times in four years. On one occasion she phoned Harry at work to tell him not to come home to the house where he had had breakfast, as she had moved them during the day to another house.

Hattie was very protective of Bud. He was nearsighted, and wore glasses from an early age. She always said he had a heart condition, but he was actually a very sturdy child. She would not allow him to play with her brother Dick's boys, who were very close in age, as she said they played too rough. To his cousins, it seemed that Bud was never in trouble like they were, but always with a book.[31]

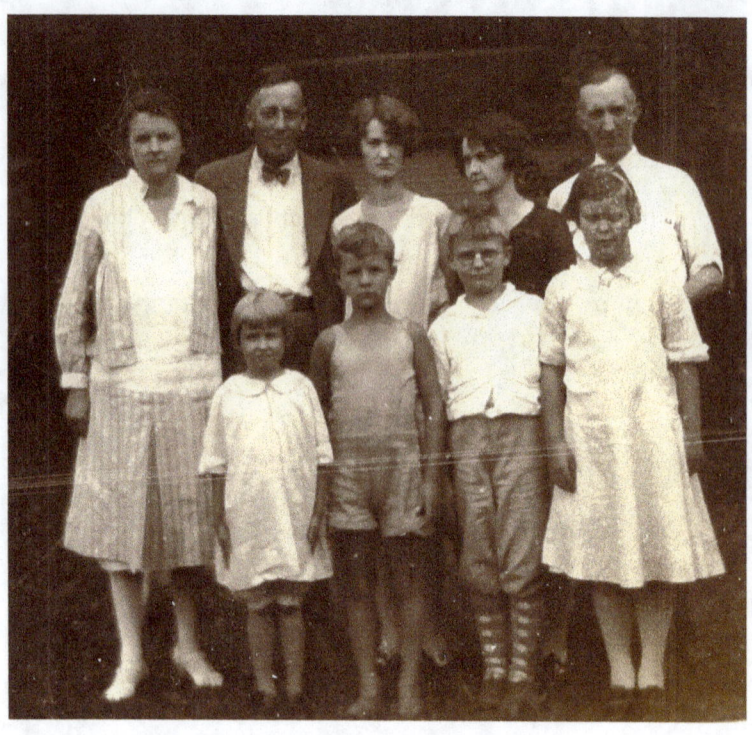

Friends. Bud is in the front row, second from the right. Verna, Hattie, and Harry are in the back row, the three people on the right.

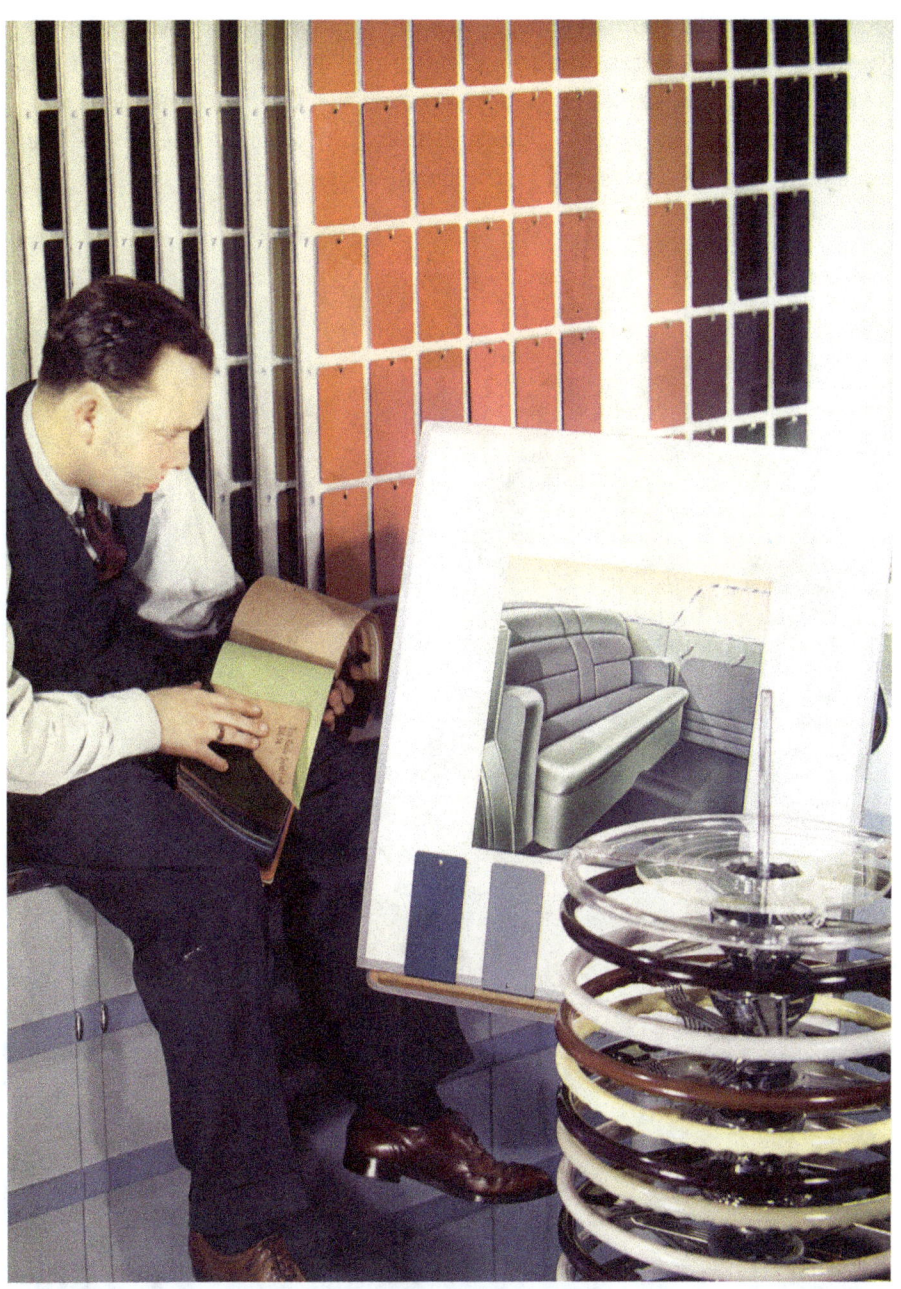

This advertisement for General Motors automobiles appeared in *Life* Magazine.
The interior of the car was painted by Harry Wilcox.

Verna was an attractive young woman. Harry and Hattie wanted to give her all the best things, but they could not afford to buy them. With a tailor for a mother and an artist for a father, however, they worked out a system. They would take her to a department store and she would try on a series of outfits, while her father sketched quietly in a corner, and her brother quietly read a book. Back at home, they would confer about the final design of the dress and Hattie would make it up.

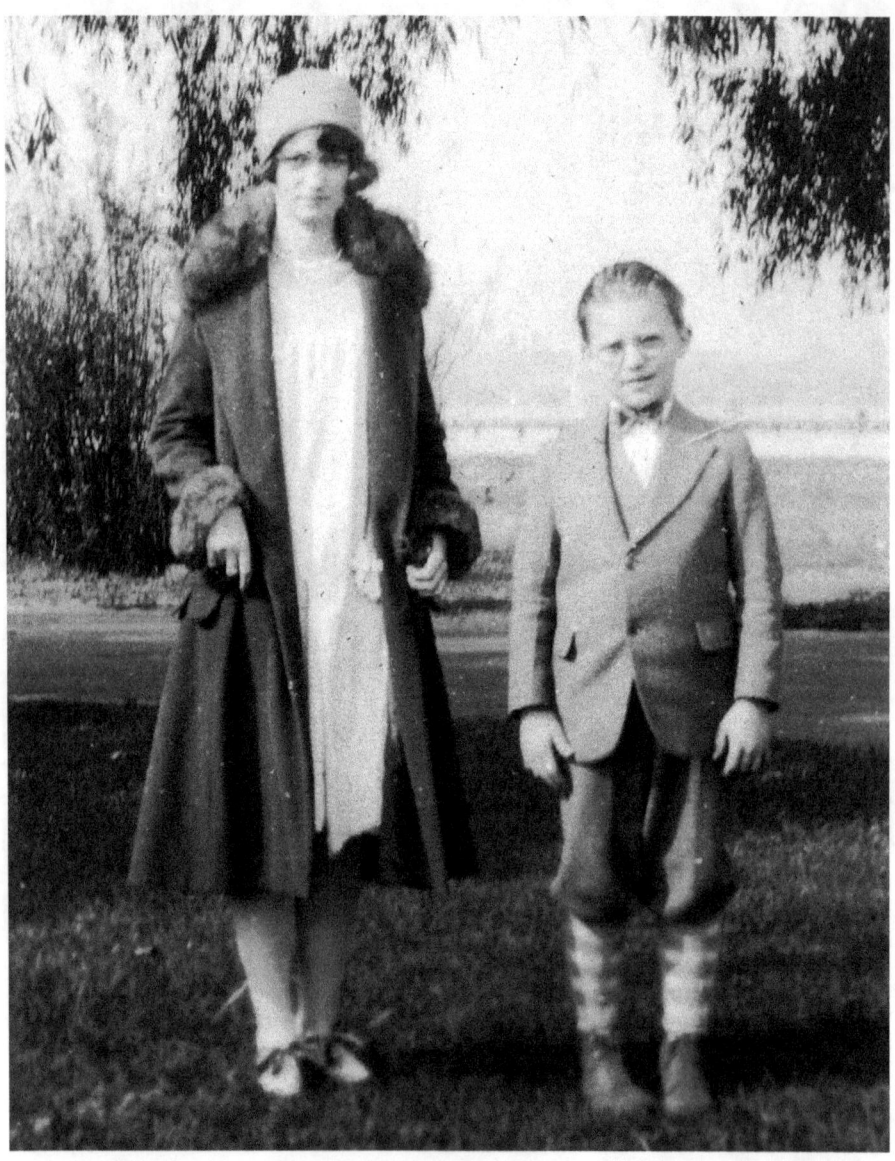

Sis and Bud, about 1926. Hattie made most of their clothes, including the coats.

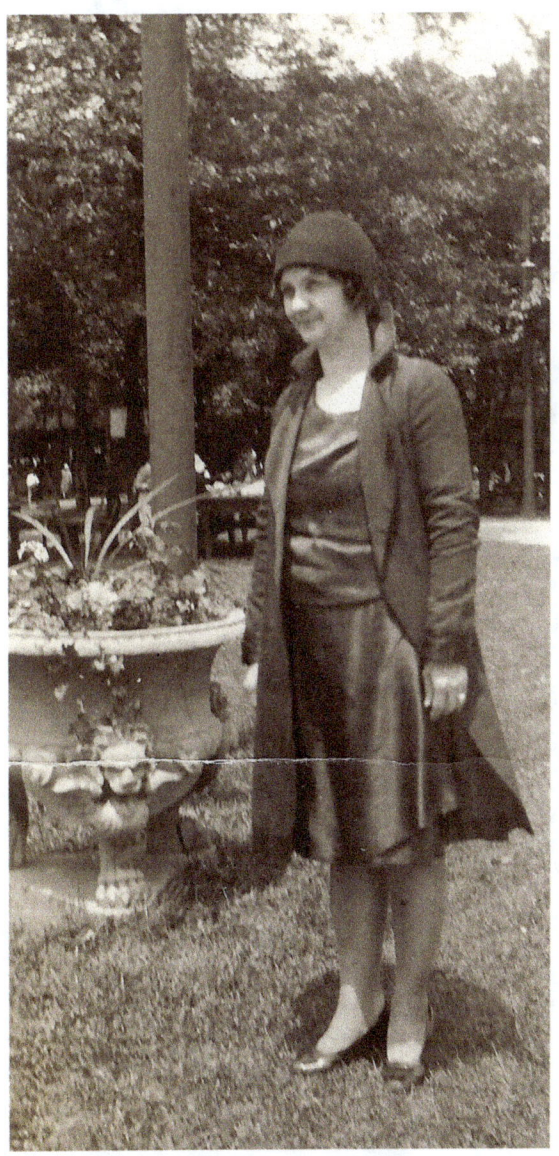

Hattie in a dark dress.

Hattie and Verna loved to go dancing; it was not Harry's idea of fun. Harry and Bud would go to the movies while Hattie and Verna went to a "cotillion." Bud saw Harry Houdini on stage in Detroit (Houdini died in 1926).

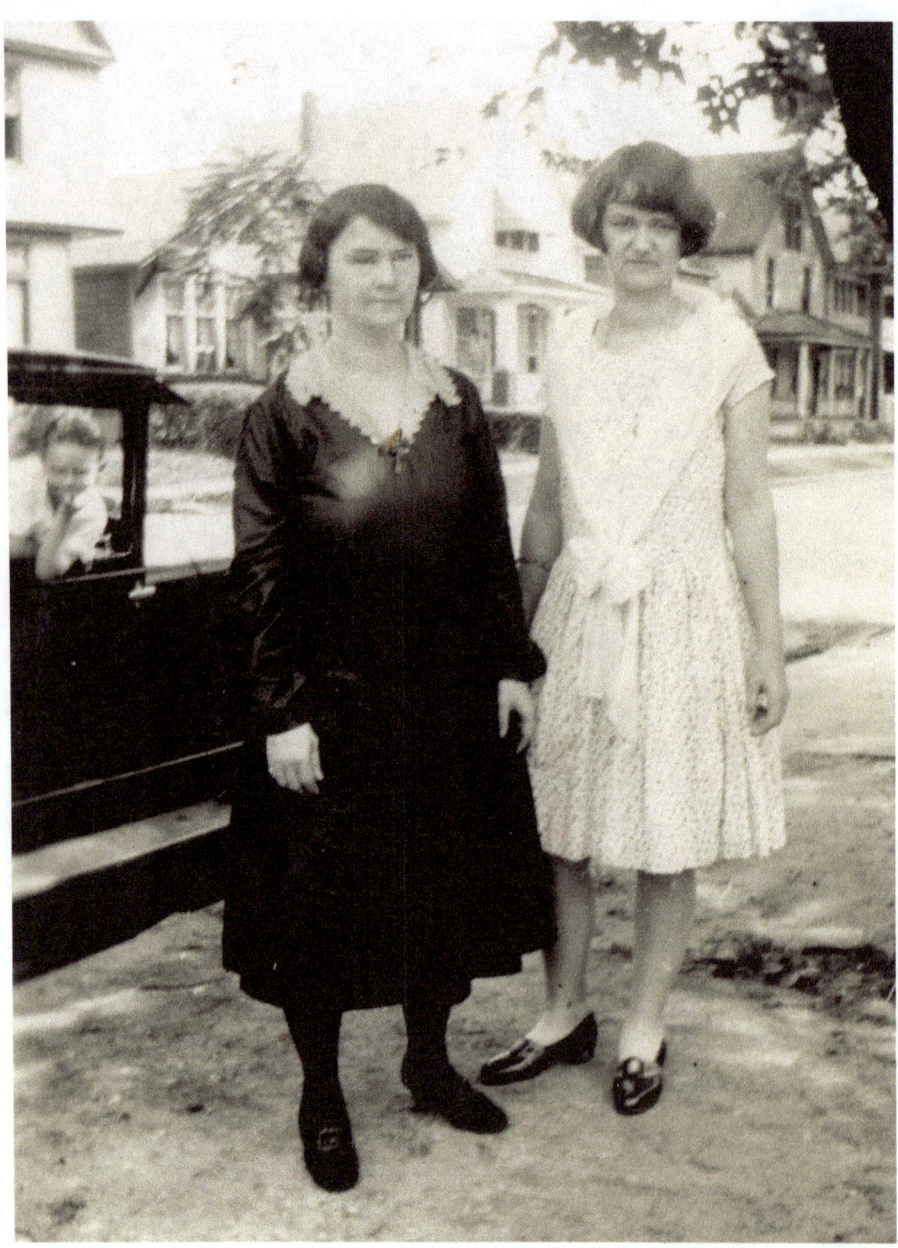

Hattie and Verna.
Bud is hanging out of the window of the car.

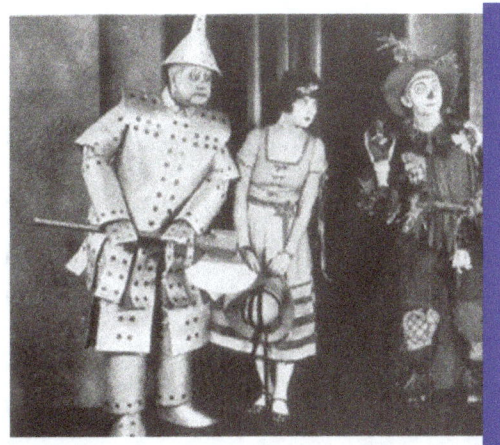

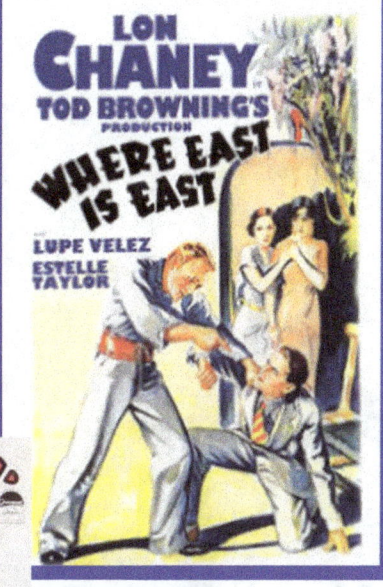

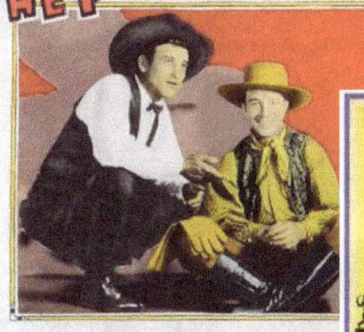

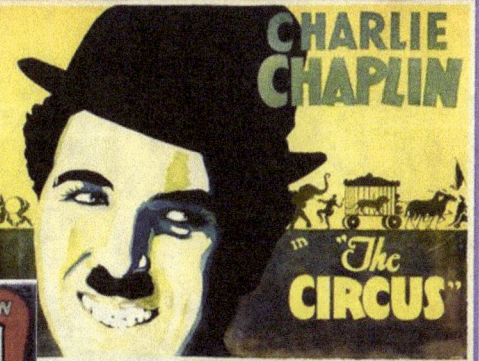

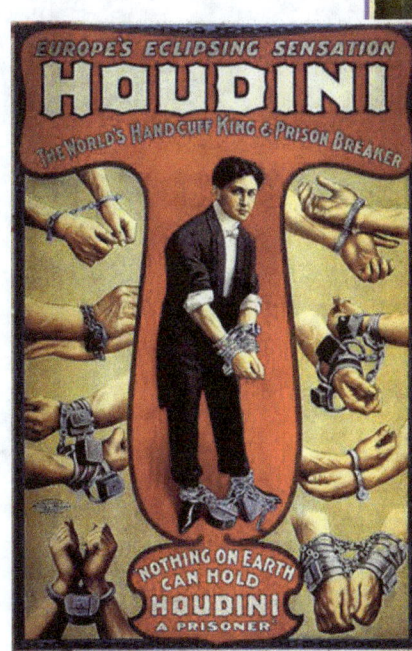

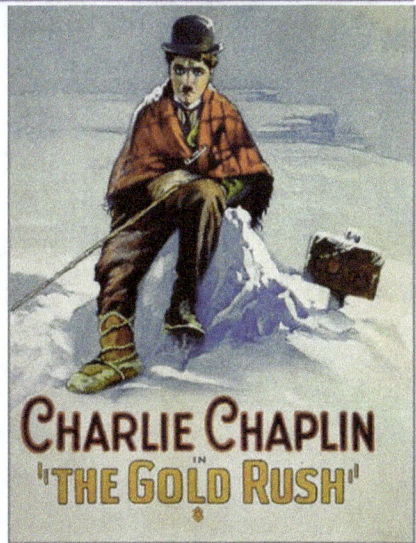

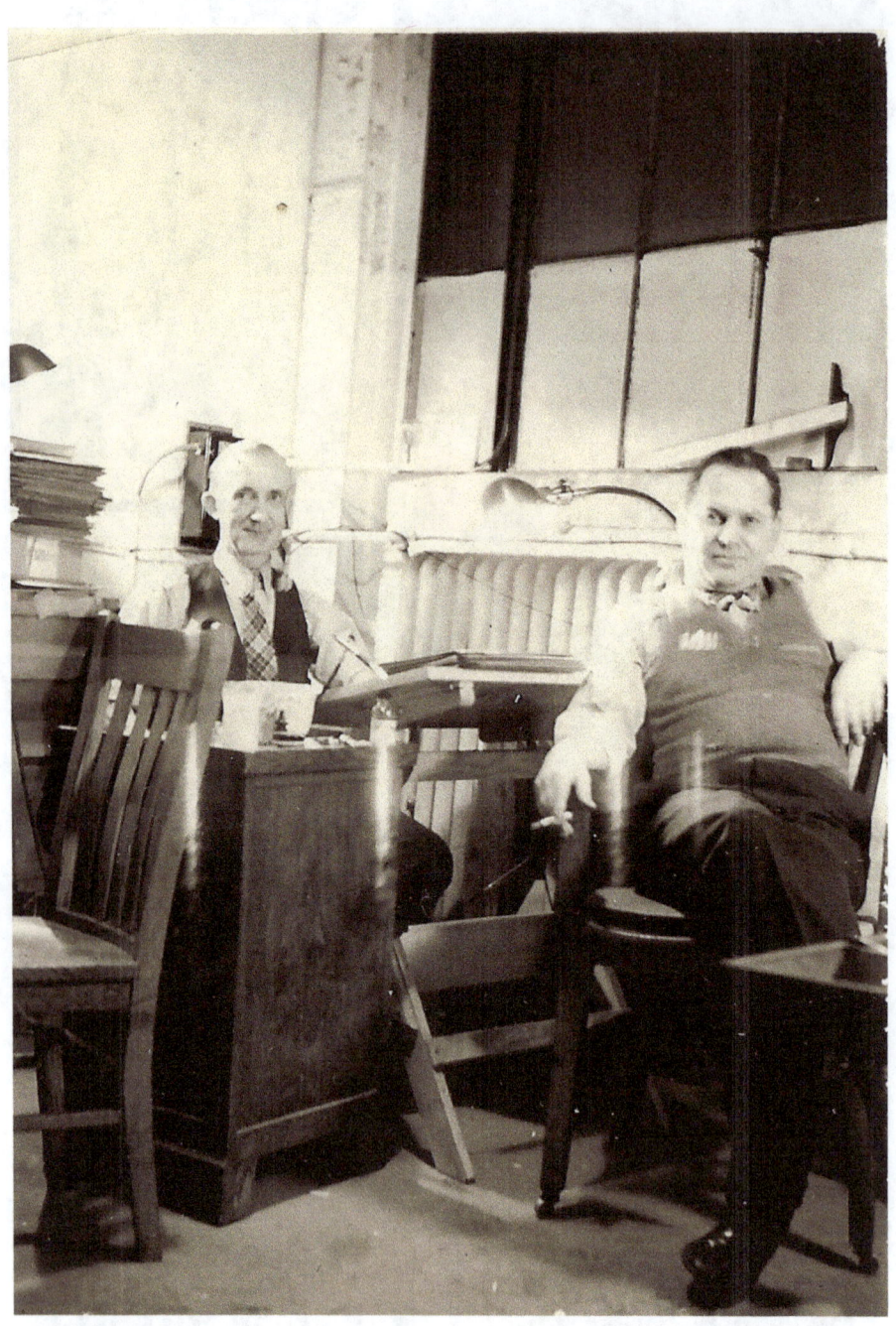

Harry and Mr. Anderson, a colleague and friend, at the office in Detroit.

Harry loved holidays. There was always a big Christmas Tree in the bay window at 1100 Isabella Street, under which miniature cowboys and wild animals scampered across fresh moss. The Fourth of July was a good excuse to bring home an abundance of fireworks to set off in the yard. He had a small toy cannon they would fire off in celebration. In Merchantville he put on a fireworks display that was more lavish than the town's municipal display.

There was always candied fruit, chocolates, and Easter candy in abundance. Hattie loved licorice and Harry loved chocolates — so of course he would present her with five pounds of Russell Stover's chocolate almond clusters for her birthday, and she would get licorice for him, often in the shape of small children. Another favorite was "railroad candy" — soft sticks of butterscotch with coconut filling from Dieter's on East Third Street.

Hattie was opinionated. Things had to be done her way. They made a ritual of doing the dishes after supper — first the glasses, then the silverware, and the pans last, Hattie washing and Harry drying. Harry was willing to comply, and their banter was usually light-hearted.

They continued to move frequently, but otherwise life was good in Detroit … until the Crash of 1929.

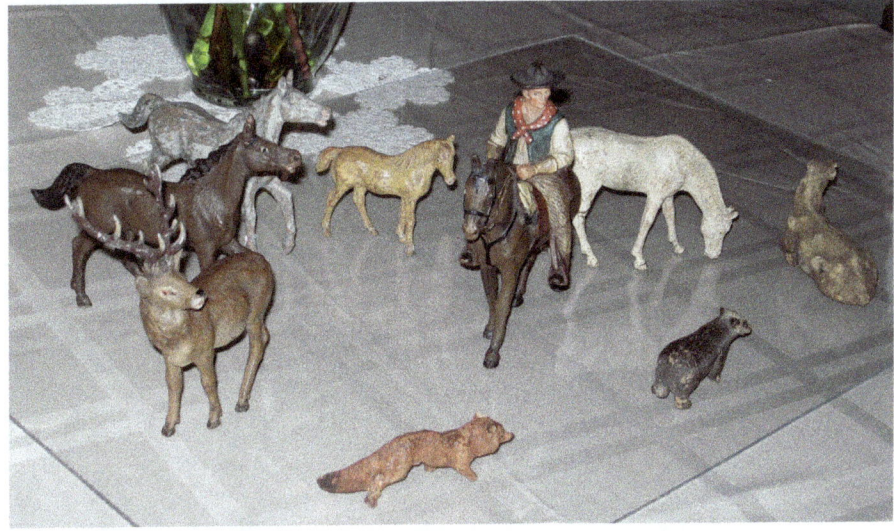

These are the original toy models of cowboys and wild animals that were used by Warren and Harry Wilcox as boys, and by Harry Jr. as a child as well. Restored by James H. Wilcox in 2011.

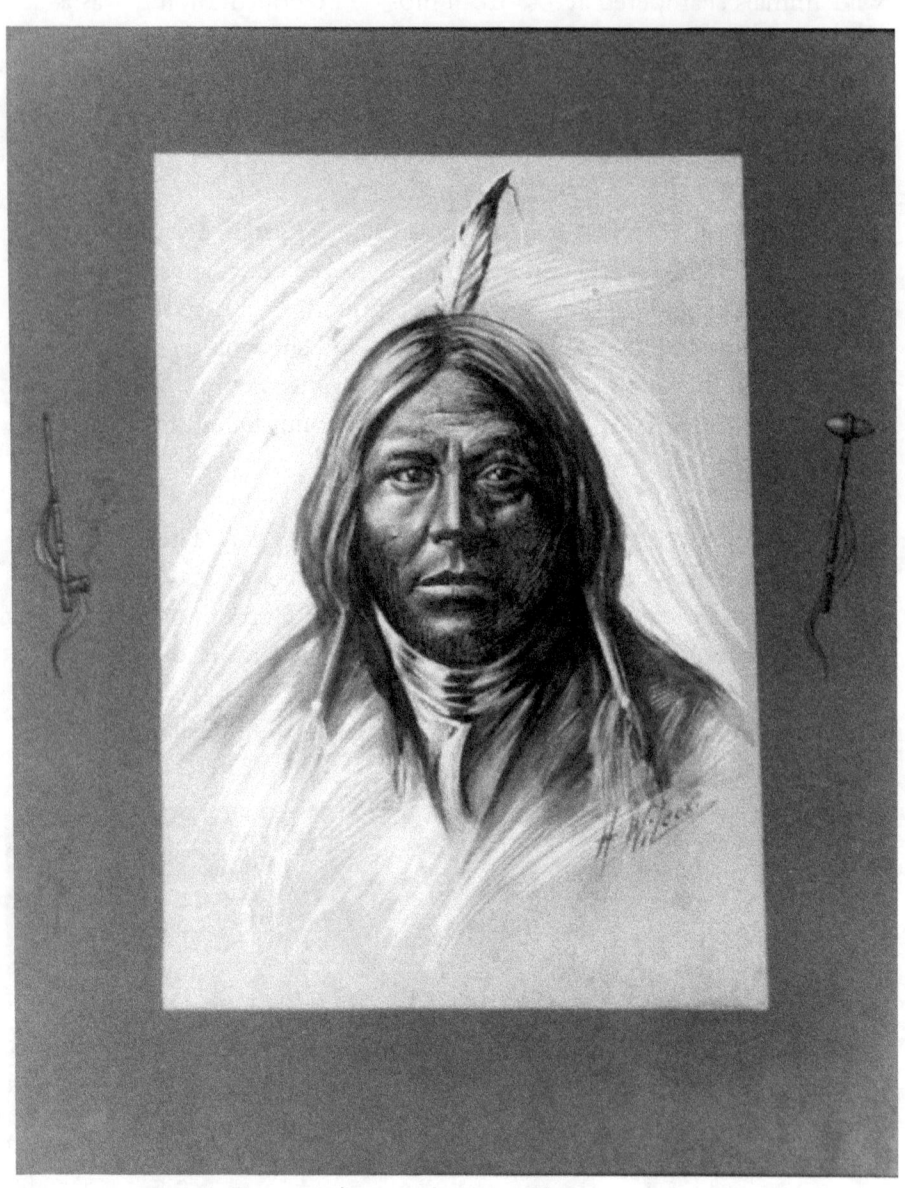

Indian man, by Harry Wilcox.
Pen and ink on scratchboard.

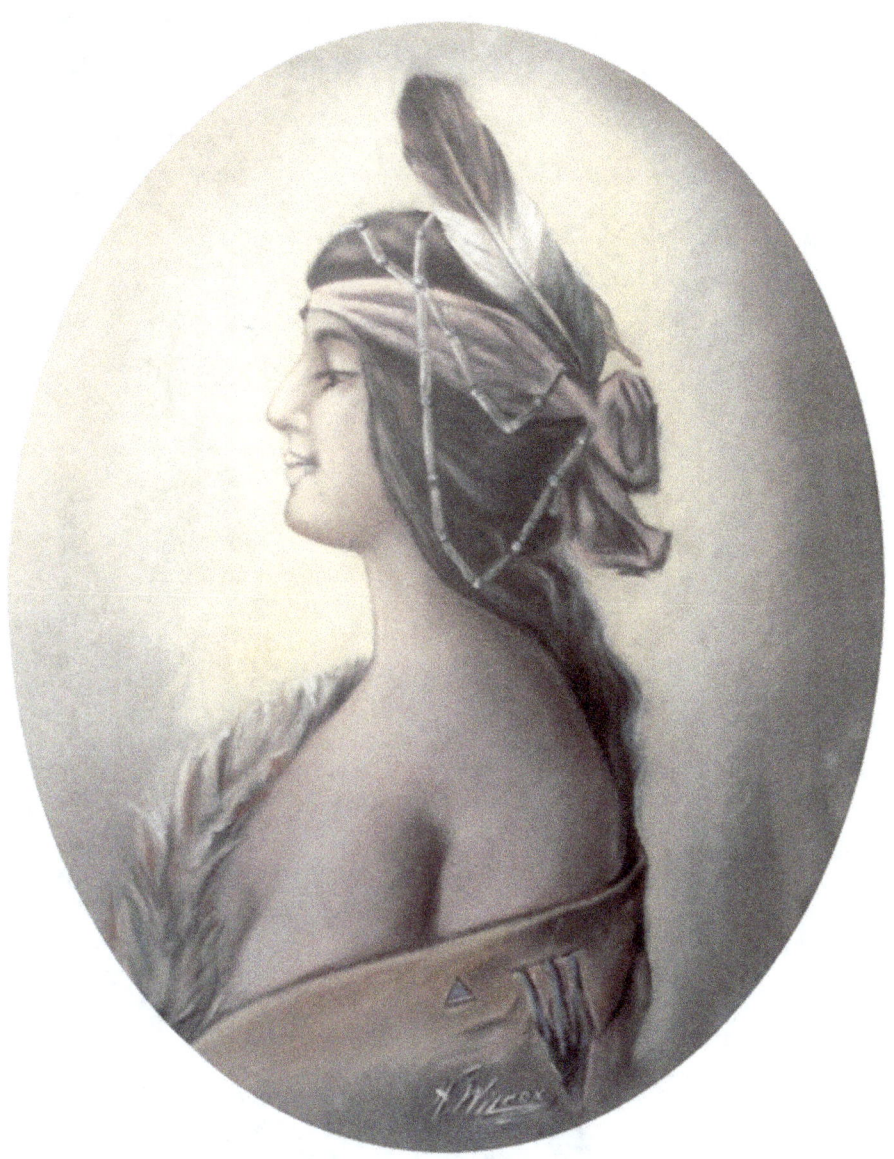

Indian maiden, by Harry Wilcox
Pastels and pencils on paper.
This painting hung in a place of honor in Hattie's living room for the rest of her life.

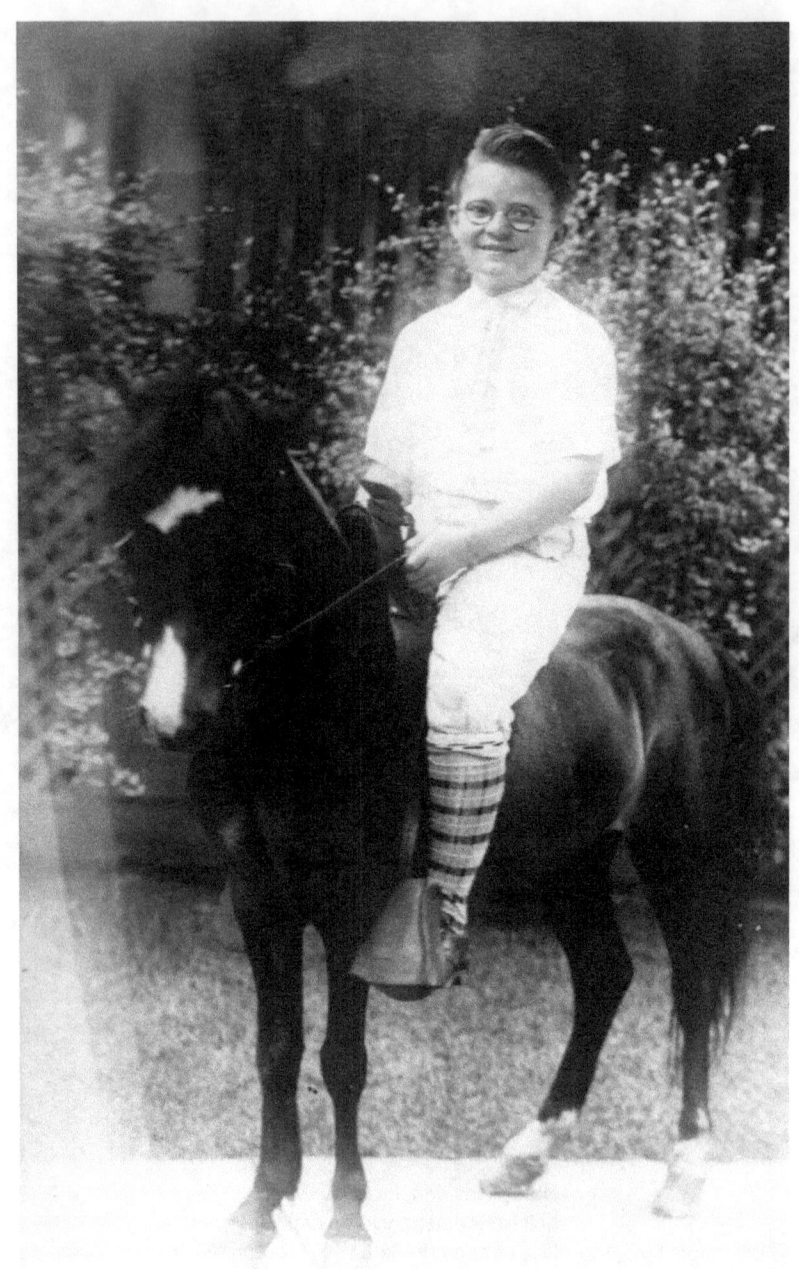

Bud on the photographer's pony, 1926.

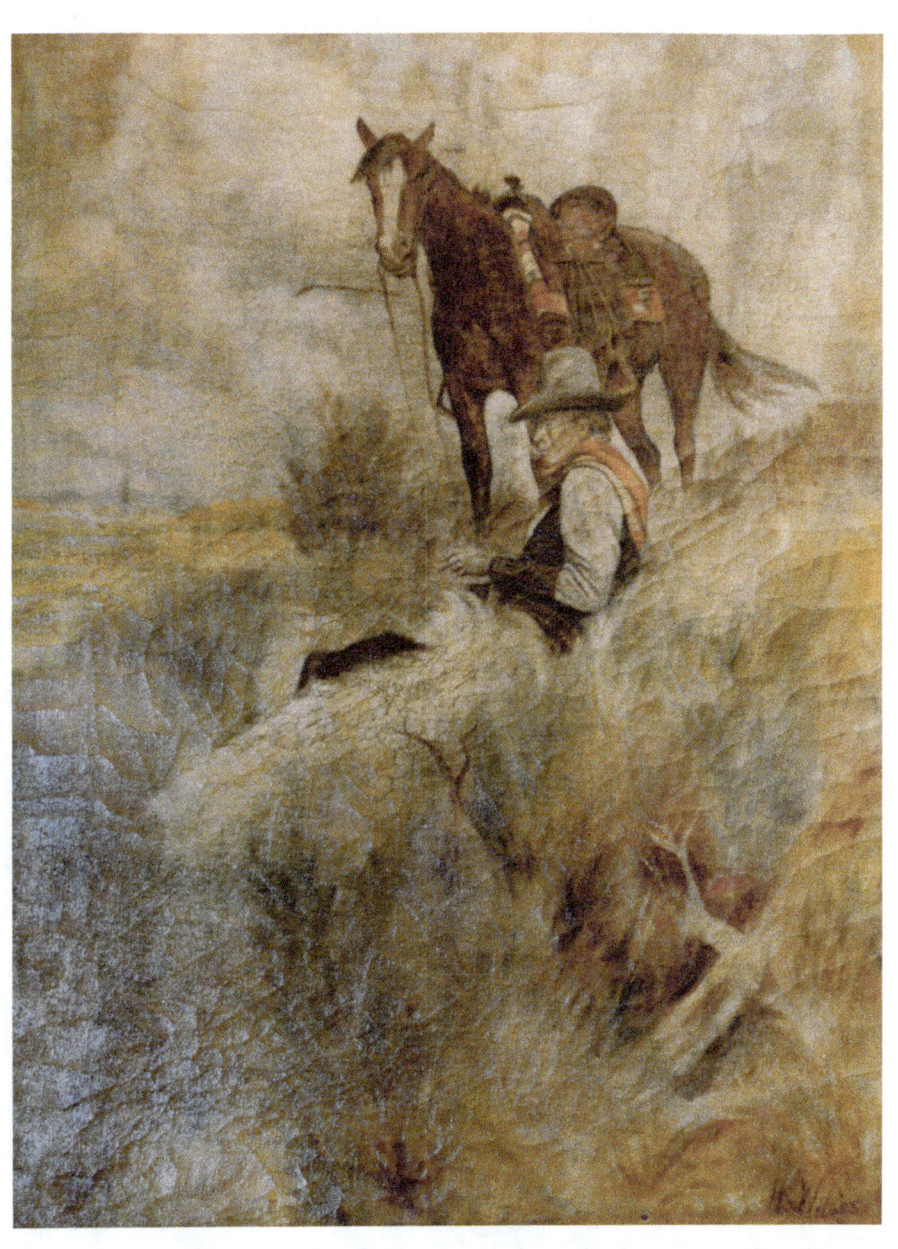

Cowboy, by Harry Wilcox
Oil on canvas.

In 1929, Harry lost his job at General Motors in the Great Depression. He continued to look for steady work in Detroit for nearly two years. He did piecework, making advertising illustrations for the newspaper, touching up furniture, or adding decorative designs. Bud remembered going with his father to a jewelry store to pick up a ring they wanted him to draw for a newspaper ad. The owner handed him the ring, Harry slipped it into his pocket, took it home, drew the illustration, and returned the ring the following day.

There were times the children went hungry. Bud remembered standing in the bread lines in Detroit, seeing people dying of starvation, sometimes collapsing on the sidewalks before the bread was handed out. At the height of the Great Depression, half of all American families were living below subsistence levels. Even 60 or 70 years later, as Bud spoke of these hard times in Detroit, his eyes would fill with tears.

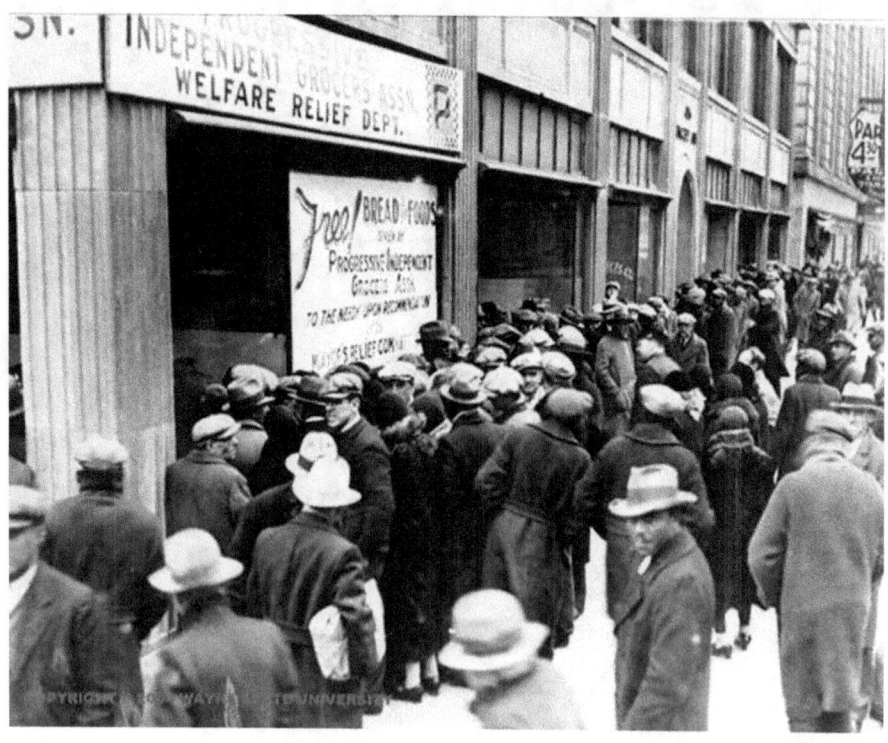

Men distributing bread and coffee to the needy.
Photo credit: Jeffrey Tucker archives, copyright Wayne State Univesity, as published on LewRockwell.com

It was a side of the Depression that most people in Williamsport never saw. The Depression came later to Williamsport, after the Rubber Company moved out. They offered to relocate their employees to their other locations, but people with ties to Williamsport stayed. Times were tough, but neighbors helped and people had gardens and food to eat.

The economics of being an artist in 1929 were clearly difficult, to say the least. Floyd Gottfredson, a Disney artist, remembers 1929:

> "I was anxious to get into the art business; that's why I had come down to Los Angeles in the first place, to try to get on one of the newpapers, and just didn't make it. I had been making $65 a week as a projectionist, which was pretty big money in 1928 and 1929. Walt [Disney] was starting everybody, except those who were trained professionals ready to go into production, at $18 a week. I was married and I had two children, so that shook me up a little bit, but I still took it. At the time, I was doing four cartoons a month for an automotive trade journal in Terre Haute, Indiana, through the mail, so between the two jobs, we were able to make it."[32]

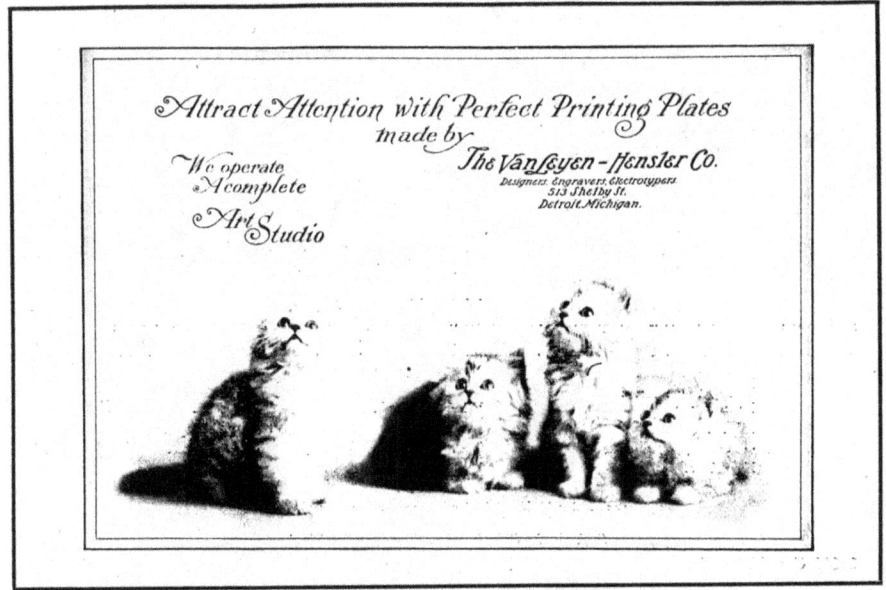

Advertisement in the Detroit City Directory, 1930, for Van Leyden-Hensler Co., photo engraving, which maintained a complete Art Studio.

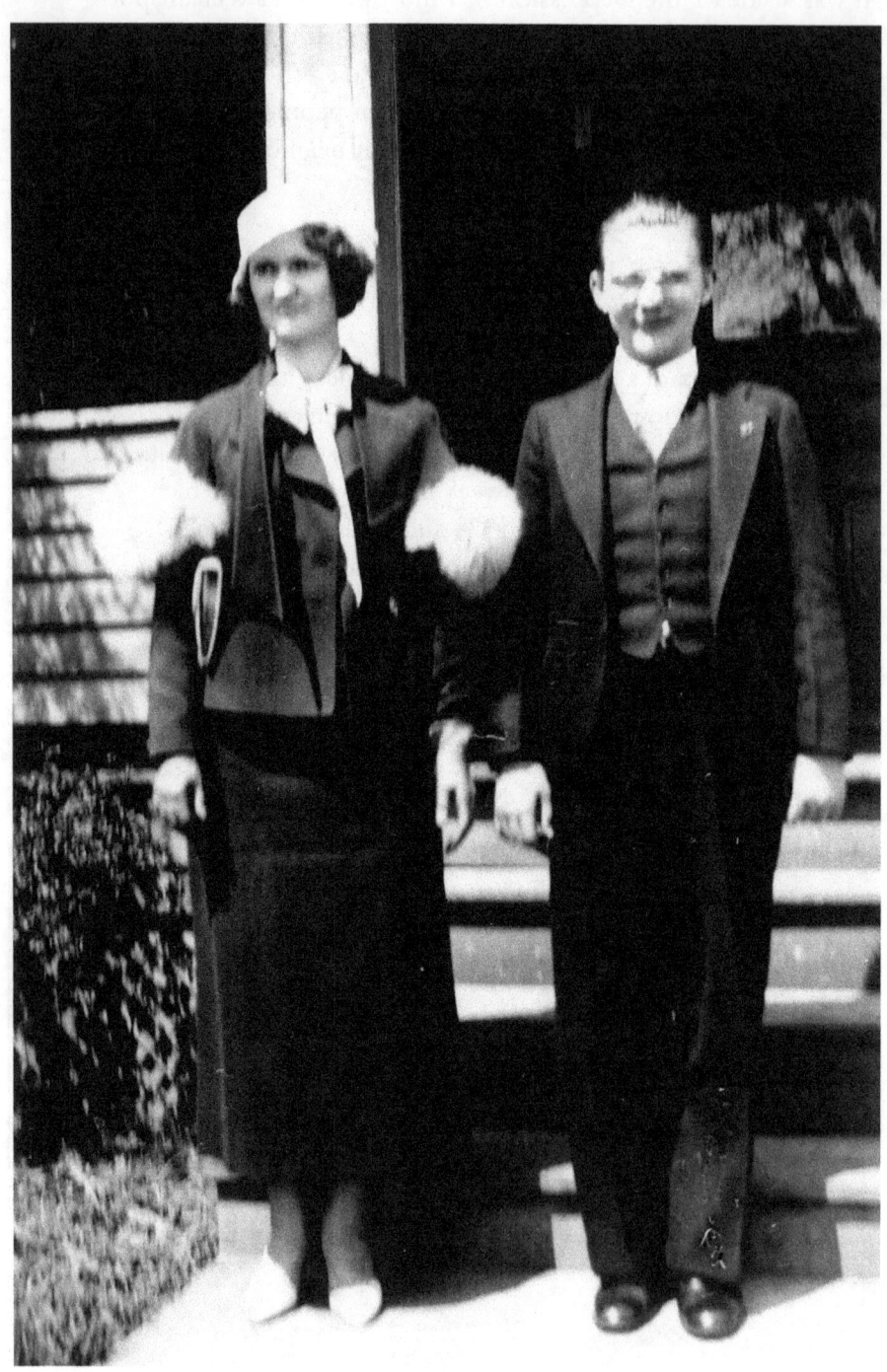

Sis (Verna) and Bud (Harry Jr), 1931 in Williamsport
at 1300 High Street. Hattie made both outfits.

In a similar way, Harry picked up piece work wherever he could, including adding decorative designs to furniture and lampshades. He is listed in the City Directory in 1930 as working for Van Leyden-Hensler Engraving Company, one of the most up-to-date photo engraving plants and art studios in the city of Detroit.[33] Nonetheless, it was only part-time work.

Finally in 1931 Harry gave up and took the family home to Williamsport, where they lived at 700 Market Street. Once again Harry was able to do some work for the *Grit* and some additional freelancing as a commercial artist and photographic retoucher. He designed Miss Sunbeam for an advertising campaign for Stroehman's Bakery, which sold their innovative packaged sliced bread to Wonder Bread.

The many moves – partly for his work, and partly instigated by Hattie – had meant that Verna and Bud had been moved through too many schools to count. Even when they were in the same city for more than one year, they were often moved among multiple school districts in that city. Both Verna and Bud had been pegged as below-average students, mostly because they were moved from one curriculum to another, missing out on the background necessary to succeed in the exams.

DETROIT HIGH SCHOOLS—SEMESTER RECORD CARD

Fill Out Carefully with Ink. For semester ending JUNE , 1929

Name in Full (Surname first) Wilcox, V rna Grade 11B Age 16

Residence 2544 Fischer Ave.

* FATHER'S Name HARRY WILCOX

" Business Address

Hour	Name of Study	C'se	Room No.	1st report	2nd report	3rd report	4th report	Final	Teacher's Name
	ENG. LIT.	1	305	E	C	E	C	E	HACKMAN
	HOME SCIENCE	3B	117	B	C	B	C	B	KEEN
	LATIN	3	310	C	D	C	D	C	STAEHLE
	MATH	S/5	308	D	C	E	C	D	WIGGINS
	ART	5	307	B	B	B	B	B	SPAFARD
	CRAFT CLUB	2	307	B	B	B	B	B	SPAFARD
	STAGE CRAFT	2	106	B	A	—	A	A?	CARTER

Verna's report card, grade 11B, age 16. Her best subjects were
Art, Craft Club, and Stage Craft, followed by Home Science.

Altogether we can document that Harry and Hattie moved 31 times —
10 times between 1911 and 1918, and another 21 times between 1918
and 1935, the children's school years. Verna graduated from High School
in 1930 in Detroit.

Three years in Williamsport, however, had allowed Bud to shine. He
attended 9th grade at Curtin Junior High School in 1931, and then
went on to Williamsport High School. The family continued to move
frequently – Market Street, Tucker Street, High Street, 6th Avenue,
Isabella Street – but he was able to continue at Williamsport High
despite the moves. He got top grades, made many lifelong friends, and
was feeling settled and successful. He was an acolyte at the church. He
learned cabinet making from Uncle Ross. His friend Walter Freed Jr.
had introduced him to his sister, June Freed, who had become Bud's
sweetheart.

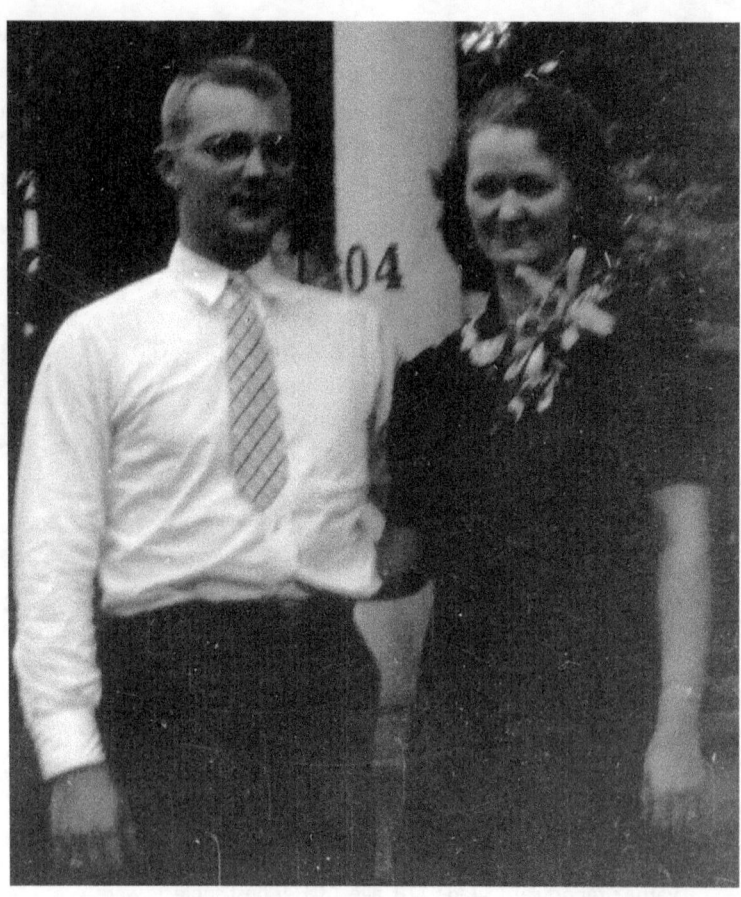

Bud (Harry Jr) and Sis (Verna) June 1934 in Williamsport.

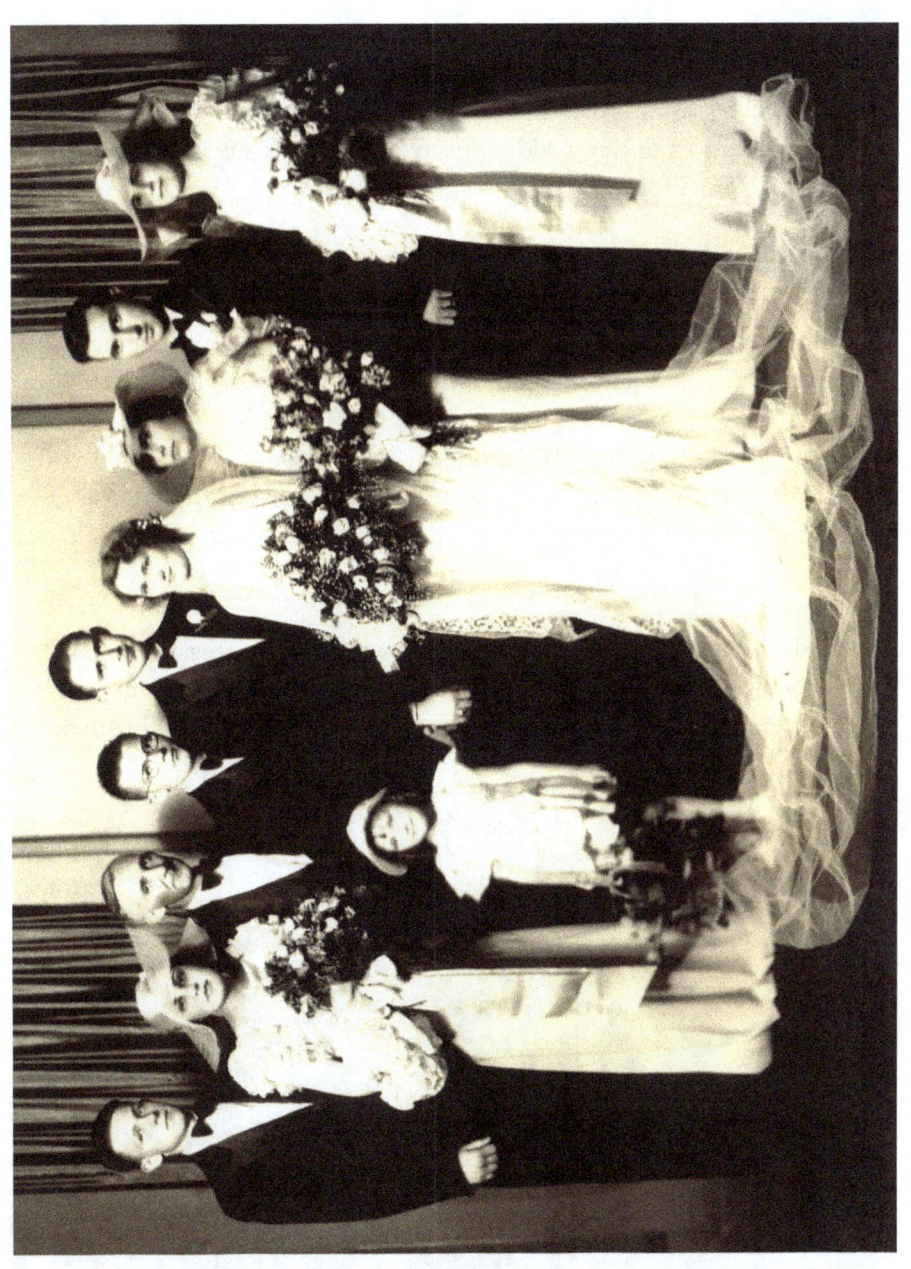

Wedding of Verna Wilcox and Meredith Alair, June 20, 1934. Left to right: George A. "Jim" Richner Jr; Vada Misho Schuchart, cousin of Hattie's; Harry Wilcox; Harry "Bud" Wilcox Jr; Meredith Alair the groom; Verna Wilcox Alair the bride; Verena Winder Cole; Austin Winder, son of Mary and James Mahlon "Doc" Winder; Ruth Conn (Barrett). The flower girl is Marian Winter, daughter of Vivian Misho Winter, Vada's older sister.

The veil Verna is wearing was that of her grandmother, Ada Virginia Kramm Wilcox. This veil was also worn by June in her wedding in 1941. It was destroyed in a house fire in the 1990's.

On June 20, 1934, Verna married her high school sweetheart, Meredith Walter Alair of Detroit. They were married at Trinity Episcopal Church in Williamsport, after which they moved in with his parents in Detroit. The many relatives in her wedding party attest to the importance of family in Verna's life.

In September 1934, as Bud was entering his senior year of high school in Williamsport, Harry and Hattie decided to move to the farm in Limestoneville to save money. Bud put his foot down. For once he wanted to stay in the same school to finish high school. He asked if he could stay in Williamsport. His Aunt Julia and Uncle Ross Conn offered to let him sleep in the back bedroom of their house at 905 Washington Boulevard. Their daughter Ruth was in the same class at the high school. Bud gratefully accepted their offer and spent a happy and productive year there.

While Harry's employment was fragile through the Depression years, Hattie's siblings had more stable incomes. Julia worked for Penn Garment making uniforms for police and postal workers; her husband

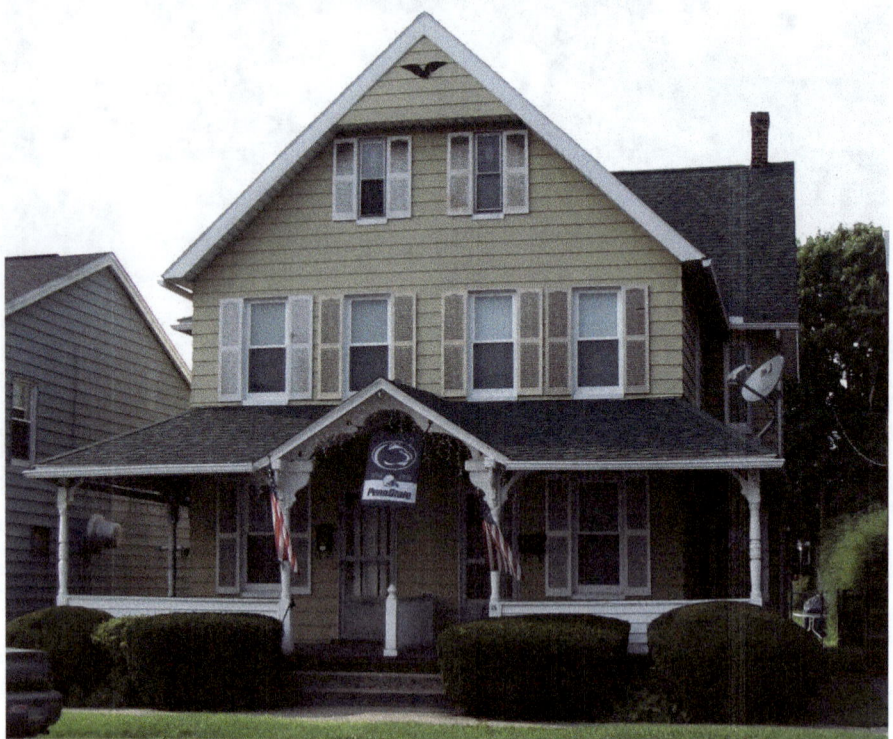

905-907 Washington Blvd, double house. Julia and Ross Conn owned the building and lived on the left; Mary and Charlie Winder lived on the right. Photo taken 2009.

Ross Conn worked at Bush and Bull Department Store, and later had a grocery store. Dick Richner was a tobacco salesman, and his wife ran their grocery store while he was on the road.[31] Charlie Winder, Mary's husband, drove a truck for a wholesale grocer, and his uncle "Doc" Winder, Emmy's husband, worked in the warehouse. Their incomes were not generous, but they were pretty steady, which was a very good thing in the Depression.

It was always fun at "the Aunties'" on Washington Boulevard. Aunt Mary, Uncle Charlie, their daughter Verena and her husband Earl Cole

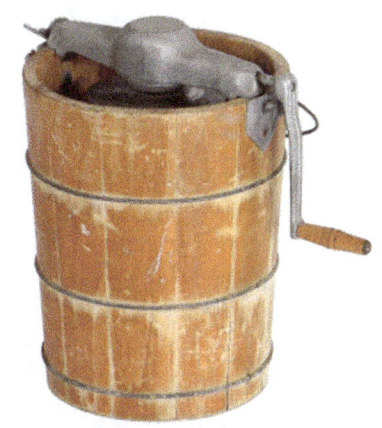

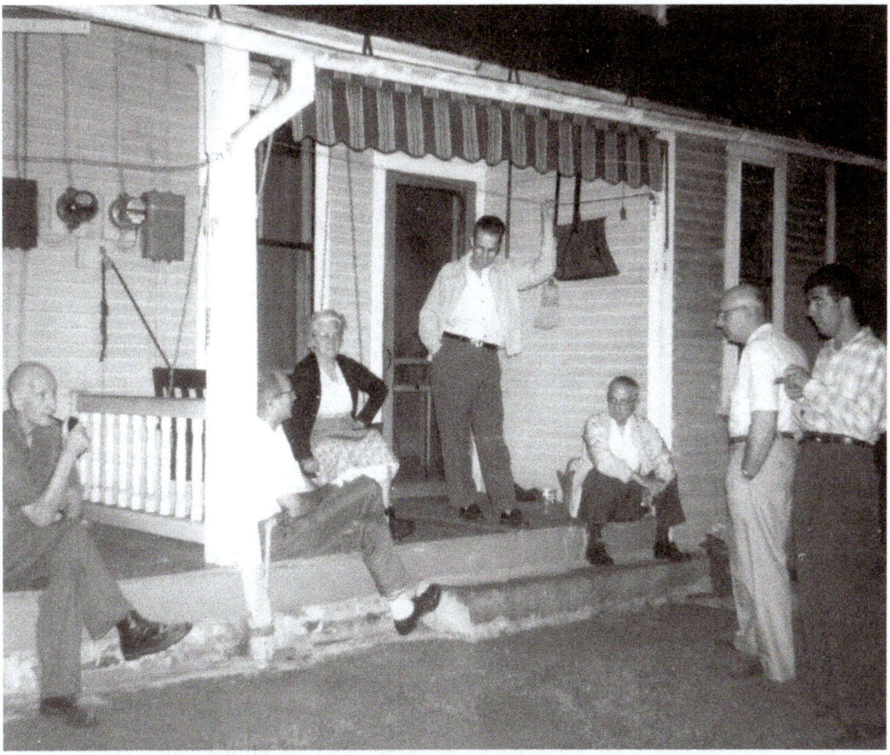

Home Ice Cream Maker. The ice cream custard is in a canister in the middle. Ice and rock salt are placed around the canister, and the crank is turned to drive the paddle inside the canister, churning the custard for about an hour until it is firm.

At the Aunties. Left to right: Uncle Charlie, Bud,ncle Dick. Standing at right: Earl Cole and Norman Cole. Photo taken 1961.

and son Norman lived in the other side of the double house at 905-907 Washington Blvd. The two halves of the house were symmetrical, with front and back porches and a shared back yard. Often there would be home-made ice cream and Verena's famous freshly grated coconut cake. The apple tree in the back yard yielded many an apple pie. Churning the ice cream was a collaborative effort – the men would take turns turning the hand crank, and would devise improvements. At one point they jacked up the car and attached the churn handle to the spokes of the car wheel. Later they attached an old washing machine motor to automate the cranking.

Grandpop Richner on Tucker Street was pretty strict and did not put up with a lot of commotion from his grandchildren. He made his own wine, which was permissible during Prohibition (1920-1933) as long as you did not sell it. He kept a store of elderberry, dandelion, grape, and white grape wines under the stairs in the basement, and was happy to share samples with visitors. Dick's sons Jim and Ed remember going to Grandpop's on Sundays, taking leftovers to him and cleaning the kitchen. Aunt Emmy would bake pies, and someone would play the piano.[34]

Many of the men in the family were fine cabinet makers: Grandpop Richner, his son Dick, and Ross Conn. Bud Wilcox learned from them all. Throughout his life he enjoyed working with wood and passed the love of woodworking to his son. Grandpop made tables for his children and doll cupboards for the little girls. Uncle Ross designed a rubber band rifle which shot circular slices of a tire inner tube about 1/2 inch wide – a formidable weapon in boys' games. All the boys had Uncle Ross's rubber band guns, with finely crafted stocks and a smooth lock mechanism that dropped the bolt and fired the rubber band with a pull of the trigger.

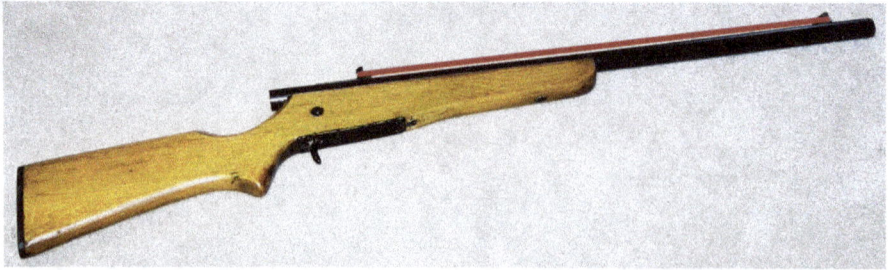

Uncle Ross' Rubber Band gun. The red rubber band shows the stretch of the rubber band, from peg to peg (20 inches), which was fired with the pull of the trigger. The overall length of the gun is 36 inches.

On Saturdays, each of the kids needed 20 cents – five cents to get into the Grand Theater or the Keystone Theater to see the serial movies, first with a piano player and later as talkies. Behind the jail there was a booth where you could get two hot dogs and a soft drink for fifteen cents.

Bud graduated from the Williamsport High School in 1935, along with his two cousins, Jim Richner (son of Dick and Kathie Richner) and Ruth Conn (daughter of Julia and Ross Conn), and Bud's sweetheart, June Freed.

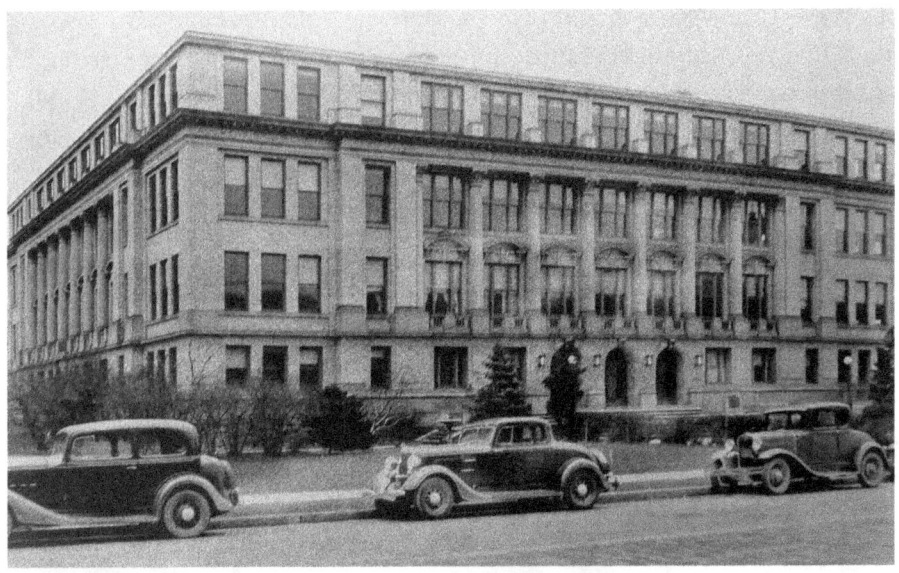

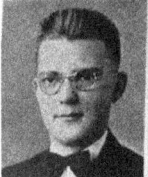
Harry H. Wilcox, Jr.
Curtin   Academic
Hi-Y 4, Math Engineers 4,
German 3-4.
"Love me, love my dog."

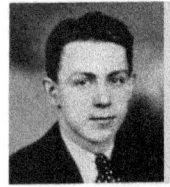
George A. Richner, Jr.
"Jim"
Curtin   Commercial
Pep Club 2-3-4
"Salesman deluxe"

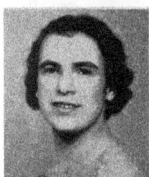
Ruth E. Conn *"Connie"*
Curtin   Academic
Glee Club 3-4, German 3,
Audubon 3, Class Basketball 2-3-4,
Orchestra 2, Secretary 304, Senior
Girls' Chorus, Accompanist 4.
Music hath charms.

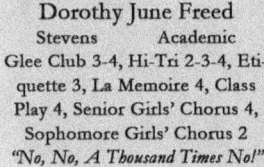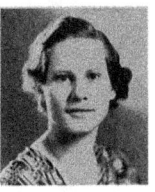
Dorothy June Freed
Stevens   Academic
Glee Club 3-4, Hi-Tri 2-3-4, Eti-
quette 3, La Memoire 4, Class
Play 4, Senior Girls' Chorus 4,
Sophomore Girls' Chorus 2
"No, No, A Thousand Times No!"

Photos from the Yearbook of the Class of 1935 of the Williamsport High School. "Curtin" and "Stevens" are the names of the Junior High Schools they attended. "No, no" refers to a song June sang in her starring role in the school play, "Growing Pains." Bud's dog Spike was a member of the cast of the same play.

When the principal of the high school asked Bud what he planned to do after graduation, Bud said he wanted to go to college. The principal asked why? Neither of his parents had even graduated from high school. His grandfather had been a butcher. What made him think he needed to go to college?

Bud was not deterred. He had made up his mind that he wanted to be a scientist.

One of Hattie's friends at Trinity Church had a son who went to the University of Michigan and loved it. Bud was sold on the idea of going to Michigan. With his father doing only piece work in the Depression, and money extremely tight, he formed a plan of how he could do it. He would go out to Michigan, spend a semester earning money and gaining in-state residency, and then would be able to afford in-state tuition, which was $50 a semester.

When Hattie learned that "Baby" wanted to go to Michigan to college, she determined that he should not be so far from home. If he was going to Michigan, then she and Harry should go too. So they packed up and left with him for Ann Arbor. On their way out of town they stopped to say good-bye to June Freed. Hattie jokingly said to June, "Absence makes the heart forget." June was startled but did not reply. Little did Hattie know, Bud and June would in fact wind up together.

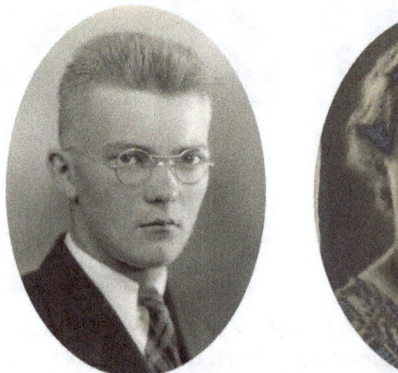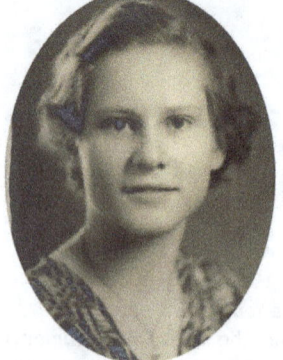

High School graduation pictures,
Harry Wilcox Jr (Bud) and June Freed.

CHAPTER 6: WARTIME IN MICHIGAN

June went off to Lock Haven State College in Pennsylvania, and Bud went off to Michigan. He had not told her he was not going to attend that first semester. Instead he helped his family settle in to a rented house on Madison Court where Hattie rented rooms to male students, and did tailoring for the department store in town. Harry found work where he was able, including some piece work for the *Grit*. Verna and Meredith worked in the Detroit area, and lived with Meredith's parents.

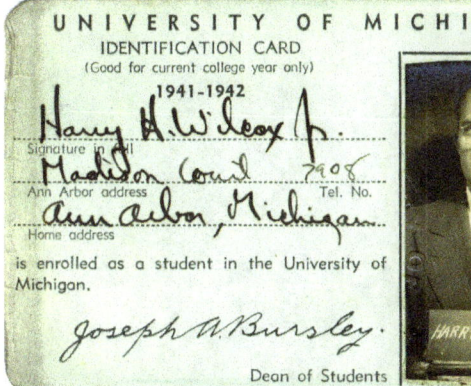

Bud worked as a waiter, a construction helper, and took courses in typing and shorthand. He saved what money he could after contributing to the household.

By January 1936, Bud was enrolled at the University of Michigan. He worked as a waiter at the League House. After waiting on Miss Gillette of the U of M library, he was offered a job in the library. They were changing the catalog system and needed more help. He continued to work in the library throughout his undergraduate years.

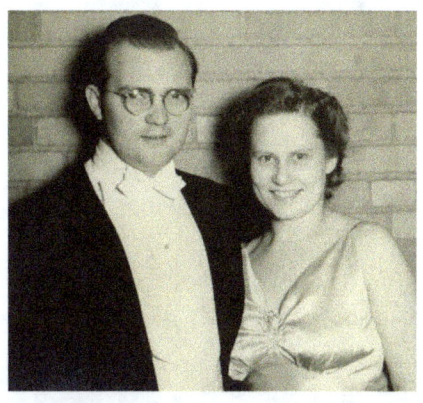

He stayed in touch with June, who came out to Michigan for the "J-Hop" and for his graduation in 1939. After they both graduated from their colleges in 1939, both went on to graduate school and completed Master's Degrees in 1940.

Bud and June at the J-Hop, Ann Arbor

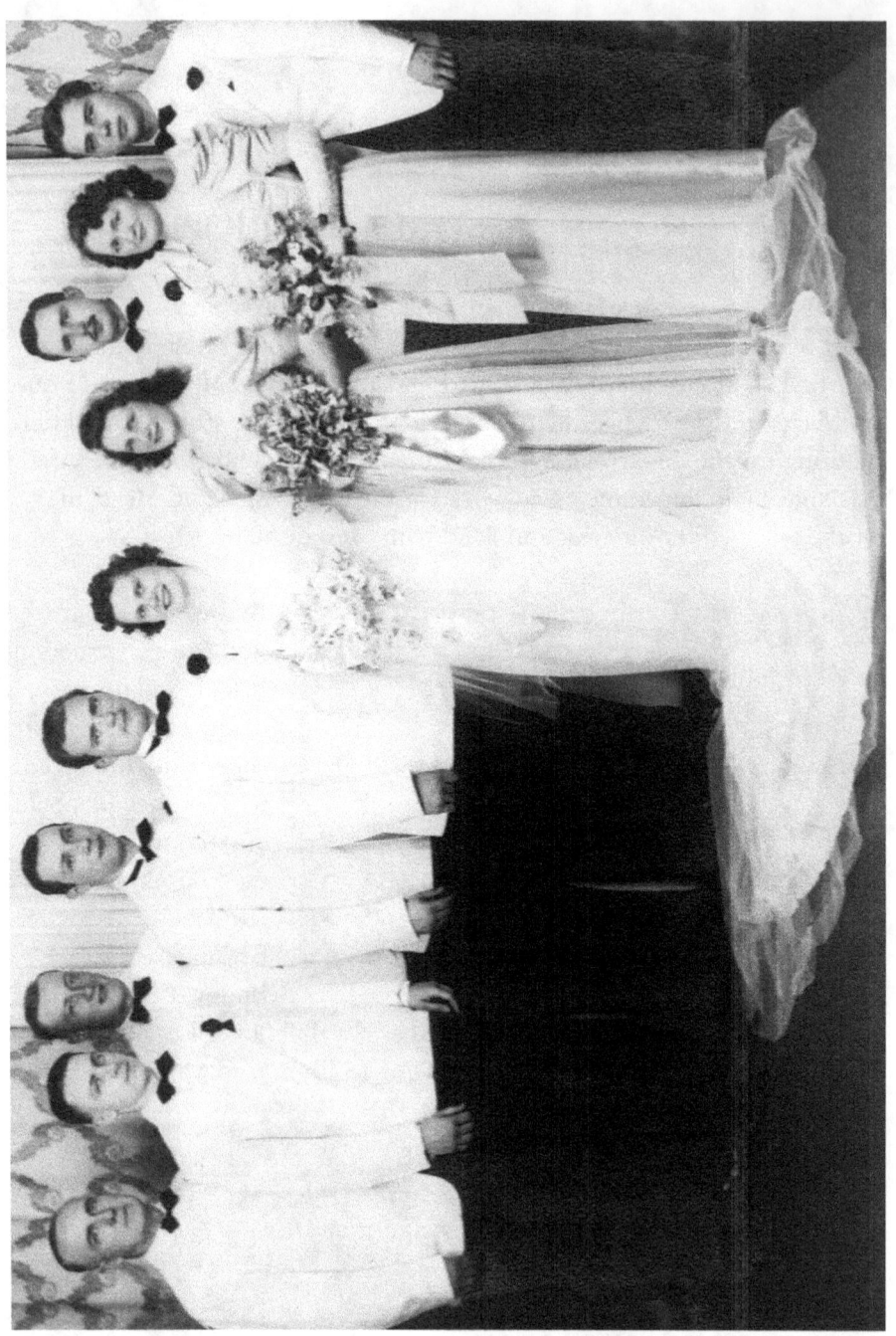

Wedding of Harry Wilcox and June Freed, June 21, 1941, St. John's Lutheran Church, Williamsport.

Left to right:

Walter C. Freed Sr, father of the bride; "Jim" Richner; Dale Freed and Walter Freed Jr, brothers of the bride; Harry "Bud" Wilcox; June Freed Wilcox; Marian Freed (Hege), sister of the bride; Meredith Alair; Verna Wilcox Alair; Franklin Hege.

The veil June is wearing once belonged to Bud's grandmother, Ada Virginia Kramm Wilcox. It was borrowed from Verna Alair.

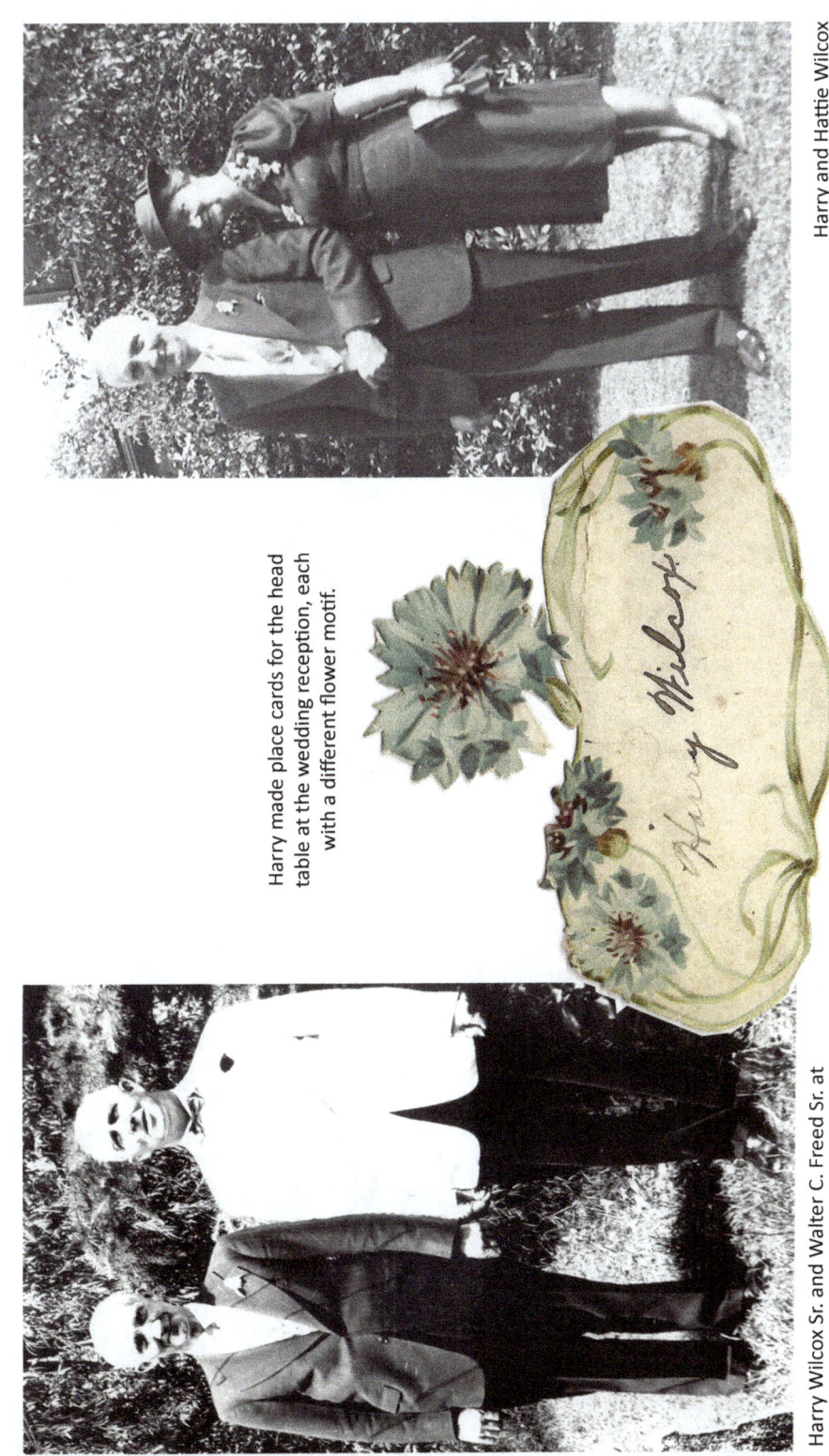

Harry and Hattie Wilcox
at their son Bud's wedding reception.

Harry made place cards for the head
table at the wedding reception, each
with a different flower motif.

Harry Wilcox Sr. and Walter C. Freed Sr. at
the wedding reception

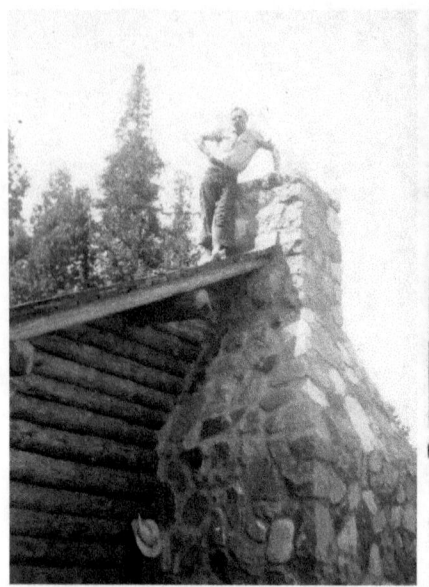

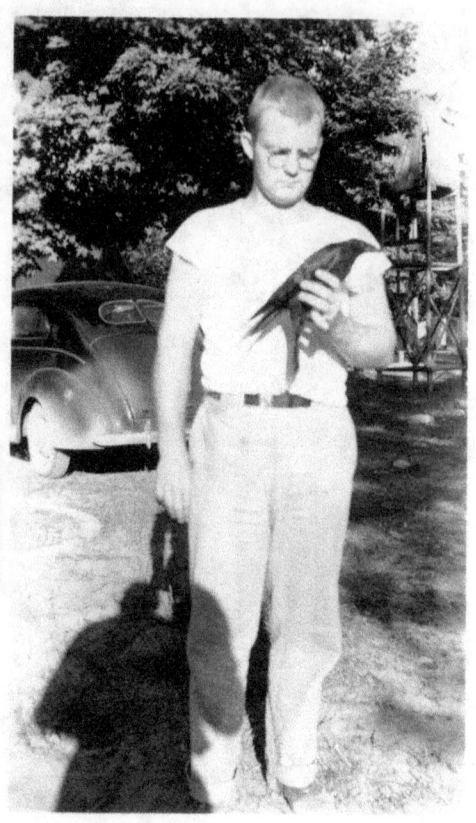

Bud atop the Lodge at the "Bug Camp," the University of Michigan Biological Station in the northern part of the Lower Peninsula of Michigan, a wildlife preserve for teaching natural science. Here, Bud was in his element, teaching and working toward his Ph.D. in comparative zoology.

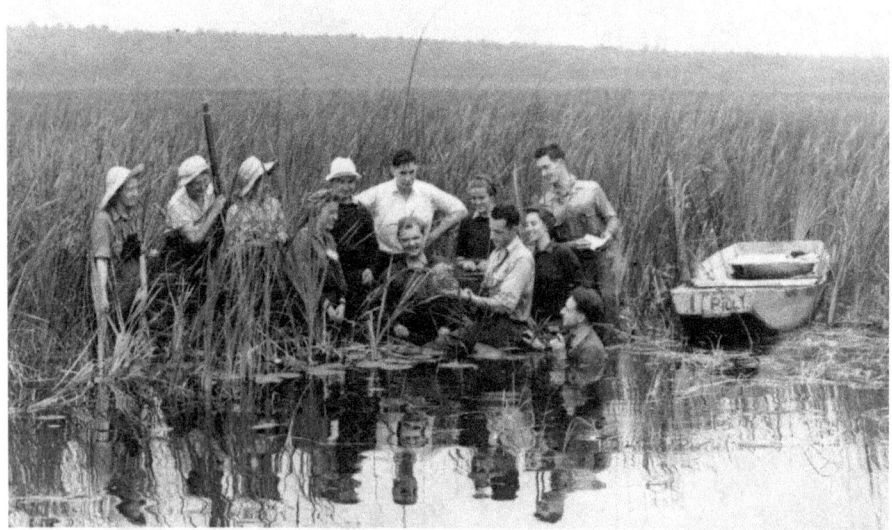

Bud taught ornithology (above) and aquatic plants (below) under the direction of Dr. Olin Sewall Pettingill. *Left to right:* Ruth Spencer, Katherine White, Peggy Muirhead, Amelia Finnaci, Ross Wagner, Harry "Bud" Wilcox, Norma Dennison, Dr. Pettingill, Jackie Clarke, Bill Brokaw, Cliff Davis. 1941.

Right:
Bud was strong and happy at the Bug Camp. He went four summers, as an undergrad and as a graduate teaching assistant, and later as a teaching associate for two summers with his new bride.

Below:
Pals? A snapping turtle offers to shorten the tail of a cat.
By Harry Wilcox, Sr,
pen and ink and colored pencil.

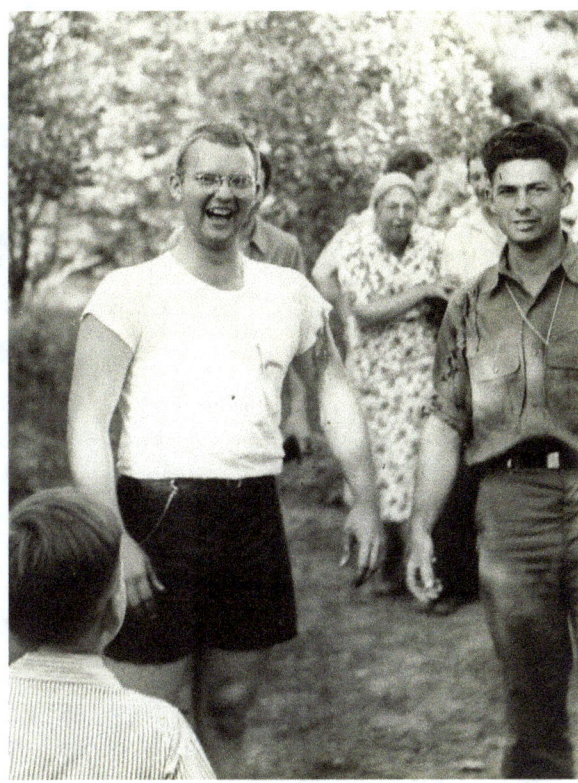

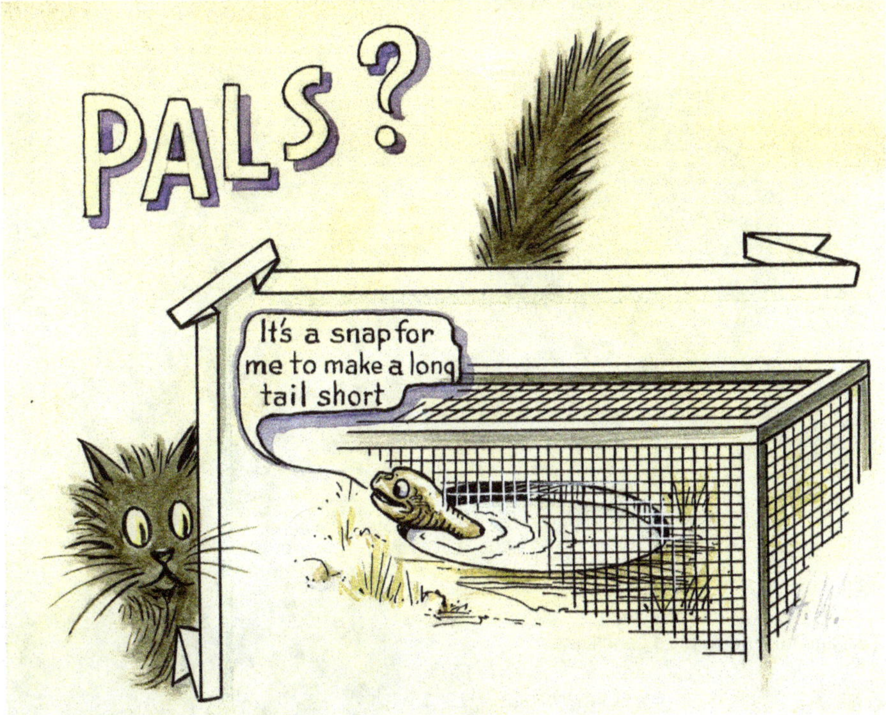

In 1941, having known each other for ten years, Bud and June married in Pennsylvania and honeymooned at the University of Michigan Biological Station in the northern part of the Lower Peninsula of Michigan, where Bud was teaching for the summer.

Meanwhile, Harry and Hattie continued to live on Madison Court. Their combination of enterprises was balancing the budget with some contributions from Bud. In the 1940 census he is listed as a "Commercial Artist for an Engraving Company" working 12 hours a week in March 1940, while Bud was working 39 hours a week as a library assistant.

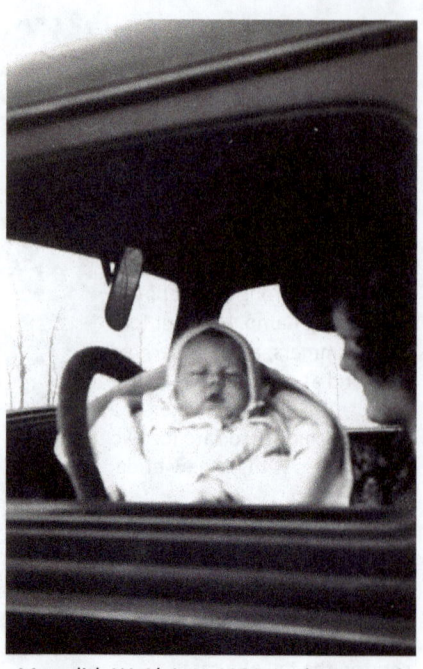

Meredith W. Alair Jr, 1939, in the car with his mother, Verna.

In addition to the roomers, they had taken on the raising of their grandson, Meredith Alair Jr., "Meredy," the son of their daughter Verna and Meredith Walter Alair. Meredy was born in 1939. Hattie had gone to

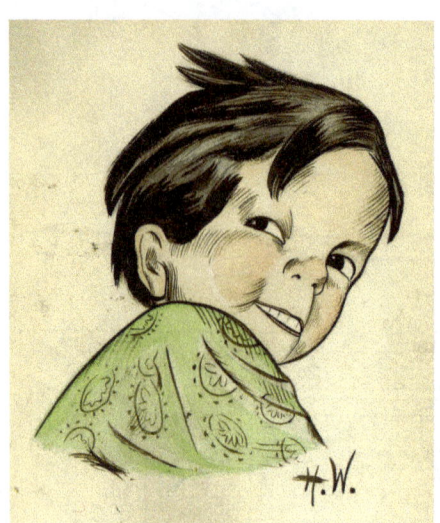

Above:
Impish boy, by Harry Wilcox
Pen and ink and colored pencil

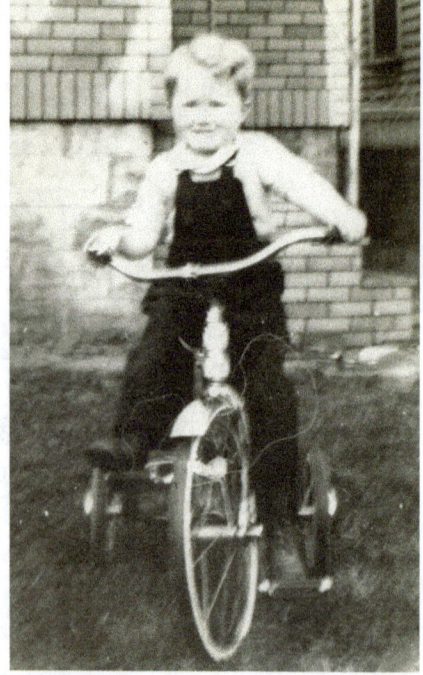

Right:
Meredith W. Alair Jr, 1941.

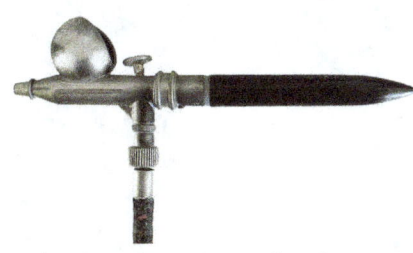

Air brush similar to the one found among the papers of Harry Wilcox. The tubing on the bottom connects to the compressor, the paint goes into the reservoir on the top.

help Verna with the new baby, and took the baby back to Ann Arbor with her to provide child care while Verna worked. Verna and Meredith came for Sunday dinner every few weeks, but the primary job of raising Meredy was with his grandparents in Ann Arbor.

When June and Bud returned from their honeymoon, they joined the full house on Madison Court. They were delighted to play with young Meredy.

Over the years, Harry had been making consistent improvements in his use of the air brush. The air brush was invented in the 1870's by Francis Stanley of Newton, Massachusetts, founder with his twin brother of the Stanley Motor Company which produced the Stanley Steamer automobile. An airbrush works by passing a stream of fast moving compressed air through an aspirator, which creates a suction that allows paint to be pulled from an interconnected reservoir. The high velocity of the air atomizes the paint into very tiny droplets as it blows past a very fine paint-metering component. The paint is carried onto paper or other surface. The operator controls the amount of paint using a variable trigger which opens more or less a very fine tapered needle that is the

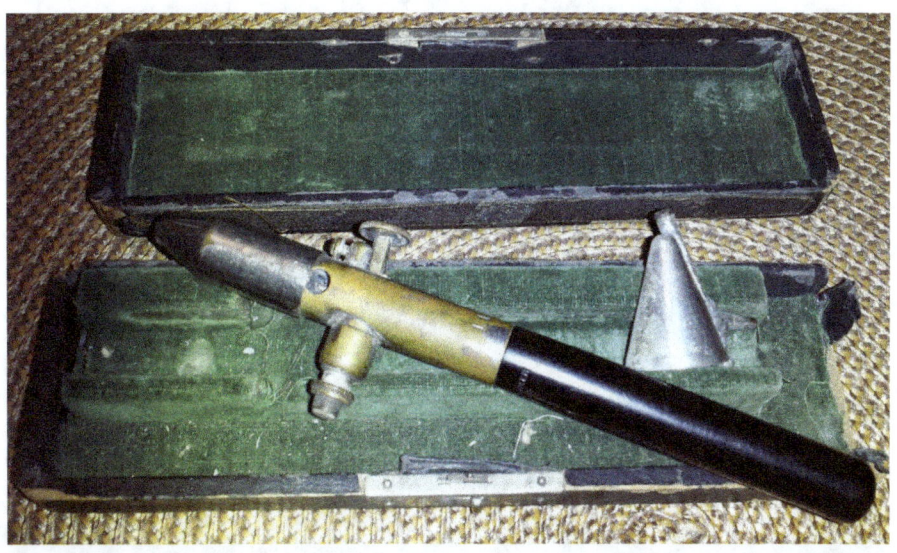

Harry Wilcox's air brush.

control element of the paint-metering component. An extremely fine degree of atomization is what allows an artist to create such smooth blending effects using the airbrush.

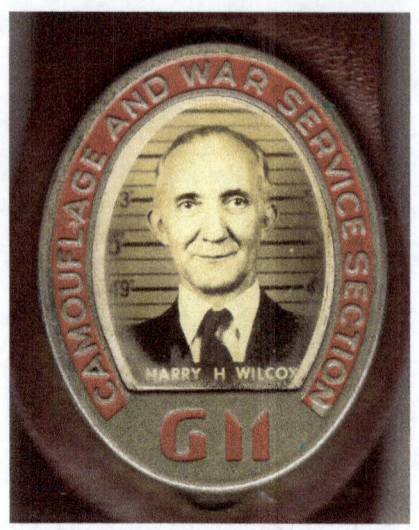

The technique allows for the blending of two or more colors in a seamless way, with one color slowly becoming another color. Freehand airbrushed images have a floating quality, with softly defined edges between colors, and between foreground and background colors. A well skilled airbrush artist can produce paintings of photographic realism

Harry's employee badge at General Motors, in the Camouflage Section.

or can simulate almost any painting medium. Painting at this skill level involves supplementary tools, such as masks and stencils, and very careful planning. Without extremely fine control, it is very easy to create a blob of paint on your work.

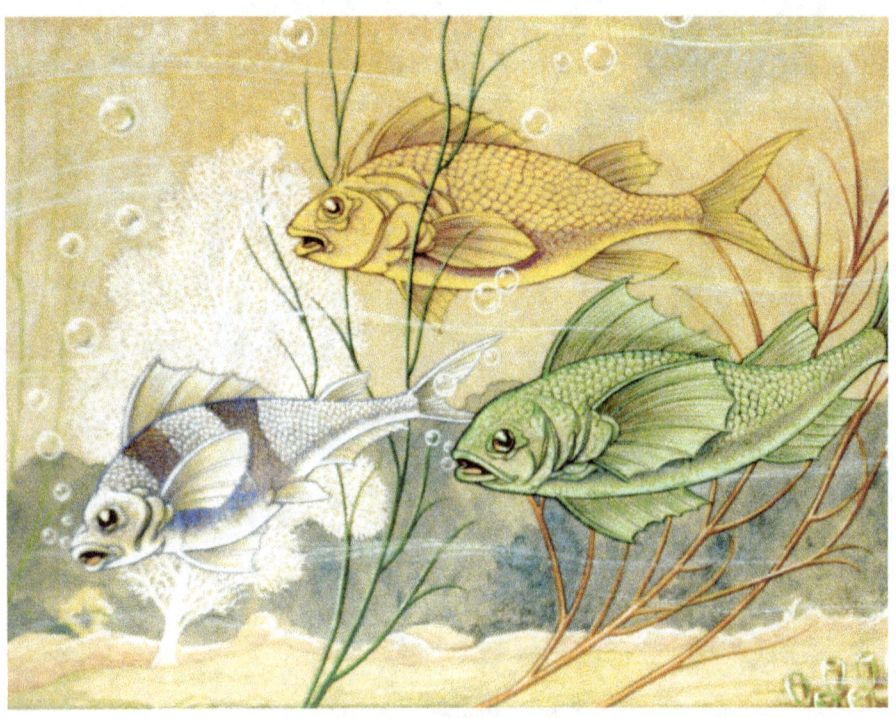

Fish, detail, by Harry Wilcox, dated 1938. See also cover art. Watercolor, air brush

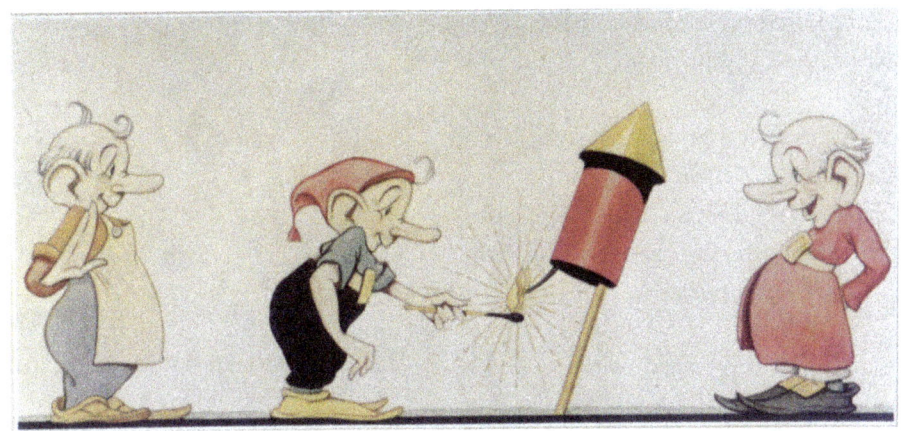

Elf Mischief, the only completed panel of a planned border for June and Bud's first child's nursery, by Harry Wilcox, 1942. Watercolor, air brush.

Harry had worked with the air brush doing photographic retouching and commercial art for 40 years now, and had honed his skill. As a demonstration of his proficiency, he did a particularly stunning painting of fish. With the fish in his portfolio, he got the job.

He also did one panel of what was intended to be a strip of cartoon characters to go around the nursery of Bud and June's first child. When

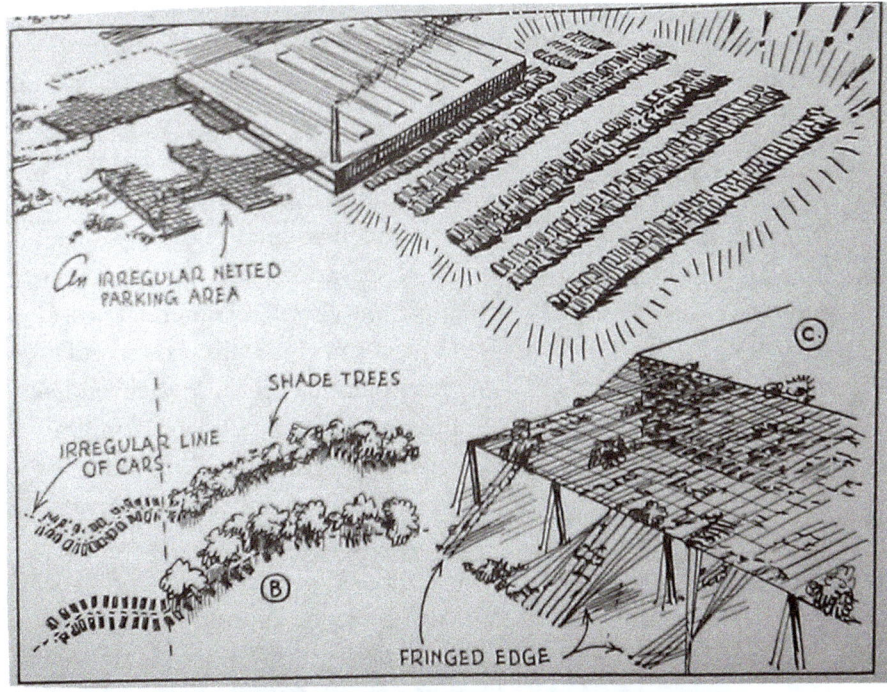

How to camouflage the automobiles in a corporate parking lot, from Eric Sloane, *Camouflage Simplified* (NY 1942), p. 58.

that pregnancy ended in miscarriage he suspended the project.

With his fish picture as his credential, he won a job offer from the Camouflage Division of General Motors, doing contract work for the War Department.

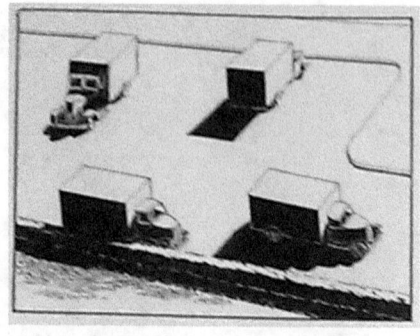

The definition of camouflage involves concealment and obscurity, whether applied to the natural coloration of animals, or to the paint schemes used on military vehicles. The methods by which concealment or obscurity are attained share a common set of strategies intended to deceive the observer. Painters and visual artists

Parking for Minimum of Shadows. "In blitz areas it is sensible to park a car or a truck in whatever direction or place will minimize its own shadow. When facing away from the sun the bulk of its shadow is broken over the hood. When left against a hedge or a wall, its shadow is in part hidden or merged with another shadow." *Precautionary Camouflage*, US Government Printing Office, 1943,

were sometimes employed in the development of camouflage, because they deal with human visual perception. It was an American artist, Abbott Handerson Thayer, who first published a scientific paper in 1892 describing the countershading technique often found in natural camouflage.

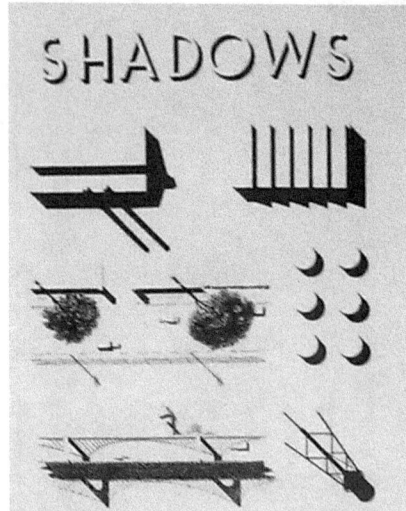

Form revealed by shadow. In this drawing, no forms whatever are delineated — only shadows which reveal the forms which cast them. *Precautionary Camouflage, p. 34.*

Military camouflage did not achieve widespread use until World War I, after the introduction of airplanes for observation made its use far more important. French gun crews wore smocks smeared with brown and green paint to break up their outlines and provide concealment from the aerial observers; it is likely that the first soldiers to try this were artists serving in the infantry, borrowing techniques from cubism. Upon seeing a camouflaged cannon for the first time, artist Pablo Picasso is reported to have said, *C'est nous qui avons fait ça,* or "it is we [artists] who have created that." This early camouflage was not restricted to just coloring, it applied to shape as well; at an early demonstration by the American Camouflage Corps, President Woodrow Wilson approached within ten feet of a soldier without noticing him. The soldier was in a foxhole covered by a *papier-mâché* cover camouflaged as a rock.[35]

Cartoonist Dick Brown's sketch in *Yank*, the U.S. Army's wartime magazine, shows two irate fighter pilots in a jungle clearing, glowering at a benign, highly self-satisfied sergeant who stands clutching a large can of paint and a dripping brush. One of the baffled pilots is growling at him, "Okay, Rembrandt – where the hell's our plane?"[36]

"One major factor would soon dramatically change the very nature and meaning of tactical concealment, and that was the growth of aerial photography; but before Pearl Harbor this wasn't yet of great importance."[37] With that deadly attack, it suddenly became important to conceal not only soldiers but trucks, munitions dumps, buildings, and industrial parks. "Industrial targets were the most lucrative and most

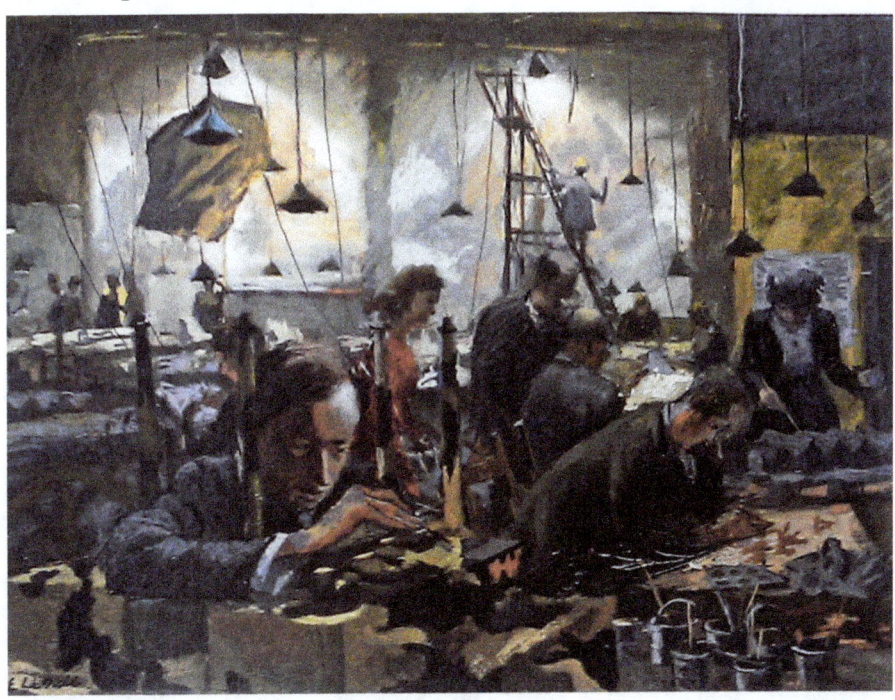

The Camouflage Workshop, oil on panel by Edwin LaDell, 1940. These civilian camoufleurs are shown at work in Leamington Spa. Sections of the finished camouflage are hung from the ceiling and could be checked from the viewing balcony. Tim Newark, *Camouflage*, Imperial War Museum, London 2007, p. 111. IWM ART LD 000322, reprinted with permission.

vulnerable objectives of bomber activity, and all the warring nations quite rightly expected their industrial base to receive a lot of attention from enemy planes."[38]

There is no available documentation of just what went on at the Camouflage Division of General Motors during that time. The work may have been similar to the work done at Leamington Spa in England, which has been documented for the Imperial War Museum in London.[39] At that camouflage workshop they developed methods to camouflage civilian and industrial sites, including nets to be used to conceal whole factories and parking lots. They painted the roofs of buildings or covered them with a painted net in order to foil photo-reconnaissance from the air.

We do know, however, that both Harry and his daughter Verna were involved in mapping activities — possibly counter-camouflage work. Photographs would be delivered, and by the next day Verna would have to turn in maps for the pilots to follow. This top-secret work was done in a vault in the Detroit area.[40]

Just as it was important to conceal, it was equally important to see through the camouflage efforts of the enemy. Seymour Reit relates a

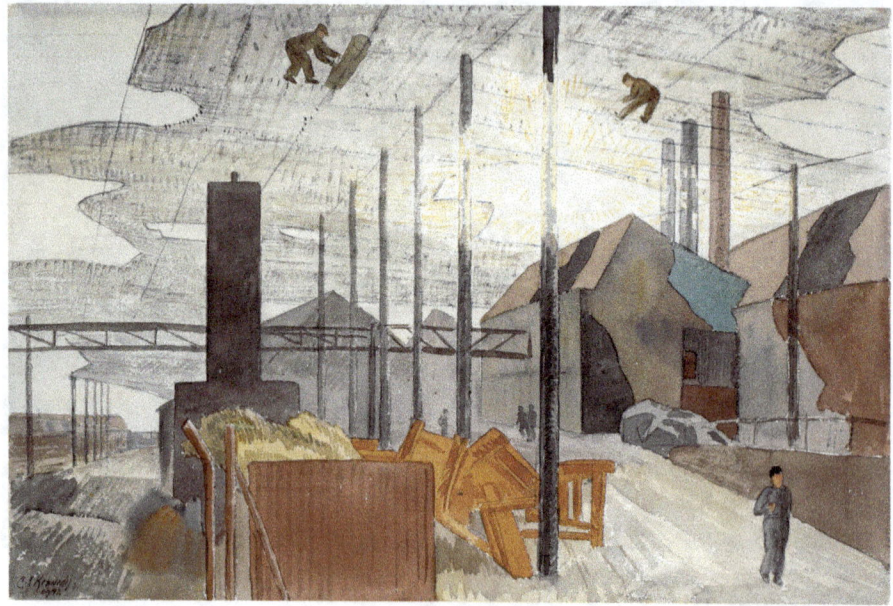

Men Fixing Netting Over a Factory. Watercolor by Cedric John Kennedy, 1942. Two men roll out camouflage material over a net framework suspended above a factory. Newark, *Camouflage*, p. 108. IWM ART LD 002757 reprinted with permission

story that illustrates the work of the counter-camouflage map-making teams in interpreting aerial reconnaissance photographs.

"The aerial prints showed a drab cluster of abandoned French farm buildings, the roofs partially collapsed and the old stone walls scarred by shellfire and bomb damage. There were no signs of life anywhere. Major Driscoll, the unit commander, studied the photographs with vague uncertainty while a young lieutenant hovered over his shoulder. "I'm fairly sure of it, Major. It's either an advance headquarters or a GCI [Ground Control Interception] center. I think they left the damage there to throw us off the train."

Driscoll picked up a small stereo device, placed it on two of the photographs, peered through and shifted the prints around, trying for the right visual effect. Under the twin magnifying lenses of the viewer (similar in design to an old-

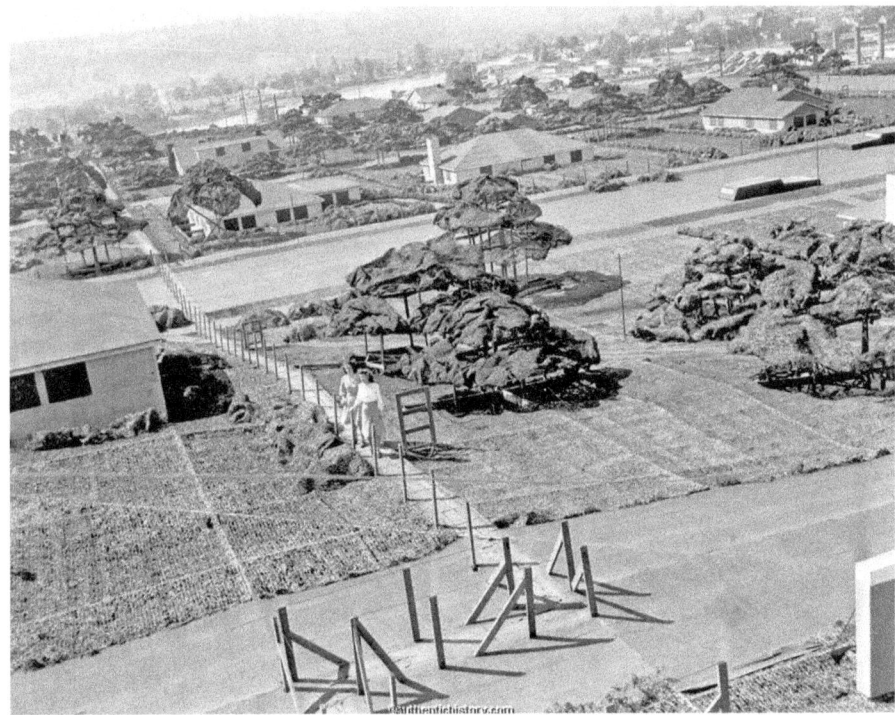

Joyce Howe and behind her Susan Heidreich walking over the camouflaged Boeing plant Number 2. Joyce was a receptionist for Boeing's engineering department and the woman behind her is her good friend who worked in another division at Boeing. Under this detailed walkable camouflage roof of fake housing, Boeing B-17 Flying Fortresses were being produced in 1942-1945. The two women show the detailing done to make it look real. Photo courtesy of The Authentic History Center, caption from Tom Philo Photography.

fashioned stereopticon), the farm buildings suddenly fused into three dimensions, almost as though he were hovering over them in a balloon, and now everything stood out with great clarity.

The Major frowned. "If you're right, the Germans are doing a good job. It looks deserted to me. Where are they keeping their transport?"

The lieutenant pointed to a patch of woods a hundred yards from the barn complex. "Their motor pool's in here under these trees. The area's much too heavily wooded — it's not normal for this time of year.

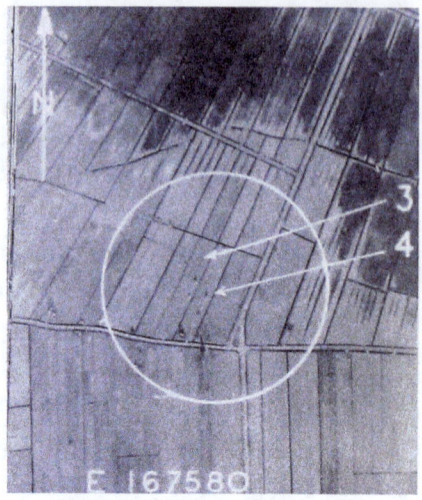

An example of photo interpretation. The circle and arrows point to four dots that were not on the previous day's photograph. Roy M. Stanley II, *To Fool a Glass Eye: Camouflage versus Photoreconnaissance in World War II*, Washington DC, 1998, p. 48.

They probably added a lot of artificial foliage." He indicated a rutted dirt road skirting the far side of the woods. "At one point the road turns in under the trees — you can just barely see it — then a little farther on it comes out again. They doctored the gap in between to make it look like the road goes straight past the woods, but it doesn't — it's their access route."

He leaned over the desk and traced a finger along the print. "From the woods they walk right along this hedgerow into the main barn. There's probably a covered path there, or a tunnel underneath. Besides, it's the wrong place entirely for that kind of hedgerow."

"Haven't you got more to go on?" he asked. "What about defenses? If this is operational, there should be heavy guns somewhere."

The lieutenant pointed again. "They're probably in these wooden sheds, which would give them a good field of fire. And look at that haystack. Farmers in this part of the country don't stack hay that way; they build low mounds, but this one is high and conical. It could be hiding antiaircraft." He put a second pair of photos on the desk alongside the first. "I checked a sortie flown ten days ago over the same area. Look at this, sir, the two wooden sheds were added since then. And compare the road coverage. The first one's fairly faint and hardly used, but since then it's been heavily traveled."

"Maybe by retreating Germans."

The interpreter persisted. "What about this clump of shrubbery? It couldn't have grown that much in ten days. I'm not sure, but I think I can see some radar equipment in there, possibly a 'Freya' [German early warning radar station]."

Driscoll studied the prints again. The new photographs had been taken at eight thousand feet, which was a relatively low altitude, but the day had been overcast and there were no clear shadows — unfortunate, since shadows often provided the best clues. He concentrated on the suspicious clump of shrubbery. Was there a faint glint of metallic edge in those bushes, a vague blur caused by a turning radar grid? Fretting over the stereo viewer, Driscoll recalled a comment by an RAF photo expert. "Don't strain too much to look for things," the veteran had said. "Just let the photos speak to you."

The half-hidden access road, the extra wooden sheds, the anomalous haystack, the shrubbery with its faint but tantalizing blur suddenly had something urgent to say. Driscoll swept the photographs together and handed them back to the interpreter. "Write it up," he said, "but don't put it through channels. Bring it back here. We'll send it direct to G-2 by air courier and start worrying."

Within the hour the lieutenant's detailed report plus an annotated print was on its way, followed by a phone call from Driscoll to Operations recommended that the target be given priority; and early the next morning a flight of P-47s lifted from an airstrip in Normandy and headed for the cluster of barns with racks of bomb under their stubby wings.

The planes ran into unexpectedly heavy ground defenses over the target and German troops erupted everywhere, but they made their drop and got safely back to base. At the debriefing, the pilots reported that the attack had apparently caused considerable fire and damage. The adjoining patch of woods had also been strafed; the fliers heard heavy explosions and saw thick columns of black smoke billowing out. A visual reconnaissance flight that afternoon confirmed that heavy smoke, the kind made by burning fuel oil, was still pouring from the woods, and several days later a report from VII Army Corps brought additional news. Allied patrols in the area had taken some prisoners who told their interrogator that the "farm" had been an important Wehrmacht communications center, heavily camouflaged. According to the POWs the bomb damage had been severe, much valuable radar and ground control equipment had been destroyed, and German operations throughout the sector had been badly disrupted.

When the report from VII Corps arrived, Driscoll made no special fuss. He simply dropped the teletype on the lieutenant's desk, tapped him approvingly on the shoulder, and hurried off to other and more pressing concerns. The interpreter, however, savored his triumph, and congratulated himself at inordinate length. It can be noted further, since the author of this account was the young officer, that for a while he became insufferably smug."[41]

Who better than an artist to note such subtle details of line, shape, shadow, and proportion?

In 1942 Harry and Hattie and Meredy moved to Nellie Avenue in Dearborn, Michigan, to be closer to his job site, and June and Bud moved to an apartment on Vaughn Street in Ann Arbor. In December of that year Harry Sr. collapsed on the street and was taken to the hospital, where he was diagnosed with Hodgkin's Disease.

At that time there were no known effective treatments for Hodgkin's Disease. Harry knew that his time was near. He wanted a garden at the house in Dearborn, but was too weak to do the work. Bud went nearly every weekend from Ann Arbor to Dearborn, carried his father out into the garden, and worked under Harry's direction to complete his vision.

Unable to paint, he focused on designing his garden and playing with his grandson, Meredy. Harry never complained. Breathing became increasingly difficult, and he often sat up at night listening to opera. He died August 12, 1943, in Dearborn.

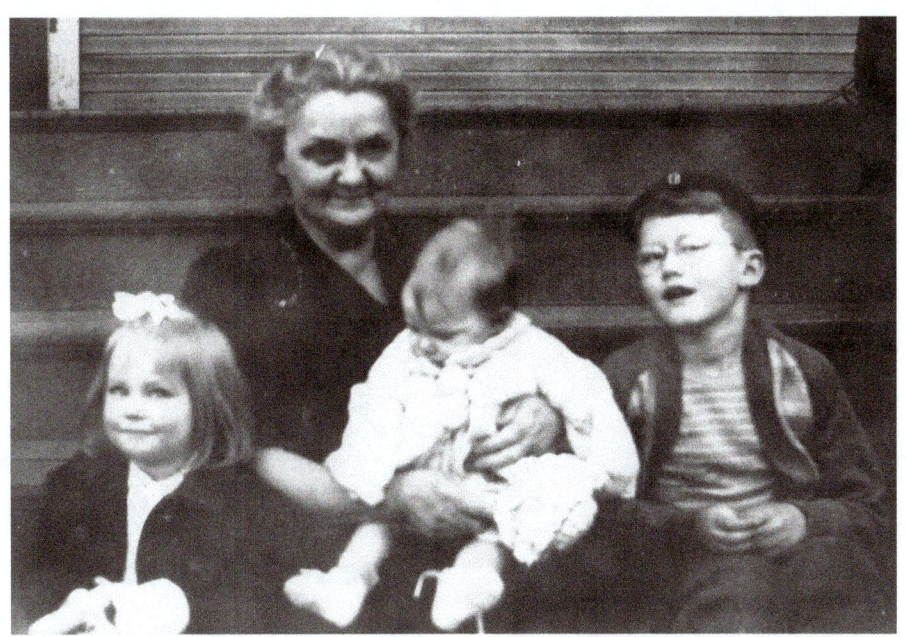

Hattie in Ann Arbor with grandchildren Joyce, Margaret, and Meredy, 1946.

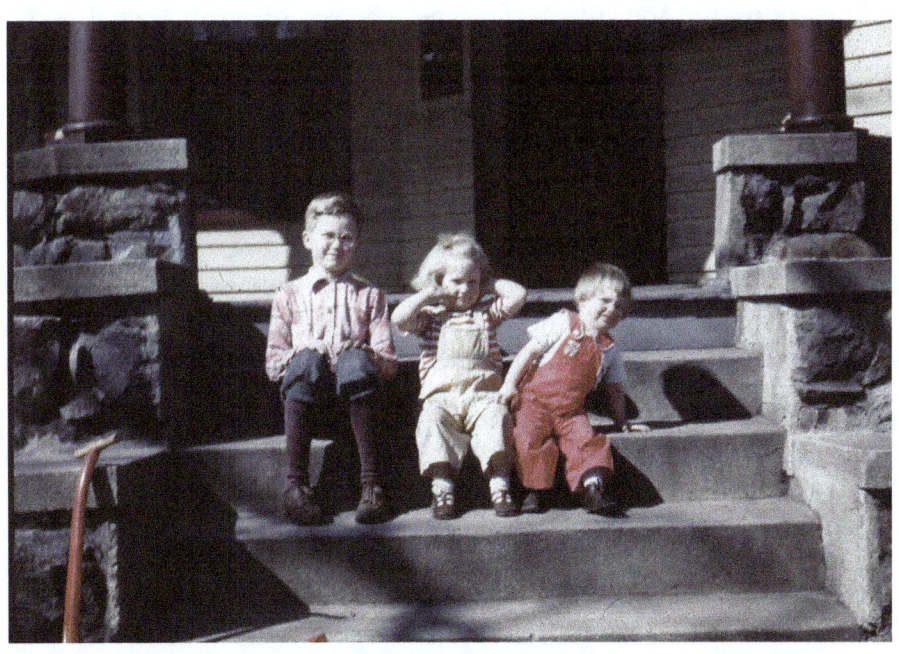

Meredy Alair, Joyce and Margaet Wilcox in
Ann Arbor, 1947.

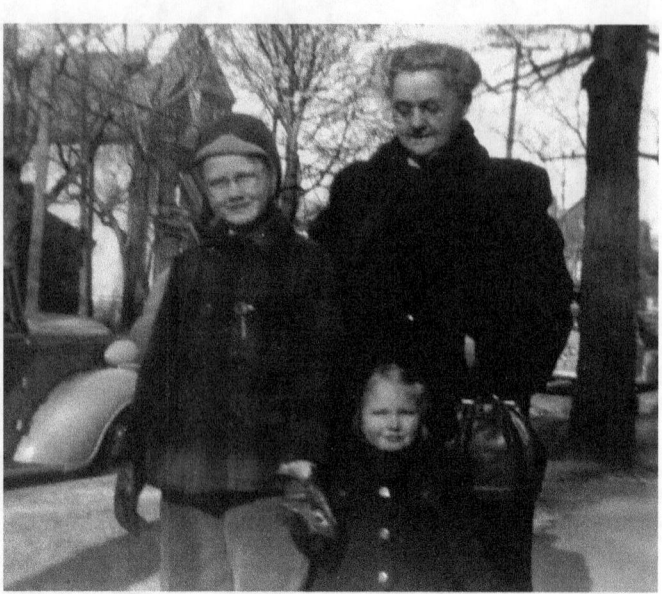

Meredy and Joyce with Grandma Hattie in Ann Arbor, 1948

Hattie, Verna, Meredy, and Bud took his body to Williamsport where he was laid out in the front parlor at the Winders' house on Washington Boulevard and then buried in the Wilcox plot in Wildwood Cemetery, along with his parents and siblings. The train trip from Michigan to Pennsylvania was too arduous for June, who was pregnant again. It was good that she did not attempt the day-long trip, as the train was terribly crowded. Verna had to sit on her suitcase the whole trip, Bud stood, and a soldier gave up his seat for Hattie with four-year-old Meredy on her lap.

Following the funeral, Hattie returned to Dearborn, and at the end of the month went to Ann Arbor where she used the life insurance money to buy a house, which would be her livelihood through most of the rest of her life. She prepared it quickly for the fall semester, to be a League House Annex, taking in female students from the University of Michigan as roomers, opening with 7 college girls. She later remodeled the third floor to add two more rooms, increasing to 11 girls.

Bud volunteered for the Navy, but flunked the Navy Dot Test — he was color blind. He then volunteered for the Air Force. He passed their test for color blindness, which was a matter of matching skeins of yarn. While he was unable to see color, he was expert at matching the intensity of colors. However the Air Force wanted him to complete his Ph.D. before enlisting. He had finished his course work, but not his dissertation. He was teaching in the undergraduate college as well as teaching nurses

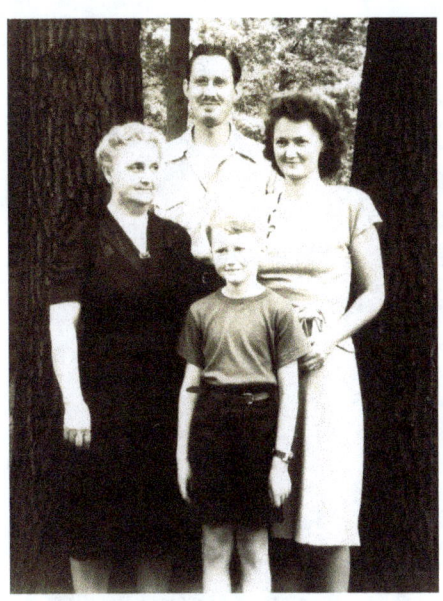

Hattie, Meredith, Verna, and Meredy
Sunday visit in Ann Arbor.

in the medical school. On the weekends he taught Survival on Land and Sea with John and Frank Craighead, the Craighead twins who went on to spend a lifetime doing conservation work and writing books and special events for the *National Geographic*.

Altogether Bud was reclassified 18 times before finally being drafted into the Army in 1945. While most draftees lost 40 pounds during basic training, Bud gained 40 pounds, being an expert in living off the land. He was shipped to the Philippines; June went home to Williamsport to be with her family and await the arrival of their second daughter, Margaret.

Hattie continued to raise her grandson Meredith until his graduation from high school in 1957. She continued to live at 629 Forest Avenue, Ann Arbor, and ran her home as a League House Annex for nearly 20 years, enjoying the many bright young women who moved through her house, making lifelong friends, and bringing vicarious adventures to her from all over the world. She made cookies and tea to celebrate their

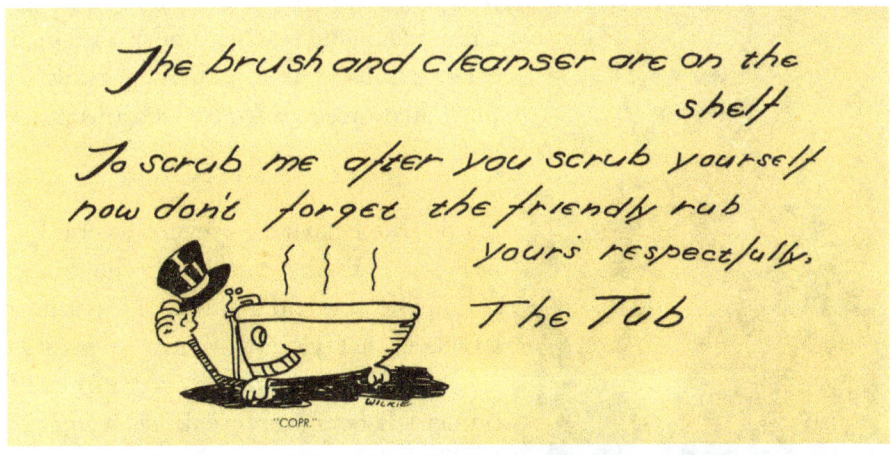

The brush and cleanser are on the shelf
To scrub me after you scrub yourself
now don't forget the friendly rub
yours respectfully,
The Tub

Hattie had this sign hanging in the upstairs bathroom which the girls shared.
A catchy rhyme, all the grandchildren can recite it. By Wilkit for COPR.

birthdays. She enjoyed the activity in the house, and the many adventures with her "girls."

She did some alterations for "the girls" in the house, but no longer took in piece work from department stores. Instead, she sold corsets. Ladies would come to her for a fitting, she would order the corsets from a company in Detroit, and then would either go by bus to Detroit to pick them up, or they would be shipped to the house.

The Harry Wilcox Jr. family would come up to Ann Arbor in the summer for at least several weeks. Joyce would read all Meredy's comic books, Peggy would tag along with Meredy and his friend Ed Faust, sitting on the floorboards of Ed's white MG with a black convertible top. Jim was under

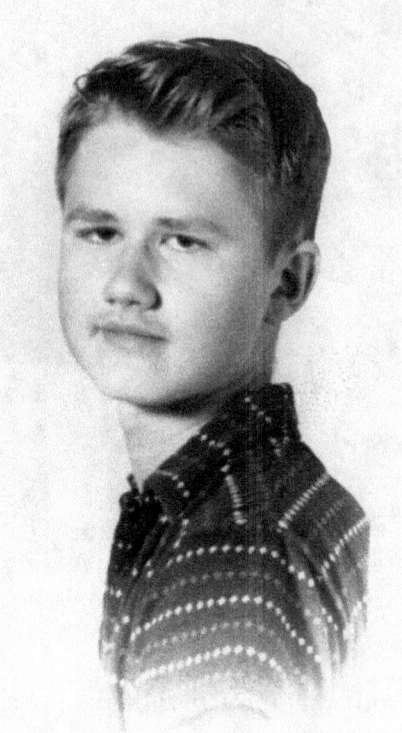

Meredith Walter Alair Jr. "Meredy"

eight years old, so he spent most of his time with his mother, June. Joyce and Peggy sometimes walked up to the summer day camp at the church

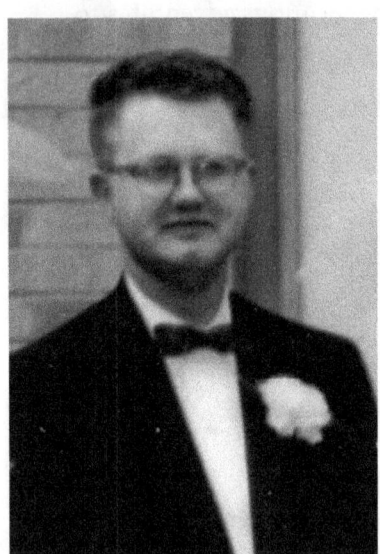

Meredith W. Alair Jr, 1961

at the end of the side street, Forest Court, to make lanyards and other small projects, or to visit Miss Pansy Johnson, a retired singing teacher whose Victorian eclectic house was a fascinating, richly decorated museum for two curious little girls.

Hattie had a canary — several at one point — in the bay window in the dining room. She also had a jungle of African violets in that window — mature plants and rootings in glass vials — that thrived on her left-over (very weak) tea water. Bud joked that she waved the tea bag over the pot and called it tea.

One of the high points of her social calendar was a visit from one of the door-to-door salesmen who visited her weekly. The Charles Chip man sold potato chips or pretzels in 2-gallon cans. The Jewel Tea man would sit with her, gossip and enjoy the latest sample of tea. He brought tea and coffee along with novelty kitchen items — a cookie dropper, push-out measuring cups, an egg separator — always a new gadget for a price she could not resist.

Hattie loved to bake cookies and pies. For dinner on Sunday there were always pies. For six guests she would offer at least four, if not six different pies: cherry, lemon meringue, chocolate, peach, butterscotch, blueberry, shoo-fly, coconut cream, and our favorite, apple pie, for dinner, or warmed with milk for breakfast.

For Christmas, she would bake hundreds of cookies, wrap them carefully in waxed paper, and store them in boxes or cans for use for the next several months. She would always send a big box of cookies to Memphis. The lebkuchen survived the trip in good shape. The animal crackers

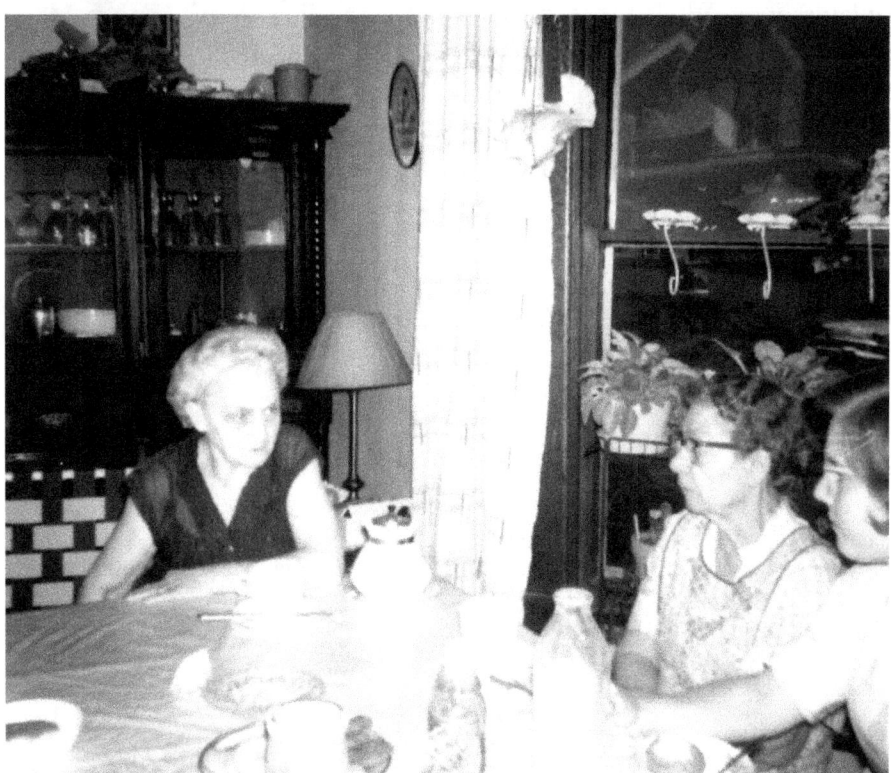

Hattie's dining room on Forest Avenue in Ann Arbor, with African violets in the bay window. Left to right: Hattie, her sister Emmy Winder, and Joyce Wilcox (Graff). Picture taken 1961.

arrived mostly with broken legs, antlers, and heads, but were nonetheless delicious.

Many of her cookie recipes were on index cards given out for free from the Detroit Edison electric company. Her own recipes were hopeless unless you watched her make them. They had no quantities listed on the card, you had to watch. One cup of nuts meant you put the cup measure into the bowl and piled nuts into it until it was overflowing into the bowl — to the extent that you could no longer see the cup. One teaspoon of vanilla meant at least a tablespoon. While the recipe called for lard, she always used double the amount of butter.

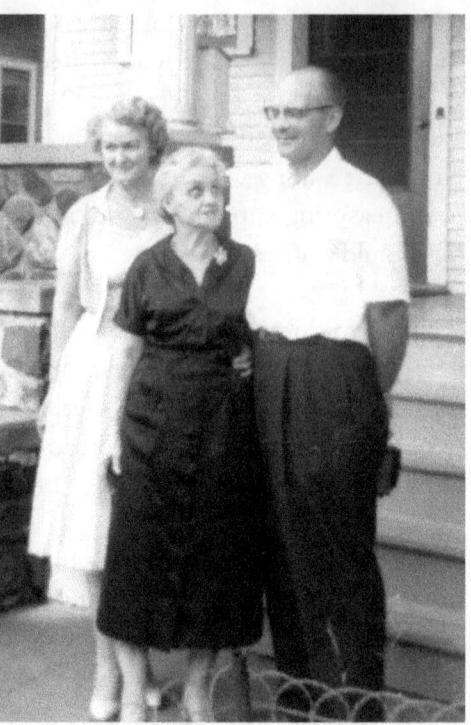

Verna, Hattie, and Bud, 1961

And there was always one ingredient in the bowl that was not noted on the card — ensuring that your rendition was never as good as her own. Nonetheless June watched, took notes, and managed to reproduce a number of her recipes.

A special treat for the grandchildren was to sit in her living room, surrounded by Harry's paintings, a baby grand piano that rarely was played, with a cowhide draped over the bench, while Grandma Hattie sang delightfully silly songs:

Camels and bears and ponies are found
Prancing around on the merry-go-round
Toodeley-oo, toodeley-ay,
on the merry-go-round!

I am from I-o-way, I-o-way
State of every land, joy on every hand
I'm from I-o-way, I-o-way
That's where the tall corn grows.

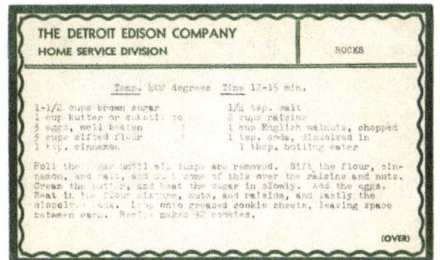
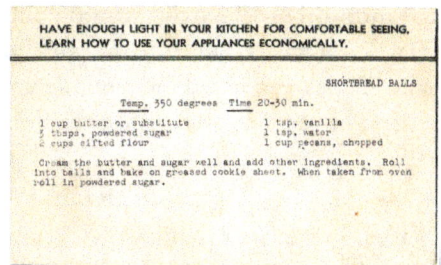

THE DETROIT EDISON COMPANY
HOME SERVICE DIVISION
ROCKS

Temp. 400 degrees Time 12-15 min.

1-1/2 cups brown sugar   1/4 tsp. salt
1 cup butter or substitute   2 cups raisins
3 eggs, well beaten   1 cup English walnuts, chopped
3 cups sifted flour   1 tsp. soda, dissolved in
1 tsp. cinnamon   1 tbsp. boiling water

Roll the sugar until all lumps are removed. Sift the flour, cinnamon, and salt, and dust some of this over the raisins and nuts. Cream the butter, and beat the sugar in slowly. Add the eggs. Beat in the flour mixture, nuts, and raisins, and lastly the dissolved soda. Drop onto greased cookie sheets, leaving space between each. Recipe makes 92 cookies.

(OVER)

HAVE ENOUGH LIGHT IN YOUR KITCHEN FOR COMFORTABLE SEEING,
LEARN HOW TO USE YOUR APPLIANCES ECONOMICALLY.

SHORTBREAD BALLS

Temp. 350 degrees Time 20-30 min.

1 cup butter or substitute   1 tsp. vanilla
3 tbsps. powdered sugar   1 tsp. water
2 cups sifted flour   1 cup pecans, chopped

Cream the butter and sugar well and add other ingredients. Roll into balls and bake on greased cookie sheet. When taken from oven roll in powdered sugar.

ROCKS

Temp: 400 degrees, Time: 12-15 minutes

1 1/2 c. brown sugar	1/4 tsp. salt
1 c. butter or substitute	2 c. raisins
3 eggs, well beaten	1 c. English walnuts, chopped
3 c. sifted flour	1 tsp baking soda, dissolved in
1 tsp. cinnamon	1 tbsp. boiling water

Roll the sugar until all lumps are removed. Sift the flour, cinnamon, and salt, and dust some of this over the raisins and nuts. Cream the butter, and beat the sugar in slowly. Add the eggs. Beat in the flour mixture, nuts, and raisins, and lastly the dissolved soda. Drop onto greased cookie sheets, leaving space between each. Recipe makes 92 cookies.

FASTNACHTKUGELS

This is a very old traditional recipe for Shrove Tuesday, the night before Lent begins, when it is traditional to have a feast before the fast. It is essentially an old-fashioned type of donut. This is likely a recipe with roots in Switzerland.

Make a dough by mixing thoroughly:

3 eggs	1 lb. flour [4 cups of flour]
1 yeast cake	1 t. salt
1 c. milk	4 tbsp. butter
1/2 c. sugar	

Roll dough and cut into rectangular pieces, about 2 x 3 inches. Slit the center and twist. Fry in deep fat and shake each one in a paper lunch bag with powdered sugar to coat.

Fast nachtkugels: Slit, Twist, Fry, and coat with powdered sugar. *Yum!*

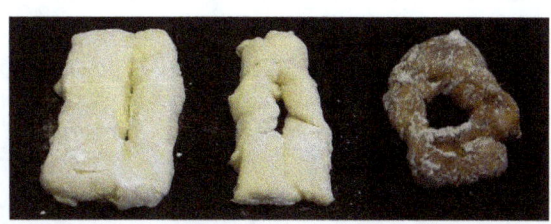

Grandmother Wilcox's animal cookies.
Hattie got this recipe from the packaging from cookie sheets. She cut the dough into shapes, decorated them with colored sugar and round red or silver balls for eyes. The red balls were called tea-berries, from the Jewel Tea man.

THREE-PART COOKIES
Part I: in a large mixing bowl, combine
  4 1/2 cups flour
  1 c. butter
  1/2 tsp. salt
 Cut the butter into the flour as for pie crust, and add the salt.
Part II: Beat 2 eggs until frothy. Add 1 c. sugar and beat again. Combine
    with the Part I mixture.
Part III: Combine in a separate bowl:
  4 tbsp. milk
  1 tsp. vanilla
  1 tsp. baking soda
 Mix with Parts I and II. Roll out for cutting, or use in a cooky press.
    Excellent filled or plain.
Each batch makes about 150 cookies. Make each batch separately.

REFRIGERATOR ROLLS
1 yeast cake or package dissolved in 1/4 c. lukewarm water

2 tsp salt (or less)	1 egg, beaten
1/2 c. butter or margarine	4 c. sifted flour
5 tbsp sugar	1 c. warm water

Dissolve yeast in lukewarm water with 1 tsp of the sugar. Cream the rest of the sugar with the butter. Add 1 c. of the flour, the yeast mixture, egg and salt. Then add the rest of the flour and mix well. Knead or stir for at least 2-3 minutes. Put the dough into a greased bowl. Cover and refrigerate for at least two hours (preferably overnight or morning to night). Roll out the dough, cut them into rounds (with a cutter or water glass). Put a small pat of butter in the center of each round, fold it over and press down with two finger. This is the shape of Parker House rolls. Arrange the rolls on cookie sheets. Cover with a cloth towel and set them in a warm place, away from drafts, for 1-2 hours until they double in size. Bake at 375 degrees for 15-20 minutes. Makes 24-30 rolls.

LEBKUCKEN
Modernized by Jim and Sedenia Wilcox, 2004

This is an old world recipe, which has been handed down through many generations. Jim and Sedenia Wilcox got this recipe from June Freed Wilcox, who got it from Hattie Richner Wilcox.

This is a large volume of mixture and requires a very large mixing bowl, a strong spoon, and a strong muscle to stir in the final cups of flour. A common household mixer is not strong enough to mix the final amounts of flour. The mixing bowl needs to be at least 16 inches across and 5 inches deep. For the mixing, it is suggested a strong, large, long wooden spoon about 12 to 16 inches long. The working guy will appreciate the ability to use both hands, or to brace the long handle along his forearm while stirring. A little extra helper holding the bowl is a valued assistant. You will use nearly five pounds of flour. A good tasting molasses is very important (Grandma's ® Original Unsulphured is currently available and recommended by June Wilcox).

The recipe came to me (Jim Wilcox) in quantities for cooking not so commonly used in the latter part of the 1900's, or now in 2004. In 2004, in most cooking recipes, the ingredients are listed by volume, not by weight such as pounds and ½ pounds, or multiples of pounds. So, as to accurately record this recipe and to make it user friendly both measurements are listed below. A very special thanks to my mother for translating some of these quantities when the recipe came to her; and more importantly for telling me some secrets that were not written down. The original measurements are listed as Old World and converted measurements are listed as Modern.

Modern	Ingredients	Old World
4 cups (1 quart)	Molasses	one quart
1/2 cup (1/4 pound)	Oleomargarine	1/2 c. lard
8 ounces	candied citron, CUT**	1/2 pound
8 ounces	candied orange peel*, CUT**	1/2 pound
8 ounces	nut meats, CUT**	1/2 pound
2 Tablespoons (6 tsp)	ground cinnamon	2 Tablespoons
1 1/2 teaspoons	ground cloves	1/2 Tablespoon
2 Tablespoons	ground nutmeg	2 Tablespoons
less than 1/4 tsp	Salt	1 pinch
2 Tablespoons	Baking soda	2 Tablespoons
1 quart	sour cream	1 quart
12 to 14 cups	All-purpose flour	nearly five pounds

* Hattie's recipes listed Lemon Peel as an optional substitute for Orange Peel, however the Orange Peel seems to be our family's favorite.

Note: CUT does NOT mean chopped into a fine dust, we want to be able to recognize that it is a nut or a piece of candied fruit. Cut the Candied Citron and Orange Peel about 1/8 inch cubes. Later when rolling the dough to about ¼ thick, the store bought 3/8" or 1/2" cubes will be too big.

In a large (4 quart) saucepan (or dutch oven) mix and heat the molasses, oleo, and sugar. Over a very low heat, slowly heat the mixture to dissolve the sugar. Stir very frequently while heating, over a very low heat. Do not overheat, just enough to melt the sugar into the molasses.

In a very large (16 inch) mixing bowl, mix the Citron, Orange Peel, Nutmeats, Cinnamon, Cloves, Nutmeg, Salt, Soda, and 4 cups of the flour (these count in your total). Mix these dry ingredients.

Pour this molasses mixture into a very large (16 inch) mixing bowl (don't waste a drop of liquid). Add and stir in the Sour Cream. Now stir in the remaining flour, slowly adding a cup at a time, perhaps a half cup at a time to the last few cups.

Cover and let the mixture sit over night in a cool place. This allows the molasses flavor to penetrate the flour and the mixture to rise a little.

Roll dough to about a ¼ of an inch thick.

A pizza wheel works well, cut the rolled dough into 1 x 1½ inch rectangles, or so. The cookie will increase in size slightly while baking.

Place about 25 cookies on a greased cookie sheet.

Bake at 350 degrees for 10 to 12 minutes (do not over bake). It is suggested to rotate the cookie sheet 180 degrees and move it to a different shelf halfway through the time to ensure even baking. They should be soft, not crispy cookies.

Glaze with a 10X sugar glaze.

1 pound   10X powdered sugar
1 Tablespoon vanilla
1 Tablespoon butter (or Oleomargarine)
3 to 4 Tablespoons milk

To make the glaze, mix 1 pound of 10X powdered sugar, with 1 Tablespoon of vanilla, 1 Tablespoon of butter, and about 3 to 4 Tablespoons of milk.

Add milk, if necessary. The glaze should be very runny and smooth.

Allow the baked cookies to cool a little before glazing; they can be slightly warm when glazed.

Apply a very thin layer to the top of each cookie. A knife is what the family has always used, but a pastry brush works even better.

For storage, pair the cookies bottom to bottom and use strips of wax paper to separate the tops.

June and Harry used an old crock which sits on the hearth. It is a popular place to seek around Christmas. It is nearly the first stop when one enters the room.

Every attempt has been made to be accurate and to reveal the family secrets. June says she generally averaged 12 to 14 cups of flour. Jim remembers Hattie saying 16 cups. The difference may be in the density of the flour when it is in the cup. Or that Hattie held out a couple of cups for the rolling and counted those. Either way the flour needed is just about 5 pounds.

June related that after several attempts at the recipe resulted in just a slight difference in taste than Hattie's, she helped Hattie make a batch and noticed that the entire procedure of heating the molasses, oleo, and sugar was a total surprise and NOT written on the recipe card. Let it be noted – after some 30 years, it was still NOT written on the recipe card, and in 2004, it was a surprise to JIM, when June mentioned it to Jim!

They say a good cook always keeps her secrets a secret.

Note from Joyce: This recipe makes enough cookies for a small army or large family. You can always divide each ingredient in half (or thirds) to make fewer cookies, and you can try a dough hook on a very strong electric mixer if you are not feeling particularly strong yourself.

Chapter 7: Heritage

Harry Wilcox's artistic talent was passed to both his children.

Verna showed an aptitude for art in school. She and her father sometimes engaged in some friendly competition. One example is the cowboy picture included in this book on page 117. Harry painted the cowboy and the horse, but he and Verna argued about the foreground. The bottom left quadrant of this painting shows signs of having been stripped and repainted multiple times, until finally one of them would frame it and hang it on the wall to stop further argument.

The entire family was very fond of dogs. Bud's dog Spike was particularly famous, having been chosen to appear in the high school play because he was so responsive to commands. Verna too had a dog Rags of whom she was very fond.

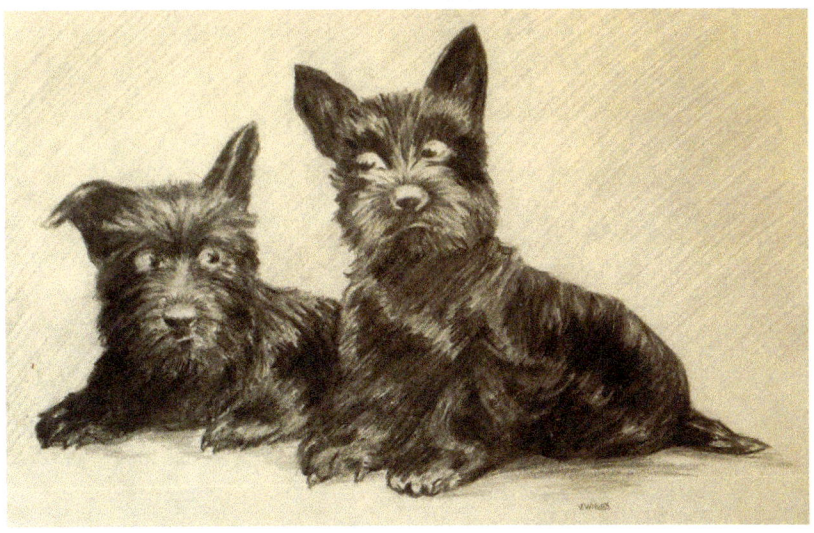

Wary Scotties, by Verna Wilcox (Alair), before 1934. Pencil.

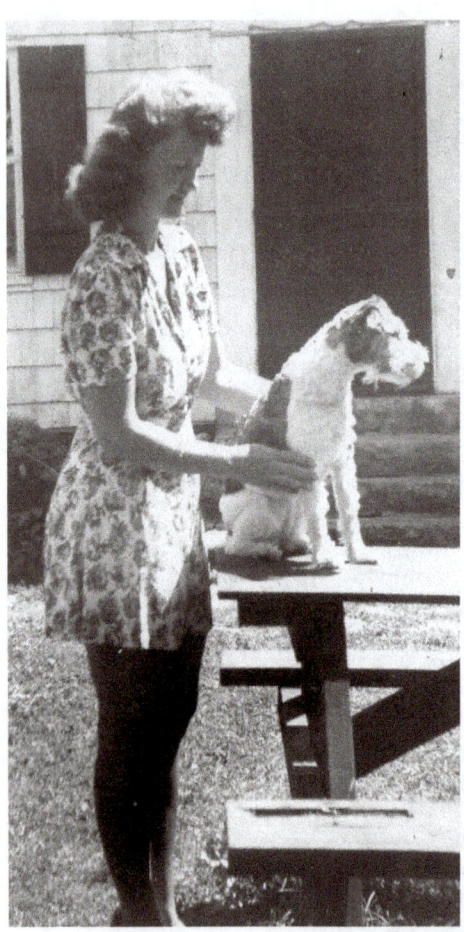

Verna with Rags, 1934 in Detroit

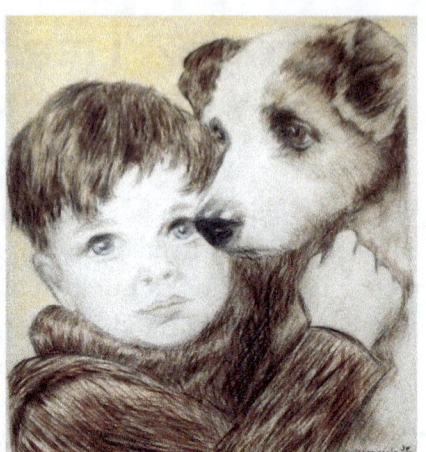

Rags and friend, by Verna Wilcox Alair, dated 1934.

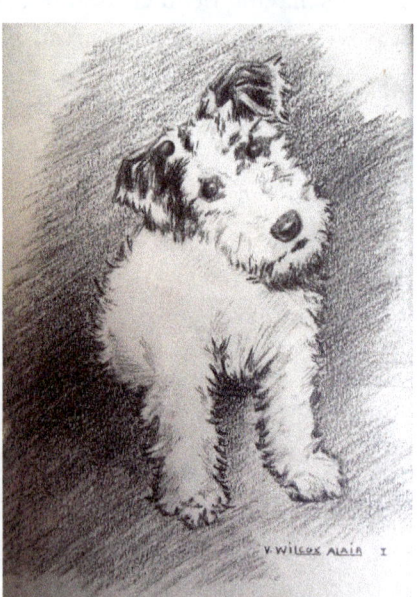

Portrait of Rags, by Verna Wilcox Alair, about 1934.

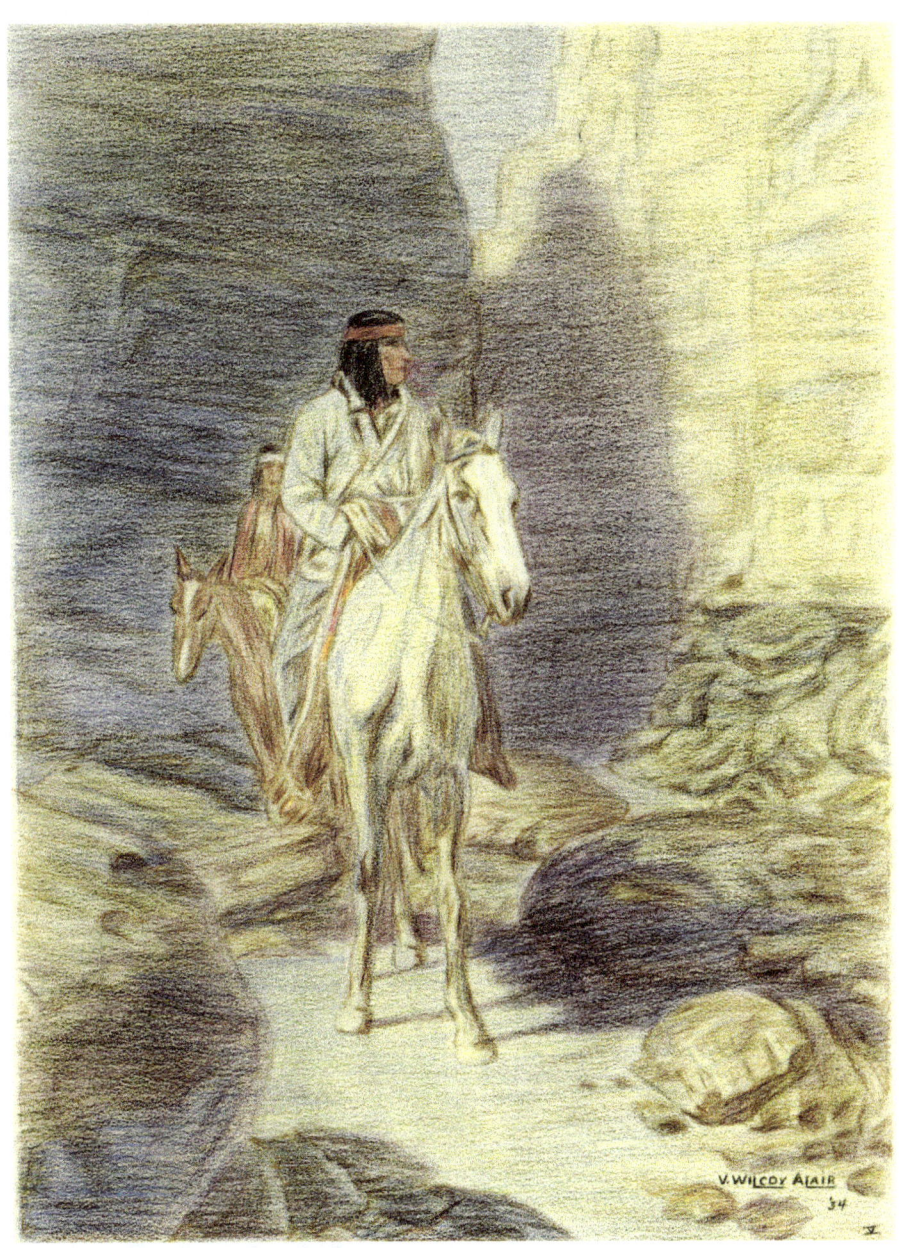

Scouting the pass, by Verna Wilcox Alair, 1934. Pencil.

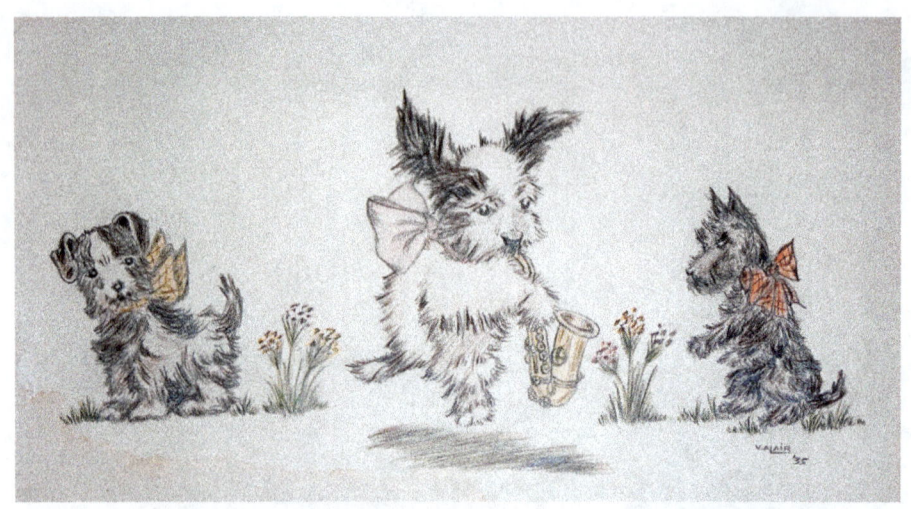

Aunt Verna's dogs. Given to Bud on his graduation from high school, 1935. Pencil.

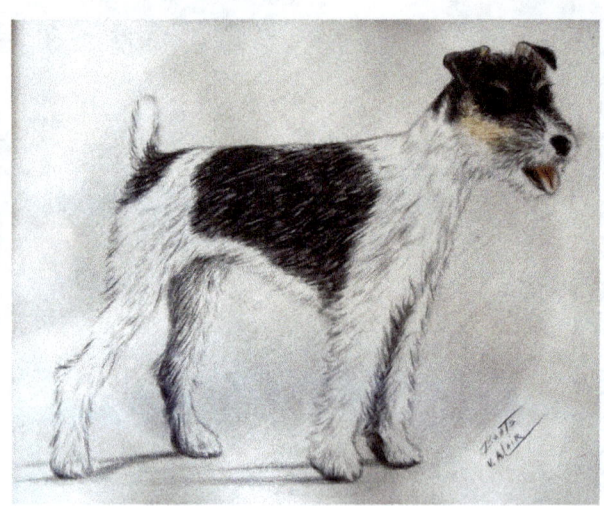

Boots, by Verna Wilcox Alair, about 1938. Pencil

Verna continued to work for the War Department through the Korean War (1950-1953) in an old four-story mattress warehouse in a seedy section of Detroit. Meredy remembers going once with his father as a teenager to drop off his mother to work. There were military police guarding the entrance. You had to have special clearance to get into the building, and higher clearance to go to the upper floors. Each night Verna had to go with her supervisor up to the vault and lock the maps she had been drawing into the vault.[42]

Later Verna worked in Hudson's Department Store, and enjoyed surrounding herself with beautiful things. She made lovely diorama boxes, like single rooms in a doll house, which she would sometimes give as gifts. In her living room she created an elegant and lavish doll house, with carpets and electric lights. June remembers once taking Joyce to that house when Joyce two years old. June put Joyce on the sofa and ordered her not to move. Everything in the room was delightfully attractive for a bright and inquisitive little girl … and also quite breakable.

At one point she embarked on making a set of china. Each place setting had a different flower as its theme. She would bring pieces to Ann Arbor to show to her mother and June, Joyce, and Margaret.

Verna particularly enjoyed jewelry making, and working with silver. She won a number of awards for her elegant pieces done in silver with polished stones which she and Meredith collected on their many road trips.

She entered pieces of her metalwork in the Exhibitions for Michigan Artists-Craftsmen at the Detroit Institute of Art in 1960, 1961, and 1966.[43] She displayed silver bowls, dishes, a jigger, and a silver and turquoise pendant. One award-winning piece was a footed silver serving dish designed to contain the uncut contents of a can of jellied cranberry sauce. She gave rose jewelry to her young nieces, and taught them to make a woven link bracelet of

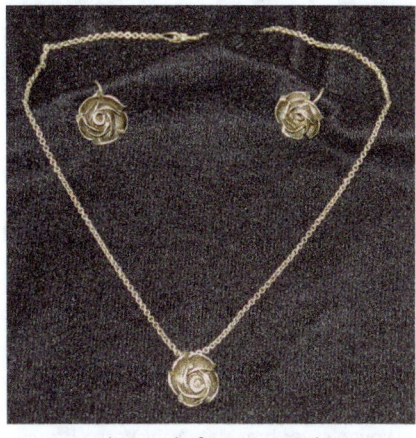

Rose jewelry made for Joyce and Margaret by Aunt Verna, 1956.

silver. For Margaret's wedding she made a lovely cross of silver with pearls, and for Joyce she made a pendant of snow obsidian mounted in silver.

Meredith was a foreman on a team at the Cadillac division of General Motors for many years. A Hollywood film producer ordered a new custom-built Cadillac every two years. He didn't want it delivered straight off the lot, he wanted it to be driven for six months to work out any bugs, and then shipped to California. Meredith would drive the Cadillac to break it in during this six months. He and Verna sometimes had outfits made to match the upholstery.

Every two years, then, Meredith and Verna had a brand new Cadillac. Harry and June drove a second-hand 1955 Chevrolet station wagon until 1963. For their children, a tour of the Alairs' latest car revealed such marvels as electric windows and windshield washers. In their brand new car, Meredith and Verna would take long road trips to the West, where they collected semi-precious stones and explored Indian art.

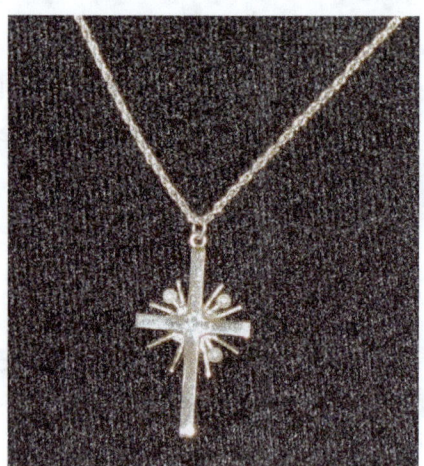

Silver and pearl cross made by Aunt Verna for Margaret's wedding.

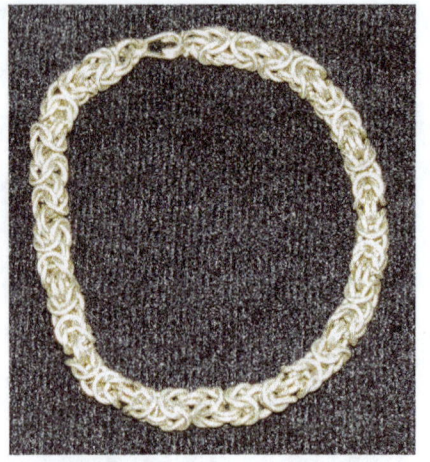

Woven silver bracelet. Aunt Verna brought materials and tools and taught Joyce and Margaret how to make these.

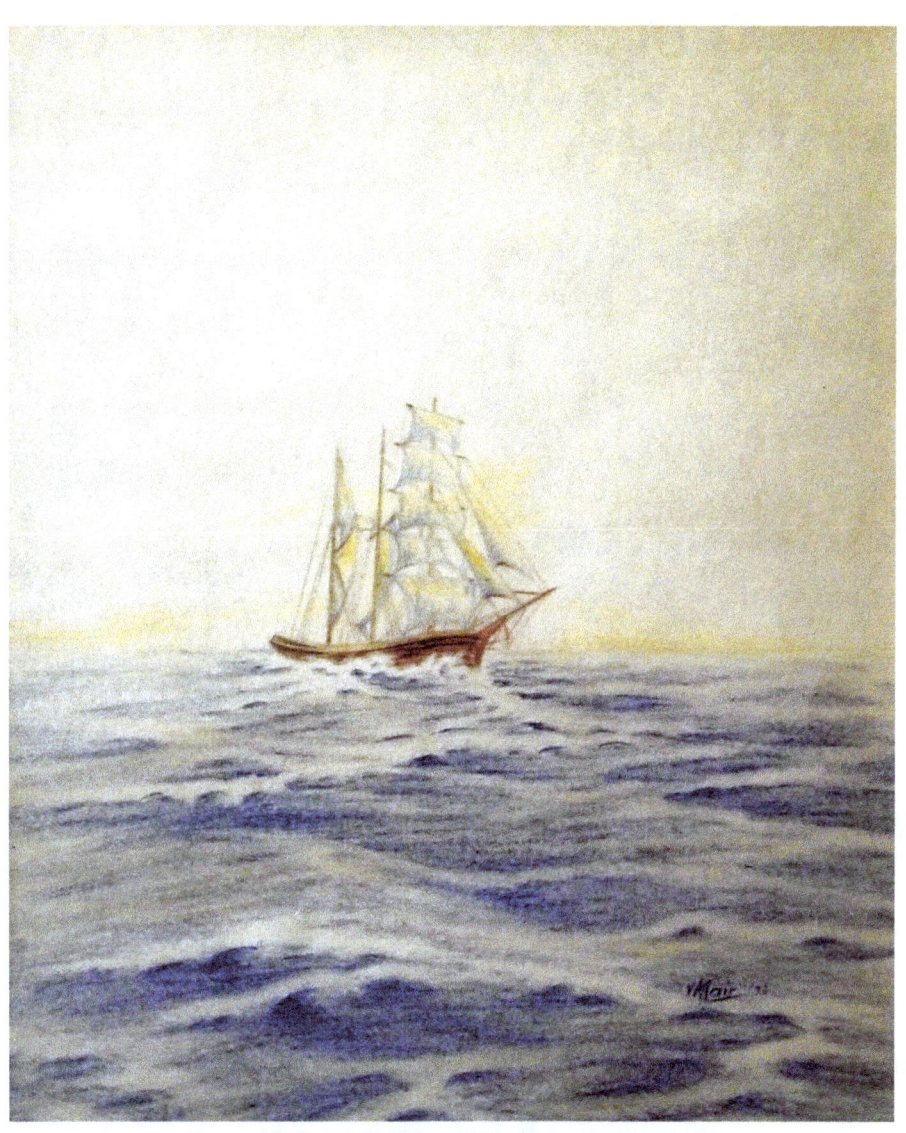

Clipper ship, by Verna Wilcox Alair, watercolor. Not dated.

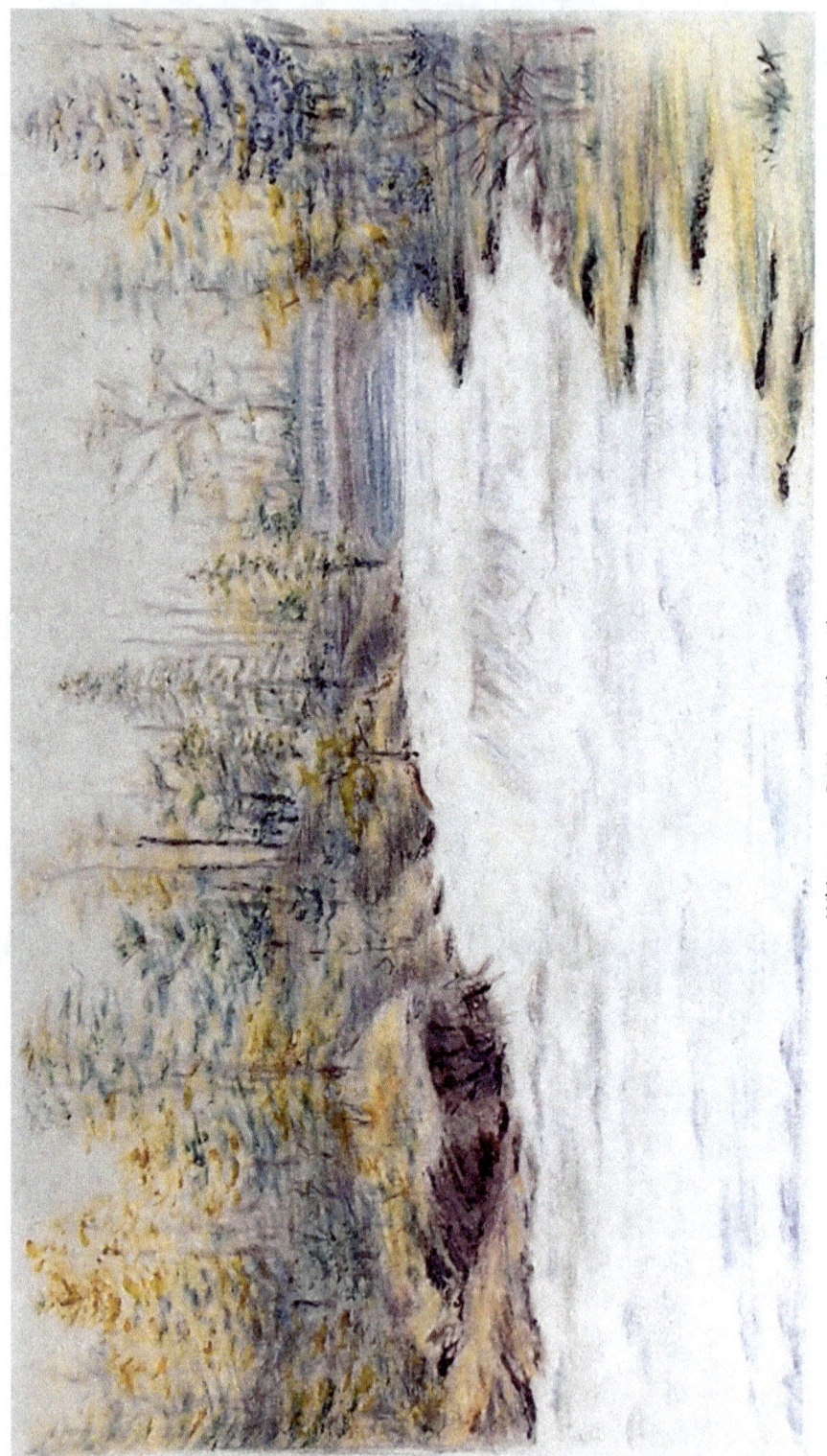

White water. By Verna Wilcox Alair.

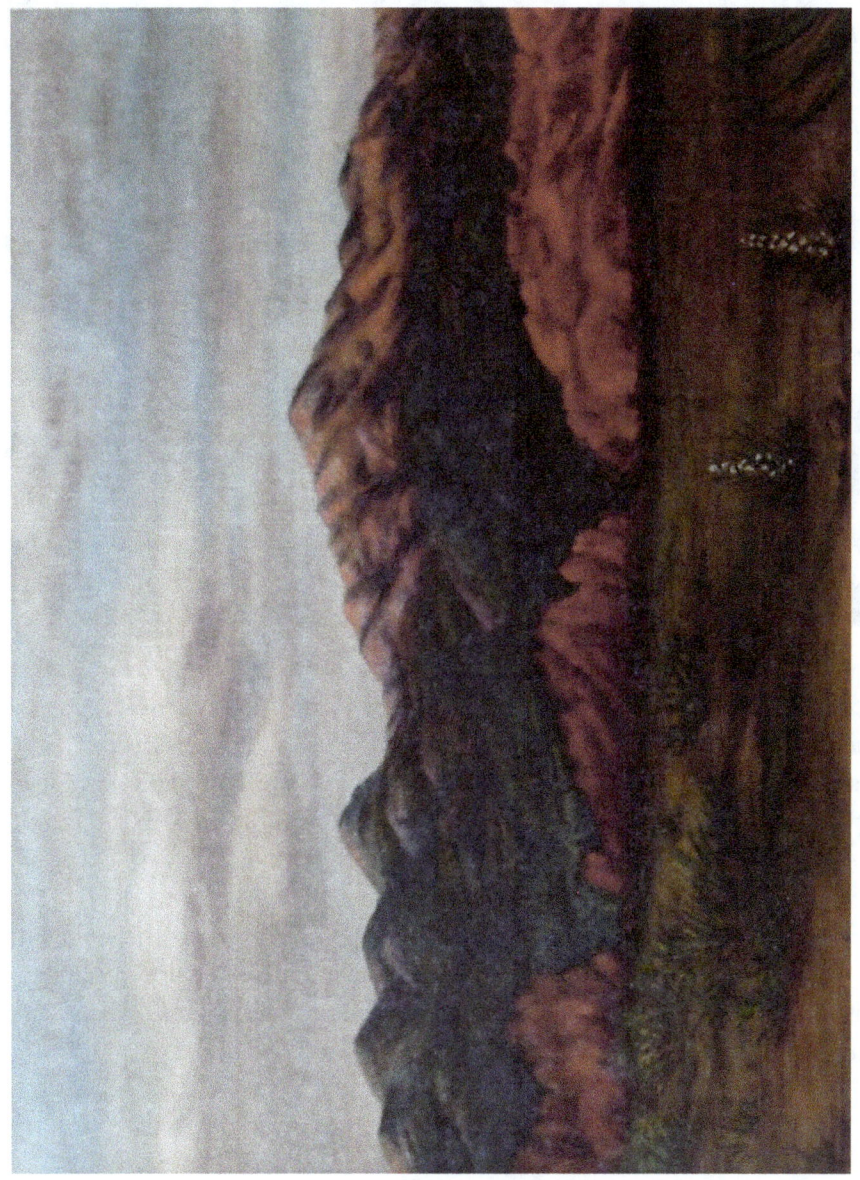

Out west. By Verna Wilcox Alair, about 1978.

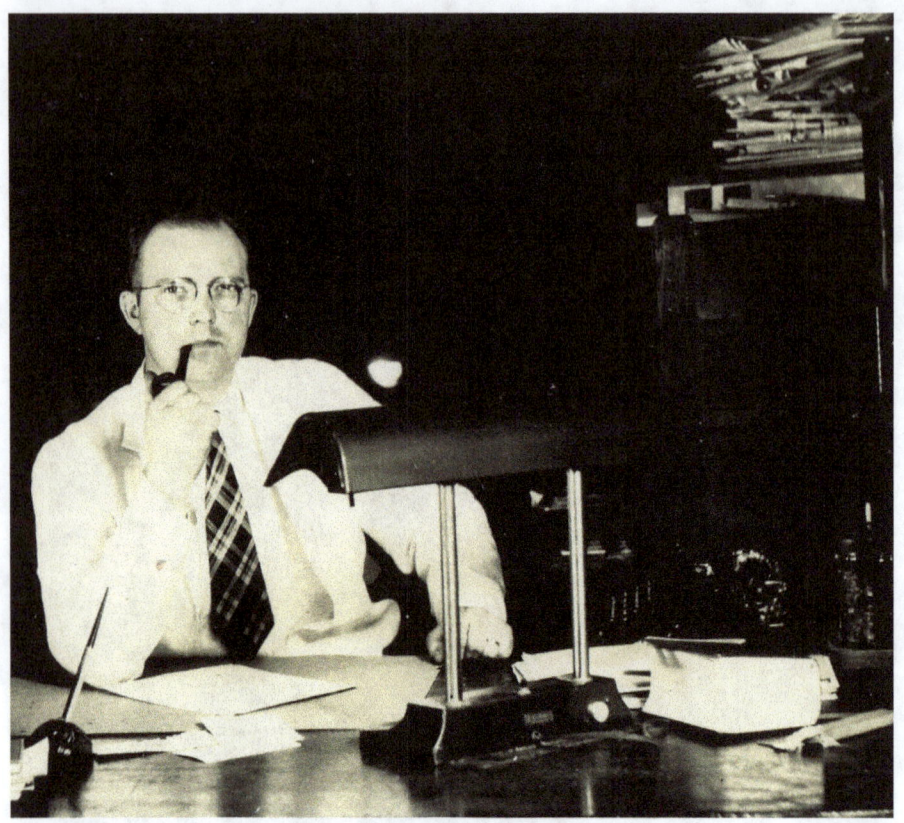
Harry Jr. in the office, 1944.

Having volunteered several times and been rejected, Bud was at last drafted into the Army. He served in the Army in the Philippines and in Japan in 1945-46, arriving home on Margaret's first birthday in the fall of 1946.

Bud was red-green-blue color blind.[44] Clearly this presented challenges to an artist. Nonetheless, he could read the color names on colored pencils. His favorite medium was certainly pen and ink — or chalk on chalkboard while teaching.

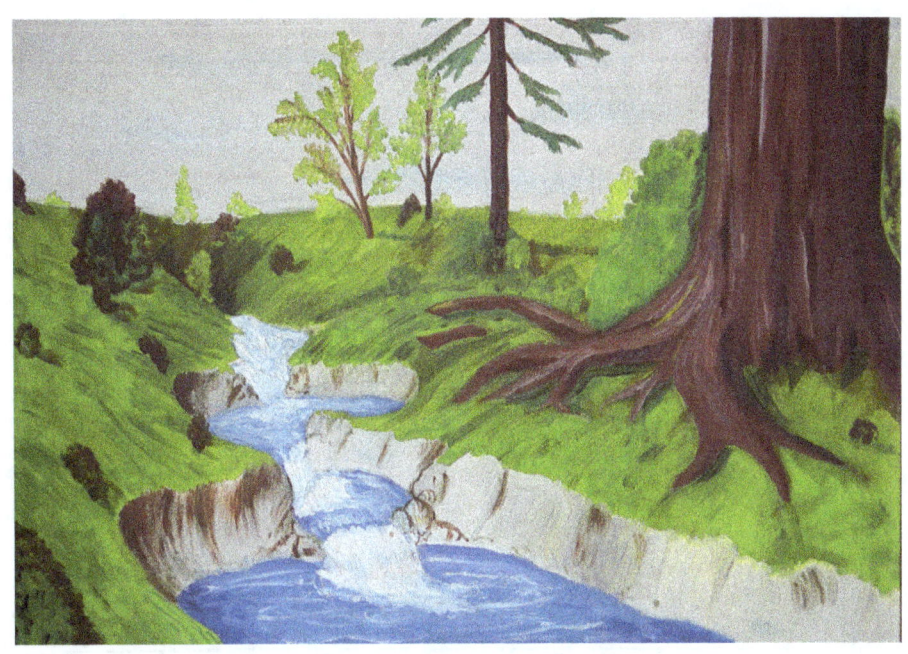

A creek in the woods, by Harry Wilcox Jr "Bud," about 1958. While it is not great art, we think it is pretty amazing for a man who is red-green-blue color blind.

For the most part he had made peace with his color blindness. He once challenged himself to paint a landscape — a tree near a brook — reading the tubes to see which paint was green or blue, and then blending the shadings and intensities of the blues or greens. He never liked it, and it is not great art, but for a man who is color blind it is pretty amazing.

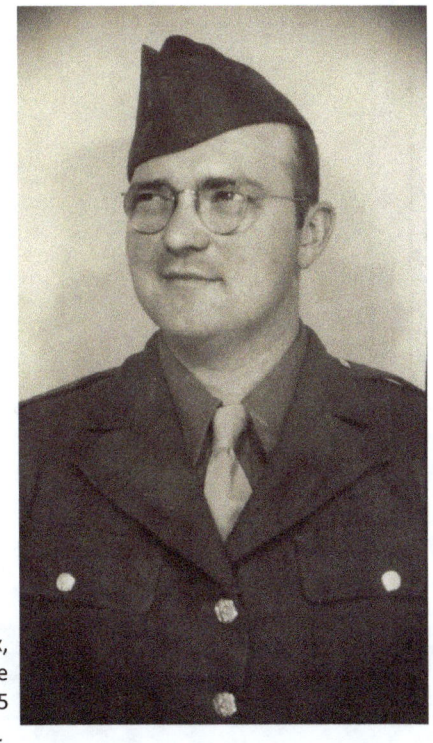

Staff Sergeant Wilcox, Army Intelligence Japan 1945

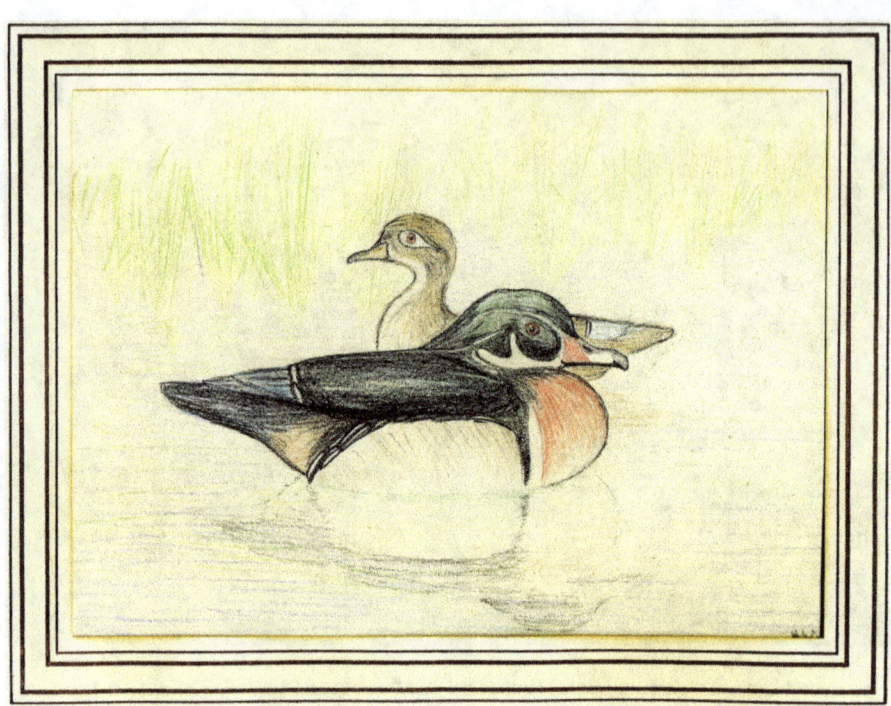

Wood ducks, by Harry H. Wilcox Jr "Bud," 1940. Pencil.

Sailboats at sunset, by Harry H. Wilcox Jr, 1940. Pencil.

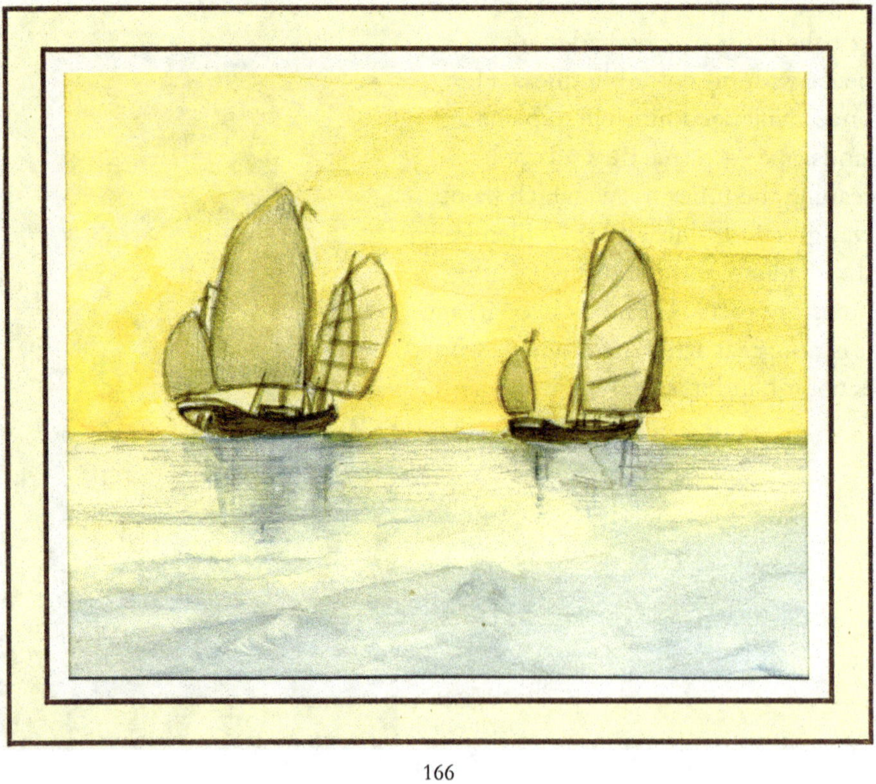

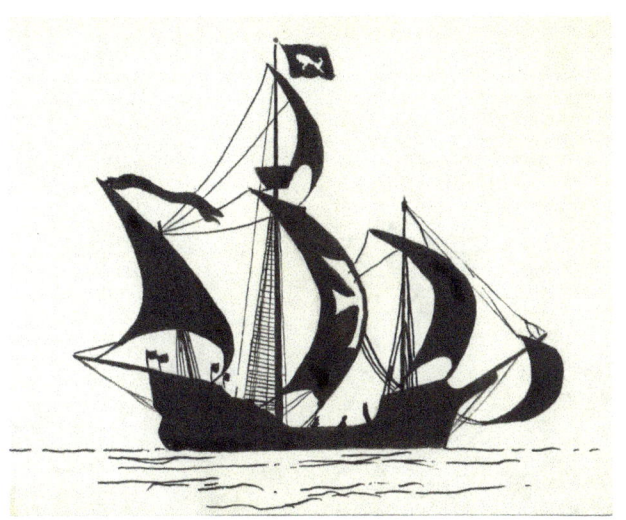

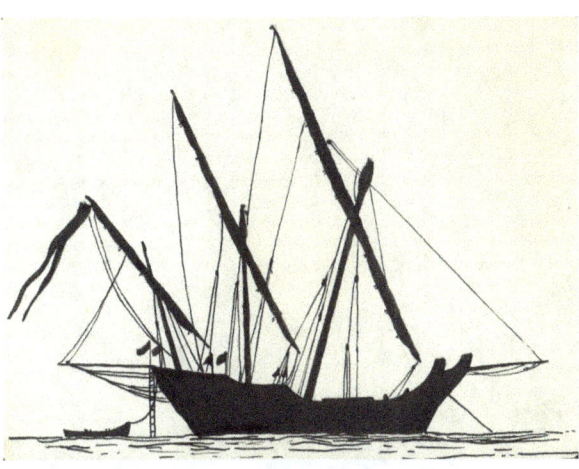

Sailing ships, by
Harry Wilcox Jr, 1940.
Pen and ink.

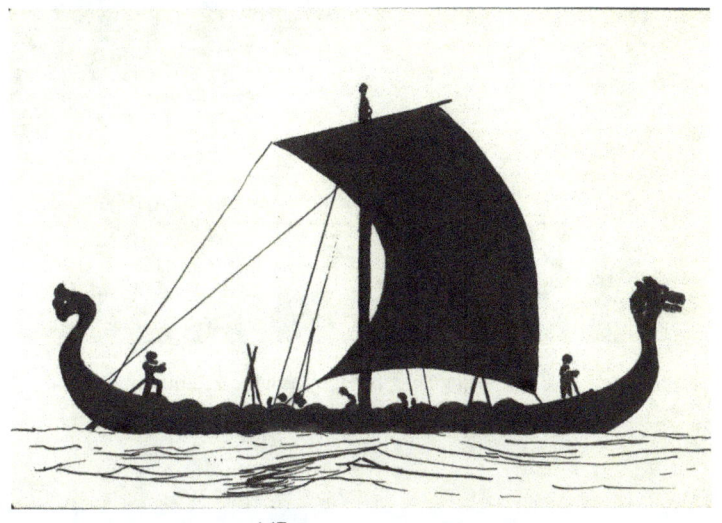

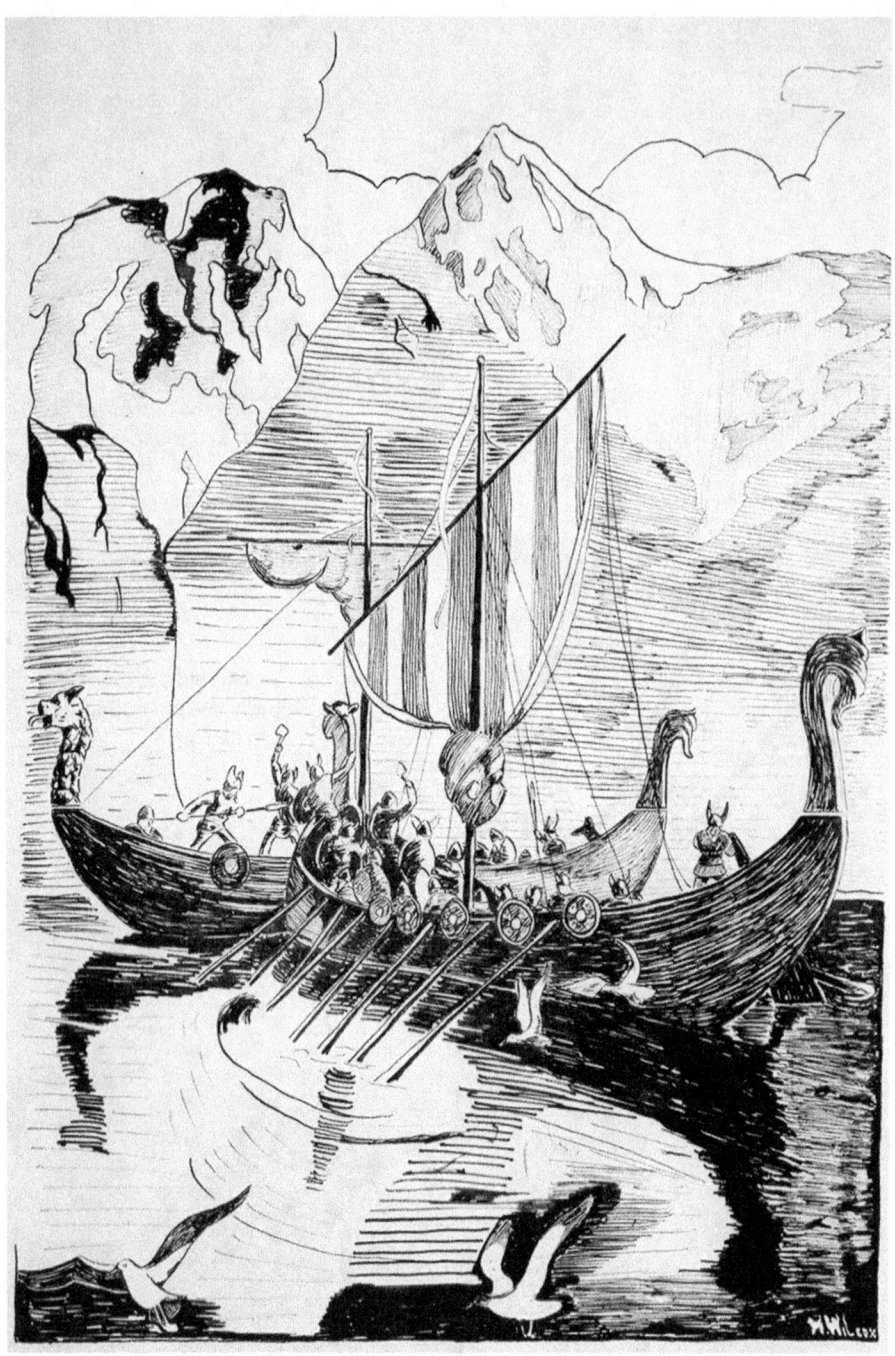

Viking Ship, by Harry Wilcox Jr "Bud," about 1948
Pen and ink on paper.

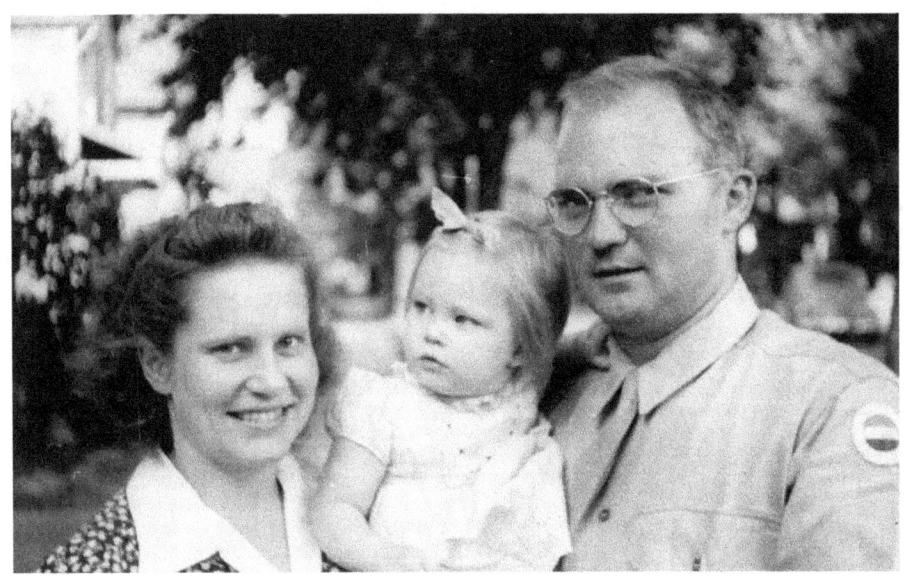

June, Joyce, and Harry Jr, early 1945

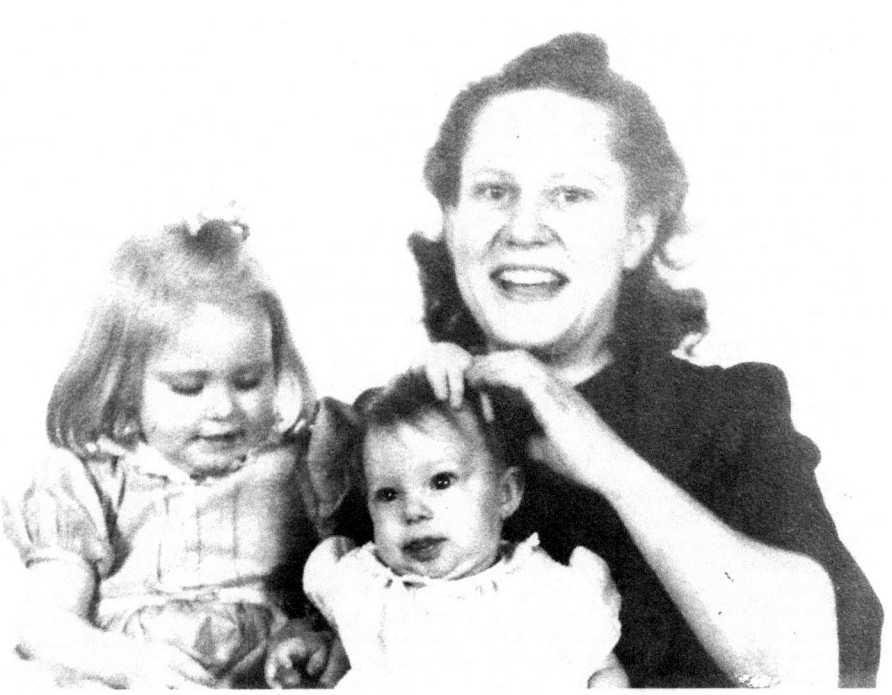

Joyce, Margaret and June, late 1945. June sent this picture to Harry shortly after Margaret's birth. He carried it in his wallet throughout the war.

Once back from the war, he resumed his Ph.D. weeks after being mustered out. As a student of comparative zoology, Bud applied his artistic talent to illustrations of anatomical features and medical drawings. His doctoral thesis on the loon includes a number of precise and beautifully rendered illustrations of anatomical features of the loon.

The loon is able to dive to great depths to fish for food. His legs, which can be tidily tucked up under his wings, can extend out to great length and with enormous power. Bud was fascinated with the elegant

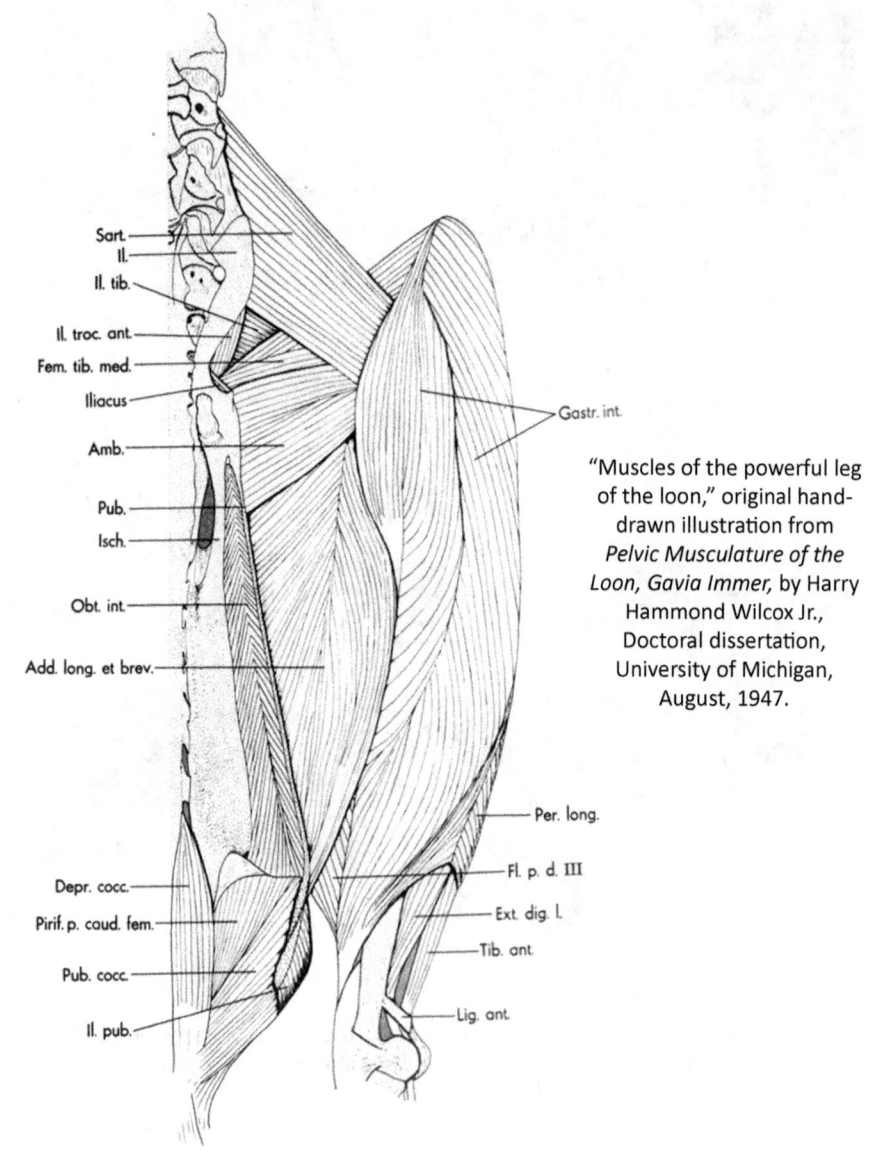

"Muscles of the powerful leg of the loon," original hand-drawn illustration from *Pelvic Musculature of the Loon, Gavia Immer,* by Harry Hammond Wilcox Jr., Doctoral dissertation, University of Michigan, August, 1947.

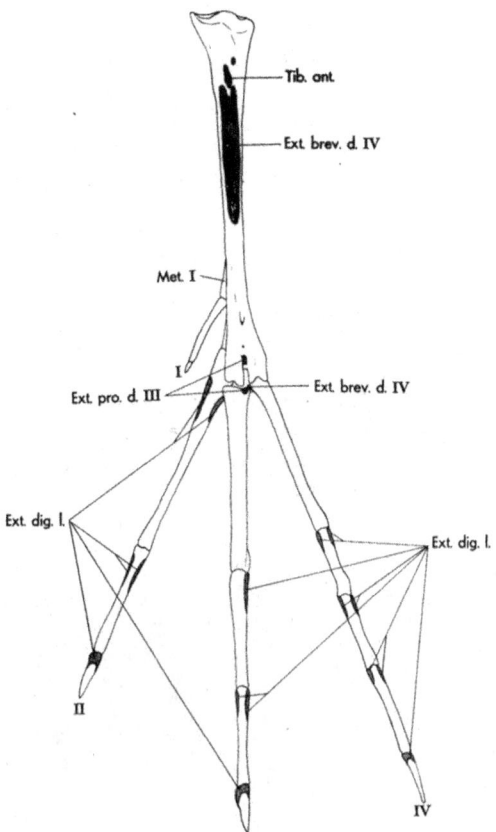

Tib. ant.

Ext. brev. d. IV

Met. I

Ext. pro. d. III — Ext. brev. d. IV

Ext. dig. l. — Ext. dig. l.

II

III

IV

"Bones of the foot of the loon" Original hand-drawn illustration from *Pelvic Musculature of the Loon, Gavia Immer,* by Harry Hammond Wilcox Jr., Doctoral dissertation, University of Michigan, August, 1947.

"engineering" of these powerful limbs, as well designed as anything manufactured for a specific purpose.

In the summer of 1947 he began teaching ornithology at Morningside College in Sioux City, Iowa. He received his actual Ph.D. diploma the following December. During that year in Iowa he discovered that his high-range hearing had been irreparably damaged in the war — he could see a bird singing but could not hear it. He realized that he would need to change from ornithology. He applied for and was awarded a teaching position in Human Anatomy at the University of Pennsylvania Medical School in Philadelphia, where he taught 1948-1952. In 1952, he accepted a position teaching anatomy at the University of Tennessee Medical Units in Memphis.

Having moved frequently as a child, he was determined to provide a steady environment for his own children to grow up and go to school in the same place. He and June settled in Memphis, where he taught for the next 35 years.

Bud and June had three children: Joyce Louise (1944), Margaret June (1945) and James Hammond (1953). With a father who taught anatomy and comparative zoology, and a mother who knew all the plants by their Latin names, a simple walk in the woods or an orphaned baby bird became a science lesson. Sewing, woodworking, and fixing nearly anything were part of the family culture from an early age.

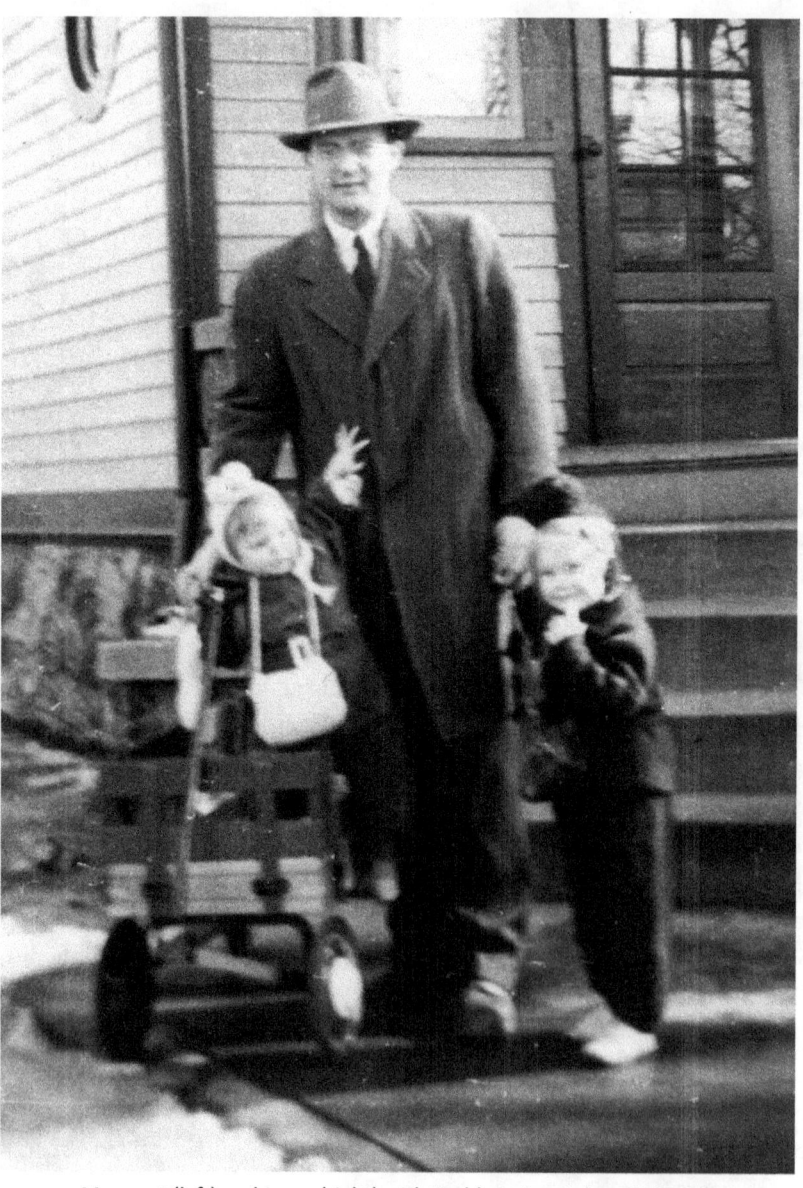

Margaret (left) and Joyce (right) with Daddy in Ann Arbor, 1946-47.

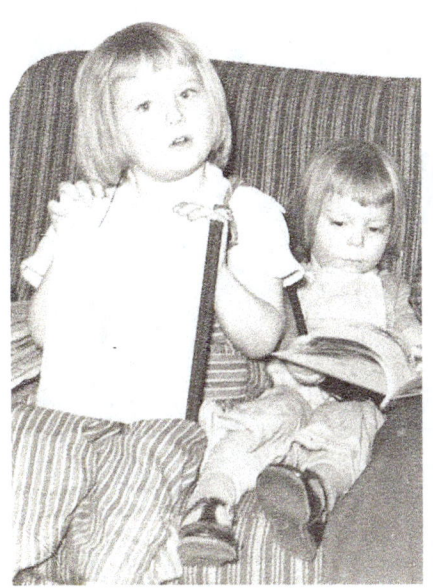

Joyce and Margaret, 1949

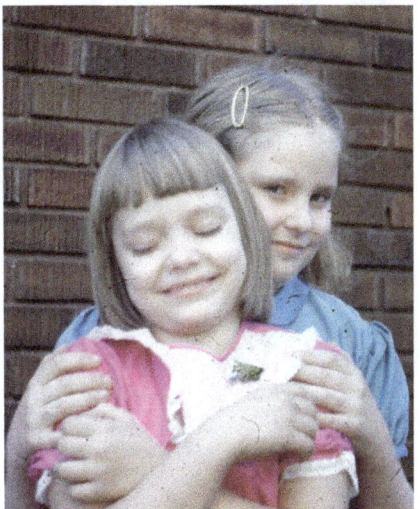

Margaret and Joyce, 1953

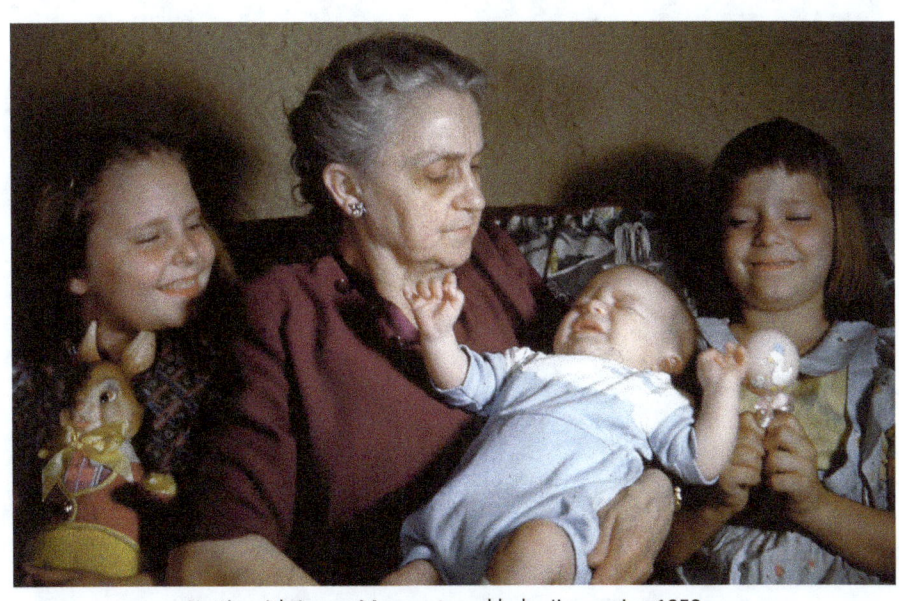

Hattie with Joyce, Margaret, and baby Jim, spring 1953.

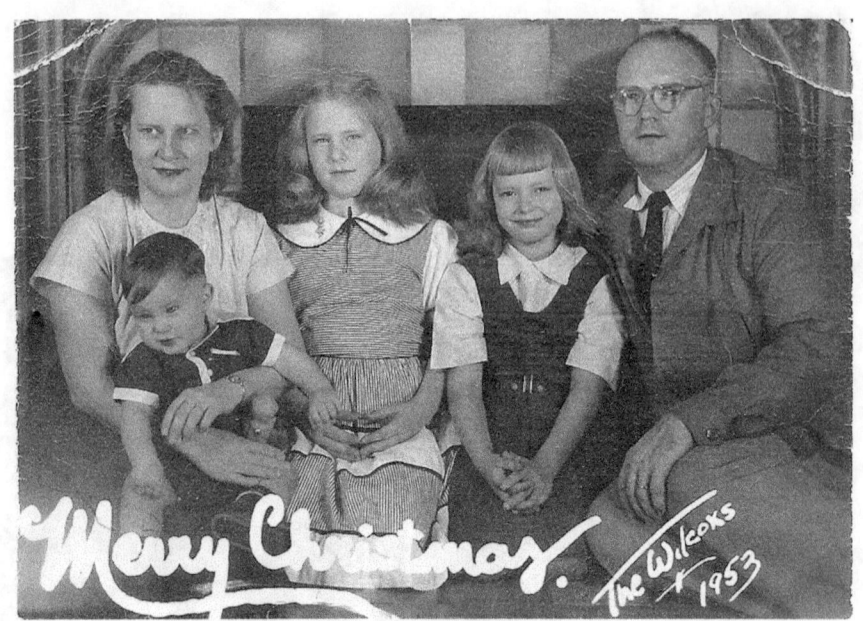

June with baby Jim, Joyce, Margaret, and Harry, 1953
in Memphis, Tennessee

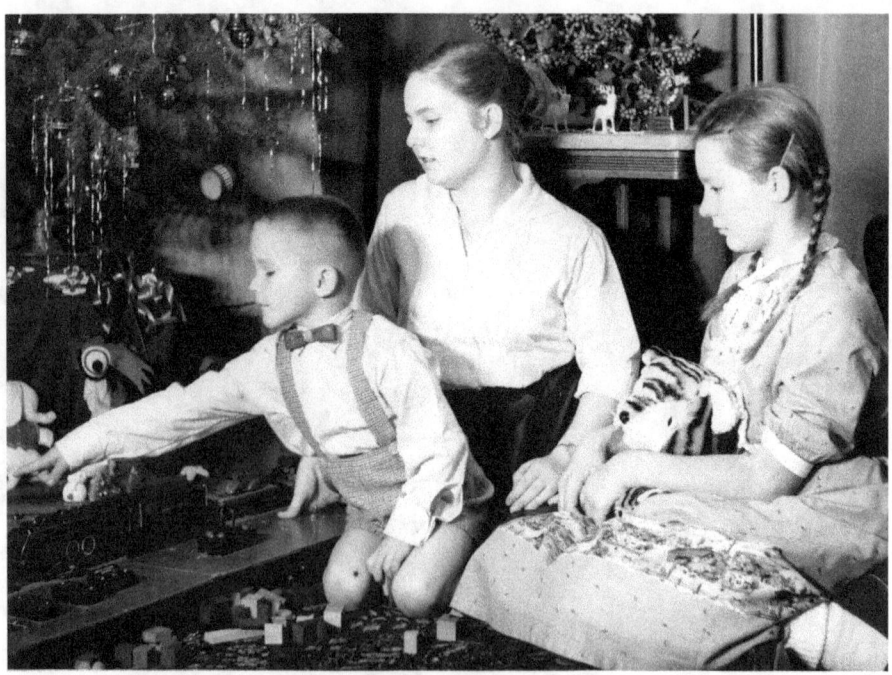

Jim, Joyce, and Margaret, 1958. The train platform was an annual treat.
It was always "Daddy's train" and an earned privilege to touch it.

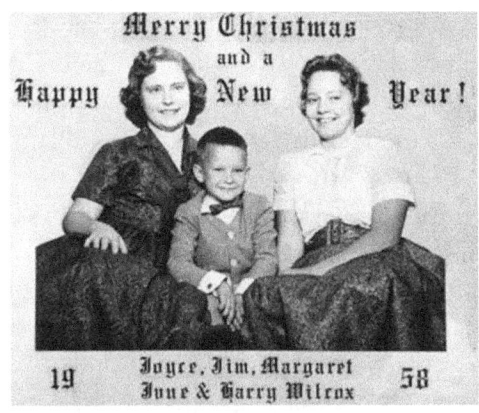

Merry Christmas and a Happy New Year!

19   Joyce, Jim, Margaret June & Harry Wilcox   58

Above:
Joyce, Jim, Margaret,
Christmas 1958

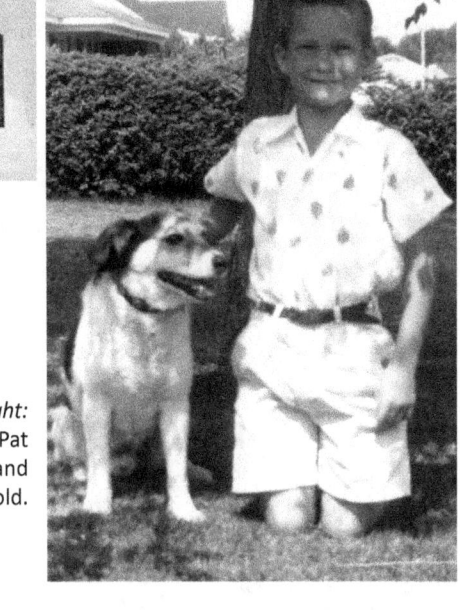

Right:
Jim with our family dog Pat
who came to us in 1949 and
lived to be 19 years old.

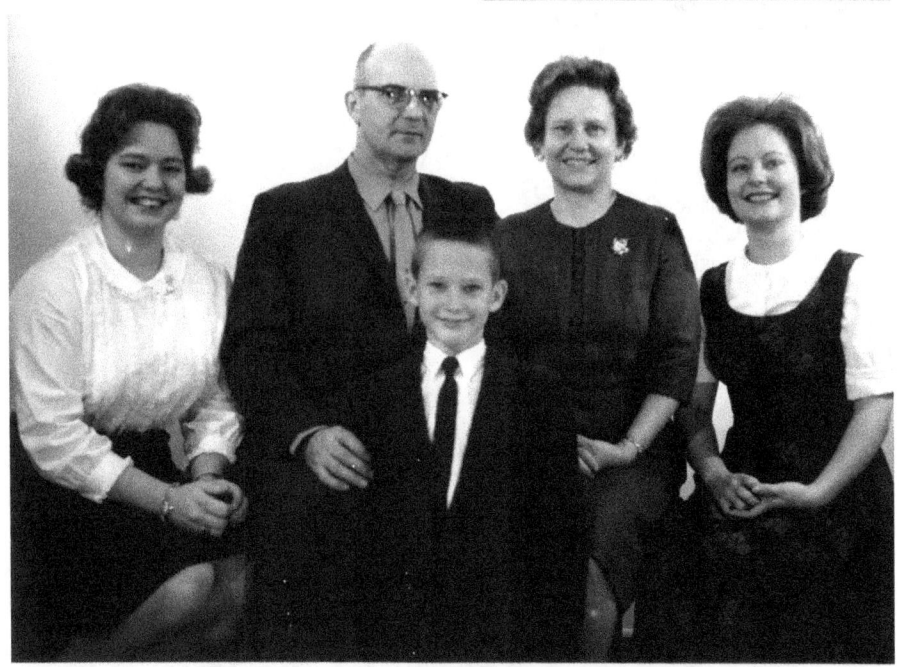

Margaret, Harry, June, Joyce, and Jim in front, 1962

In Memphis, most of Harry Wilcox Jr's research and publication had to do with neuro-anatomy, with a focus on the effects of aging on the brain. He was a Professor of Anatomy at the University of Tennessee Medical Units in Memphis, now the Center for the Health Sciences.

Nonetheless, his love of comparative zoology was never far behind. In 1950, he published a paper on the "Histology of the Skin and Hair of the Adult Chinchilla" in *The Anatomical Record,* the premier journal of anatomists, of which he was one of the editors for many years. The article included a number of original drawings. He was fascinated by the unique configuration of chinchilla hair, having many strands of hair in bundles from a single follicle, contributing to its particularly soft fur.

Original drawings by Harry Wilcox Jr. from "Histology of the Skin and Hair of the Adult Chinchilla" in *The Anatomical Record,* 108:3, November 1950, pp 387ff. Among his papers we found the desiccated pelt of a chinchilla, which June gave to Rhodes College.

Right:
Figure 1 shows that bundles of hair emerge from a single follicle, whereas in most mammals each follicle houses a single hair.

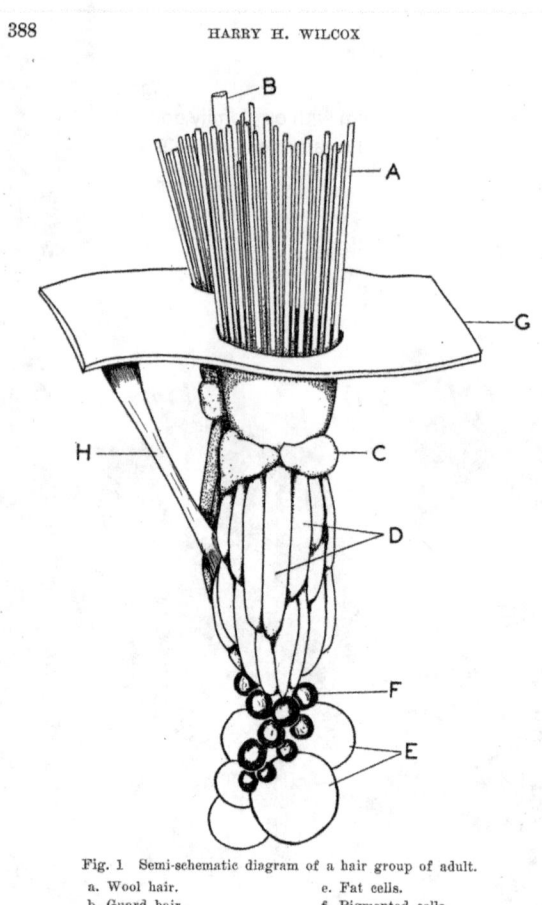

Fig. 1 Semi-schematic diagram of a hair group of adult.

a. Wool hair.	e. Fat cells.
b. Guard hair.	f. Pigmented cells.
c. Sebaceous gland.	g. Epidermis.
d. Follicles.	h. Arrector pili muscle.

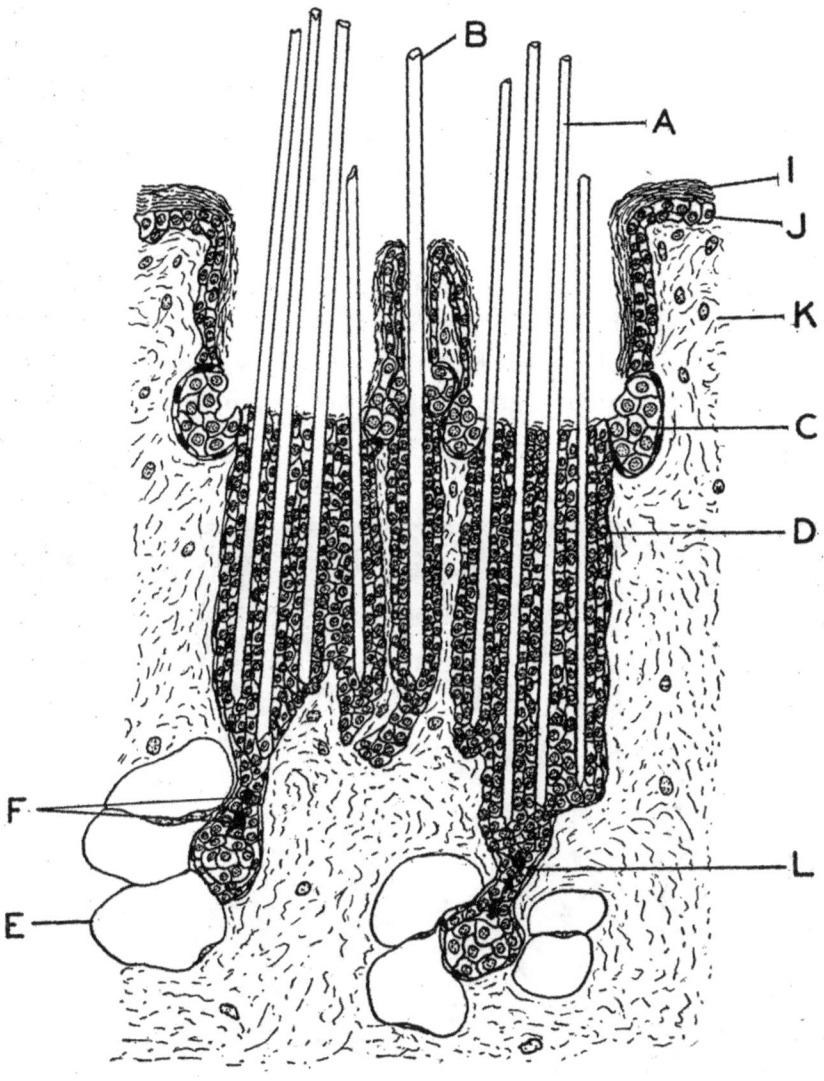

Fig. 2   Diagram of a longitudinal section of a hair group of adult.

            i. Stratum corneum.
            j. Stratum germinativum.
            k. Corium.
            l. Proliferating follicle.

Other labels as in figure 1.

Figure 2: A cross-section of the hair follicle in an adult chinchilla. Original drawing by Harry Wilcox Jr. from "Histology of the Skin and Hair of the Adult Chinchilla" in *The Anatomical Record,* 108:3, November 1950, pp 387ff.

Mark Richner recalls that Bud once took him and others "to a small stream outside of Duboistown to look for salamanders. I remember looking under a lot of rocks! My mother told me NOT to bring anything home. I think I would have been about 10 or 12 years old."[45]

In 1962, after a series of falls and broken bones, Hattie moved to Memphis to be nearer to her son and his family. She bought a house one block away from Bud and June and their family. That same year Joyce went from Memphis to Cornell University to attend college. Hattie and Joyce traded overcoats — Joyce's cloth coat would be too thin for winters in Ithaca, and Hattie's 1930's sealskin coat would be too heavy for Memphis. Joyce wore that "grizzly fur" coat through the next ten winters in the North.

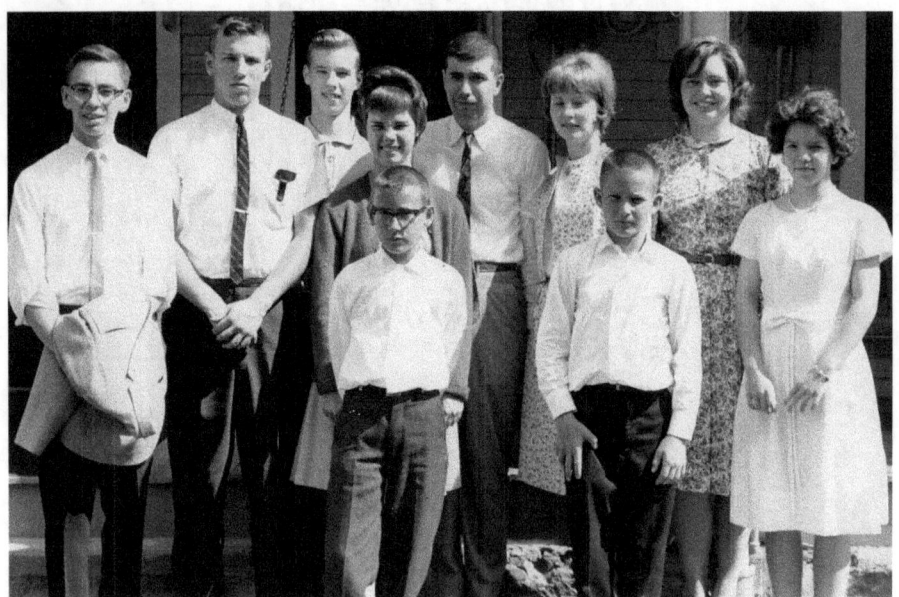

The Richner cousins, who attended Julia and Ross Conn's 50th wedding anniversary celebration 1963. *Left to right:*
Mark Richner (son of Eddie Richner and Phyllis Maneval, grandson of Dick),
Sam Barrett (son of Ruth Conn and Fred Barrett, grandson of Julia),
Richard Winder (son of Austin Winder and Doris Hunter, grandson of Emma),
Loraine Winder (daughter of Austin Winder and Doris Hunter, granddaughter of Emma),
Norman Cole (son of Verena Winder and Earl Cole, grandson of Mary),
Joyce Wilcox Graff, Margaret Wilcox (Smith), and
Beth Richner (Porter), sister of Mark.
The two boys in front are Fred "Bif" Barrett (son of Ruth Conn and Fred Barrett, grandson of Julia), and Jim Wilcox.

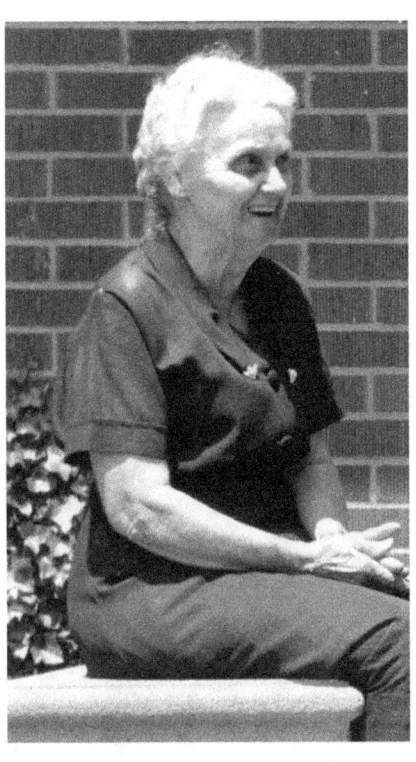

Left:
Hattie in the sunshine — smiling! — at 2525 Four Mile Drive, Montoursville, at the 50th wedding celebration of Walter and Dorothy Youngman Freed, 1966.

Below:
Brother and sisters at
Julia and Ross Conn's
50th wedding anniversary, 1963.
Left to right: George A. "Dick" Richner,
Mary Winder, Emmy Winder,
Hattie Wilcox, and Julia Conn.

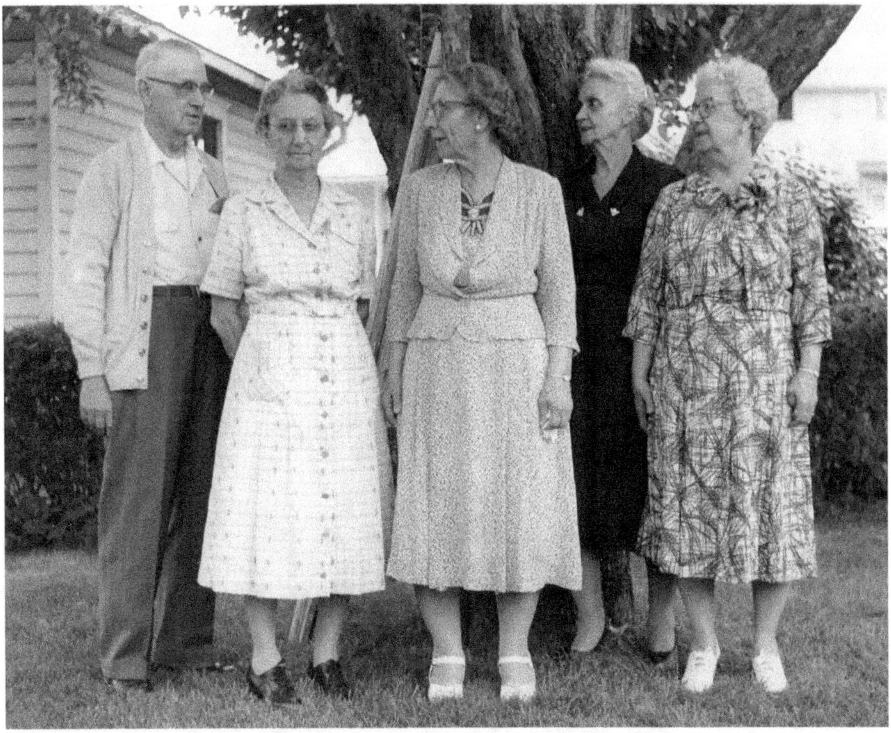

With Grandmother, the family traveled north nearly every summer. In 1963 Julia and Ross Conn celebrated their 50th wedding anniversary, and in 1966 June's parents, Walter and Dorothy Freed also celebrated 50 years together. Both were good reasons for family gatherings.

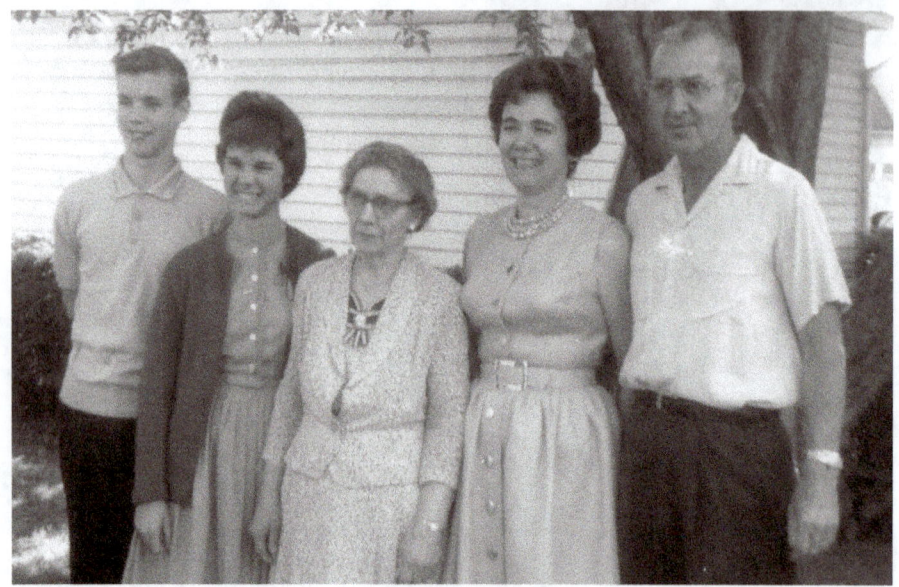

Aunt Emmy's family
Richard, Loraine, Emma, Doris, and Austin Winder. 1963.

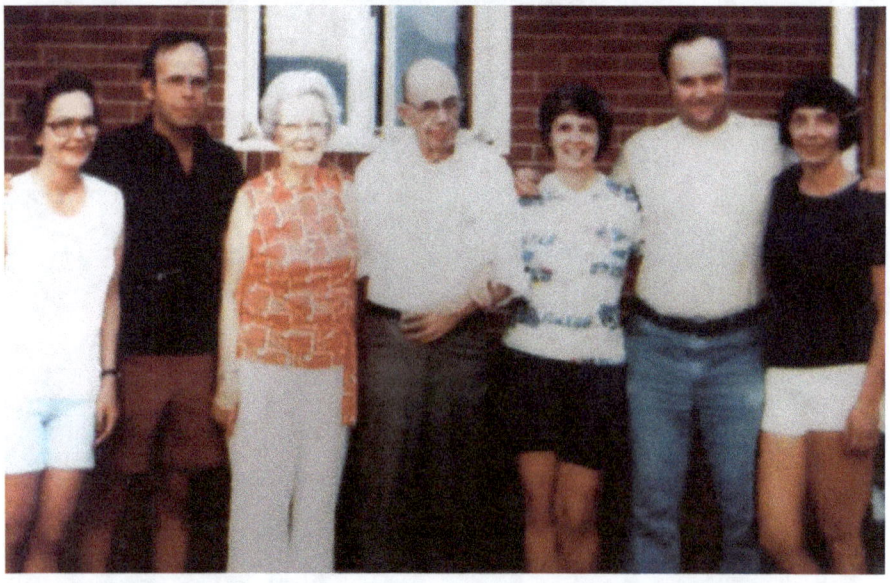

Lois (Workman), Thomas, Louise, Mahlon, Dolly (Bastian), James,
and Eleanor (Halibeit) Winder, about 1963.

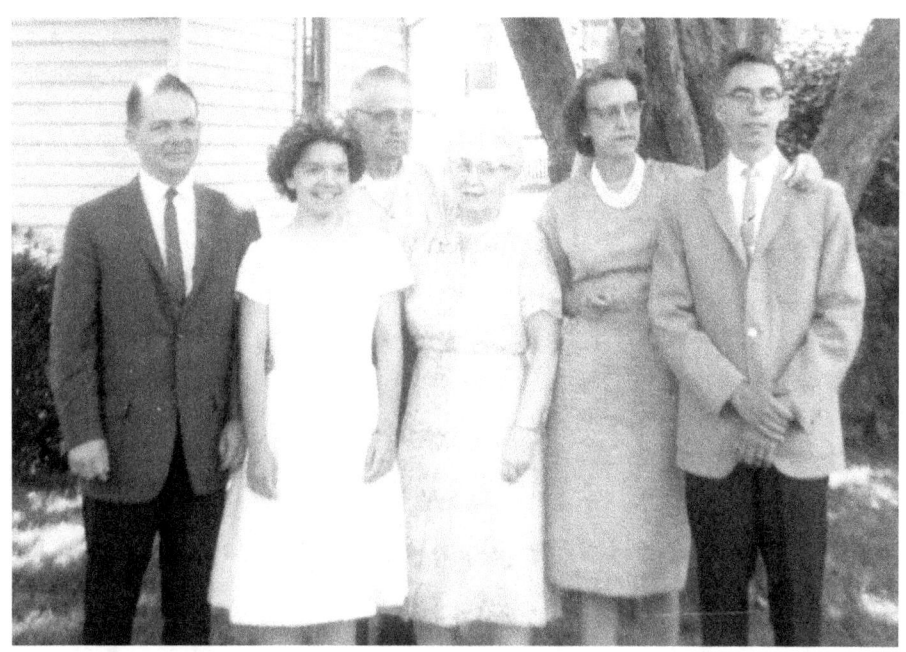

Uncle Dick's family
Eddie, Beth, George A Sr "Dick," Kathie, Phyllis, and Mark Richner.

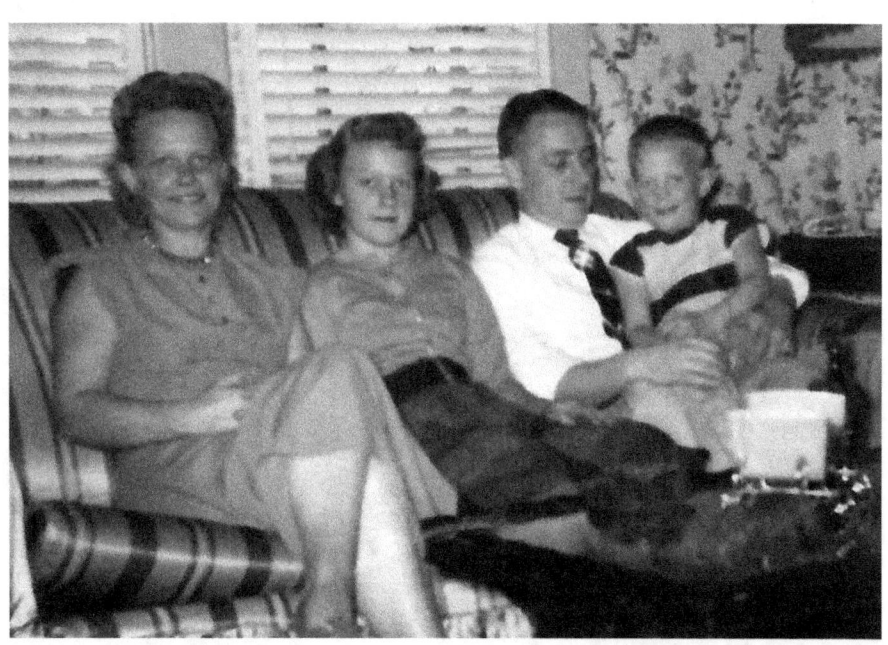

Kate, Carol (Gallagher), George A. Jr "Jim" and Stephen.

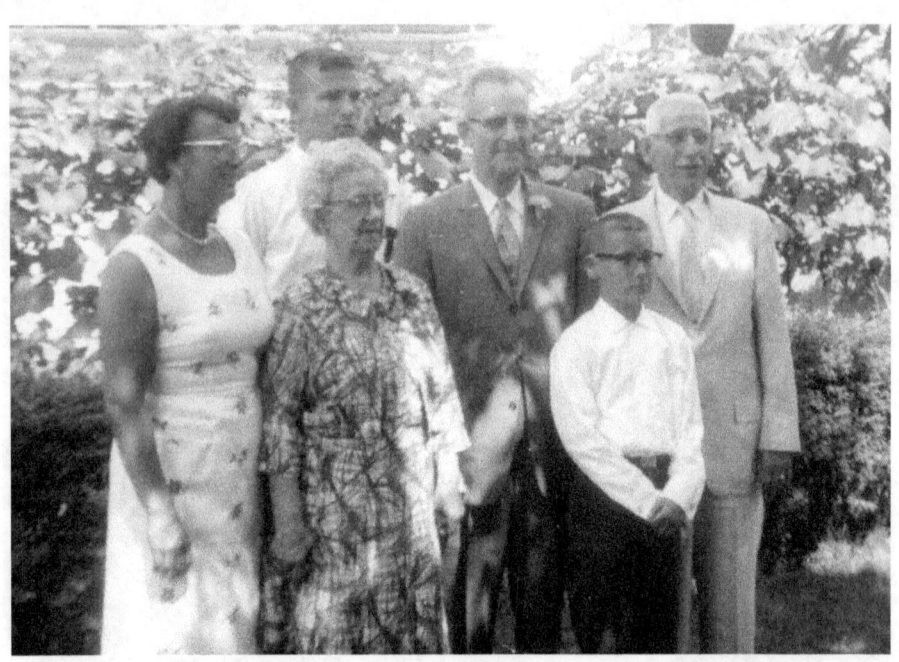

Aunt Julie's family
Back: Ruth Conn Barrett, Sam Barrett, Ross Conn, Fred Barrett
Front: Julia Conn, Fred Barrett Jr "Bif"

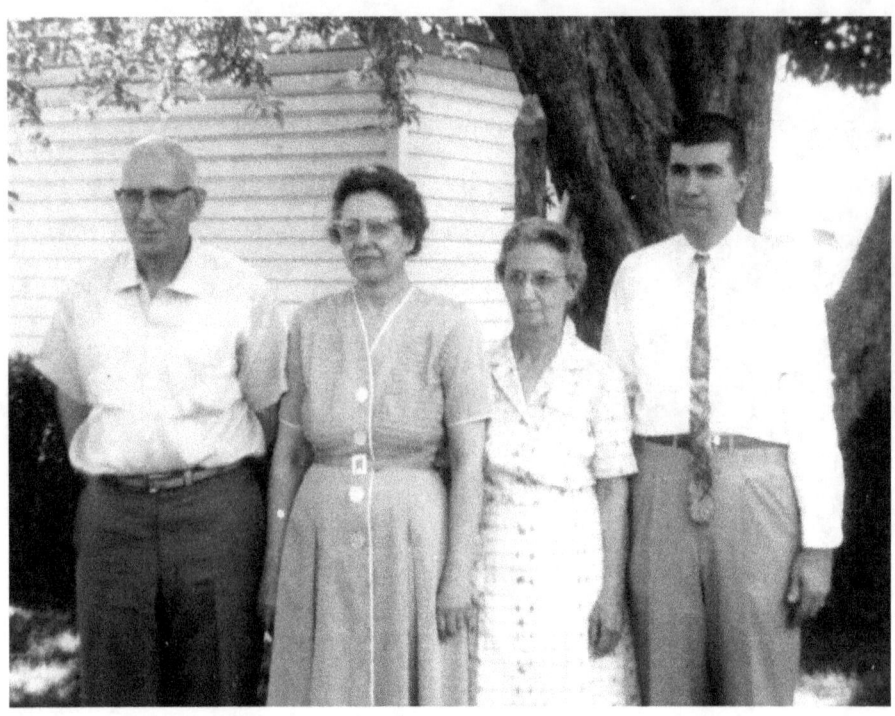

Aunt Mary's family
Earl and Verena Winder Cole, Mary Winder, Norman Cole

In 1967 Bud was honored as a teacher by the University of Tennessee. *Commercial Appeal*, May 2, 1967:

"Teacher's "infinite patience" pays off with honor at UT
By J. Whitley Perry

"Dr. Harry H. Wilcox has been named the third faculty member of the University of Tennessee Medical Units here to receive the Goodman Professorship in recognition of outstanding accomplishments in teaching.

Dr. Wilcox, professor and deputy chairman of the UT Medical Units' department of anatomy, will receive a $2,000 annual salary supplement as part of this award.

Supported by the Abe Goodman Fund Advisory Committee, the professorship was established in 1961 to recognize outstanding scholarly pursuits of the faculty. The only other faculty members to receive the honor are Dr. Lemuel W. Diggs of the department of medicine and Dr. Simon R. Bruesch of the department of anatomy.

"I'm very flattered by it," said Dr. Wilcox. "I don't know what to say, except that I like my subject, and I just enjoy teaching it."

In 1965 Dr. Wilcox was the first faculty member to receive The Golden Apple, the highest award the students can bestow upon a faculty member. It was presented to him by the Student American Medical Association for "excellence in teaching."

According to students and teachers, Dr. Wilcox displays a strong interest in the students and their welfare. One former class member remembers him as "a man of infinite patience, able to take a complex subject in anatomy and make it simple, then build it back up so that its complexities are made plain."

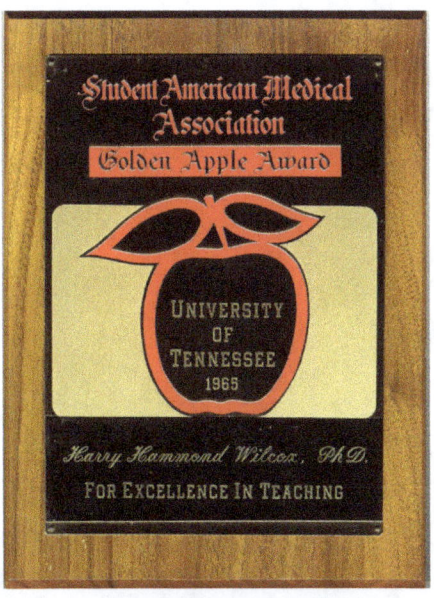

The Golden Apple Award

Dr. Wilcox is a member of the American Association of Anatomists, American Society of Zoologists, American Academy of Neurology, and the Biological Stain Commission. He has been active in the Quintard House, the Episcopal Center for the medical students. He also joined in the move to build the Interfaith Center planned for construction at the UT Medical Units. He received his doctorate in zoology from the University of Michigan in 1948 and came to UT in 1952 as an assistant professor. He lives [in Memphis] with his wife, June Wilcox, who teaches fifth grade at Grahamwood School. They have three children: Joyce, Margaret, and Jim."

In 1969 Hattie fell and broke her pelvic bone, two days before her granddaughter Margaret's wedding. After two months in the hospital and two months in a nursing home, she spent the last nine years of her life bedridden in a room in the home of June and Harry Jr. She enjoyed making beautiful afghans of hairpin lace. She died in 1977.

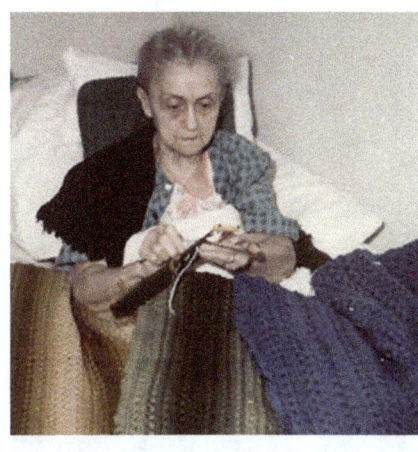

Grandmother Hattie
making a hairpin lace
afghan in shades of green.

Joyce remembers once sitting with her grandmother Hattie in her room, watching a news broadcast with some footage about the astronauts walking on the moon. Hattie turned to Joyce and said, "You know … I remember Kitty Hawk."

It was awe-inspiring to think how much change had transpired in her lifetime. From Kitty Hawk to the moon in a single lifetime. The revolution in commercial art — from line drawing to air brush to computer graphics — is no less awesome.

Each of us has witnessed a piece of that revolution, and has contributed some small bit to it.

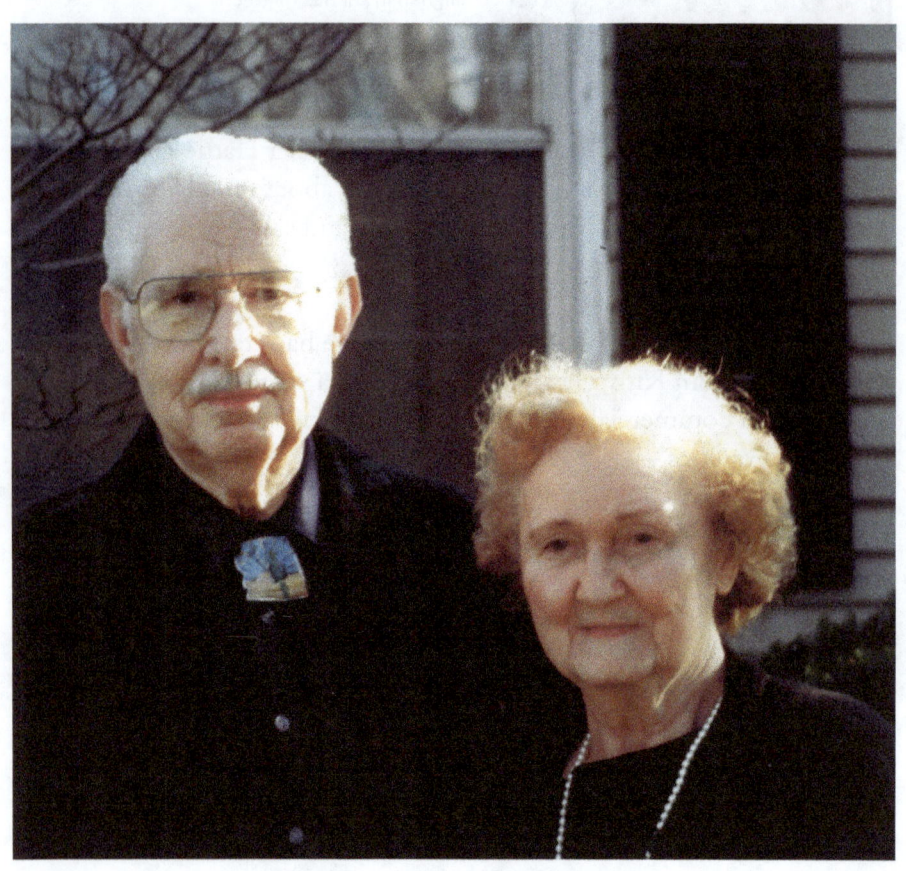

Meredith and Verna Wilcox Alair, 1987

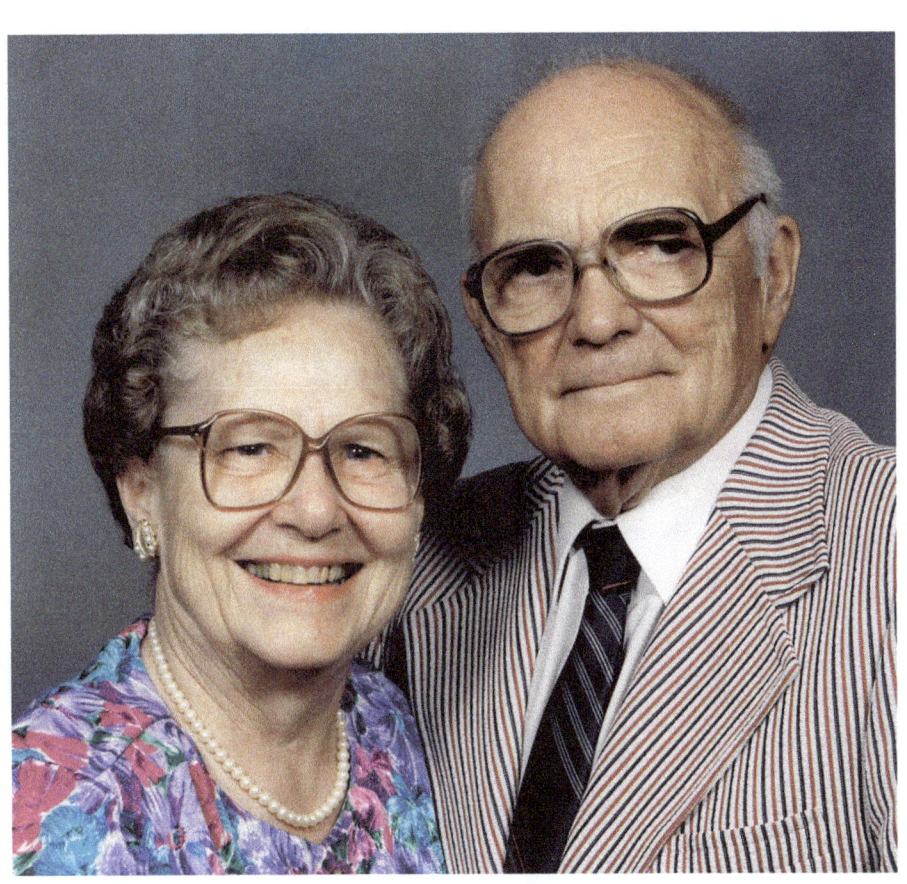

Harry and June Freed Wilcox, 1993

Appendix:
Lydel Sims Interviews Harry Jr.

Lydel Sims was a long-time columnist for the Memphis *Commercial Appeal*. His many readers enjoyed every day his humorous view of the human condition. In 1977 Sims interviewed Harry Wilcox Jr. for a column, giving us a glimpse into the sly humor that Harry and his father shared.

Assignment: Memphis, by Lydel Sims
Commercial Appeal, July 21, 1977.

Dispute over body weight presents issue to take sides on

"It's amazing," the man told me, "what a group of retired men will argue about."

I don't know about that. Some people might think amazing means foolish or frivolous — even scandalous. But what this fellow and his friends had been arguing about wasn't any of those things. Deep is more like it.

"We were discussing," he explained, "which side of the human body weighs the most."

Before you snort, try answering the question.

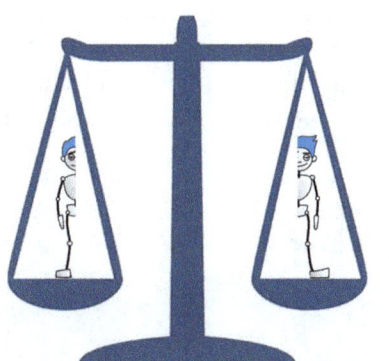

Which side, in fact, does weigh more? The right, or the left?

And how do you know the answer isn't significant? Did you take quarks seriously before the scientists started poking around amongst them?

All right, then.

Eager to get to the bottom

(the side?) of the matter, I called the office of Dr. E. William Rosenberg, acting dean of the College of Medicine at the University of Tennessee Center for the Health Sciences.

He was at a meeting, but I left the message. Later, his office called back.

Dean Rosenberg wasn't sure, but he thought perhaps the right side weighed more in the case of a right-handed person, and vice versa, of course, for southpaws.

He hadn't comments on ambidexterity. But then I hadn't asked.

And he suggested that I consult Dr. Harry Wilcox, who, as they say at medical college, is "in anatomy."

"I don't know if anybody ever split anybody down the middle to find out," Dr. Wilcox confessed when I posed the question. I said yes, but did he have an opinion? Would the right side of a right-hander weigh more?

At this point the professor introduced a new element into the equation: compensation.

The upper half of a right-hander might well weigh more, Dr. Wilcox conceded, but one must consider the lower area of the body as well. Would there not be a compensatory shift of the center of gravity down there to keep the individual from listing rightward? Would that perhaps not result in additional weight in the lower left portion, thereby balancing the scales?

Would he say, then, that each side weighed the same?

Not necessarily. One side or the other probably weighs just a little bit more, for one reason or another, but it is doubtful that there is any identifiable consistency in the fluctuations.

That left us both pondering.

Then, I asked, didn't the continuing mystery arouse his curiosity? Would he be prepared to perform experiments to find an answer?

"Sure," he said cheerfully. "If there are any volunteers."

It was a statement of fact, but it almost sounded like a question. Nay, even an invitation. I thanked him somewhat nervously and said goodbye. It may well be that, important as they are, some questions are best left for speculation and debate.

Any volunteers?

Genealogy

The primary purpose of this book is to collect and catalog the work of Harry Wilcox Sr. and to describe it in the context of his times.

There is of course a great deal of family history in this book, and learning some of it will often stimulate the appetite for more.

The illustration of the family tree on page 194 depicts four generations prior to Harry and Hattie Richner Wilcox. Within that four generations, the Richners and the Steinbachers immigrated to the United States. Some reviewers asked why we did not also put the immigration information for the Wilcoxes and the Kramms on the tree — simply put, because they were already here. The Wilcoxes came to America about 1635, settled in Massachusetts Bay Colony, left with Roger Williams to found what became the state of Rhode Island, and fought in the Revolutionary War. The Kramms immigrated in the late 1600's through Philadelphia and also fought in the War of Independence.

The purpose of this section is to fill in some of those blanks. It does not intend to be a complete genealogical record. Jim has data on more than fifty thousand relations going back to England, France, Germany, and Switzerland. This will give you a picture of the direct line of the Wilcox family beginning in 1565 in England, and participating in the building of America.

If you are interested in more, please contact James H. Wilcox, ancestry@wilcoxkids.net.

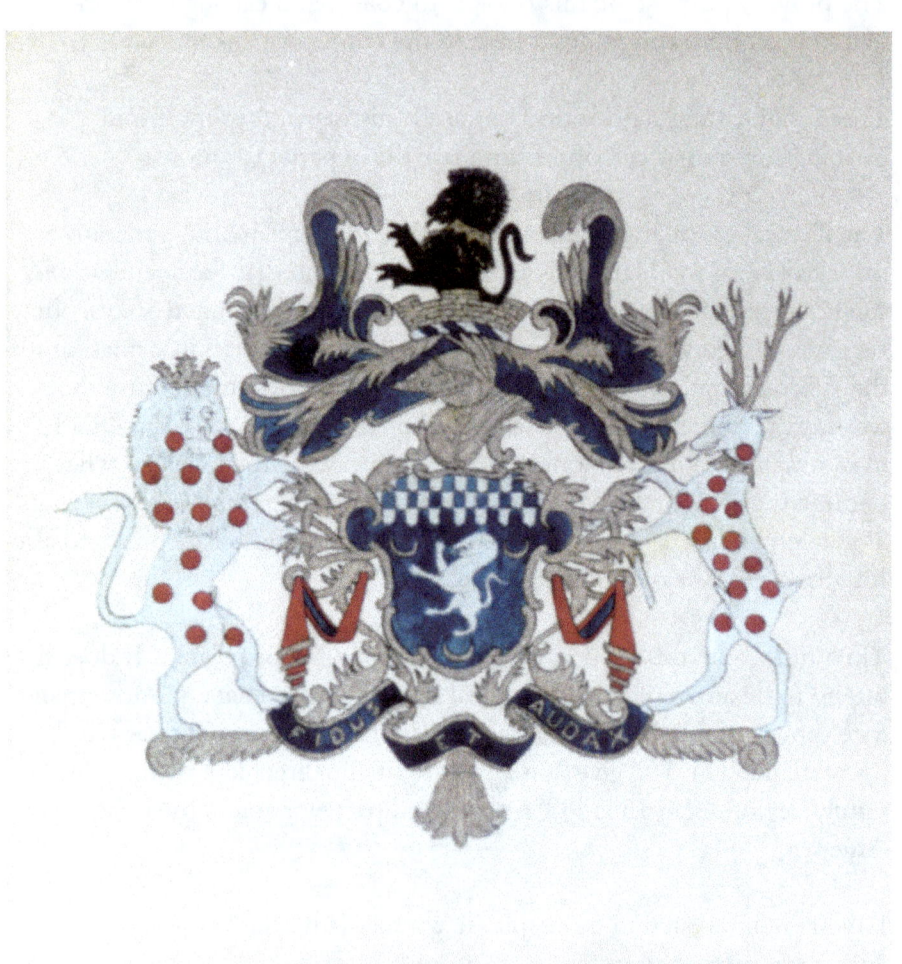

The Wilcox family crest, drawn and colored by Harry Wilcox Jr.
Copied from the letterhead of a letter to Sarah Verna Creasy Wilcox (Mrs. Daniel Wilcox, 1860-1948) of Berwick, Pennsylvania, from a relative in England.

The Wilcox Line

by William Richard Cutter[46]

The Wilcox family is of Saxon origin, and was seated at Bury St. Edmunds, county Suffolk, England, before the Norman conquest. Sir John Dugdale, in the Visitation of the County of Suffolk, mentioned fifteen generations of the family previous to the year 1600. This traces the lineage back to the year 1200, when the surname came into use as an inherited family name.

On old records the spelling Willcox, Wilcocks, Wilcoxon, and Wilcox are used interchangeably. It is of interest to note that the names Northington and Southington were names of communities in England where the Wilcox family were prominent as peers before their migration to America.

The Wilcox family had a coat of arms of which account is found in a number of heraldic works. From a member of the family in Connecticut was secured a reproduction of the original arms brought from England, the features of which were the mantling motto, crest, lion, rampant, and demi-lion sable issuing out of the mural crown and collared with a ducal crown. The ducal crown indicated the relation of the person to the crown who bore the arms, that of a duke, and the highest next to a prince or sovereign, and usually a son or brother or near relation of the sovereign.

The significance of the lion rampant is that the person bearing the arms had, as general of the army of England, won great victories and honor to the crown.

The motto, Fidux et audax, means faithful and true, or faithful and bold. The supporters here shown are the same as used by the Earls of Norfolk, a branch of the family, and recognizable in the fact that the family were seated in Northington, Connecticut, a place of the same name as in England. Northington is a community in Norfolk, England, the history of which is the most rich in antiquity as connected with the progress of Anglican civilization, and at one time nearly all of the eastern part of England was governed or controlled as one province by this same family.

A branch of the family were dukes of Suffolk directly south of Suffolk, but political changes caused them to be submerged, and only ancient history discloses these facts.

Four Generations before
Harry and Hattie Richner Wilcox

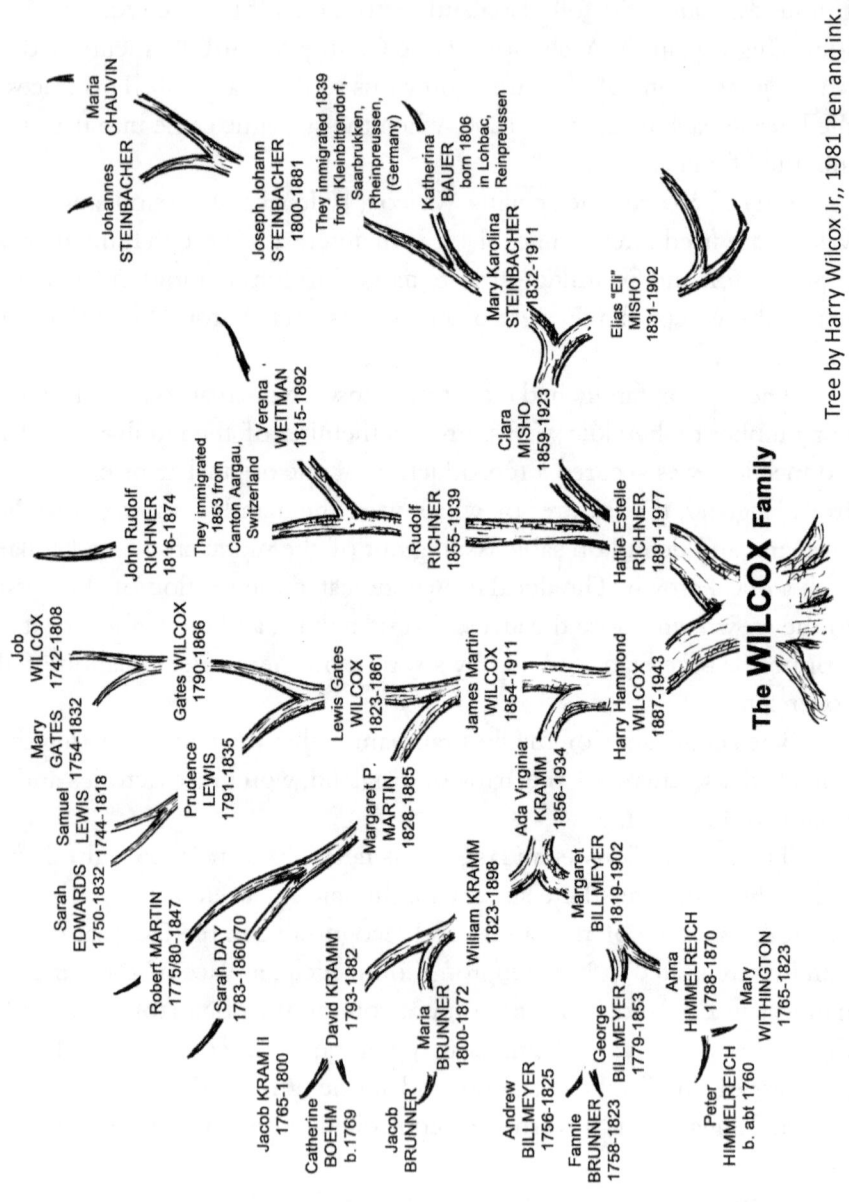

Tree by Harry Wilcox Jr., 1981 Pen and ink.

Maria CHAUVIN

Johannes STEINBACHER

Joseph Johann STEINBACHER 1800-1881

They immigrated 1839 from Kleinbittendorf, Saarbrukken, Rheinpreussen, (Germany)

Katherina BAUER born 1806 in Lohbac, Reinpreussen

Mary Karolina STEINBACHER 1832-1911

Elias "Eli" MISHO 1831-1902

John Rudolf RICHNER 1816-1874

They immigrated 1853 from Canton Aargau, Switzerland

Verena WEITMAN 1815-1892

Rudolf RICHNER 1855-1939

Clara MISHO 1859-1923

Hattie Estelle RICHNER 1891-1977

Job WILCOX 1742-1808

Mary GATES 1754-1832

Gates WILCOX 1790-1866

Samuel LEWIS 1744-1818

Prudence LEWIS 1791-1835

Lewis Gates WILCOX 1823-1861

Sarah EDWARDS 1750-1832

Margaret P. MARTIN 1828-1885

James Martin WILCOX 1854-1911

Harry Hammond WILCOX 1887-1943

The WILCOX Family

Robert MARTIN 1775/80-1847

Sarah DAY 1783-1860/70

Ada Virginia KRAMM 1856-1934

Jacob KRAM II 1765-1800

David KRAMM 1793-1882

Margaret BILLMEYER 1819-1902

Catherine BOEHM b. 1769

Maria BRUNNER 1800-1872

William KRAMM 1823-1898

Jacob BRUNNER

Andrew BILLMEYER 1756-1825

George BILLMEYER 1779-1853

Anna HIMMELREICH 1788-1870

Fannie BRUNNER 1758-1823

Peter HIMMELREICH b. abt 1760

Mary WITHINGTON 1765-1823

Mapping your tree forward from
Harry and Hattie Richner Wilcox

for privacy and security, names and details of living persons have been
omitted from this book. Use this page and add paper as needed
to map your own lineage from Harry and Hattie to you.

THE WILCOX FAMILY

Harry Hammond Wilcox 1887-1943	m.	Hattie Estelle Richner 1891-1977
James Martin Wilcox 1854-1911	m.	Ada Virginia Kramm 1856-1934
Lewis Gates Wilcox 1823-1861	m.	Margaret P. Martin 1828-1885
Gates Wilcox 1790-1866	m1.	Prudence Lewis 1791-1835
Job Wilcox 1742-1808	m.	Mary Gates 1754-1832
Abraham Willcox 1695/1706 – 1800/1810	m.	Lydia Harrington 1723-1807
Thomas Willcox 1663/4 – 1728	m.	Martha Hazard 1668-1753
Stephen Willcox 1633-1690	m.	Hannah Hazard
Edward Willcox 1602/4 – before 1660	m2.	Susana Thomson b.1607
Daniel Willcox 1565-1605	m.	Esabel (Isabel) ___

The Wilcoxes were among the earliest settlers from England to America. We do not know the exact date or ship on which they came, but in 1634 they were in Lincolnshire, England, and in 1638 they were in Aquidneck (now Rhode Island) where Edward signed the charter for what became North Kingston, Rhode Island.[47] He was intimately involved in the founding of Rhode Island and the controversy headed by Roger Williams.

Beginning in 1620 the Pilgrims established the colony of

Massachusetts Bay. The first major wave of immigration began in 1630. Roger Williams, an ordained minister of the Church of England, did not go with the first wave, but by the end of the year he decided he could no longer remain in England under the corrupt administration of Archbishop William Laud.

By the time he and his wife boarded the *Lyon* in early December 1631, he had arrived at a Separatist position.

When Roger and Mary Williams arrived at Boston on February 5, 1631, he was welcomed and almost immediately invited to become the Teacher (assistant minister) in the Boston church to officiate while Rev. John Wilson returned to England to fetch his wife. He shocked them by declining the position, saying that he found that it was "an unseparated church." In addition he asserted that the civil magistrates may not punish any sort of "breach of the first table [of the Ten Commandments]," such as idolatry, Sabbath-breaking, false worship, and blasphemy, and that every individual should be free to follow his own convictions in religious matters. Right from the beginning, he sounded three principles which were central to his subsequent career: Separatism, freedom of religion, and separation of church and state.

As a Separatist he had concluded that the Church of England was irredeemably corrupt and that one must completely separate from it to establish a new church for the true and pure worship of God. His search for the true church eventually carried him out of Congregationalism, the Baptists, and any visible church. Years later in 1802, Thomas Jefferson, writing of the "wall of separation" between Church and State echoed Roger Williams in a letter to the Danbury Baptist Association.

The Salem church was much more inclined to Separatism, so they invited Williams to become their Teacher. When the leaders in Boston learned of this, they vigorously protested, and the offer was withdrawn. By the end of the summer of 1631, Williams had moved to Plymouth colony where he was welcomed, and informally assisted the minister there. He regularly preached and, according to Governor Bradford, "his teachings were well approved."

After a time, though, he realized that the Plymouth church too was not sufficiently separated from the Church of England, and his study of the Native Americans had caused him to doubt the validity of the colonial charters. Governor Bradford later wrote that Williams fell "into some strange opinions which caused some controversy between the church and him."[48]

In December 1632, Williams wrote a lengthy tract which openly condemned the King's charters and questioned the right of Plymouth (or Massachusetts) to the land without first buying it from the Indians. He charged that King James had uttered a "solemn lie" when he asserted that he was the first Christian monarch to have discovered the land. Subsequently, he moved back to Salem by the fall of 1633 and was welcomed as an unofficial assistant in the church.

In April, he so vigorously opposed the new oath of allegiance to the colonial government that it became impossible to enforce it. He was summoned again before the Court in July to answer for "erroneous" and "dangerous opinions," and the Court declared that he should be removed from his church position. Finally, in October 1635, he was tried by the General Court and convicted of sedition and heresy. The Court declared that he was spreading "diverse, new, and dangerous opinions."[49]

He was ordered to be banished. The execution of the order was delayed because Williams was ill and winter was approaching, and he was allowed to stay temporarily provided he ceased his agitation. He did not cease, so in January 1636, the sheriff came to pick him up, only to discover that Williams had slipped away three days before. He walked through the deep snow of a hard winter the 105 miles from Salem to the head of Narragansett Bay. There he was rescued by his friends, the Wampanoags, and taken to the winter camp of their chief sachem, Massasoit.

In the spring of 1636, Williams and a number of his followers from Salem began a settlement on land that Williams had bought from Massasoit, only to be told by Plymouth that he was still within their land grant. They warned that they might be forced to extradite him to Massachusetts and invited him to cross the Seekonk River to territory beyond any charter. The outcasts rowed over to Narragansett territory, and having secured land from Canonicus and Miantonomi, chief sachems of the Narragansetts, Williams established a settlement with twelve "loving friends." He called it "Providence" because he felt that God's Providence had brought him there. He said that his settlement was to be a haven for those "distressed of conscience," and it soon attracted quite a collection of dissenters and otherwise-minded individuals.

Williams established a temporary trading post at North Kingston, Rhode Island, at the intersection of two major Native American thoroughfares, the Pequote Path (now Post Road) and the major east-west route of the Marraansett People between their winter and summer villages (now Stony Lane). This seasonal trading outpost was also adjacent to the home of his friend Narragansett Chief Sachem

Canonicus. Williams was followed by two additional seasonal traders, Richard Smith and **EDWARD WILLCOX**, in 1693. Willcox left the area after a time and relocated to the region that was to become Westerly, Rhode Island. Smith in 1641 and Williams, in 1643, decided to make North Kingston their home. Williams stayed for the next eight years, farming, raising goats, and trading with the Narragansett People for fur and wampum.[50]

Richard Smith stayed on permanently. He established a trading house, giving free entertainment to travelers passing through that section. He became a very large proprietor of lands, estimated at approximately nine miles long by three miles wide. In addition to his property in Rhode Island, Smith also owned land in "the Dutch Islands" [Manhattan and Long Island]. Roger Williams gave a tribute to him after his death:

"Being now near to four scores years of age [near 80], yet (by God's mercy) of sound understanding and memory, I do humbly and faithfully declare that Richard Smith, Senior, deceased, who for his conscience toward God, left a fair possession in Gloucestershire and adventured with his relatives and estates to New England, and was a most acceptable and prime leading man in Taunton in Plymouth Colony, for his conscience sake (many differences arising) he left Taunton and came to the Nanhigansick country, where (by the mercy of God and the favor of the Nanhigansick sachems) he broke the ice (at his great charge and hazard) and put up in the thickest of the barbarians, the first English house amongst them. I humbly testify that about forty-two years from this date he kept possession, coming and going, himself, children and servants, and he had quiet possession of his housing, land and meadows, and there in his own house, with much serenity of soul and comfort, he yielded up his spirit to God (the Father of spirits) in peace."[51]

Edward Willcox died probably at Narragansett before 1648, and in 1653 Richard Smith acted as guardian for eight children supposed to have been those of Edward Willcox. Willcox was owner of the ship *Abigail*, and was actively engaged in trading along the Atlantic coast. In partnership with Smith and Williams, he operated at New Netherlands [New York], and he is supposed to have owned land at Bushwick, Long Island, in 1638. He was an enterprising and aggressive trader and appears at one time in Virginia and again in Delaware in the Swedish colony. Among his children were Stephen and Daniel and a daughter Mary.[52]

The colony of New Sweden (1638–1655) was located along the Delaware River with settlements in modern Delaware (e.g., Wilmington), Pennsylvania (e.g., Philadelphia) and New Jersey (e.g., New Stockholm and Swedesboro). The colony was conquered by the Dutch, who perceived the presence of Swedish colonists in North America as a threat to their interests in the New Netherland colony, now New York.

Edward's son **STEPHEN WILLCOX** had a grant of 16 acres in 1657. In 1658, his father-in-law Thomas Hazard deeded to him an additional 34 acres as his daughter's dowry. He was listed among the free inhabitants of Westerly, Rhode Island, in 1669. He was one of the first deputies from Westerly to the colonial government. He married Hannah, daughter of Thomas and Martha Hazard of Portsmouth. Thomas was a ship carpenter by trade and had come from Wales to Boston about 1635. In the Hutchinson contention, he was driven from Massachusetts and settled on Aquidneck.[53]

Stephen's son **THOMAS WILLCOX** married Martha Hazard, daughter of Robert and Mary Brownell Hazard, and granddaughter of the above Thomas Hazard, so they were cousins. This was not very uncommon in the very early colonies since there were only a few English families.

Martha's mother Mary Brownell (daughter of Thomas and Anne Brownell) was born in 1639 in Braintree, Massachusetts, and died 12 January 1739/49 in South Kingston, Rhode Island.

> "Mary Brownell Hazard's obituary in *The Boston Gazette* for February 12, 1739, stated that she died in her 100th year, had 500 children, grandchildren, and great-grandchildren, of whom 205 were still living. It also says she was the grandmother of George Hazard, the late Deputy Governor of Rhode Island that "she was accounted a very useful gentlewoman, both to poor and rich and particularly among sick persons for her skill and judgment, which she did gratis."

Thomas and 17 others bought 2000 acres of vacant lands sold by the Assembly. He and Martha had nine children.

ABRAHAM WILLCOX married Lydia Harrington. Her great-great-grandfather Edward Wighman was one of three people executed for witchcraft on 11 April 1612 in Litchfield, England, said to be the last person burned at the stake in England. A great-grandfather was the physician Gysbert Op Dyck (Gilbert Updike), born in Wesel, Germany, who immigrated to America in 1635. Gilbert married Katherine Smith, a daughter of Richard Smith (born in 1596 in Gloucestershire, England, and died in 1666 in Wickford, Narragansett, Rhode Island). In 1645 Gilbert signed a treaty of peace with the sachems of Mohicans, Hackensacks and other tribes. He and seven others were chosen to deliberate on Indian Affairs and Safety. In 1657, he was the Commander of Fort Good Hope, and subsequently he was the Assessor in charge of collecting a tenth of crops or "quit rents" from farmers on Long Island.[54] Quit rents were fees paid in lieu of required labor.

Abraham and Lydia had 13 children, of whom the second is our ancestor.

JOB WILLCOX (1743-1808) served as a corporal in the Rhode Island militia during the Revolutionary War.[55] He and his wife Mary Gates Willcox had twelve children, of whom their tenth child, Gates Willcox, is our ancestor.

In addition to Job, there are many others of the ancestors of Harry Wilcox who served in the American Revolution and the earlier conflicts:

☆ ☆ ☆

Ancestors who served in the American Revolution

Robert Hazard (1635-1710) Military Commander of
   Portsmouth, Rhode Island, during King Philip's War.
   He is a grandfather of Abraham Willcox.

Job Willcox (1742-1808) served in the American
   Revolutionary War 1781-1784 as a Corporal, Rhode Island
   unit under Capt. David Harrington in Colonel Smith's
   Regiment[56]

John Philip Boehm (1747-1816) American Revolutionary War
   as Lt. Col. He is a grandfather of David Kramm.

Peter Withington III (1732-1777) served in the American
   Revolutionary War as a Captain commanding a company
   in the 12th Pennsylvania Regiment of the Continental
   Line. He died in Reading Berks Co., Pennsylvania, after
   becoming sick near Philadelphia, Pennsylvania, during the
   American Revolutionary War. He is a grandfather of Anna
   Himmelreich.

Jacob Kram I (d. 1798)
   - served in the Revolutionary War in the Militia Units of

Northampton Co.
- served in the 6th Class of the 4th Company Militia, 4th Battalion (1782).
- served in the 4th Class of the 4th Company Militia, 1st Battalion (1783).[57]

Jacob Kram II (1763/1765-1800)
- Served in the 2nd Class of the 4th Company, 4th Battalion of Militia, (1782), commanded by Lt Col. Philip Boehm (his father-in-law to be)
- Served in the 2nd Class of the 2nd Company, 2nd Battalion of Militia (1785)[58]

Peter Himmelreich (1756/7-1828) was one of the Hessian soldiers who joined with the Americans in fighting the British in the American Revolution. He married Mary Withington, daughter of Peter Withington III, and is the father of Anna Himmelreich.[59]

☆ ☆ ☆

In addition to these there are several brothers, uncles, and cousins that answered the call for military service.

GATES WILLCOX was a prominent lumberman in Williamsport, when it was one of the centers of the lumber industry. He married three times and had seven children. It was during his lifetime that the Willcoxes dropped the double-L to Wilcox.

He built the first grist mill in McDonough County, New York, in 1808, on the outlet of the Genegantslet Lake. A grist mill is for milling corn or wheat into flour. "This mill was subsequently replaced by a stone one from the same man."[60]

Lewis D. Burdick, a grandson of Mary Wilcox Lewis who married Clark Lewis (a brother of Prudence Lewis Wilcox, first wife of Gates Wilcox) published this account of the mill in 1898:

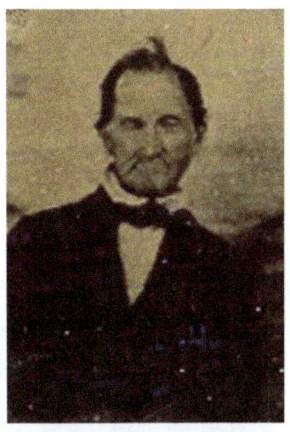

Gates Wilcox, tintype
Inscribed on the back: "Presented to Scott Willcox by his brother in law Edgar Cole. Scott, keep this as long as you live."

203

"For a mile below the outlet of the lake the stream, although not large, is a most attractive one. This mile of the stream has played an important part in the history of the town. Before the days of electricity and steam, its waterpower sites were regarded of great value. The old stone mill is one of the oldest landmarks. The builder was Gates Wilcox, three quarters of a century ago.

An old history of Chenango records that Samuel Lewis came from Voluntown, Rhode Island, in 1803, with covered wagons to Preston, New York, starting March 1st and arriving April 1st. This Samuel Lewis and three of his brothers were soldiers in the Revolution. His daughter Prudence married Gates Wilcox and moved to McDonough and afterwards moved [135 miles southwest] to Wellsboro, Pennsylvania, where both he and his wife died. Few of the oldest inhabitants now remember him, but the old stone mill is still an object of interest and value.

There is one more mark of his sojourn here. An infant's grave in the cemetery has a brown stone slab with the inscription "Sarah Ann, daughter of Gates Wilcox died August 23, 1826, aged one year, six months and eighteen days.

Come parents all with us behold
The tombstone at the head

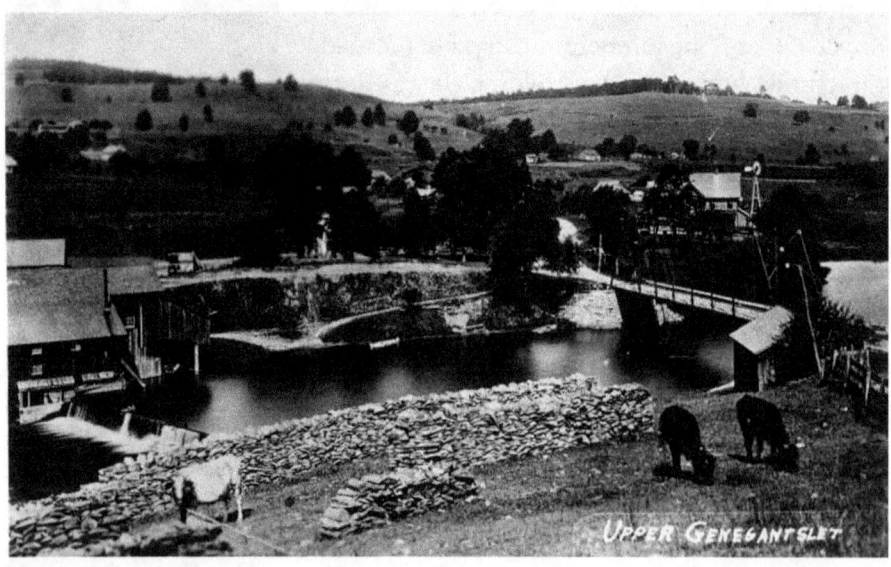

Mill built 1808 by Gates Wilcox at Upper Genegantslet, New York

Of this our little infant's grave

That rests among the dead."[61]

The town of Wellsboro, Pennsylvania, was incorporated in 1830. Five years later, in 1835, Gates Wilcox was listed as the head of one of the 59 families living within its limits. In 1835 he built a saw mill on Pine creek in western Lycoming County, Pennsylvania. Pine Creek flows from Wellsboro southward to the Susquehanna River.

In 1838 Gates Willcox built another Saw Mill, this time along the west side of the Loyalsock creek, near Montoursville, Pennsylvania, which also flows to the Susquehanna River at Williamsport.[62]

The lumber mill was torn down in 1905.

"History of the Mill

"One by one the saw mills are becoming fewer in number around Williamsport and the nearby towns along the river that only a few years ago depended principally on the lumber business for the thrift [income]. What has been known for many years as the Fisher Mills, on the west side of Loyalsock creek near Montoursville, will soon be no more. The big structure is being torn down.

"Site Long Occupied by Saw Mills

"The first building on the site of the present Fisher mill was a water power plant to prepare lumber for market. It was erected in the year 1838 by Gates Wilcox. At the time Wilcox sawed lumber and timber from rafts floated down the river and towed from the river or canal to the mill. Afterwards a more modern mill on the site of the old water mill was operated by different owners, including Wilcox, Smith, F.S. and W. S. Fisher, and the Loyalsock Lumber Company, until the property was purchased by the Emery Lumber Company, about [1899]."[63]

Gates died in 1866 near Wellsboro, Tioga county, Pennsylvania.

LEWIS GATES WILCOX was the eldest son of Gates and Prudence Lewis Wilcox. He married Margaret P. Martin and was given a parcel of ten acres of land in Montoursville, Pennsylvania, as her dowry from her father. Lewis Gates and Margaret had seven children, six boys and one girl, who are pictured in this book on page 10. Their son James Martin Wilcox is our ancestor. Lewis died in 1861 in Williamsport, leaving his wife to raise their young children. Their youngest son, Lewis Gates Wilcox, Jr, was born 6 1/2 months after his father's death.

No. 740,962.

PATENTED OCT. 6, 1903.

L. G. WILCOX.
PENCIL SHARPENER.
APPLICATION FILED JAN. 26, 1903.

NO MODEL.

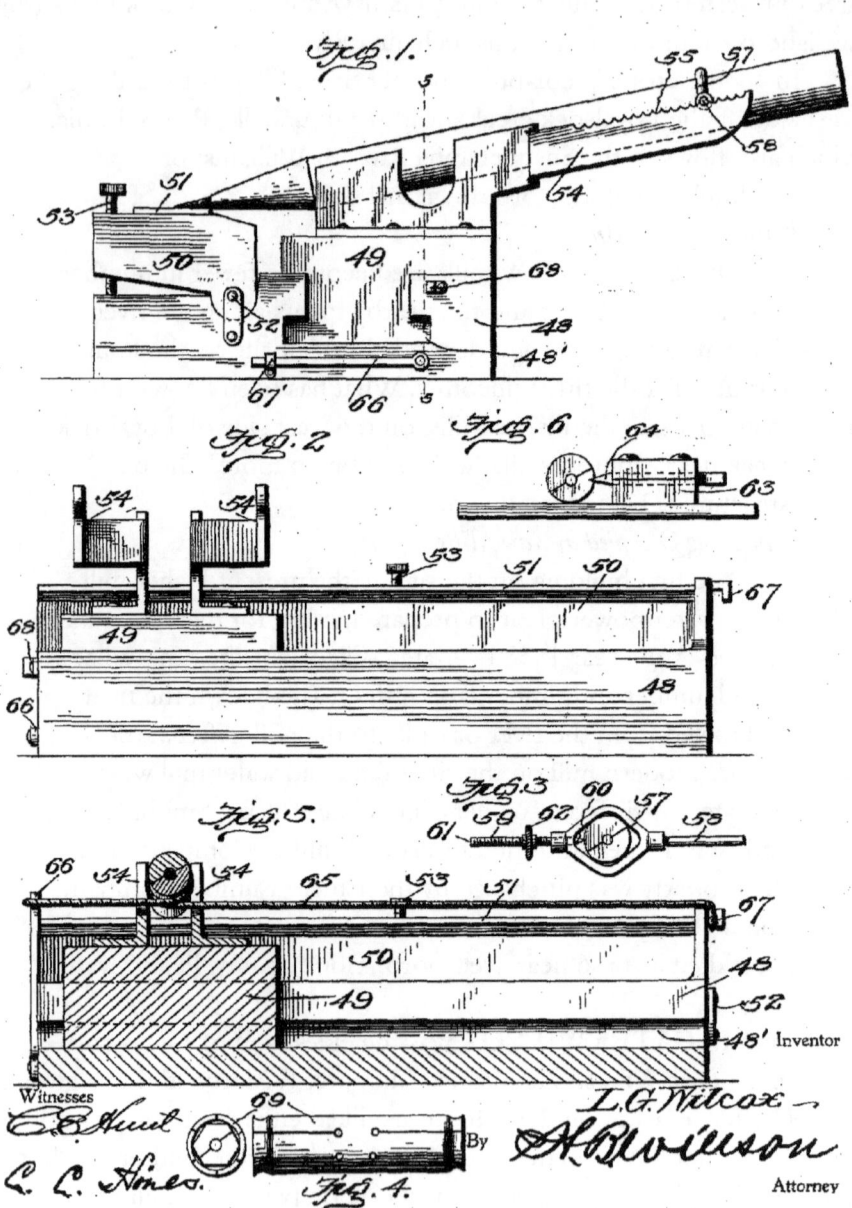

Pencil-Sharpener. Figures from the Letter of Patent filed January 1903,
by Lewis Gates Wilcox Jr, Mechanical Engineer.

Lewis Gates Jr., our uncle, completed a college education and was a mechanical engineer and inventor. He was the head of the Department of Inspection for the Railroad commission of New York. Among his more notable patents is one for a mechanical pencil sharpener, filed in 1903 when he was living in Philadelphia.[64]

"The purpose of my invention is to provide a device by which unfinished pencils from which the wood has been trimmed by a sharpener may be conveniently and expeditiously finished or painted." The device may be used to sharpen the point to a "wedge form with parallel sides," or to form a long round point. The numbers in the following description refer to the illustrations (Figures 1 through 5) enclosed with the patent application and shown on page 206.

"When it is desired to form a long round point, the pencil is placed in the holder 57, and the spindle 59 reversed to bring its blunt end 61 into position to bear upon and form a bearing against which the pencil in the holder may turn. A cord 65 is then looped around the pencil, the pencil placed in position between the two flanges 54, and one end of the cord secured to a pivoted bar 66 and the other end to a hook 67 on the opposite end of the support from said bar, as indicated in Fig. 5 [page 206]. By then sliding the block 49 the cord 65 will alternately rotate the pencil in opposite directions, thus causing the point end thereof to be dressed down to a round or tapered surface by the file 51."

JAMES MARTIN WILCOX was a butcher in Williamsport, working for at least two different grocers in his career. He married Ada Virginia Kramm of Limestoneville. The couple had three children, of whom Harry Wilcox is the subject of this book. See pages 10 and following.

Generations in America

I.   EDWARD WILLCOX

Born February 12, 1602/04. Edward was the son of Daniel (Danyell Willcocke) (born about 1565 in Lincolnshire, England) and Esabel (Isabel) __. Daniel died in 1605 in South Elkington, Lincolnshire, England

Edward died before 13 April 1660, age 57.[65]

    MARRIED twice:

    FIRST to Mary __ in England. Mary died in June 1630 in Croft, Lincolnshire, England. She was buried 7 June 1630 in Croft.

    SECOND to Susana Thomson. They were married in Orby, Lincolnshire, England, on 12 May 1631. She was the daughter of Amos Thompson and presumably his wife Carynthaphuch Jackson.[66]

    CHILDREN:

      Stephen, b. 1633. See II. below

      Daniel, b. 1635

      Mary who married Eber Sherman, son of Phillip Sherman

II.   STEPHEN WILLCOX

Born 1633 in Croft, Lincolnshire, England

Died before 6 Feb 1689.

    MARRIED Hannah Hazard in 1658 in Portsmouth, Westerly, Rhode Island. Hannah was a daughter of Thomas and Martha Hazard.

    NINE CHILDREN:

    Edward, Thomas, Daniel, William, Stephen, Jeremiah, Hannah, Elizabeth, Bethia

III.   THOMAS WILLCOX

Born 18 February 1663/4 near Westerly, Rhode Island

Died about 1726 near Exeter, Washington County, Rhode Island.

    MARRIED Martha Hazard in 1710. Martha was born about 1668 at Portsmouth, Rhode Island, and died 9 January 1753. She was a daughter of Robert and Mary Brownell Hazard

NINE CHILDREN:
Sons Robert, Stephen, Jeffrey, Thomas, <u>Abraham</u>, George, and
  Edward, and daughters Hannah Place and Investory.

IV. ABRAHAM WILLCOX

Born between 1695 and 1706
Died between 1800 and 1810, likely in Washington County, Rhode Island.
  MARRIED Lydia Harrington on 5 June 1739 in Exeter,
    Washington County, Rhode Island. Lydia was born about
    1723 and may have died 23 May 1807. Lydia was a daughter
    of Job Harrington and Alice Wightman.
  Lydia's father was Job Harrington, the son of Job Harrington
    and Martha Elizabeth Weeden. Her father's great-grandfather
    was Benjamin Harrington, who was born in England in 1618.
    He was in Providence, Rhode Island, in 1646 and in Lynn,
    Massachusetts, in 1647. In 1648, he married Elizabeth White
    and they had 9 or 10 children.
  Abraham and Lydia had 13 CHILDREN:
John, <u>Job</u>, Martha, Abraham, Isaac, Robert, Alice, Jacob,
  Ebenezer, Hannah, Larkin, Whitman, Lydia

V. JOB WILLCOX

Born 4 February 1742/3 in Exeter, Washington County, Rhode Island
Died in January 1808 in Oxford, Chenango County, New York.
He served in the American Revolution.
  MARRIED Mary Gates in 1771 in Rhode Island. Mary Gates
    was born 11 July 1754 in Preston, Windham County,
    Connecticut, and died 22 October 1832 in Chenango County,
    New York
  They are buried in the Wilcox Cemetery on Tyner Road in
    Chenango County, New York
  CHILDREN born at Exeter:
Asa, April 7, 1772
Nathan, August 16, 1774
Esther, August 20, 1776
Simon, September 3, 1778
Eunice, August 17, 1780
Job, March 12, 1782

Harrington, September 22, 1783
Mary, August 22, 1785
Prudence, April 2, 1787
<u>Gates</u>, September 21, 1790
Hannah, October 7, 1794
Thurston, November 2, 1796

VI.   GATES WILLCOX

Born 21 September 1790 in Exeter, Washington County, Rhode Island
MARRIED three times:

(1) Prudence Lewis, born 17 August 1791 and died 21 March 1835, age 43, following an illness of several months. They had four children:

<u>Lewis Gates</u>, Margaret, Sarah Ann, and Daniel.
Prudence Lewis Wilcox is buried in Academy Hill Cemetery, in Wellsboro, Tioga County, Pennsylvania.[67]

(2) Elizabeth Mathers in 1835, likely in Pennsylvania. They had one son

Dewitt Clinton Wilcox (1837-1908).
Elizabeth was born about 1795 and died 4 April 1845 in Montoursville, Lycoming County, Pennsylvania. Elizabeth was a daughter of John Mathers and Jane McKeever.

Dewitt Clinton Wilcox was born 29 March 1837 in Williamsport, Lycoming county, Pennsylvania, and died 26 November 1908 in Emporia, Lyon County, Kansas. He was married in December 1857 in Bradford County, Pennsylvania to Ellen Gay, daughter of Gilbert and Lucinda Gay.

Dewitt and Ellen had three children:

a. Ray Wilcox, born 1853 in Pennsylvania and died after 1899, probably in Kansas or west.

b. Lynn Gay Wilcox was born 21 March 1859 in Jamestown, NY and died 30 January 1924 in Topeka, Kansas. Lynn married Annie M. Jones. The *Topeka Daily State Journal* reported 30 January 1924, "L.G. Wilcox, 65, father of Clinton T. Wilcox, of the Topeka Wholesale Grocery company died this morning in his apartment in the Throop Hotel. Mr Wilcox was born in Jamestown,

New York, March 21, 1859, and came to Kansas February 22, 1879, settling in Emporia, where he was in the retail grocery business until 1910 when he came to Topeka. He has been retired since that time. Besides his son he is survived by a sister, Mrs. P. J. Heilman of Guthrie, Oklahoma. Mrs. Wilcox died last August and his only daughter, Mrs. Edna Wilcox Wiley, died less than three years ago."

c. Nellie A. Wilcox was born 31 October 1862 in Jamestown, New York, and died 26 July 1946 in Guthrie, Logan County, Oklahoma. Nellie married Phillip J. Heilman.

"Mr. Heilman was born January 18 1853 in Bermersheimer, Germany, youngest son of Hans Valentine Heilman, a burgomaster and church elder. He left his family to come to America at age 11, and joined an uncle already in the U.S., settling in Tifflin, Ohio. He spoke only German and never went to school. He worked for his uncle until about the age of 17 at which time he and a boy friend ran off to Kansas, settling in Emporia, where he eventually had a harness business. He married Nellie Wilcox January 27, 1881. They had two children, Earl Clinton (1881) and Norma Louise (1889) born in Emporia. In 1890 he sold his business and boarded a train for Galveston, Texas. On board he heard people talking about Guthrie and the land rush of '89. He got off the train in Guthrie, liked it, and decided to stay.

"At that time it was only a tent city with many outlaws and saloons. He returned to Kansas to move his family. He began in the harness business again, but because of pending law suits his first business at First and Oklahoma Streets was under Nellie's name. He owned much land around Guthrie, as well as places of business. His business was called the "Guthrie Tent, Awning and Harness Co," which he ran until his death in 1931.

"He hired a well-known architect, Joseph Foucard, to construct his home which was started about 1893 and completed in 1895. The stones were hand cut in the street. Interior walnut woodwork was carved on the premises and the arched windows were composed of tiny handcut pieces, placed side by side. Some of the fancy work was shipped from Pennsylvania.

"He was very afraid of storms so his home was built to be tornado-proof of massive stone construction with 18" thick walls. It was the first stone and brick home built in Oklahoma Territory, and was of Gothic Victorian design.

"Governors and Senators were among their many friends. Many lavish parties were held at the Heilman home, with dances held on the large front porch. He died in the home he loved so well in September 1931. His son, Earl, took over his business.

"One day during the Depression in the 1930's he came home, took two nickels out of his pocket, and told his wife that was all he took in all day at the harness shop. Yet for a man of no education he owned a lot of property and built one of the most lavish homes in Guthrie, which still stands in very good shape."[68]

(3) Gates married Rebecca Durflinger, widow of Andrew Gamble, who was also in the lumbering business in Tioga and Lycoming counties. Rebecca was born in 1814 and died 21 April 1869. Gates Willcox died in 1866 near Wellsboro, Tioga County, Pennsylvania. Gates and Rebecca are buried in the West Franklin Cemetery in Bradford County, Pennsylvania.

Rebecca and Andrew Gamble had five children: Elizabeth, Mannel, George, Mercy and Thomas Andrew Gamble.[69]

Thomas Andrew Gamble became a physician practicing in East Troy, New York, where he established a lucrative business "and stands among the most successful practitioners in the county." Dr. Gamble married Almeda, daughter of Enoch and Lucy (Snyder) Lloyd of Lycoming County.

Rebecca and Gates Willcox had two CHILDREN:

(a) Prudence Wilcox was born 1848 in Williamsport, Pennsylvania, and died 1916 in San Francisco, California. She married Edgar Cole before 1870.

(b) Winfield Scott Wilcox was born 14 March 1851 in Pennsylvania and died 14 September 1915. He married Emma __. They had two children:

1. Lula Wilcox, born 1873
2. Harry G. Wilcox, born October 1880, who married first Lura E. __, Their daughter Eloise was born in New Jersey. Harry G. married second Sue A. Smith. Their daughter was Jane Wilcox, born in New York.

VII. LEWIS GATES WILCOX

Born in 1823 in New York and died 25 August 1861 in Pennsylvania MARRIED Margaret P. Martin on 18 July 1846 in Lycoming County, Pennsylvania.

Margaret was born in 1828 in Pennsylvania and died 31 March 1885. Family stories cite Margaret as the youngest of the 13 children of Robert Martin and Sarah Day. Her father Robert Martin was born between 1775 and 1780, possibly in New Jersey or Pennsylvania, and died before 1847 in Lycoming County, Pennsylvania. Her mother Sarah Day was born in 1783, likely in Pennsylvania, and died between 1860 and 1870. For more information on the Martin family, see page 252.

CHILDREN:
1. Robert Bruce Wilcox was born in May 1847 and died 8 Sept 1919. He married Mary F. Vollmer about 27 Mar 1878 in Williamsport, Lycoming Co., Pennsylvania. Mary was born in Dec 1844 in Maryland and died 20 Jan 1940 in Williamsport. Robert Bruce was a dairy farmer and made his home deliveries by horse drawn wagon. See photo page 72.
They had SIX CHILDREN:
a. Minnie D. Wilcox was born 12 Jan 1880 and died 7 Sept 1968 in Caldwell, Essex Co., New Jersey. She married Alfonso Chandler Von Dreele, then divorced. He was born 15 Apr 1882 in Lycoming County, Pennsylvania, and died in Nov 1971 in Shelton, Fairfield Co., Connecticut. They had 4 children:
1. Nellie Francis Von Dreele, born 17 June 1902 in Williamsport and died 27 July 1932 in Bloomfield, New Jersey.
2. Bruce Franklin Von Dreele Wilcox, born 26 Nov 1903 in Williamsport and died in Feb 1974 in Benson Johnston Co., North Carolina. During World War II, Bruce was working for the military in Washington, D.C.,

and was concerned that the anti-German sentiment in America during WWII, might jeopardize his employment, so he legally changed his name to Wilcox.

    3. Carl Wilcox Von Dreele, born 19 Oct 1905 in Williamsport and died 12 Oct 1988 in Arden, Delaware.

    4. Grace Elmira Von Dreele, born 7 Sept 1907 in Philadelphia and died in November 1979 in Ocean Grove, Monmouth County, New Jersey.

b. Clarence Lee Wilcox was born 15 Aug 1882 and died 21 Feb 1964 in Williamsport, Pennsylvania. He married Rachel Harris. They had 3 children:

    1. Robert Harris Wilcox, born in 1903 in Williamsport and died in Feb 1973 in Warren, Pennsylvania. He married Gladys Mines. They had 2 sons.

    2. Caroline Emaline Wilcox, born 20 Sept 1905 and died 9 Mar 1997 in Williamsport, Pennsylvania. She married Frank Edward Frey. They had 3 children.

    3. Martha Frances Wilcox, born 7 Aug 1907 and died in Feb 1986. She married Gerald Fenderson.

c. Frederick Lewis Wilcox was born 14 Jul 1884 and died Feb 1966 in Williamsport, Pennsylvania.

d. Margaret A. Wilcox was born in 7 Jun 1886 and died 12 Nov 1942. She married Louis Bolle.

e. Frank Raymond Wilcox was born 20 Jan 1888 and died 12 Jun 1928 in Williamsport, Pennsylvania. He married Sarah M. Fry. They had four children:

    1. Mary Evelyn Wilcox, born 15 Sept 1918 and died 2 Feb 2008. She married Ronald L. Weigle.

    2. Lewis Gates Wilcox, born 12 May 1921 and died 27 Aug 1992 in Riverside, California. He married Helen Patterson.

    3. Ella Bernadine Wilcox, born 9 Mar 1923 and died 28 Feb 2000 in Victorville, California. She married Michael Anthony Catrambone.[70]
    They had 6 children.

    4. Sylvester Eugene Wilcox, born 11 June 1925 and 13 January 1987 in Pomana, California.

f. Caroline Virginia Wilcox was born 7 Sept 1892 and Dec 1893.

2. Sarah "Sade" Virginia Wilcox was born 6 Jul 1849 and died 20 Jul 1922. She married Peter Follmer on 2 Nov 1875.

Peter Follmer was a widower. He first married Lavina Metzger.

They had:

    a. Alice R. Follmer, born in 1861 and died 22 June 1927

    b. Annie L. Follmer, born 8 Sept 1862 and died 7 Apr 1935

    c. Alva E. Follmer, born 6 July 1867 and died 6 Feb 1934

    d. Estella Follmer, born in July 1869.

Sarah "Sade" Virginia Wilcox and Peter Follmer had four children:

    e. William Wilcox Follmer, born 1877 and died in 1902

    f. Margaret Emma Follmer, born in Aug 1878 and died 15 Aug 1967 in Danville, PA. She married Harry H. Wilson in 1904.

    g. Mabel Follmer, born 9 Mar 1882 and died in Jan 1972. She married Charles W. Heiney in 1904.

    h. Clinton Lee Follmer, born 12 Feb 1889 and died 9 Jan 1963. He married Katherine Vera Aldridge.

3. Adolphus Lee Wilcox was born 17 Jan 1852 and died 1 Jan 1922 in Chicago. Illinois. He married Jane A. ___. They had a daughter:

    a. Kittie D. Wilcox was born 2 Nov 1883 in Maucelena, Michigan. She married Leo H. Waters 12 Jan 1904 in Benton Harbor, Berrien Co. Mchigan.

    They had two children:

    1. Jane K. Waters

    2. Richard Waters, born 12 July 1909 and died 24 June 1979 in Benton Harbor, Michigan

    Kittie D. Wilcox also married James R. Brown and a Mr. Fletcher.

4. James Martin Wilcox married Ada Virginia Kramm (See below.)

5. Daniel Clinton Wilcox was born in 1858 and died 24 Apr 1929 in Berwick, PA. He married Sarah A. "Verna" Creasy. She was born Jan 1860 and died 22 Aug 1948. They had no children.[71]

6. William A. Wilcox was born in 1860 and died 12 Dec 1863

7. Lewis Gates Wilcox Jr. was born 14 Mar 1862 and 11 Feb 1925 in Philadelphia, Pennsylvania. Lewis Gates Jr. was actually born 6 ½ months after the death of his father.

VIII.   JAMES MARTIN WILCOX

James Martin Wilcox was born 4 Mar 1854 in Lycoming Co. Pennsylvania, and died 4 Feb 1911 in Williamsport, Lycoming Co., Pennsylvania.

MARRIED Ada Virginia Kramm on 14 Dec 1880 in Limestoneville, Montour Co., Pennsylvania. She was born 10 Nov 1856 in Limestoneville, Montour Co., Pennsylvania. She was the daughter of William Kramm and Margaret Billmeyer. They had four children, all born in Limestoneville, Pennsylvania:

1. Warren Kramm Wilcox, born 18 Jan 1882 and died 30 Dec 1954 in Williamsport, Pennsylvania. He never married.[72]
2. Adolphus Lee Wilcox, born 13 July 1884 and died 31 July 1892.
3. <u>Harry Hammond Wilcox.</u> See below
4. Verna Margaret Wilcox, born 14 Apr 1892 and 31 Oct 1918 in Williamsport, Pennsylvania. She married John Grenfall Emminger on 18 Sept 1916 at Erie Ave Baptist Church in Williamsport, Lycoming Co. Pennsylvania. John was the son of Letitia and Daniel Eminger.[73] They had two children born in Williamsport, Pennsylvania:
   a. Jane Ann Emminger, born 28 Oct 1917 and died 15 Jan 1987 in Erie, Pennsylvania. She married first Harry A. Morgan. They had a daughter:
   1. Verna Margaret Morgan born 1937 and died in 1997. Jane married second Howard H. Caldwell. They had a daughter,
   2. Sally Esther Caldwell.
   b. Daniel J. Emminger, born 20 Oct 1918 and died 10 Dec 1981 in Clark, Mercer Co., Pennsylvania. He married Mary Mikulas.

John accepted a position with American Steel and Wire in Sharon, Pennsylvania, as bookkeeper and company telegrapher. John later moved to Titusville to accept a position as Physical Director of the YMCA until 1928 when he took a position with the Kewanee Oil Company as bookkeeper. He was a secretary and song leader of the Kiwanis Service Club in Titusville. During this time he served as high school basketball coach and later officiated in both basketball and football.

John remarried Grace C. Vanderschot in 1920. They had one daughter. Mrs. Grace Emminger died in 1935.

c. Annetta Emminger, born 11 Apr 1922 and died 14 Jan 2004 in Langhorne, Bucks Co., Pennsylvania. Annetta married Frank Hesch of Warminster, Pennsylvania. Frank was born 7 Jun 1919 and died 13 Apr 2008 in Langhorne, Bucks Co., Pennsylvania.

After the death of Grace, John married Alice E. Jacobson of Titusville. In 1947 he was transferred to Tulsa, Oklahoma, to the offices of the Kewanee Oil company where he served as chief accountant until his retirement in 1957. He was a member of the finance and music committee of the White City Baptist Church of Tulsa where he sang in the choir. At his death in 1964 he was survived by his wife Alice, three children, six grandchilren, and two great-grandchildren.

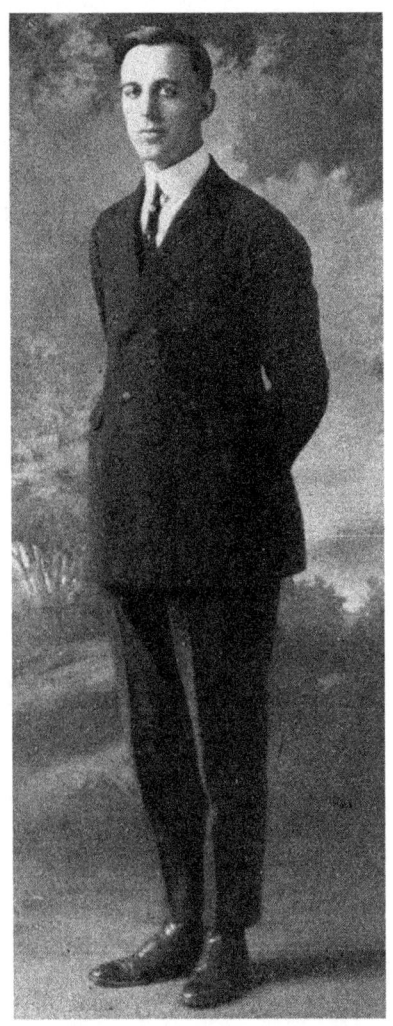

Basketball Coach John G. Emminger, from *The Optimist*, Titusville School Yearbook, 1923.

IX. HARRY HAMMOND WILCOX I

Harry Hammond Wilcox born 25 June 1887 in Limestoneville, Montour Co., Pennsylvania, and died 12 Aug 1943 in Dearborn, Wayne Co., Michigan.

MARRIED Hattie Estelle Richner on 24 Aug 1911 in Williamsport, Lycoming Co., Pennsylvania. Hattie was born 11 June 1891 in

Williamsport, Pennsylvania, and died 23 June 1977 in Memphis, Shelby Co., Tennessee.

Harry and Hattie had 3 CHILDREN:

1. Verna Kathryn Wilcox was born 21 Aug 1912 in Williamsport, Pennsylvania, and died 13 Feb 1998 in Superior twp. Washtenaw Co., Michigan. She married Meredith Walter Alair. They had one son.
2. Harry Hammond Wilcox Jr. was born 31 May 1918 and died 22 Jan 2010 in Memphis, Shelby Co., Tennessee. He married Dorothy June Freed on 21 June 1941. Harry Jr and June had three children. At his death he was survived by three children, 8 grandchildren, and 15 great-grandchildren.
3. Lewis Richner Wilcox, born 21 Feb 1921 in Pennsaken twp. Camden, New Jersey, and died 1 Mar 1921 in Merchantville, Camden, New Jersey.

To map your descent from these ancestors, please see page 195.

THE KRAMM FAMILY

Harry Hammond Wilcox 1887-1943	m.	Hattie Estelle Richner 1891-1977
James Martin Wilcox 1854-1911	m.	Ada Virginia Kramm 1856-1934
William Kramm (1823-1898)	m.	Margaret Billmeyer (1846-1902)
David Kramm (1793-1882)	m.	Maria Brunner (1800-1872)
Jacob Kram II (1863/5-1800)	m.	Catherine Boehm (d. 1769)
Jacob Kram I (d. 1798)	m.	Barbara ____

I.   JACOB KRAM I

Jacob Kram I was born in Germany. He came to America before 1789, and served in the American Revolutionary War.
- served in the Militia Units of Northampton County.
- served in the 6th Class of the 4th Company Militia, 4th Battalion (1782).
- served in the 4th Class of the 4th Company Militia, 1st Battalion (1783).[74]

He married Barbara __. He died in 1798. After Jacob died, his children were put into a series of Guardian Homes.

Jacob and Barbara had at least one son, Jacob.

II.   JACOB KRAM II

Jacob Kram II was probably born in Germany about 1763 or 1765. He is shown in the census records for 1790 as living in Lower Saucon township, Northumberland County, Pennsylvania. He served in the

American Revolution:

Jacob Kram II (1763/1765-1800)
- Served in the 2nd Class of the 4th Company, 4th Batallion of Militia, (1782), commanded by Lt Col. Philip Boehm (his father-in-law to be)
- Served in the 2nd Class of the 2nd Company, 2nd Batalion of Militia (1785)[75]

He married Catherine Boehm about 1784. Catherine was the daughter of John Philip Boehm, his commanding officer in the Revolution.

Jacob died 1 May 1800. After Jacob's death, Catherine remarried to George or Henry Roseberger in 1806, and had two additional children by her second husband.

CHILDREN of Catherine Boehm and Jacob Kram are:
1. Mary Magdalena Kram, born 1785
2. Susannah Kram, born 1786. Married Rinker.
3. Elizabeth Kram, born 1788. Probably married Dill. Elizabeth was baptized 11 Apr 1804, Lower Saucon, Northampton Co. Pennsylvania, sponsored her grandmother Barbara Boehm, wife of Philip Boehm Sr.
4. Jacob Kram III, born 1791
5. David Kramm, born 26 January 1793, Lower Saucon Township, Northampton C., Pennsylvania. Died 28 Sept 1882.
6. Joseph Kram, born about 1795. Married Maria Mill 1 Sept 1816.
7. Samuel Kram, born about 1798. Married Hannah Buckwalter.

CHILDREN of Catherine Boehm and Mr. Roseberger are:
8. Nancy Roseberger
9. Elizabeth Roseberger

For more information on Catherine Boehm and her antecedents, see page 250.

III.   DAVID KRAMM

David Kramm was born 26 Jan 1793 in Lower Saucon, Northampton Co. Pennsylvania, and died 28 Sept 1882. He is a son of Jacob Kram and Catherine Boehm.

David married Maria Brunner 16 Jan 1821. Maria Brunner was born

13 Feb 1800 in Lehigh Co. Pennsylvania, and died 4 Sept 1872.
They had 14 CHILDREN:

1. Samuel Kramm, born 24 Aug 1822 and died 9 Mar 1887. He married Mary Ann Derr.
2. William Kramm, born 3 Oct 1823 and died 2 Sept 1898. (See below)
3. Edward B. Kramm, born 16 Nov 1824 and died after 1896. He married Elizabeth Woolever.
   a. their son Harry Hammond Kramm, both 1868, married Carrie N. Geise in 1888. Harry was in the lumber business with his father. They branched out into bicycles in 1890, which became their main business by 1891. See photos page 5.
4. Sarah Ann Kramm, born 9 Mar 1826 and died 30 Aug 1905. She married Charles Ravert.
5. Maria Kramm, born 10 Oct 1827 and died 9 Dec 1899. She married Martin Billmeyer II (1821-1863).
6. Eayan Kramm, born 10 Aug 1829 and died 20 Nov 1901
7. Matilda Kramm, born 19 Feb 1831 and died 20 Nov 1901. She married Charles Billmeyer (1827-1891).
8. Ephraim Kramm, born 27 May 1832 and died after 1900. He married Anna Maria Garbutt.
9. Tavilla Kramm, born 25 Apr 1834 and died in 1920's. She married Daniel Koch.
10. Reuben H. Kramm, born 24 Oct 1835 and died 4 Aug 1915. He married Anna Maria Kemmerer.
11. Christianna C. Kramm, born 27 Oct 1837 and died 1928. She married Joseph Bird.
12. Susan Elizabeth Kramm, born 23 Sept 1839 and died 1909. She married William Hunsinger.
13. Alavesta Kramm, born 8 Aug 1842 and died 3 Nov 1890. She married Thomas J. Hillard.
14. David Jacob Kramm, born 5 Sept 1844 and died 13 Dec 1862 at Fredericksburg, Virginia, during a Civil War battle The 10 living children of David Kramm attended the Golden Wedding Anniversary celebration in 1896 for William Kramm and Margaret Billmeyer. See the photo on page 17.

David, Kramm, 1881

IV.   WILLIAM KRAMM

William Kramm was born 3 October 1823 and died 2 September 1898. William Kramm and Margaret Billmeyer were married 5 Feb 1846 in Liberty twp., Montour Co., Pennsylvania. She was a daughter of George Billmeyer I and Anna Himmelreich (daughter of Peter Himmelreich and Mary Withington). Margaret Billmeyer was born 13 Nov 1819 and died 13 Sept 1902. They had four children:

- a. Anna Matilda Kramm, born 11 Jun 1847 and died 28 May 1931. Married Kaufman.
- b. Francis Uranah Kramm, born 5 Jan 1855 and died 24 Feb 1857
- c. Ada Virginia Kramm, born 10 Nov 1856 and died 30 Aug 1934. Married Wilcox.
- d. William Hammond Kramm, born 16 July 1859 and died 6 Feb 1905. Married Huldah Fisher. "W. Ham Kramm, postmaster and merchant at Limestoneville and well known in Milton, died at his home on Tuesday night, about 11 o'clock from the effects of a paralytic stroke which he sustained about three weeks ago. He was from from his late home on Friday, at 10:30 o'clock. Internment was made at Milton in Harmony Cemetery. He was in his "fourth-seventh" [47th] year and is survived by his wife and two sisters, Mrs. Kauffman of Limestoneville and Mrs. Wilcox of Williamsport."72. We are extremely grateful for the photo album of Warren Wilcox, which he passed to his nephew, Harry Wilcox Jr." on page 273[76]

The large family photo taken on the wedding day of William Hammond Kramm and Huldah Fisher in 1881 is believed to contain the only photo of David Kramm, the groom's grandfather, shown on page 221. It certainly would be near the last, having been taken the year before David Kramm died.

V.   ADA VIRGINIA KRAMM

Ada Virginia Kramm was born 10 Nov 1856 in Limestoneville, Montour Co., Pennsylvania. She was the daughter of William Kramm and Margaret Billmeyer.

She married James Martin Wilcox on 14 Dec 1880 in Limestoneville, Montour Co., Pennsylvania.

James Martin Wilcox was born 4 Mar 1854 in Lycoming Co., Pennsylvania, and died 4 Feb 1911 in Williamsport, Lycoming Co., Pennsylvania.

They had four children, all born in Limestoneville, Pennsylvania.

For more information, see Wilcox section, page 216.

THE BILLMEYER FAMILY

Harry Hammond Wilcox 1887-1943	m.	Hattie Estelle Richner 1891-1977
James Martin Wilcox 1854-1911	m.	Ada Virginia Kramm 1856-1934
William Kramm (1823-1898)	m.	Margaret Billmeyer (1846-1902)
George Billmeyer (1779-1853)	m.	Anna Himmelreich (1788-1870)
Andrew Billmeyer (1756-1825)	m.	Fannie Brunner (1758-1823)
Johann Leonhardt Bihlmeier (b. 1706)	m.	Anna _____

Our thanks to Harold Robinson for his research on the Billmeyer family and to Carol Joiner for her research on the Crawford family.

I. JOHANN LEONHARDT BIHLMEIER

Johann Leonhardt "Leonhardt" Bihlmeier was born about 1706. He married Anna _____. Leonhardt and Anna immigrated from the German Palatinate by way of Rotterdam, arriving in Philadelphia in 1731 on the ship *Britannia* of London.

Their CHILDREN:

> Johann Leonhardt Billmeier, son of Leonhardt and Anna: born March 7, 1749; baptized March 9, 1749
>
> Johann Michael Billmeyer, son of Johann Leonhart and Anna: born October 20, 1751; baptized October 20, 1751
>
> Johann Georg Bielmayer, son of Leonhart and Anna: born March 21, 1755; baptized March 23, 1755
>
> Andreas "Andrew" Buhlmayer, son of Leonhart and Anna: born November 23, 1756; baptized November 28, 1756, died 2 Feb 1825, Liberty Township, Columbia Co., Pennsylvania.

II.   ANDREW BILLMEYER

Andrew Billmeyer was born 22 Sept 1756 in Lancaster, Pennsylvania, and died 2 Feb 1825 in Liberty Township, Columbia Co., Pennsylvania. He married Fannie Brunner, daughter of Jacob Brunner. (She is variously listed as Fannie, Frances, or Faronica) She was born 23 Aug 1757, and died 8 Feb 1823 in Liberty Township, Columbia Co., Pennsylvania.

Andrew Billmeyer served as a private in Captain Martin Weybright's 7th Company, 8th Battalion, Lancaster County Militia 1782-83 in the 8th Class under Col. James Ross.

In 1796 Andrew Billmeyer was an Inn Keeper at West Buffalo, Pennsylvania.

In the summer of 1873 John Lesher tore down the old house known as BILLMEYER TAVERN and afterwards as "Gebharts." On taking off the weathered boards, a log building, about forty four feet square was disclosed. In the logs were marks of arrows and many bullet holes. Between the flooring he found a shingle on which was written "James Tabor built 1775," the name no doubt of the carpenter. William McCandish died in the fall of 1785 and the tavern was sold to Andrew Billmeyer (grandfather of Philip Billmeyer of Lewisburg) who sold it on 21st of May 1812 to Philip Gebhart. It was the place of rendezvous for the people in the lower end of valley during subsequent indian troubles 1776-1785.[77]

During the Whiskey insurrection of 1794, Troops under Captain Robert Cooke traveling from Northumberland to the West passed through Buffalo Valley. At Andrew Billmeyer's a little beyond Lewisburg a pole [sign] had been erected but the report of the advancing troops got there before they did and the pole was cut down and hidden. The soldiers could not find it and took their revenge in drinking up all the whiskey, eating everything in the house, leaving word that Uncle Sam would pay the bill.[78]

CHILDREN of Andrew Billmeyer and Fannie Brunner were:
  a. Jacob Billmeyer, born 23 Dec 1776; died 1805; married Ms. Derr.
  b. Martin Billmeyer, born 9 Aug 1777, Liberty, Columbia Co. (later Montour Co.) Pennsylvania; died 6 Dec 1855, Montour Co., Pennsylvania and died 6 Dec 1855 in Montour Co, Pennsylvania. He married Margaret Himmelreich 21 Jun 1807

in Buffalo Valley, Pennsylvania. Margaret was the daughter of Peter Himmelreich and Mary Withington. Margaret was born 14 Feb 1790 in Pennsylvania, and died 4 Mar 1870. Martin was a farmer and distiller of rye, apples and peaches, and was a prosperous and well known man of his time.

c. George Billmeyer (born 1779, died 1853), 8 Jan 1779, Northumberland (now Union) Co., Pennsylvania Rev War; died 21 Jun 1853, Montour co, Pennsylvania married Anna Himmelreich

d. Martha Billmeyer, born 9 Aug 1782.

e. Magdalena Billmeyer, born 8 Mar 1785.

f. Frances Billmeyer, born 18 Dec 1790, Pennsylvania; died 17 Apr 1835. married James Cummings in 1817. He was born 1794 and died in 1830.

g. Andrew Billmeyer II, born 1 Aug 1793; died 3 Feb 1843. married Margaret Klein in 1817. She was born 1792 and died in 1841.

h. Mary Billmeyer, born 15 Oct 1795, Pennsylvania; d. 15 Sept 1873. married Philip Lesher in 1815. He was born in 1791 and died in 1844.

i. Margaret Billmeyer, born 1798; died 1 Oct 1842. Married Benjamin Knauss. He was born in 1787 and died in 1881.

j. Catherine Billmeyer, born 10 Sept 1800; died in Danville, Pennsylvania. Catherine married Martin Kelly I in 1820. He was born in 1803. She died before her husband Martin.

III.   GEORGE BILLMEYER

George Billmeyer I was born 8 Jan 1779 in Northumberland (now Union) Co., Pennsylvania. He served in the Revolutionary War and died 21 Jun 1853 in Liberty Township, Montour Co., Pennsylvania. He married Anna Himmelreich August 1805. Anna was the daughter of Peter Himmelreich and Mary Withington. She was born 4 Mar 1788 and died 25 Dec 1870.

"Among the early settlers are the descendants of the Billmeyers. This was a large and influential family noted for their frugality, prosperity and enterprise as farmers. John Steinman built a saw-mill about half mile above Billmeyers, in 1812, and in 1814 a turning-lathe on the old mill property. John Auten built a saw-mill also in 1812, and in 1814 he added to his saw-mill a grist-mill. The lumber for his house and grist-mill was cut at his own saw-mill, and these buildings were erected as soon as he could secure the lumber. The grist-mill was worn out and torn down. The saw-mill still stands in the shape of a modern built mill as a successor to the first one. These two saw-mills and the grist-mill were the only ones in this part of the county at this time, and here for many years the people in the vicinity had their grain ground and their lumber cut.

"John Wilson purchased land adjoining the Billmeyer place. He improved about 175 acres and on this farm made his residence until he died. In olden time every neighborhood imperatively needed a weaver to weave cloth from wool and flax for weaving apparel for the people. The hatter, the weaver and the itinerant shoemaker were the only sources of supply for the average person's clothes of that day of rural simplicity and frugality.

"The entire scheme of social economy is now wholly changed—a change wrought mostly by the wonderful mechanical inventions and appliances of the American people. There are but few of the industries now carried on in which machinery has not been introduced whereby one man can do the work of the seven to ten men, and in no occupation has greater improvement been made than in that of weaving, and yet we note the singular fact that wearing apparel is much more expensive now than it was three-quarters of a century ago. The spinning Jenny and the cotton-gins have taken away much the larger proportion of the time and toil upon each yard of cloth, as compared with half a century ago. These remarks are parenthetical to the fact that in the early times George Wagner, a weaver, located in the township. After working here some years he removed to Limestone, and stopping there some time he again removed, this time to Washingtonville, where he remained until he died about 1862. Of this family there were a number of children. James and John McMahon were of the first settlers. These two brothers were noted Revolutionary soldiers, as were the two Billmeyer brothers, George and Martin. The McMahons settled just west of Mooresburg. Another family that to this day are closely allied with the history of this part of the county, the Siningtons, sent John and Peter to the war of 1812-1815. This particular family of the Billmeyers settled in the Chillisquaque. One of that name is now living in the house built by his great grandfather.

"The oldest church in the northwest part of the county is the Chilliequaque Church. It is still a church regularly offering its ministrations to the living and its hopes and consolations for the dead. Their present building was erected in the early 'fifties' [1850's]. The minister in attendance is Rev H. C. Finney, who also serves at Mooresburg. The church at the latter place was erected about forty years ago."[79]

CHILDREN of George Billmeyer and Anna Himmelreich:
a. Frances Billmeyer, born 27 Nov 1806, Pennsylvania; d. 9 Nov 1879, Woodstock, McHenry Co. Illinois. Frances married Charles Crawford in 1826. He was born in 1804 and died in 1870 in Woodstock, McHenry Co., Illinois.
Charles served as a trustee of the incorporated village of Woodstock for the year of 1861.[80]
"Died — in this city [Woodstock, Illinois] Tuesday, Nov. 17th, 1879, Mrs. Frances Crawford, aged 73 years. Deceased was born in Union county, Pennsylvania; was married in March 1826 and came to Illinois in 1850, living on a farm five miles southeast of this city. In 1857 her family moved to DeKalb where they resided until the fall of 1858, when they returned to Woodstock and she had lived here from that time until her death. She leaves seven children, Andrew, Newcomb, Mrs. Caroline Bliss, Jacob, Mrs. R.S.W. [Mary Ellen] Ely, Mrs. W.B.[Margaret] Boss and Charley ... Through life her aim was to live not for herself alone but to promote the happiness and comfort of those around her; and the remembrance of some kind act or gentle, consoling word will bring the tears to the eyes of many who have known her."[81]
CHILDREN of Charles Crawford and Frances Billmeyer:
1. Andrew Crawford, born about 1829, married in 1859 to Sarah A. Brown (born 1840, died 1910-1920).
2. Newcomb Crawford, born April 1831, married in 1865 to Harriet A. Barber (born 1846, died 1910-1920)
3. Caroline Crawford, born about 1833, married in 1852 to John D. Bliss (born 1832, died 1880-1900)

4. Jacob Crawford born about 1835, married in 1859 to Louise Barber (born 1841)
5. Anna Matilda Crawford born about 1838, died 1878-1880, married in 1857 to Albert H. Deitz (born 1824)
6. Mary Ellen Crawford born about 1839, married in 1858 to Richard S. W. Fly (born 1835)
7. Margaret A. Crawford, born about 1841, married in 1864 to Henry A. Blood.
8. Susanna E. Crawford, born about 1843, married in 1866 to Arthur G. Murphy (born 1840)

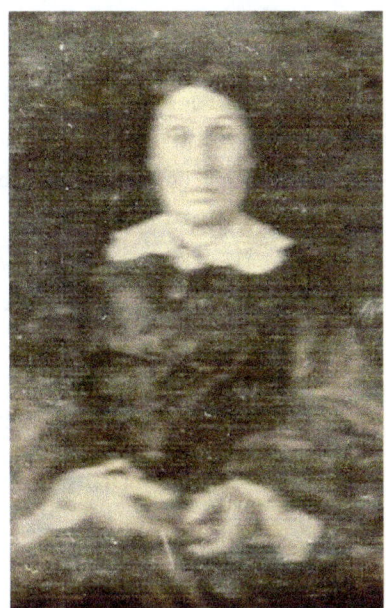

Frances Billmeyer Crawford, daguerreotype, ca. 1860

9. Charles Crawford Jr., born about 1845
10. Henry Crawford, born in 1846 and died in 1850[82]
11. Clareme Crawford, born in 1849 (twin)
12. Calvin H. Crawford, born in 1849 (twin) and died in 1850 Township, Pennsylvania. He died 24 February 1850 in Muncy at the age of about 8 months.[83]

b. infant Billmeyer, born May 1809.

c. Andrew Billmeyer, born 13 Aug 1810, Northumberland (now Union) Co., Pennsylvania; died 16 Apr 1883, Liberty Township, Montour Co., Pennsylvania. married Mary Ann Lichtenthaler in 1826. She was born in 1826 and died in 1901. CHILDREN of Andrew Billmeyer and Mary Ann Lichtenthaler:

1. Williams H. Billmeyer (born 1841)
2. Mary Frances Billmeyer (born July 1852) married in 1874 to Jacob Umstead (born 1848)
3. Margaret Billmeyer (1857-1935) married in 1878 to James Clarence Heddens (1855-1933)
4. Griffeth Billmeyer (1859-1931) married in 1886 to Elizabeth Bothwell (born 1870)
5. Charles Crawford Billmeyer (1862-1926) married in 1889

to Anna Hewett McFarland (1866-1919)

    6. Frank W. Billmeyer (1867-1948) married in 1889 to Ida M. Krock (1873-1926)

d. George Billmeyer II, born 1 Sept 1812, Pennsylvania; died 16 Sept 1897. George married Abigail Boudeman in 1837. She was born in 1816 and died in 1884.

CHILDREN of George Billmeyer II and Abigail Boudeman:

1. Margaret A. Billmeyer (1837-1877) married to Robert E. Auten Jr. (1834-1912)
2. Mary E. Billmeyer (1839-1848)
3. Jane Billmeyer (1841-1869) married to George Irvin
4. Frances Billmeyer (1844-1912) married in 1866 to William Howard Taylor (1841-1917)
5. George Billmeyer III (1845-1856)
6. James P. Billmeyer (1847-1848)
7. Isaiah R. Billmeyer (1848-1850)
8. Daniel Boudeman Billmeyer (1850-1930) married to Sarah E. Ryan (1851-1929)
9. Charlotte Billmeyer (born1852) married to George Irvin
10. Peter Billmeyer (1854-1934) married in 1907 to Annie F. Cummings (1855-1917)
11. Andrew Billmeyer (1856-1912) married in 1879 to Sarah Ellen Deiterick (1856-1941)

e. Phillip Billmeyer, born 10 Oct 1814, Liberty, Columbia Co. (now Montour Co.) Pennsylvania; died 5 Sept 1885. Phillip married Susan Follmer in 1841. She was born in 1821 and died in 1874.

CHILDREN of Philllip Billmeyer and Susan Follmer:

1. Mary E. Billmeyer (1842-1926) married in 1867 to James Merrill Linn (1833-1897)
2. Margaret Billmeyer (1843-1898) married before 1870 to Augustus Green Walls (1837-1890)
3. Sarah A. Billmeyer (1848-1911) married in 1861 to Henry C. Wolfe (1843-1924)
4. Emma Jane Billmeyer (1850-1940) married in 1872 to George S. Matlock (1851-1893)
5. Clara Follmer Billmeyer (1852-1855)
6. Alverda F. Billmeyer (1857-1939)

f. Mary Billmeyer, born 10 Apr 1817, Pennsylvania. Mary married Thomas Shurtz

CHILD of Mary Billmeyer and Thomas Schurtz:

1. George B. Shurtz (born 1838)

g. Margaret Billmeyer, born 13 Nov 1819; died 13 Sept 1903. Margaret married William Kramm (son of David Kramm). See next section.

h. Peter Billmeyer, born 07 Aug 1822, Pennsylvania. married Sarah ____

CHILDREN of Peter Billmeyer and Sarah ___:

1. Andrew Billmeyer (born1846)
2. John G. Billmeyer (Feb 1848 - Dec 1848)

i. Elizabeth Billmeyer, born 07 Dec 1824, Pennsylvania; died 3 Mar 1902. Elizabeth married Franklin Ryan He was born in 1820 and died before 1860. After his death she remarried (2) Johnson or Johnston.

CHILDREN of Franklin Ryan and Elizabeth Billmeyer:

1. Mary A. Ryan (1845-1918) married in 1864 to Martin Kelly II (1835-1905)
2. Emma Jane Ryan (1847-1925) married to William Billmeyer (1848-1920), son of Martin Billmeyer (1821-1869) and Maria Kramm (1827-1899)
3. Sarah E. Ryan (1851-1929) married to Daniel Boudeman Billmeyer (1850-1930)

j. Charles Billmeyer, born 24 Jan 1827, Pennsylvania; died 17 Jul 1891. Charles married Matilda Kramm (daughter of David Kramm). The 1900 census finds Matilda Kramm Billmeyer in Cass, Clayton County, Iowa. The following year Matilda died in Milton, Pennsylvania.

CHILDREN of Charles Billmeyer and Matilda Kramm:

1. Clarence K. Billmeyer (1852-1891)
2. Harry N. Billmeyer (1857-1900) married to Mary Rebecca Sharp (born 1861)
3. Adah M. Billmeyer (1858-1937) married to William D. Steinbach (born 1856, died 1910-1920)
4. George M. Billmeyer (born 1863, died 1920-1930) married in 1893 to Phila Elizabeth Ferry (born 1864, died after 1931)

k. Anna Billmeyer, born 5 Jan 1830; died 17 Mar 1851.

l. Sarah Billmeyer, born 19 Oct 1832, Pennsylvania; died 14 May

1857. married Andrew Lesher before 1857. He was born in 1829 and died in 1878.

CHILDREN of Sarah Billmeyer and Andrew Lesher

1. Anna M. Lesher (1856-1891) married to William Robbins (1838-1931)
2. infant son Lesher (1857-1857)

m. Charles Paul Billmeyer, born 1840.

IV.   **MARGARET BILLMEYER**

William Kramm and Margaret Billmeyer were married 5 Feb 1846 in Liberty twp., Montour Co., Pennsylvania. See photograph taken on their Golden Wedding celebration, page 17. She was a daughter of George Billmeyer I and Anna Himmelreich (daughter of Peter Himmelreich and Mary Withington). Margaret Billmeyer was born 13 Nov 1819 and died 13 Sept 1902.

They had four children.

For more information, see Kramm family, page 222.

THE HIMMELREICH AND
WITHINGTON FAMILIES

Harry Hammond Wilcox 1887-1943	m.	Hattie Estelle Richner 1891-1977
James Martin Wilcox 1854-1911	m.	Ada Virginia Kramm 1856-1934
William Kramm (1823-1898)	m.	Margaret Billmeyer (1846-1902)
George Billmeyer (1779-1853)	m.	Anna Himmelreich (1788-1870)
Peter Himmelreich (b. about 1760)	m.	Mary Withington (1785-1823)
Peter Withington III (1733-1777)	m.	Eve Christina Albert (1739-1833)
Peter Withington II (b. 1712)	m.	Jane Hutchin
Peter Withington I (1675-1715)	m.	Sarah ____
David Withington (1650-1713)	m.	Elizabeth ____ (d. 1707)
Charles Withington (b. about 1600)	m.	Jonne ____

Peter Withington II, is our ancestor who immigrated to America. We have included information about three generations before him in England.

CHARLES WITHINGTON was born about 1600, and died 1662 in Ower Green, Southampton, Hampshire, England. He married Jonne ____ (say "Joan"). Charles is buried in Fawley, Southampton, England.

CHILDREN of Charles and Jonne Withington are:
1. <u>David Withington</u>, born about 1650 in Fawley, Southampton, England; died August 1713 in Fawley.
2. Charles Withington, died 1704. Married Mary ___.
3. Elizabeth Withington

DAVID WITHINGTON was born about 1650 in Fawley, and died August 1713 and is buried in Fawley. He married Elizabeth ___, who died in 1707.

CHILDREN of David and Elizabeth Withington are:
1. <u>Peter Withington I</u>, born about 1675, and died 1715 in England..
2. Mary Withington, born about 1675 in Fawley, Southampton, Hampshire, England. Married John Ayles 31 October 1699 in Fawley.

PETER WITHINGTON I was born about 1675 in England, died, and was buried 8 February 1715 in Fawley, Southampton, England. He married twice: (1) Ann Boon 20 June 1699 in Fawley. Ann died and was buried 1 June 1709 in Fawley churchyard, Fawley, Hampshire, England. He married (2) Sarah ___ some time after 1709.

CHILDREN of Peter Withington and Ann Boon are:
1. Anna Withington, born 23 August 1704 in Fawley
2. Elizabeth Withington, born 1706, baptized 8 March 1706 in Fawley, died 1707 in Fawley.
2. May Mary Withington, born May 1708, baptized 6 May 1708 in Fawley; died 1709.

CHILDREN of Peter Withington and Sarah ___ are:
1. <u>Peter Withington II</u>, born May 1712, Fawley, Southampton, England.
2. Mary Withington, born 28 November 1710, Fawley, Southampton, England
3. Richard Withington, born 8 November 1714.

Generations in America

I. PETER WITHINGTON II

Peter Withington II was born May 1712 in Fawley, Southampton,
England. He was baptized May 1712 at Fawley, England.
He married Jane Hutchin on 9 Sep 1731 in Fawley, Southampton,
England. Jane was the daughter of Edward Hutchin and Mary Hayle. She
was born about 1707 in Fawley, Southampton, England.

Peter and his family immigrated to America, and died in Pennsylvania.

Peter and Jane had seven CHILDREN, all of whom were baptized in the
church at Fawley, England.
1. <u>Peter Withington III,</u> born January 17, 1733, ; died 11 May
   1777, Reading, Berks Co. Pennsylvania.
2. Jane Withington, born August 5, 1734, England
3. Sarah Withington, born January 27, 1736
4. Mary Withington, born June 13, 1738
5. David Withington, born February 19, 1740
6. Anna Withington, born May 4, 1743
7. Henrietta Withington, born October 23, 1747

II. CAPTAIN PETER WITHINGTON III

Peter Withington III was born 17 Jan 1733 in England, and died 11
May 1777 in Reading, Berks Co. Pennsylvania. He married Eve Christina
Albert (or Albright or Albrite) about 1759, the daughter of Johan Albert
and Maria Reinacher. Eve was born 8 Oct 1739 in Warwick, Lancaster
Co. Pennsylvania, and died 27 Jun 1833 in Youngmanstown (now
Mifflinburg), Union Co. Pennsylvania. Some DAR records list her as
Eve Schepler, which might have been a subsequent married name, as she
outlived her husband by 50 years..
Peter Withington, (1733-77), raised and equipped a company of
soldiers for the Revolutionary War, which he commanded until his death.
Peter was captain in Col. William Cooke's regiment. His company left
Sunbury in boats, December 18, 1776, for service in New Jersey. He fell
ill near Philadelphia, was sent home sick, and died of camp fever May 11,
1777.[84]

The Society of Cincinnati was founded in May 1783 by Continental Army officers who fought in the American Revolution. The Society was named for Lucius Quintus Cincinnatus, a Roman farmer of the Fifth Century B.C., who like Washington was called from his fields to lead his country's army in battle. Cincinnatus, as did Washington, returned from war a triumphant leader, declined honors, and went back to his farm. Washington, as did Cincinnatus, lived up to the Society's Motto: "He gave up everything to serve the republic."

There is a list of some of the original members of the Pennsylvania society, and some officers who died in service. Descendants of these officers are eligible to apply as hereditary members to the Society, including descendants of Captain Peter Withington (who died in Service) of the 12th Pennsylvania Regiment.[85]

> "The Twelfth Pennsylvania Regiment of the Continental Line, of which four companies were from Northumberland County and the others from Northampton County, was raised by authority of Congress, and among the last acts of the convention which had assembled in Philadelphia, to form a State Constitution, was the choice of its field officers, from its members, on September 28, 1776.
>
> "William Cook, delegate from Northumberland, was made Colonel; Neigal Gray, who, after the war, moved to White Deer township, Union County, and died there in 1786, was made lieutenant-colonel; and James Crawford, delegate from Northumberland County, was chosen major.
>
> Peter Withington was the first captain, appointed by the Council of Safety on October, and three days later, with the field officers, took the qualification directed by the convention. On the same day (October 4th) Nichlolas Miller and Hawkins Boone were appointed captains; Thomas Brandon and Hananiah Lincoln, first lieutenants; and Robert King and James Williams second lieutenants. It was resolved that the commissions of the captains and subalterns should be dated October 1st. On the 14th of October, John Brady and Major John Harris, both of Northumberland County, were appointed captains; Christopher Gettig, first lieutenant; and Francis Allison, sergeant.[86]

The regiment went immediately into active service. Being composed mainly of good riflemen, large drafts were made upon it for picket and skirmish duty. A portion, under Boone, was sent into the northern army, and assisted in the capture of Burgoyne. At Brandywine, the regiment lost heavily in officers and men, and at Germantown; so that after the wintering at Valley Forge, the field officers were mustered out, the supernumerary line officers discharged into the Third and Sixth Regiments, which arrangement went into effect July 1, 1777. Captains John Brady and Hawkins Boone, Lieutenants Dougherty and Robert King were ordered home by General Washington to assist Colonel Hartley in protecting the West Valley. Captain Brady . . . was killed by Indian scouts near the town of Muncy, April 11, 1779, and Captain Boone fell near Fort Freeland on the 29th of July, in the same year, while Dougherty also lost his life in the defence of the frontier after passing safely through the hard campaigns of the Continental army. Their names will reappear in this history.

Captain Peter Withington, commissioned October 1, 1776, took sick in Philadelphia in December, 1776; sent home to Reading, where he died May 11, 1777; his widow, Eve, survived him over fifty years, and died in Mifflinburg.[87]

Eve also received compensation from the Army for service:

Withington, Eve, was credited with Lb5.5.10 Due her On her acct [for] boarding 20 state prisoners at Reading for one week.[88]

Eve lived in Mifflinburg for the rest of her life. "Her enjoyment of novels was well known and *The children of the Abbey* was one of her favorite books."[89]

CHILDREN of Peter Withington and Eve Albert are:
1. Mary Withington, born 18 Jul 1765; died 9 Aug 1823.
2. Sarah Withington

III.   MARY WITHINGTON and
PETER HIMMELREICH

Mary Withington was born 18 Jul 1765, and died 09 Aug 1823. She married Peter Himmelreich. Peter was born 1756/57 in Bruendersen, Hesse, Germany; and died 2 November 1828 in Union County, Pennsylvania.

Mary is buried in the Dreisbach Cemetery in Union County, Pennsylvania. "Here lies the remains of Mary Heimmelreich, consort of Peter Heimmelreich and daughter of Peter and Eve Withington, was born July 18th and departed this life August 9th 1823, aged 58 years."[90]

Peter Himmelreich, whose name means "Kingdom of Heaven," was one of the Hessian soldiers who joined with the Americans in fighting the British in the American Revolution.

Mary and others in Pennsylvania would have been able to converse with the Hessians, and were delighted to have their expert assistance in the war.

> "Intermarriage between the various German immigrants, among whom the dialects of the Palatinate, Franconia, etc., predominated, has resulted in the formation of a dialect which is known as "Pennsylvania German." This more strongly resembles some of the Bavarian dialects than any other of the German, as was recognized by the present writer during his service as staff-surgeon in the Prussian army during the war of 1870-71. Although Pennsylvanians read German newspapers and books, they are generally unable to converse in that language, and experience great difficulty in understanding a recent German immigrant, whom they regard in the light of a foreigner, as much as do people of English descent."[91]

Peter Himmelreich and Mary Withington were likely married during the early years of the revolution. He arrived in America sometime between 1776 and 1783.[92]

We find Peter Himmelreich in the 1790 Census at Heidelberg, Berks County, and in subsequent censuses in Penns, East Buffalo, and Buffalo, Northumberland and Union Counties, Pennsylvania.

CHILDREN of Peter Himmelreich and Mary Withington:[93]

1. Sarah Himmelreich
2. George Himmelreich, born 1805; d. 1895, Ohio.
3. David Himmelreich
4. Harry Himmelreich
5. Anna Himmelreich, born 4 Mar 1788, died 25 Dec 1870. Married Billmeyer.
6. Margaret Himmelreich, born 14 Feb 1790, PA; died 4 Mar 1870. Married Martin Billmeyer.
7. Peter Himmelreich II, born 1792.
8. Elizabeth Himmelreich
9. Polly Himmelreich
10. Fannie Himmelreich, married John Ready[94]

IV. ANNA HIMMELREICH

Anna Himmelreich was born 4 March 1788 and died 25 December 1870. Her birth date was calculated from age and death date on her tombstone.

She married George Billmeyer I in August 1805.

George was the son of Andrew Billmeyer and Fannie Brunner. He was born 8 January 1779 in Northumberland (now Union) County, Pennsylvania. He served in the Revolutionary War and died 21 June 1853 in Liberty Township, Montour County, Pennsylvania.

For more information, see the Billmeyer section, page 226.

THE BOEHM FAMILY

Harry Hammond Wilcox 1887-1943	m.	Hattie Estelle Richner 1891-1977
James Martin Wilcox 1854-1911	m.	Ada Virginia Kramm 1856-1934
William Kramm (1823-1898)	m.	Margaret Billmeyer (1846-1902)
David Kramm (1793-1882)	m.	Maria Brunner (1800-1872)
Jacob Kram II (1863/5-1800)	m.	Catherine Boehm (d. 1769)
John Phillips Boehm (1747-1816)	m.	Anna Barbara Deshler (1747-1832)
Anthony William Boehm (1714-1766)	m.	Hannah Phillis
Rev. John Philip Boehm I (1683-1749)	m.	Anna Maria Stehler (d. 1720)
Rev. Philip Ludwig Boehm (1646-1723)	m.	Maria Engelhard (1651-1693)
Johann Boehm	m.	—

The REV. PHILLIP LUDWIG BOEHM was born 1646 in Dorheim, Wetterau (later the Grand-duchy of Hesse), Germany, and died 23 Jan 1723 in Ravolzhausen, Germany. He married Maria B. Engelhard about 1679, daughter of Johann Engelhard and Maria Balde. She was born 21 Sep 1651, and died 29 Jun 1693.

His ancestors came from a section of Germany called Bohemia, as the name Boehm means one who came from Bohemia (home of Boii). Boehm is the English spelling of German Bohm, with other English spelling being Behm, Boehme, Boehmer and Bohm.[95]

The Rev. Boehm's father was Johann Boehm, the earliest known Boehm ancestor, who lived in Dorheim, county of Fritzlar, Homberg, Germany. Johann's son, Philip Ludwig, was born in Dorheim in 1646. There are no records of any other children of Johann, but it is assumed that Philip Ludwig was not an only child, since his brother-in-law, Johannes Hassenpflug, was a sponsor at the baptism of Philip Ludwig's son, John Philip. It follows that Hassenpflug was married to Philip Ludwig's sister, whose name we do not know.

The Rev. Philip Ludwig Boehm performed his first wedding in Hochstadt, February 19, 1680. About this same time Philip was married and his first child was born in Hochstadt in 1681. Phillip married Maria B. Engelhard about 1681. Maria was the daughter of Johann Christoph Engelhard, a winemaster in Hanau, and Maria Balde, his wife. Maria, Philip's wife was born September 21, 1651, and died June 29, 1693.

After the death of his wife Maria, Phillip married again January 11, 1694, to a widow, the daughter of Jacob Bernes. In this marriage there were frequent quarrels, which caused the Consistory to cite the Rev. Boehm for his domestic troubles. Therefore, in January, 1701, he was transferred to Rumpenheim on the Main River, near Frankfort.

The CHILDREN of Rev. Philip Ludwig Boehm and Maria Engelhard:
1. John Daniel Boehm, born about 1677. John enrolled in the Latin school at Hanau, June 6, 1684, and on June 17, 1691, the University of Marburg. Later he received financial help from the Consistory to continue his studies at Bremen. June 12, 1705, John Daniel followed in the steps of his father and became a minister. John Daniel accepted the job of Court preacher to the Count von Donau at Guntersblum.
2. Clement Lewis Boehm, born 1679. Clement entered the Latin school of Hanau with his brother John, June 6, 1684.
3. Margaretha Boehm. Margaretha was born on October 4, 1681, at Hanau, and was baptized on October 9, 1681.
4. The Rev. John Philip Boehm I, born in November, 1683 in Hochstadt, Germany; died 29 Apr 1749, Hellertown, Pennsylvania (in a house, now 766 Main Street.)

Generations in America

I.   REV. JOHN PHILIP BOEHM I

REV. JOHN PHILIP BOEHM I was born Nov 1683 in Hochstadt, Germany, and died 29 Apr 1749 in Hellertown, Pennsylvania (in a house, now 766 Main Street). He married (1) Anna Maria Stehler about 1708. She died before 1720. He married (2) Anna Maria Scherer before 1720, the daughter of Philip Scherer.

The Rev. John Philip Boehm is the most well known of all our ancestors. The Rev. Boehm is considered to be the founder of the Reformed Churches (now United Church of Christ) in Pennsylvania. He was the first minister to organize churches and establish church government. Due to his tremendous influence in early America, there have been many books and articles written about his life and work.[96]

The Rev. John Philip Boehm was born in November 1683 and he was baptized at Hochstadt, the place of his birth, November 15, 1683. His Baptism record translates as follows: "In the village of Hochstadt, township of Hanau, Phillippus Ludivicus Boehm, pro tempore pastor of this place, and Maria, his wife, brought a son for baptism November 25, 1683. His name of Johnnes Philipp. Sponsors were: Mr. Johannes Hassenpflug, pro tempore praeceptor in the third class (of the Latin School) at Hanau-on-the-Main, a brother in law."[97]

Many people of the German Reformed faith had been invited to settle in Worms to help rebuild the city that had been destroyed by King Louis XIV of France. In 1708, Rev. John Philip Boehm was formally elected schoolmaster.

"John Philip's time as a schoolmaster in Worms was filled with conflicts, which stemmed from opposition caused by Christopher Schmidt. Mr. Schmidt had nominated someone else for schoolmaster and after Boehm won the election, Schmidt took the part of sore loser. Quarrels seemed to be an everyday affair in Worms. Boehm's salary was illegally withheld, which he protested. Others stopped at nothing to cause Boehm problems and make him defend himself. Finally, Boehm gave up and handed in his resignation, November 22, 1715.

During his stay in Worms, Rev. Boehm had four children baptized. These children were born to his first wife, Anna Maria Stehler, who probably married Boehm before his arrival in Worms.

After leaving Worms, John Philip Boehm became a schoolmaster at Lambsheim. There, in the year 1717, his yearly salary was 145 florins, which placed him in the upper middle class. Boehm, however, got into a quarrel with the town council over the distribution of lands. The electoral government decided in favor of schoolmaster Boehm.

At Lambsheim, after the death of his first wife, John Philip married for the second time. His second marriage was to Anna Marie Scherer, a daughter of Philip Scherer, a citizen of Lambsheim.

Disillusioned by continuing conflicts—both religious and secular—in Germany, Boehm decided to emigrate to the young community in Pennsylvania where there was greater freedom of religion. On the 30th of August 1720, along with some 400 others from the German Palatinate fleeing religious persecution, he arrived in Philadelphia on the ship *Laurel* from Rotterdam by way of Liverpool and Cork.

The governor of Pennsylvania was alarmed at the arrival of so many German-speaking nationals in British territory. He required that the ship's captain supply a list of the names and occupations of all the passengers, and that all males on board over the age of 16 had to swear allegiance to the English King. Their fears were soon allayed, however.

> "In 1738, for example, Governor George Thomas, in a message to the Provincial Assembly, declared: This Province has been for some years the asylum of the distressed Protestants of the Palatinate, and other parts of Germany; and I believe it may with truth be said that the present flourishing condition of it is in great Measure owing to the Industry of those people; and should any discouragement divert them from coming hither, it may well be apprehended that the value of your Lands will fall, and your Advances to wealth be much slower; for it is not altogether the goodness of the soil, but the Number and Industry of the People that make a flourishing Country."[98]

An article in the 1907 Pennsylvania-German newspaper states that Boehm came "bearing testimonials that he had been a faithful master of the parish school and precentor (choir director) of the Reformed Church at Worms, Germany, for seven years and had been driven thence by the persecutions of the Catholics."[99]

By 1730, there were more than 15,000 people in Pennsylvania, scattered over 300-400 miles, who considered themselves members of the German Reformed Church, but there were no regular pastors.[100]

In September 1736, John Philip Boehm purchased 200 acres of land in Whitpain township, Philadelphia (now Montgomery) County. There he settled with his family. He took up farming to support himself, although in later life he was called a "rich plantation owner." He owned and operated the Stage Inn at Lambsheim, Pennsylvania, in his early years. He became a citizen there 14 Apr 1706.[101]

There were no ordained ministers of the German Reformed Church in Pennsylvania at that time. The German people who settled in Pennsylvania gathered to worship in homes, barns, and the wide open spaces. Boehm became a "Reader" in their services, a position for which he was well qualified, reading the Bible and printed sermons, and serving as schoolmaster. After five years, the community decided not to wait for an ordained minister to arrive, and begged Boehm "the pious schoolmaster" to take on the additional duties of minister. "They hungered and thirsted for the Word as the hart panted for the water brooks. Especially was this the case when death entered their abodes. They longed for the consolation of religion."[102]

He finally agreed, drew up a system of church government, and on October 15, 1725, he served communion to 40 members of the Faulkner Swamp Church, the date now used as the founding of the German Reformed Church in America. He subsequently also served communion to 37 members at Skippack, and to 24 members at Whitemarsh. He was now the *de facto* minister of the community, but not officially ordained. Word spread and other groups requested his services so he became a circuit rider for Philadelphia, Montgomery, Bucks, Berks, Lehigh, Northampton, Lancaster, Chester, and Lebanon counties.

When an ordained minister, George Michael Weiss, arrived in 1727 he denounced Boehm's ministry and challenged the validity of his ministerial acts, such as marriages and baptisms.

Finally Boehm and his most prominent elder, William Dewees, went to New York to confer with the ministers of the Dutch Reformed Church. These ministers advised them to present their case to the Classis of Amsterdam and to petition them to legalize Boehm's ministry. The Dutch Reformed Church had its headquarters in Holland and had been informed of the needs of the German people in Pennsylvania by the Upper Consistory at the Palatinate.[103]

The Classis at Amsterdam concluded that Boehm's call "originating as it did, out of the very heart of the congregation, must be considered as valid." They directed that he be ordained by the ministers in New York. Upon receiving word that he was to be ordained, Boehm proceeded to New York with a representative from each congregation, namely: Frederick Antes[104] from Falkner Swamp, Gabriel Schuler from Skippack, and William DeWees from Whitemarsh. All four men confirmed their faith to the Heidelberg Catechism and the Formulas of Unity. They also promised to correspond with the Classis and to pay Boehm a salary. Thereafter, Boehm was publicly ordained in the Dutch Reformed Church of New York, Sunday afternoon, November 23, 1729.

He owned several tracts of land and evidently supplemented his income with other pursuits since he advertised in the 1 Aug 1755 Sower's newspaper "good rum and molasses for sale cheap."

On April 10, 1741, the Rev. Boehm was naturalized by the Supreme Court of Pennsylvania.

Rev. Boehm spent most of the rest of his life as a circuit riding preacher. He covered a region bounded by the Susquehanna River, the Blue Mountains, The Lehigh River, The Delaware River, and the Mason-Dixon line. He covered this territory on horseback and foot, traveling 104 miles a month, and in a ministry of over twenty years he had traveled over 25,000 miles.[105]

As the Rev. Boehm became older, his work, although a joy, became a greater burden. He was pleased to hear of the arrival in Pennsylvania of Rev. Michael Schlatter from Switzerland who had been sent to Pennsylvania by the Synod of Holland to organize the Reformed Churches into a permanent religious body. Sept 7, 1746, the Rev. Schlatter met the Rev. Boehm at Boehm's home in Whitpain Township. The Rev. Boehm gave his full support to the Rev. Schlatter and a definite organization of Reformed Churches took place, September 29, 1747, in Philadelphia. At the second meeting of the Committee from September 28-30, 1748, the Rev. Boehm was elected president.

The last church that the Rev. Boehm organized was, with the help of the Rev. Schlatter, in his own home, February 3, 1747. This church claims to have started in 1740, but the Rev. Hinke gives the 1747 date. This church in Whitpain township at Blue Bell, is today known as Boehm's Reformed Church, United Church of Christ.[106]

His theological discussions with the Moravians were frequent and warm. One of the Moravians, Mr. Neisser, calls him "Der veiche Plantagemann," because of his wealth. He secured land cheap, and died a very rich man. He deeded this tract to his son Anthony in 1747.[107]

John Philip Boehm died at his son Anthony's farm near Hellertown, Pennsylvania. He was buried under the altar of his church in Whitpain, near what is called Boehm's Church, in Montgomery County. "He had been a prudent and successful manager of his temporal affairs. After debts were paid, his estate was valued at 348 pounds and included many books."[108]

Boehm's second wife, Anna Maria Scherer, outlived him and she was given money by the Classis of Holland in 1752. The Rev. Boehm left no will. His estate which was valued at over 400 pounds was settled by his son John Philip Boehm, Jr. who received Letters of Administration in Philadelphia County. The estate was finally settled in 1755, at which time Boehm's widow, Anna Maria, received one-third, which amounted to 130 pounds. John Philip Boehm Jr. received the lands in Whitpain township, with the responsibility of caring for his grandfather, Philip Scherer.

> "In the Rev. John Philip Boehm, a most worthy character stands at the head of our ancestral line in America. A strong good man who served his day and generation well. His labors made for righteousness. He has long since entered into rest. Let successive generations esteem it a privilege to cherish his memory and honor his name. And let us, his descendants, especially strive to prove ourselves worthy of the heritage, which his faithfulness, with God's blessing, has secured to us. No worship of ancestors do we commend, and none of that sickening pride of ancestry by which degenerate children disgust the world, but an uplifting purpose.

> "To live to learn their story
> Who've suffered for our sake,
> To emulate their glory,
> And follow in their wake;
> Bards, patriots, martyrs, sages,
> The noblest of all ages,
> Whose deed crown history's pages
> And Time's."[109]

The Rev. John Philip Boehm had eight CHILDREN, four by his first wife, Anna Maria Stehler, and four by his second wife, Anna Maria Scherer. Boehm's children were as follows:

CHILDREN of John Philip Boehm and Anna Maria Stehler:
1. Johanna Sabina Boehm. Johanna was born in Worms, Germany, May 2. 1709 and was baptized, May 4, 1709. She

married Ludwig Bitting in America and they were living in 1749 in Lower Milford township of Bucks (now Lehigh) County. He was born in 1703, and from 1758 to 1760 he served in the State Assembly as a representative from Northampton County. He outlived Sabina, since by the time of his death, December 27, 1775, his wife was Elizabeth. Their children were Ludwig, Henry, Anthony, Philip, Peter, Anna Maria, Elizabeth, Dorothea, Mary Catherine, and Christina.

2. Franciscus Ludovicus Boehm. Franciscus was born in Worms, Germany, July 24, 1711, and baptized, July 26, 1711. He died in infancy.

3. John Christopher Boehm. John was born in Worms, Germany, May 4, 1713. He died the same year, August 2.

4. <u>Anthony William Boehm.</u> Anthony was born April 27, 1714, in Worms, Germany. Anthony is our ancestor.

CHILDREN of John Philip Boehm and Anna Maria Scherer:

5. Anna Maria Boehm. Anna Maria married Adam Moser. In 1749 they were living in Philadelphia.

6. Elizabeth Boehm. Elizabeth married George Shamboh, a weaver. In 1749 they were living in Upper Milford township.

7. Maria Philippona Boehm. Maria married Cornelius DeWees, a son of William DeWees,[103] one of the Rev. Boehm's elders at Whitemarsh. Cornelius was a cooper (a barrel-maker) and by 1749 they were living in Gloucester County, New Jersey.

8. John Phillip Boehm II. John was born May 1, 1734. He married Anna Maria Yost, August 2, 1753. Her ancestry is recorded in *The Spare Family*, a 1931 genealogy. About 1760 they made their home in Philadelphia and had several children baptized in the First Reformed Church, in which he served as a deacon and elder. John Philip served as a Justice of the Peace for the County of Philadelphia and worked as a grocer and merchant on Second Street. John Philip died in September, 1790, and was buried in the cemetery of the Race Street Reformed Church, now known as Franklin Square. John Philip and Anna Maria had nine children, namely:

a. Jacob (born 1755 died 1765)

b. Elizabeth (born September 1757 died 1765)

c. Philip (born July 28, 1761 died 1765)

d. Daniel (born March 14, 1764 died 1765)

e. Mary (born 1765 and married William Peltz)

f. Philip (born August 13, 1766)

g. Jacob (born October 29, 1768 died 1773)

h. Daniel (born March 21, 1771 and married Catherine Peltz)

i. Elizabeth (born 1778 died 1788)

II.   ANTHONY WILLIAM BOEHM

Anthony William (Wilhelm) Boehm was born 27 Apr 1714 in Worms, Germany, and died 6 Apr 1766. He married Hannah Phillis about 1746. Notes for ANTHONY WILLIAM (WILHELM) BOEHM:

Anthony came with his family from Germany on the ship *Laurel* to Philadelphia.

According to Patton, "Hannah was again made a widow by the death of her second husband, Anthony, April 6, 1766. He was buried in a private cemetery on his farm in Upper Saucon Township. One hundred and thirty years later his tombstone was discovered: its inscription reads "Hier Ruben in Gott Anton Wilhelm BOEHM ist geboren den 27 April 1714, in Worms, Ist geStorben April 6, 1766. Seines Alters 52 Jahr." [Here lies with God Anthony William Boehm, born 27 April 1714 in Worms, died 6 April 1766. He was 52 years old.] This tombstone has been moved to the graveyard of the Friendsville Church, which is about two miles from its original location."

CHILD of Anthony William Boehm and Hannah Phillis:

1. Lt. Col. John Phillips Boehm, born 14 Dec 1747, Hellertown, Pennsylvania. He served in the Revolutionary War. He died 10 January 1816, at the age of 69 years and 2 months.

III.   JOHN PHILLIPS BOEHM

Lt. Col. John Phillips ("Philip") Boehm was born 14 Dec 1747 in Hellertown, Pennsylvania. He served in the Revolutionary War, and died 10 Jan 1816 at the age of 69 years and 2 months.

He married Anna Barbara Deshler about 1768. Anna was the daughter of Adam Deshler and his wife Apolonia. She was born 2 Nov 1747, and died 10 Oct 1832.

Philip Boehm's real claim to fame came as a result of his love for his country and the outbreak of the Revolutionary War. The Colonial

Records and Pennsylvania Archives refer to him several times. At the beginning of the War, March 6, 1777, his name is mentioned in a letter sent to General Washington from the Council of Safety. Part of this letter states that, "Lt. Col. Boehm of Col. Geiger's battalion of militia of Northampton County, now in Camp, informs us that they are uneasy under an apprehension that it is intended to keep them in service more that the allotted time for the militia (6 weeks) on account of some of the said Battalion deserting . . ." The volunteers often felt they had already been away too long, endangering their crops and thus food for their families for the winter.[110]

The letter also states that the said Militia had "been very active suppressing the Tories in their County, and [is] the principal support of the cause in that part of the Country ..."

On August 27, 1777, Philip Boehm was made Paymaster of the Northampton County Militia, a position which he held until 1781. In 1779, the Council of Safety wrote Philip asking why the militia had not been paid, but later the same year they sent 3,000 pounds for that purpose.

Philip quickly obtained rank (an elective opposition) in the militia. In June of 1777 he was a quartermaster. He later had the ranks of Colonel and Lt. Colonel. Philip certified the returns of several units (Battalions and Militia) and was the field commander of others. Philip's units were:
- 2nd Batt. Mil. (October 18, 1782); 4th Co. Mil. 4th Batt. (1782);
- 3rd Class 4th Batt. (two months active service starting June 11, 1782);
- Capt. Peter Hay's Co. 4th Batt.; 4th Batt Mil. (May 1780);
- Lewis Stacker's Co. (1781);
- 2nd Batt. (May 14, 1783);
- 7th Co. Batt. Mil. (May 19, 1784);
- 7th Co. Sebent Batt. (April 28, 1785);
- 8th Co. 2nd Batt. (April 19, 1875; and
- Rangers of the Frontiers (177801783).

Philip was not only part of the Militia, but he did see active service. His name appears among those of the Continental Line from Northampton County and among those who received Depreciation Pay.

After the war, Philip settled down with his family and continued living in Lower Saucon Township. The first census of the United States in 1790 shows his family of five males (two over 16 and three under) and three females. By 1800 all of his family, except one daughter, had married; on the census for that year he is listed as over 45, his wife is listed as over 45, and one female between the ages of 16 and 26 was still at home. He was buried 15 Feb 1816 at the First Reformed Church, Easton, Pennsylvania.

CHILDREN of John Phillips Boehm and Anna Deshler are:
1. <u>Catherine Boehm</u>, born 1769. Married Kram.
2. Anthony Boehm, born 17 Jan 1770; died 25 Sep 1848.
3. John Boehm, born 1772.
4. Magdalena Boehm, born 18 Oct 1772. Magdalena was baptized 15 Nov 1772 at Allentown Church.
5. Mary Boehm, born 1774. Mary married Jacob Haas.
6. Susanna Boehm, born 15 Jul 1774. She may have died young, or this may be the same as Susanna (born 14 June 1776) who married Jacob Ochs. Susanna was baptized 31 Jul 1774, at Allentown Church.
7. Johanna Christiana Boehm, born 13 Mar 1776; probably died young. She was baptized 24 Mar 1776, at Allentown Church - Zion Reformed.
8. Susanna Boehm, born 4 Jun 1776; d. 19 Dec 1846.
9. Philip Boehm II, born 7 Mar 1778; died 28 Jun 1869.
10. David Boehm, born 1780. Confirmed 1796 at Lower Saucon Church
11. Elizabeth Boehm, born 28 May 1784.

IV.   CATHERINE BOEHM

Catherine Boehm was born 1769. She married (1) Jacob Kram II, son of Jacob Kram I and Barbara. Following Jacob's death she married (2) George or Henry Roseberger in 1806.

Catherine had the following children:

CHILDREN of Jacob Kram I and Catherine Boehm:
1. Mary Magdalena Kram, born 1785.
2. Susannah Kram, born 1786. Married Rinker.
3. Elizabeth Kram, born 1788. Probably married Dill.
4. Jacob Kram III, born 1791
5. <u>David Kramm</u>, born 26 Jan 1793, Lower Saucon Township, Northampton Co., Pennsylvania. Died 28 September 1882.
6. Joseph Kram, born about 1795. Married Maria Mill 1 Sept 1816.

7. Samuel Kram, born about 1798. Married Hannah Buckwalter

CHILDREN of Catherine Boehm and Mr. Roseberger are:
8. Nancy Roseberger
9. Elizabeth Roseberger

For more information on David Kramm and his descendants,
see Kramm section, page 220.

THE MARTIN FAMILY

Harry Hammond Wilcox 1887-1943	m.	Hattie Estelle Richner 1891-1977
James Martin Wilcox 1854-1911	m.	Ada Virginia Kramm 1856-1934
Lewis Gates Wilcox 1823-1861	m.	Margaret P. Martin 1828-1885
Robert Martin (1775/80-1847)	m.	Sarah Day (1783-1860/70)

The research on this family is still on going and has been very challenging: We invite you to submit additions or corrections to ancestry@wilcoxkids.net.

Robert Martin was born between 1775-1780 (possibly in New Jersey or Pennsylvania) and died before about 1847 in Lycoming Co., Pennsylvania.

Robert married Sarah Day, born in 1783 (likely in Pennsylvania) and died between 1860-1870.

The CHILDREN of Robert Martin and Sarah Day are:
1. Deborah Martin died before 1850, married Joseph Wallis, who was born 1798 in Pennsylvania.
2. Mercy Ann Martin born about 1804, married William King Jr. on 6 Jul 1837 in Lycoming Co., Pennsylvania.
3. Sophia Martin was born in 1806 in Pennsylvania. She married Jacob Huff, who was born in 1813 in Pennsylvania and died in 1856 in Fort Madison, Lee Co., Iowa.
   They had two daughters:
   a. Gertrude Huff, born in 1846
   b. Debora Huff, born in 1848
   Nothing else is known about Sophia and her daughters after 1860 in Fort Madison, Iowa.
4. Elizabeth Martin was born in 1806 in Pennsylvania. On 29

Apr 1830 in Loyalsock, Lycoming Co. Pennsylvania, she married Edward Wallis, who was born in 1787.

Their children were:

a. Robert Wallis, born Jun 1831 and died between 1900-1910.

b. Elizabeth Wallis, born 1834

c. Mary Wallis, born in 1836

d. Thomas Wallis, born in 1838 and died in 1921

e. Abigail Wallis, born in 1842

f. Margaret Wallis, born in 1849

5. Benjamin F. Martin was born in 30 Jun 1808 and died 17 Jan 1882. He married Mercy about 1830-1835. They lived in LeBouff, Erie Co., Pennsylvania.

Their children:

a. Catherine Martin, born in 1836

b. Mary C. Martin, born in 1839

c. Margaret Martin, born 12 May 1842 and died 29 Nov 1913

d. James R. Martin, born in 1845

e. George P. Martin, born in 1847

f. Elizabeth Martin, born in Sept 1848 and died 20 Mar 1893

g. Robert B. Martin, born in 1853 and died 18 Feb 1882

6. Lewis Martin, born about 1808 married Margaret. Their children:

a. Richard Martin, born about 1840

b. Robert Martin, born about 1842

c. James C. Martin, born in Mar 1846

7. Richard Martin, born about 1813

8. a boy

9. Anna Eliza Martin, born in Mar 1825 and died 1 Mar 1918 in Williamsport, Lycoming Co., Pennsylvania. She married Cornelius Shearer in 1844. He was born 28 Oct 1818 in Glasgow, Scotland, and died 12 Dec 1891 in Williamsport, Lycoming Co., Pennsylvania. Cornelius was a lumberman and worked for the railroad. His lengthy obituary appeared on page 1 of the *Grit* on Dec 13, 1891. Their twelve children were:

a. James B. Shearer, born in 1846 in Pennsylvania and died 2 Nov 1898 in Galveston, Texas. He married Louisa Frederika Wilamena Baumgarden on 11 Jan 1868 in Texas.

b. Robert M. Shearer, born in Aug 1848 and died 9 Feb 1918 in Osceola Mills, Fairfield Co., Pennsylvania. He married

Adelaide ____.

    c. William T. Shearer, born in Oct 1850

    d. Elizabeth Shearer (twin) born in 1851

    e. Samuel T. Shearer (twin) born in 1851

    f. Cornelius G. Shearer, born in Nov 1853

    g. John D. Shearer, born in 1855

    h. Freman Shearer, born in 1857

    i. Harry R. Shearer, born in 1859 and married Lillie M. Horn

    j. Ida May Shearer, born in Nov 1862 and married Fred Houck, one of the grocers James Martin Wilcox worked with as a butcher.

    k. Joseph Shearer, born in Jul 1863

    l. Edward H. Shearer, born in 1867

10. Robert B. Martin, born in 1826 and died after 1900 in California. He was a blacksmith. He married Ellen Gurley on 27 Jan 1848 in LaSalle Co., Illinois. After her death, he married Waltie on 22 Dec 1864 in Trinity, California. Waltie was a Native America woman. They had about 11 children.

11. <u>Margaret P. Martin</u> married Lewis Gates Wilcox.

For more information, see Wilcox section, page 213.

THE RICHNER FAMILY

<table>
<tr><td>Harry Hammond Wilcox
1887-1943</td><td>m.</td><td>Hattie Estelle Richner
1891-1977</td></tr>
<tr><td>Rudolf Rufus Richner
(1859-1939)</td><td>m.</td><td>Clara Misho
(1859-1923)</td></tr>
<tr><td>Johan Rudolf Richner
(1821-1874)</td><td>m.</td><td>Verena Weitman
(1815-1892)</td></tr>
</table>

The Richner line in America begins with Johan "Rudolf" Richner, who came from Canton Aargau, Switzerland.

He took the oath to become a citizen on 6 Oct 1854 in Philadelphia.

We are grateful to our cousins Lou-Jean Rehn and Mark Richner for their research and notes.

I. JOHAN RUDOLF RICHNER

Johan "Rudolf" Richner was born about 1821 in Switzerland and he died 9 Feb 1874 in Williamsport, Pennsylvania. He married Verena Weitman in Switzerland/Germany. She was born 6 July 1815, likely in Switzerland, and died 11 Jan 1892 in Waterville, Marshall Co., Kansas.
They had 8 CHILDREN:

    1. Jacob Richner, born 5 Aug 1842 in Switzerland and died in 1919 in Williamstown, Dauphin Co., Pennsylvania. He left Williamsport and changed his name to Jacob Moyer and set up in Williamstown, Pennsylvania.

    Jacob married

    (1) Susan Ziegler. They had 3 children:

    a. Mamie Moyer, born Aug 1874. She married William F. Williams 15 Mar 1892 in Williamstown, Pennsylvania. They had 6 children:

        1. Emma Amelia Williams, born Sept 1898

        2. Edith M. Williams, born Feb 1893

        3. John Rudolph Williams, born Mar 1896

4. Ruth C. Williams, born about 1899

5. Amelia Williams, born about 1904

6. Margaret Williams, born about 1906

b. Rudolph R. Moyer, born 10 Oct 1876 and died in 1960 in Williamstown, Dauphin Co., Pennsylvania. He married Bertha May Lower 10 May 1898 in Dauphin Co., Pennsylvania.

They had 11 children.

c. Emma Moyer, born Aug 1879

(2) Jacob Moyer married second Ida Riegler 15 Nov 1904 in Harrisburg, Pennsylvania. They had 5 children:

d. William Moyer (1906-1981)

e. Harry Moyer (1907- 1986)

f. Pearl Moyer (about 1910-)

g. Ida Moyer (1912-1995)

h. Charles Moyer (about. 1914 -)

2. Elizabeth Richner, born 2 May 1844/46 in Switzerland and died before 1854 in Switzerland.

3. John Richner, born December 14, 1845, in Canton Aargau, Switzerland. John enlisted as a musician in the Union Army in 1863 at the age of 18 years and 1 month, and took part in General David Hunter's expedition to Lynchburg, Virginia. He was taken prisoner and held at Andersonville, and later at Florence Stockade. He died of "acute colitis" 26 Jan 1865 in the Florence Infirmary, Florence, South Carolina, while a prisoner of the Confederates during the Civil War. He is interred in the Florence National Cemetery.[111]

4. Varina "Fannie" Richner, born 21 Oct 1850 in Switzerland and died 20 Nov 1902 in Centralia, Nemaha Co., Kansas. She married Michael Niggly 2 Apr 1872 in Waterville, Marshall Co., Kansas. He was born 9 Sept 1839 in Federis, Canton Gruwbunden, Switzerland, and died 23 Jan 1893 in Salt Lake City, Utah. They had 6 children:

a. infant son, born and died Nov 1872 in Waterville, Kansas

b. infant son, born and died Dec 1873 in Waterville, Kansas

c. infant son, born and died 1874 in Waterville, Kansas

d. infant girl, born and died 1876 in Waterville, Kansas

e. Laura Matilda Niggly, born 17 Sept 1878 and died 14 Oct 1889 in Waterville, Kansas

f. Florence Alfretta "Flossie" Niggly, born 2 Apr 1889 and

4 Sept 1981 in San Diego, California. Florence married in 1908 in Marshall Co. Kansas to Jay Thompson (1881-1941). They had 3 CHILDREN:

1. Jean Dale Thompson (1909-1972) married in 1936 to Dorothy Pauline Branch
2. Carol Jaylette Thompson (1913-1977) married in 1937 in Greeley, Colorado to Lewis Eugene Holland (1914-1992)
3. Muriel Arlene Thompson.

g. In addition to these six children of their own, Fannie and Michael raised Michael's Nephew, Josiah or Joseph Niggly (born 1874 in Arkansas) who is listed in some census records as their son. "He was the son of Michael's brother Peter and his wife Margaret Walley. After Margaret died Peter dropped the older children off with Margaret's parents, took baby Joe and headed to Colorado to seek his fortune in gold. Along the way he dropped baby Joe off with Michael and Fanny. Michael and Fanny raised him. My Grandmother Flossie always thought of him as an older brother, but he was her cousin."[112]

5. Anna Aba Richner. According to the family lore she was born at sea (about 1 Jan 1854) though she claimed New York as her place of birth, where her birth was first officially recorded. This was traditional practice at the time. She died 9 Jan 1920 in Williamsport, Pennsylvania.

6. <u>Rudolf Rufus Richner</u>, born 11 Nov 1859 in Norristown, Pennsylvania. (See below)

7. Mary Ann Richner, born 10 Nov 1855 in Norristown, Pennsylvania, and died 4 July 1935 at Fort Mead, South Dakota. She married Lyman Hawley Bennett on 22 June 1885 in Marysville, Marshall Co. Kansas. He was born 9 Dec 1842 in Franklinville, New York.

They had one daughter:

a. Verena Ann Bennett, born 2 Dec 1888 in Centralia, Nemaha Co., Kansas, and died 13 Apr 1936 at Fort Mead, South Dakota.

8. Emma Pauline Richner, born 2 June 1868 in Williamsport, Pennsylvania, and died 6 Feb 1941. She married Joseph A. Craig 31 May 1887 in Waterville, Marshall Co. Kansas.

They had one son:

a. Monte Cristo Craig, born 13 May 1895 Manitoba, Canada, and died 16 Sept 1959 in Saskatoon, Saskatchewan, Canada.

II.   RUDOLF RUFUS RICHNER

Rudolf Rufus Richner was born 11 Nov 1859 in Norristown, Pennsylvania, and died 12 Dec 1939 in Williamsport. He was a son of Johan (Rudolf) Richner and Verena Weitman.

Rudolf married Clara Misho in 1883 in Williamsport, Pennsylvania. Clara was born 8 May 1859 in Pennsylvania and died 6 Apr 1923 in Williamsport, Pennsylvania. They had 6 children, all born in Williamsport, Pennsylvania:

1. Emma Elizabeth Richner, born 8 Aug 1883 and died 12 Jan 1969 in Muncy, Pennsylvania. She married James "Doc" Mahlon Winder on 9 Jan 1907 in Williamsport, Pennsylvania. He was born 10 Sept 1883 in Warrensville, Pennsylvania, and died 16 Jan 1955 in Montgomery, Pennsylvania.

They had two sons:

a. Mahlon Aden Winder, born 29 Dec 1907 in Williamsport, Pennsylvania, and died in Feb 1983 in Montgomery, Pennsylvania. He married Louise Clark. They had 5 children.

b. Austin Rudolf Winder, born 5 July 1910 in Williamsport, Pennsylvania, and 1 Dec 1973 in Williamsport, Pennsylvania. He married twice: (1) Beryl Scheffler. She was born 21 Jan 1905 and died 1 Apr 1972 in Muncy, Pennsylvania.

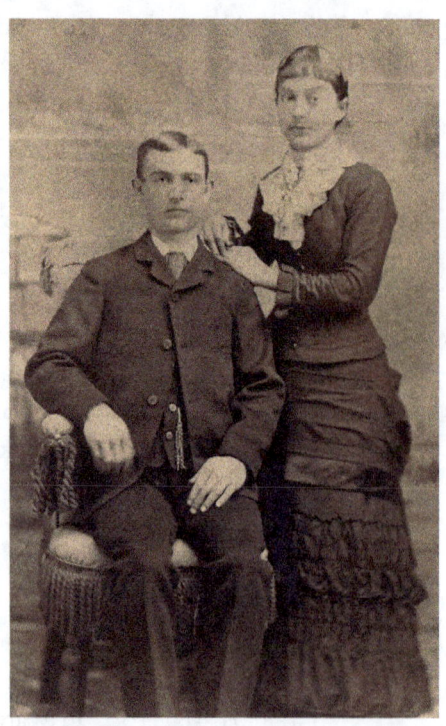

Rudolf and Clara Misho Richner, 1883.

They had 2 daughters.

(2) Doris Hunter was born 27 Apr 1946 in Lock Haven, Pennsylvania.

They had 2 children.

2. Mary Olivia Richner, born 11 Apr 1886 and died 15 Aug 1974 in Williamsport, Pennsylvania. She married Charles Aden Winder on 20 Jan 1909. He was born 20 Feb 1886 and died 3 Aug 1961 in Williamsport, Pennsylvania. They had one daughter:

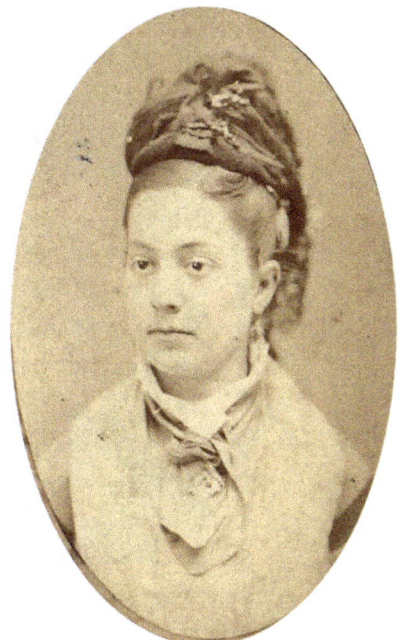

Clara Misho (Richner), 1885, about age 17.

a. Verena Harriett Winder, born 25 Oct 1909 and died 28 May 1999 in Williamsport, Pennsylvania. She married Franklin Earl Cole on 26 June 1933 in Williamsport, Pennsylvania. He was born 1 Mar 1906 in Montoursville, Pennsylvania, and died 22 Jan 1971 in Williamsport, Pennsylvania. They had one son.

3. Julia Gertrude Richner, born 21 Dec 1888 and died 14 March 1980 in Williamsport, Pennsylvania. She married Ross Lester Conn, on 17 June 1913. He was born 29 May 1889 in Jackson Twp., Lycoming Co., Pennsylvania, and died 5 January 1979 in Williamsport, Pennsylvania. Their daughter:

   a. Ruth Eleanor Conn, born 23 Oct 1917 and died 30 May 2002 in Utica, Macomb Co., Michigan. She married Frederick Irvin Barrett on 20 Aug 1942 in South Williamsport, Pennsylvania. He was born 21 Sept 1902 in Williamsport, Pennsylvania, and died 27 Dec 1969 in Bellevue, Ohio. They had 2 sons.

4. Hattie Estelle Richner, born 11 June 1891 and died 23 June 1977 in Memphis, Tennessee. She married Harry Hammond Wilcox on 24 Aug 1911 in Williamsport, Pennsylvania.

   They had 3 children. For more on the descendants of Harry and Hattie Richner Wilcox, see page 217.

5. George Austin Richner, born 9 Sept 1893 and died 28 May

1977 in Williamsport, Pennsylvania. He married Kathryn Reed Harrison 12 June 1916 in Williamsport, Pennsylvania. She was born 8 June 1895 in Williamsport, Pennsylvania, and died 20 June 1981 in Williamsport, Pennsylvania. They had 2 sons:

a. George Austin Jr. "Jim" married Katherine Bernstine (1919-1997). They had a daughter and a son.

b. Edward M., married Phyllis Maneval (1921-1995). They had a son and a daughter.

6. Ruth Omelia Richner, born 10 Oct 1895 and died in Jan 1897 in Williamsport, Pennsylvania. Her parents gave a stained glass window to Saint Mary's Episcopal church, Williamsport, in memory of Ruth.

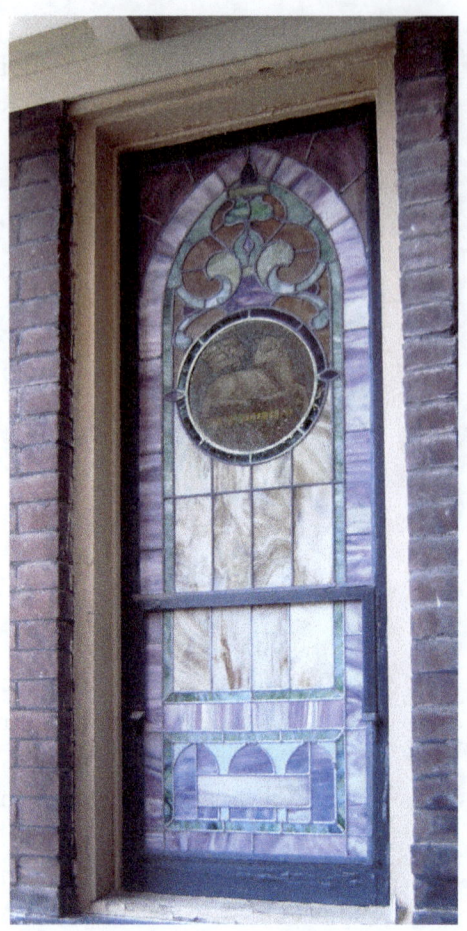

Window in memory of Ruth Omelia Richner (1895-1897), in the former St. Mary's Episcopal Church, 912 Almond Street, Williamsport.

III. HATTIE ESTELLE RICHNER

Hattie Estelle Richner, born 11 June 1891 and died 23 June 1977 in Memphis, Tennessee. She married Harry Hammond Wilcox on 24 Aug 1911 in Williamsport, Pennsylvania. They had 3 children.

For more on the descendants of Harry and Hattie Richner Wilcox, see page 217.

THE MISHO FAMILY

Harry Hammond Wilcox 1887-1943	m.	Hattie Estelle Richner 1891-1977
Rudolf Rufus Richner (1859-1939)	m.	Clara Misho (1859-1923)
Elias Misho (1831-1902)	m.	Mary Steinbacher (1832-1911)

Clara Misho was the daughter of Elias "Eli" Misho and Mary Karolina C. P. Steinbacher.

Elias "Eli" Misho was born about 1831, in Pennsylvania, and died 1 Dec 1902 in Williamsport, Lycoming Co. Pennsylvania.

He married Mary Steinbacher about 1850. She was born 11 Aug 1832 in Kleinbittendorf, Saarbruchen, Rheinpreussen (Germany) and died 13 May 1911 in Williamsport, Pennsylvania.

Eli worked as a laborer at a number of jobs, including working in a saw mill. Lumbering was one of the major industries in Williamsport at the time. He registered for the draft in the Civil War, but evidently was not called up. On his draft registration and in the 1900 census he lists his father as having been born in France, and his mother in Germany.

His obituary lists a "half-brother," Rev. O. P. Farling. It is possible that his mother remarried and had additional children by the name of Farling. This may be the Rev. Obediah J. Farling (1839-1927) of Harrisburg, who had a brother John H. Farling (1844-1909). Their father may likely be Jacob Farling (1800-1854). The name Misho (of French origin) is sometimes spelled Mishow or Michau or similar variants.

Eli and Mary had 10 children:

1. Margaret Helen Misho, born in 1855. She married Oliver W. Trowbridge.
2. Clara Misho, born 8 May 1859. Married Rudolf Richner.
3. George E. Misho, born Nov 1862 and died 30 Oct 1940. He married Mary Adah Stinson.
   They had 5 children:
   a. Blanche May Misho, born in Mar 1885

b. Ruth Misho

c. Bruce F. Misho, born Feb 1889 and died 14 Apr 1910 at Mt. Alto Tuberculosis clinic, Pennsylvania.

d. Louise Kathryn Misho, born June 1891 and died 1981. She married Guy N. Flohr.

e. John Thomas Misho, born 29 May 1905 and died 7 Mar 1907.

4. Hattie Estelle Misho, born in 1863. She married Harry W. Levering on 25 June 1884.

They had 5 children:

a. Rachel Sidney Levering, born 28 Apr 1885 and died about 1936.

b. Charles Eli Levering, born 12 Apr 1888 and died about 1934.

c. Thomas H. Levering, born 6 Apr 1902 and died 3 June 1968 in Williamsport, Pennsylvania. He married Isabell H. Crone on 25 Sept 1925. Thomas Levering was the mayor of Williamsport from 1955 to 1963.

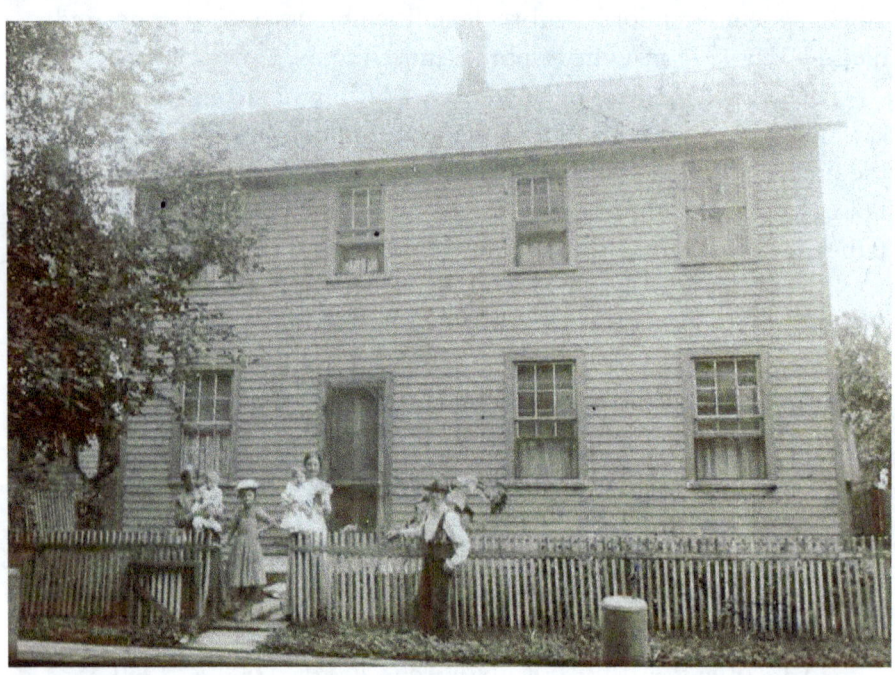

The Mishos at 93 Meade Street in Williamsport, about 1902. Left to right: Aunt Ellen (Susan Gertrude Misho McKenna) with Helen Margaret McKenna (age 3), Hattie Richner (Wilcox) age 11, Aunt Julia Misho Patterson with Charlotte Busler (age 2), Elias Misho. The house number was later changed by the post office and is sometimes reported as #1100.

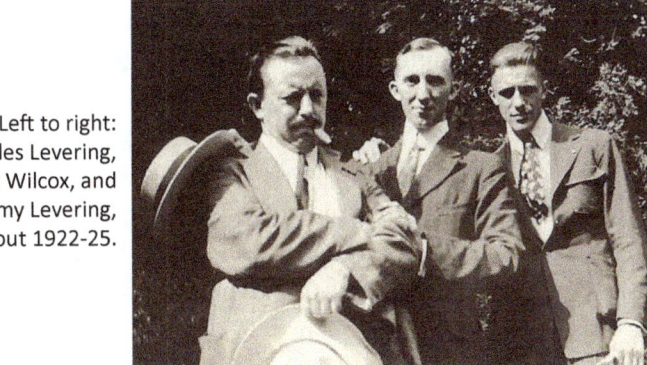

Left to right: Charles Levering, Harry Wilcox, and Tommy Levering, about 1922-25.

d. Edward Albert Levering, born 4 Apr 1892 and died 8 Sept 1892.

e. infant

5. John Misho, born in 1864 and died 23 June 1943 in Carlisle, Pennsylvania.

6. Lucy G. Misho, born 1867 and died before 1880.

7. Elizabeth Lenore Misho, born Feb 1869 and died 9 Sept 1962. She married Norman Charles Busler (or Bussler) on 25 Feb 1897 in Williamsport, Pennsylvania. They had 2 daughters, and moved to Cleveland, Ohio.

   a. Charlotte Busler, born Feb 1900 and died 11 May 1993 in Williamsport, Pennsylvania. She married George Buehner.

   b. Rachel Busler, born 1908. She married James T. Harter.

8. Julia "Jewell" Misho, born in 1871. She married Henry Clay Patterson in 1906.

  They had a daughter:

   a. Elizabeth Patterson

9. Charles Elias Misho, born 7 Sept 1874 and died 8 Apr 1953. He married Lois Adella Allen in 1905. She was born 31 May 1882 in Virginia and died 22 Feb 1958. They had 5 children:

   a. Oliver Randolph Misho, born 10 Apr 1906

   b. Vivian L. Misho, born in Nov 1909. Married Winter.

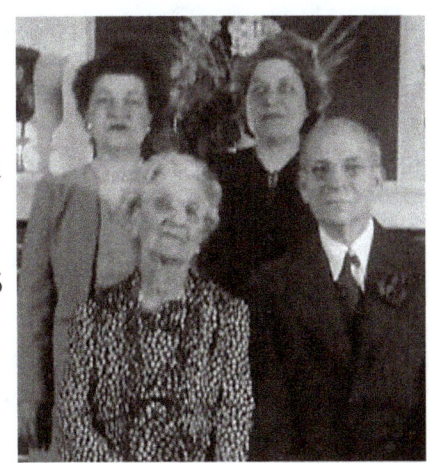

Sitting: Elizabeth Misho Busler, Norman Charles Busler. *Standing:* Rachel Busler (Buehner), Charlotte Busler (Harter).

c. Vada Leona Misho, born 18 July 1914

d. Bernadine Misho, born in Dec 1917 and died in 1980.

e. Charles C. Misho, born in Oct 1919

10. Susan Gertrude "Ellen" Misho, born in Feb 1880 and died before 1910. She married Alfred McKenna on 3 May 1899. They had 2 children:

a. Helen Margaret McKenna, born in Dec 1899

b. Frederick Obadiah McKenna, born 9 Dec 1903

II.   CLARA MISHO

Clara Misho was born 8 May 1859 in Pennsylvania and died 6 Apr 1923 in Williamsport, Pennsylvania. She married Rudolf Richner in 1883 in Williamsport, Pennsylvania.

Rudolf Rufus Richner was born 11 Nov 1859 in Norristown, Pennsylvania, and died 12 Dec 1939 in Williamsport. He was a son of Johan (Rudolf) Richner and Verena Weitman.

They had 6 children, all born in Williamsport, Pennsylvania.

For more information, see Richner section, page 258.

THE STEINBACHER FAMILY

<table>
<tr><td>Harry Hammond Wilcox
1887-1943</td><td>m.</td><td>Hattie Estelle Richner
1891-1977</td></tr>
<tr><td>Rudolf Rufus Richner
(1859-1939)</td><td>m.</td><td>Clara Misho
(1859-1923)</td></tr>
<tr><td>Elias Misho
(1818-1902)</td><td>m.</td><td>Mary Steinbacher
(1832-1911)</td></tr>
<tr><td>Joseph Johann Steinbacher
(b. 1800)</td><td>m.</td><td>Katherine Bauer
(b. 1806)</td></tr>
<tr><td>Johannes Steinbacher</td><td>m.</td><td>Maria Chauvin</td></tr>
</table>

Mary Karolina C. P. Steinbacher was born 11 Aug 1832 in Kleinbittendorf, Saarbruchen, Rheinprussia (Germany) and died 13 May 1911 in Williamsport, Pennsylvania. She was a daughter of Joseph Johann Steinbacher. Mary came to America about 1839.

Joseph and his family came with his two brothers. Mary's uncles were the Reverend Father Nicholas Steinbacher, the first Priest of the Immaculate Conception Church in Bastress, Lycoming Co., Pennsylvania; and Johann Theodore Steinbacher, who died 13 Feb 1856 in Bastress, Lycoming Co., Pennsylvania, after he split open his foot while cutting timber.

I. JOSEPH JOHANN STEINBACHER

Joseph Johann Steinbacher was born in 1800 in Kleinbittendorf, Germany, son of Johannes Steinbacher and Maria Chauvin). He married Katherine Bauer on 19 Jul 1825. Katherine was born in 1806 in Lohbach, Rheinpreussen.

The 13 children of Joseph Johann Steinbacher and Katherine Bauer are:
1. Heinrich Steinbacher, born 25 Sept 1826
2. Margaretha Steinbacher, born 8 May 1830
3. Mary Karolina Steinbacher, born 11 Aug 1832

4. Johann Baptist Steinbacher, born 4 Feb 1834

5. Nicholas C. Steinbacher, born in 1835

6. Susanna Steinbacher, born 5 Dec 1837

7. Katherine Steinbacher, born in 1839

8. Mary Magdalena Steinbacher, born 20 Sept 1840

9. Anna Steinbacher, born 8 Aug 1842

10. Barbara Lucia Steinbacher, born in 1844

11. Aloeseus Steinbacher, born in 1846

12. Joseph John Steinbacher, born in June 1848

13. Peter Ludwig Steinbacher, born 14 July 1851

II. MARY KAROLINA STEINBACHER

Mary Karollina Steinbacher was born 11 August 1832. She married Elias Misho.

For more information, see page 261.

Notes and References

1. David Kramm is found in the 1850 Census with real estate valued at $12,100; in the 1860 census land valued at $11,100; in the 1870 census the real estate was listed at $4000, probably because he was breaking up his original land into family farms for his children.

2. William Kramm is found in the 1860 Census with real estate valued at $5000 and in the 1870 with land valued at $29,200 — quite a sizable farm for the day. William Kramm was born 1823 in Lehigh Co. PA and died in 1898. His wife Margaret Billmeyer, a daughter of George and Anna (Himmelreich) Billmeyer was born 1819 and died in 1902.

3. Lewis Gates Wilcox (1823-1861) and Margaret P. Martin (1828-1885) had seven children:
   Robert Bruce Wilcox 1847-1919 married Mary F. Vollmer
   Sarah Virginia "Sadie" Wilcox 1849-1922 married Pete Follmer
   Adolphus Lee Wilcox 1852-1922 married Jane A.
   James Martin Wilcox 1854-1911 married Ada Virginia Kramm
   Daniel Clinton Wilcox 1858-1929 married Verna (Sarah A.) Creasy
   William A. Wilcox 1860-1863 (died young)
   Lewis Gates Wilcox Jr 1862-1925 (did not marry)
   For more information, see pages 197ff. and 213.

4. Article by Garr in the Sunday *Grit*, 22 April 1913. Garr quotes a letter written to him by Adolphus Lee Wilcox, then residing at 60 Dearborn Street, Chicago, Illinois, responding to an illustrated article printed in the paper on 9 February 1913, showing and describing the new concrete bridge. Garr continues, "Mr. Wilcox will be remembered by residents of Montoursville and this city [Williamsport]. He was a student at Dickinson Seminary in 1873, and since he left school he has written several books."

5. According to the Williamsport City Directories, which list professions and sometimes business addresses, James Martin Wilcox worked for J. B. Gibson & Son 1904-1905; as a clerk with the Grand Tea

Company 1906-1909; and as an agent with the Great Atlantic and Pacific Tea Company in 1910.

6.   Daniel B. Emminger (Eminger) enlisted 1 July 1861 and was discharged 7 July 1864. He served as a Private in Company E, 39th Pennsylvania Infantry, and later in Company I, 191st Pennsylvania Infantry. He was granted Invalid benefits in 1889, and Letitia was granted widow's benefits in 1892. Civil War Pension Index (ancestry.com), and 1890 Veteran Census for Pennsylvania Clarion Co.

7.   *Judge* magazine cover image and quote from the story are reprinted with permission from the website graphicwitness.org.

8.   "Man of Grit: Dietrick Lamade and Sunday *Grit*," *Williamsport Sun Gazette.* August 17, 2008.

9.   Robin Van Auken, *Sunday Grit: A Newspaper Legacy,* Williamsport, 2008, p. 20.

10.   Robin Van Auken, *Sunday Grit: A Newspaper Legacy,* Williamsport, 2008, p. 18.

11.   *Sunday Grit* newspaper, September 6, 1908.

12.   John Rudolf Richner left Canton Aargau, Switzerland, with his wife and four children and arrived in America with another daughter, Anna, who was born at sea. He took the Oath of Intent to be Citizen of the United States on October 6, 1854. Three more children were born to this family. Rudolf was the next to the youngest, born in Norristown, Pennsylvania in 1859. John Rudolf Richner was a stonemason by trade. He was working to put up a building and fell onto a pile of stones, which left him an invalid until his death in 1874. His widow Verena (Weitman) Richner moved to Waterville, Marshall Co., Kansas, and died there in 1892. See pages 255ff.

13.   Rudolf died in Williamsport in 1939. In 1883 he married Clara Misho (daughter of Elias "Eli" and Mary Caroline (Steinbacher) Misho in Williamsport, Pennsylvania. They had six children. One daughter died young. Their four girls and their baby brother all lived well past 80. Hattie Estelle was the fourth daughter. She was born in 1891 in Williamsport, Pennsylvania, and died in Memphis, Tennessee in 1977. See pages 258ff.

14.   Interview with Jim and Ed Richner, sons of Hattie's brother George

Austin "Dick" Richner, Williamsport, April 2011.

15. Source: a letter from the Principal, collection of JHW.

16. Warren is listed in the 1910 census as working in a restaurant as a waiter. In 1904, Warren was working and had been working for a number of years at the Lycoming Rubber Company (source letter of recommendation from the papers of Warren Kramm Wilcox, collection of JHW).

17. Interview with Jim and Ed Richner, Williamsport, April 2011.

18. In this church there is a window in memory of Hattie's youngest sister Ruth who died young. See photo page 260.

19. From the obituary of John Emminger in the Titusville newspaper, 1964, provided by his granddaughter, Sally Iesue, August 2009.

20. For more on John Emminger's later years, see pages 216 ff.

21. Fox New Services, "Mutt and Jeff visited at their studio," mimeographed news release, February 16, 1917. Museum of Modern Art Collection. As quoted in Donald Crafton, *Before Mickey: The Animated Film 1898-1928* (Cambridge, Massachusetts, 1982), p. 164

22. Richard Fleischer, *Out of the Inkwell: Max Fleischer and the Animation Revolution*, Lexington, Kentucky, 2005, p. 29.

23. Lewis Richner Wilcox was born 21 Feb 1921 in Pennsauken township, Camden Co. New Jersey and died eight days later, 1 Mar 1921, in Merchantville, Camden Co. New Jersey

24. Interview with Norman Cole, son of Verena and Earl Cole, and grandson of Mary and Charlie Winder, 2010.

25. Hattie may have been Rh-negative, as one of her granddaughters is Rh-negative. When the mother is Rh-negative and the father is Rh-positive, the fetus can inherit the Rh factor from the father. This makes the fetus Rh-positive too. Problems can arise when the fetus's blood has the Rh factor and the mother's blood does not. If the mother is Rh-negative, she may develop antibodies to an Rh-positive baby. If a small amount of the baby's blood mixes with her blood, which often happens, her body may respond as if it were allergic to the baby. Her body may make antibodies to the Rh antigens in the baby's blood. This means she

has become sensitized and her antibodies can cross the placenta and attack the baby's blood. They break down the fetus's red blood cells and produce anemia (the blood has a low number of red blood cells). This condition is called hemolytic disease or hemolytic anemia. It can become severe enough to cause serious illness, brain damage, or even death in the fetus or newborn. This might have been the cause of baby Lewis' death. Today there is a shot to prevent the development of antibodies in the mother's body and prevent problems in future pregnancies. However, in 1920 this condition was not yet understood. (Information on Rh factor from the American Pregnancy Association.)

26. Interview with Les Clark, page 131, from the book *Working with Walt: Interviews with Disney Artists,* by Don Peri, 2008.

27. Interview with Dick Huemer, page 45, from Peri, *Working with Walt.*

28. Neal Gabler, *Walt Disney: The Triumph of American Imagination,* p. 86

29. Interview with Ben Sharpsteen, page 3, from Peri, *Working with Walt.*

30. Donald Crafton, *Before Mickey,* page 298.

31. Interview with Jim and Ed Richner, April 2011.

32. Interview with Floyd Gottfredson, page 111, from Peri, *Working with Walt.*

33. *Detroit City Directory, 1930,* and *The City of Detroit, Michigan, 1701-1922,* by William Stocking and Gordon K. Miller, (Detroit 1922), p. 605.

34. Interview with Jim and Ed Richner, April 2011.

35. "A Chronology of Camouflage: A Pastiche in a Bouillabaisse," introductory address by Roy R. Behrens at the International Camouflage Conference, April 22, 2006, University of Northern Iowa. As quoted in Wikipedia, "Theory of Camouflage"

36. Seymour Reit, *Masquerade: The Amazing Camouflage Deceptions of World War II* (NY 1978), p. 91

37. Reit, *Masquerade,* p. 66.

38. Roy M. Stanley II, *To Fool a Glass Eye: Camouflage versus Photoreconnaissance in World War II,* Washington, DC, 1998, page 139.

39. Tim Newark, *Camouflage*, Imperial War Museum, London, 2007.

40. Interview with Meredith W. Alair, Jr.

41. Seymour Reit, *Masquerade*, pp 98-101.

42. Interview with Meredith Alair Jr., 2012.

43. Our thanks go to Nicolet V. Elert, Intern, Research Library & Archives, Detroit Institute of Arts, for searching their collection of exhibition catalogs to find these listings.

44. Bud was red-blue-green color blind, and one of his grandsons and one great-grandson inherited the same trait. It is a trait passed to a male child from his mother, which means that Hattie's father or grandfather would also have been color blind.

45. Interview with Mark Richner, 2012.

46. Quoted from William Richard Cutter, ed., *New England Families, genealogical and memorial: a record of the achievements of her people in the making of commonwealths and the founding of a nation,* page 2014.

47. History of North Kingston, Rhode Island, as posted on the Town's website, http://www.northkingstown.org, History

48. As quoted in Edwin Gaustad, *Liberty of Conscience: Roger Williams in America,* Judson Press, 1999, p.28.

49. FaFantasie, Glenn W., ed., *The Correspondence of Roger Williams,* University Press of New England, 1988, vol. 1, pp. 12-23

50. History of the Town of North Kingston, Rhode Island, from their website, www.northkingstown.org

51. Austin, *Genealogical Dictionary of Rhode Island.*

52. Wm. Richard Cutter's *Genealogical and Family History of Central New York,* Vol. III, Pages 1435-6:

53. Cutter, *Genealogical and Family History of Central New York,* Vol III:1436; and John Osborne Austin, "The Genealogical dictionary of Rhode Island: comprising of three generations of settlers who came before 1690"

54. John Osborne Austin, *Genealogical Dictionary of Rhode Island.*

55. American Genealogical Research Institute, *Wilcox Family History,* Heritage Press, Washington, DC, 1978, page 67

56. Connecticut Historical Society, *The Record of Connecticut Men in the Military and Naval Service During the War of the Revolution, 1775-1783,* pp. 368-369, Colonel Swift's Regiment . . . during the War of the Revolution.

57. Reference: Vol 8, fifth Series, Pennsylvania Archives

58. Notes from Harry Wilcox Jr.

59. Peter arrived in 1776, 1777, 1780, or 1783 depending which of four Peter Himmelreichs he may be. See Records 3067.30 p 74, 3067.32, 3067.30 in "Hessische Truppen im Amerikanischen Unabhaengigkeitskreig (Hetrina): Index nach Familiennamen. (Marburg: Archivschule) (Veroeffentlichungen der Archivschule Marburg, Institut fuer Archivwissenschaft, Nr. 10)." Band I. Marburg, 1976; Auflage, 1984, p.74; Band III. Marburg, 1976; Auflage, 1984, p.205

60. Hamilton Child, editor, *Gazetteer and Business Directory of Chenango County, New York,* for 1869-70

61. Published in *Oxford New York Times,* 1898, written by Lewis D. Burdick. Burdick sent a copy of this article with a handwritten note to Daniel Clinton Wilcox (1858-1929). It was passed by his widow Verna C Creasy Wilcox to Warren Kramm Wilcox (1882-1954), who then passed it to our father, Harry ("Bud") Wilcox (1918-2010), who passed it to us.

62. *History of Lycoming County Pennsylvania,* edited by John F. Meginness, 1892, Chapter 56, entry concerning Nathaniel C. Johnson who worked for Gates Wilcox.

63. Article on the mill published in the *Williamsport Gazette and Bulletin,* August 17, 1905.

64. U.S. Patent Office, patent No. 740,962, filed January 26, 1903, and granted October 6, 1903.

65. Sam Behling's Register Report.

66. Jane Fletcher Fisk (NEHDR Vol. 147, p.188 April 1993)

67. John L. Sexton Jr, *History of Tioga County, Pennsylvania* (NY 1883)

68. Gene Decker, "Philip John Heilman," in the Logan County (Oklahoma) History 1889-1977.

69. George Keil, editor, *1892 Medical and Dental Registry Directory and Intelligencer for Pennsylvania, New Jersey, and Delaware, Philadelphia*, 1892.

70. We are grateful to our friend the late Michael Anthony Catrambone for his research and notes about our family.

71. We are thankful for the notes, photos, and letters they passed on by Daniel and Verna Creasy Wilcox to our father Harry Wilcox Jr.

72. We are extremely grateful for the photo album of Warren Wilcox, which he passed to his nephew, Harry Wilcox Jr.

73. Daniel B. Emminger (Eminger) enlisted 1 July 1861 and was discharged 7 July 1864. He served as a Private in Company E, 39th Pennsylvania Infantry, and later in Company I, 191st Pennsylvania Infantry. He was granted Invalid benefits in 1889, and Letitia was granted widow's benefits in 1892. Civil War Pension Index (ancestry.com), and 1890 Veteran Census for Pennsylvania Clarion Co.

74. Reference: Vol 8, fifth Series, Pennsylvania Archives

75. Notes from Harry Wilcox Jr.

76. Pennsylvania *Grit*, Local News Section, February 12, 1905, page 3, column 4.

77. John Blair Linn, *Annals of Buffalo Valley, Pennsylvania*, p. 72.

78. Linn, *Annals of Buffalo Valley*, p. 297.

79. J. H. Battle, ed., *History of Columbia and Montour Counties*, 1887, p. 132.

80. *History of McHenry County, Illinois : together with sketches of its cities, villages and towns, educational, religious, civil*, p. 555.

81. Woodstock, Illinois, *Sentinel* Newspaper, November 19, 1879. Supplied by Alice Hostetter of Spokane, Washington, e-mail dated 21 May 2008.

82. Obituary, *Muncy Luminary Newspaper* in Muncy, Pennsylvania,

February 24, 1850 "Henry, son of Charles CRAWFORD, died in this Borough on Sunday evening last, aged 3 years and 2 months."

83.   Obituary, *Muncy Luminary Newspaper* in Muncy, Pennsylvania, 18 May 1850.

84.   Lineage book, National Society of Daughters of the American Revolution, Volume 7, pp. 97-98, # 6285 also # 2547.

85.   This is the documentation needed to apply:
Military History of Peter Withington according to the Pennsylvania Society of Cincinnati:
1 Oct 1776 Captain 12th Penna. Reg - Illness, Philadelphia
Dec 1776 Captain 12th Penna. Reg - Sent Home, Sick
11 May 1777 Captain 12th Penna. Reg - DIS (Died In Service)
Northumberland County, Military Records of the 12th Penna. militia, "History of that part of the Susquehanna and Juniata Valleys, Embraced in the Counties of Mifflin, Juniata, Perry, Union and Snyder In The Commonwealth of Pennsylvania." Philadelphia, 1886, In Two Volumes, Vol 1, pp 97-99.

86.   *Colonial Records,* Vol. X. P. 756; Archives (Second Series), Vol. X. P 759.

87.   Source: http://files.usgwarchives.net/pa/northumberland/military/12thpa01.txt

88.   CG. Grand Account.CCLIX . . . p112, Bp540 as quoted in http://66.43.27.42/th/read/WOODRINGTON/2005-07/1121761401 reference provided by Barry Wetherington, cbarrfly@comcast.net

89.   From a letter from Bertha E. Kemmerer, 1218 Walnut Street, Philadelphia, Pennsylvania, to Mr & Mrs Harry M. Billmeyer, Pottsgrove, Pennsylvania, dated Sunday, February 28, 1954.

90.   Letter from Harold A. Deiterick to Harry Wilcox Jr.

91.   "According to Folk-Lore of the Pennsylvania Germans." Part I. from W. J. Hoffman, M. D., *Journal of American Folk-lore, 1888,* 1:2 pp. 125-35.

92.   Peter arrived in 1776, 1777, 1780, or 1783 depending which of four Peter Himmelreichs he may be. See Records 3067.30 p 74, 3067.32, 3067.30 in "Hessische Truppen im Amerikanischen

Unabhaengigkeitskreig (Hetrina): Index nach Familiennamen. (Marburg: Archivschule) (Veroeffentlichungen der Archivschule Marburg, Institut fuer Archivwissenschaft, Nr. 10)." Band I. Marburg, 1976; Auflage, 1984, p.74; Band III. Marburg, 1976; Auflage, 1984, p.205

93.   List of names from Harold Robinson, Gettysburg, Pennsylvania. Birth sequence is not yet determined.

94.   Source: Notes of Harry Wilcox Jr.

95.   Alfreda Patton Davidson, *David Kramm: his Ancestors and Descendants,* booklet published, 1978.

96.   The first major work on the life of the Rev. Boehm was contained in a book called *Proceedings of the ReUnion of Apple's Church and of the Boehm Family,* September 14, 1895, written by the Rev. A. P. Horn and published 1902. In 1916 a book of 501 pages was written and edited by the Rev. William J. Hinke entitled *Life and Letters of the Rev. John Philip Boehm.* The Rev. Hinke devotes 151 pages to the Rev. Boehm's life, ancestry, and descendants and to early church history. The remaining pages in the book are letters written from the Rev. Boehm to the Classis of Amsterdam, Holland, and their replies to the Rev. Boehm. This book has recently been reprinted in a series called "Religion in America" and is available in the original without charge online at Google books.

97.   Alfreda Patton Davidson, *David Kramm: his Ancestors and Descendants,* booklet published, 1978.

98.   As quoted in *Colonial Records of Pennsylvania,* Vol IV (1735-1745), p. 315.

99.   Alfreda Patton Davidson, *David Kramm: his Ancestors and Descendants,* booklet published, 1978.

100. Estimated by Rev. John Wilhelmius in a report to the Synod of South Holland, July 4-14, 1730. *Pennsylvania German Pioneers,* pp 64-113.

101. Carrie E. Bodensteiner, information shared at ancestry.com.

102. From a memorial elegy by Rev. Wilson F. More of Catasauqua, Pennsylvania, as quoted in *Proceedings of the Re-Union of Apple's Church and of the Boehm Family,* 1902, New Jerusalem Reformed and Lutheran Church, Leithsville, Northampton County, Pennsylvania, pp. 71-80.

103. William DeWees is one of the ancestors of June Freed Wilcox. See Graff and Wilcox, *A Freed Family History*, 1981, pages 79-83.

104. Antes is also an ancestor of June Freed Wilcox. See Graff & Wilcox, *A Freed Family History*, pp 49-66.

105. Alfreda Patton Davidson, *David Kramm: his Ancestors and Descendants*, booklet published, 1978.

106. Hinke, *Life and Letters of the Rev. John Philip Boehm*.

107. William W. H. Davis, *History of Northampton Co, Pennsylvania*, 1877.

108. Betty I. Ralph, as quoted by Carrie E. Bodensteiner, ancestry.com

109. Rev. Wilson F. More, as quoted in *Proceedings of the Re-Union of Apple's Church and of the Boehm Family*, 1902, pp. 71-80.

110. Patton Davidson, *David Kramm*, page 32.

111. We are grateful to Mark Richner for his diligent and persistent research on John Richner and his death as a prisoner of the Confederacy. He wrote up his findings in the article Mark Richner with Brian Mathias, "Tracking the Fate of Private John Richner, a Pennsylvania Volunteer in the Civil War," *The Journal of the Lycoming County Historical Society*, Volume 44:1-2, 2008.

112. Correspondence with LouJean Rehn, June 2012.

BIBLIOGRAPHY

Academy Hill Cemetery, Wellsboro, Tiago Co. PA

Alair, Verna Wilcox, all original art and jewelry are privately held and are reprinted with permisson.

American Genealogical Research Institute, *Wilcox Family History,* Heritage Press, Inc, Washington, D.C. 1978

Ancestry.com. Provo, Utah

Austin, John Osborne. *The Genealogical Dictionary of Rhode Island: comprising three generations of settlers who came before 1690,* Baltimore, Genealogical Pub. Co, 1978,1969 Vol. VIII.

Authentic History Center, authentichistory.com, and correspondence with Michael Shawn Barnes, for photographs of the camouflage of the Boeing aircraft factory complex.

Battle, J. H. *History of Columbia and Montour Counties.* 1887

Behrens, Roy R. "A Chronology of Camouflage: A Pastiche in a Bouillabaisse." Paper presented to the International Camouflage Conference, 2006.

Benton Harbor, Michigan, City Directory, Kimball Publishing, 1896 Benton Harbor, Michigan

Billmeyer Cemetery in Montour County, Pennsylvania

Bradsby, H. C. *History of Bradford County Pennsylvania.* 1891

Brown, James V. Library, Williamsport, Pennsylvania, local history collection.

Burdick, Lewis D. Handwritten and typed notes to Dewitt Clinton Wilcox.

Canton Ohio, City Directories

Child, Hamilton. *History of McDonough, New York: Gazetteer and Business Directory of Chenango County, New York, for 1869-70.* Syracuse, New York, 1869

Connecticut Historical Society, *The Record of Connecticut Men in the Military and Naval Service During the War of the Revolution, 1775-1783.*

Crafton, Donald. *Before Mickey: The Animated Film 1898-1928.* Cambridge, Massachusetts, 1982.

Cutter, William Richard, ed. *New England Families, genealogical and memorial; a record of the achievements of her people in the making of commonwealths and the founding of a nation,* Volume III.

Cutter, William Richard. *Genealogical and Family History of Central New York*

DAR Lineage Records: Miss Myra Louise Shattuck 67105, DAR Vol 113

P. 209 # 112641 Mrs Anna Foote Eccleston Gibbs: Descendants of Corp. Job Willcox (1743-1808)

Davis, William W. H. *History of Northampton County, Pennsylvania.* 1877

Decker, Gene. *Logan County (Oklahoma) History 1889-1977*

Detroit, Michigan, *City Directories*

Detroit Edison Company, original recipe cards from the collection of Joyce Graff.

Detroit Institute of Art, Research Library and Archives, records of their Artists-Craftsmen Exhibitions.

Dobson, John Blyth. "Genealogy Page of John Blythe Dobson." A nicely researched and referenced site including the Wilcox line. http://cybrary.uwinnipeg.ca/people/dobson/genealogy/

Emporia (Kansas) *Weekly Republican* Newspaper, Emporia, Kansas

Emporia (Kansas) *Daily Gazette,* Emporia, Kansas

FaFantasie, Glenn W., ed., *The Correspondence of Roger Williams.* 1988, vol. I.

Family Photographs and memorabilia collected and preserved by Harry Wilcox Sr., Warren Wilcox, Harry Wilcox, and many others. From the papers of Dr. Harry H. Wilcox Jr.

Fisk, Jane Fletcher. "Edward Wilcox of Lincolnshire and Rhode Island"

Fleischer, Richard. *Out of the Inkwell: Max Fleischer and the Animation Revolution.* Lexington, Kentucky, 2005.

Flock's Brewery, Williamsport. Correspondence and photos of memorabilia from Shawn Flock, whose ancestor Henry Jacob Flock came to America from Prussia in the mid-1800's, moved to Williamsport and bought the city brewery. The business stayed in the family until the 1940's. flockweb.com

Franklin Center Christian Church Cemetery, Franklin, Bradford Co. Pennsylvania.

Gabler, Neil. *Walt Disney: The Triumph of American Imagination.* New York, 2006.

Gaustad, Edwin. *Liberty of Conscience: Roger Williams in America.* 1999.

Gazette & Bulletin Newspaper. Williamsport, Lycoming Co., Pennsylvania.

Graff, Joyce W. and June Freed Wilcox. *A Freed Family History.* Baltimore, 1981.

Grit Newspaper. Williamsport, Pennsylvania. Microfilm at James V. Brown Library; some paper copies at Taber Museum, Lycoming County Historical Society

Harmony Cemetery in Milton, Pennsylvania

Hinke, William John. *Life and Letters of the Rev. John Phillip Boehm.*

Hinke, William John. *Pennsylvania German Pioneers.*

History of Chenango and Madison Counties, New York: with illustrations and biographical sketches of some to its prominent men by James H. Smith. Syracuse, N.Y. 1880

History of McHenry County, Illinois.

History of Tioga County, Pennsylvania. New York, 1883.

History of the Town of North Kingston, Rhode Island. From the Town website.

Hoffman, W. J., M.D. "According to the Folk-lore of the Pennsylvania Germans." *Journal of American Folklore,* 1888.

Judge Magazine, 1905 issue, reprinted with permission from graphicwitness.com

Keil, George, ed. *1892 Medical and Dental Registry Directory and Intelligencer for Pennsylvania, New Jersey, and Delaware.* Philadelphia, 1892.

Leybourne, Kit and John Canemaker, *The Animation Book,* 1979, 1998.

Linn, John Blair. *Annals of Buffalo Valley, Pennsylvania.*

Lycoming County Historical Society, original research.

Maplewood Cemetery Record, Emporia, Kansas.

Meginness, John F. *History of Lycoming Co. Pennsylvania,* 1892

Military records for the various wars, through printed sources and ancestry.com

Milton Cemetery in Milton, Pennsylvania

Moriarty, G. Andrews. Citing "One Branch of the Rhode Island Wilcox Family," TAG 19 (1942).

New England Historic Genealogical Society, v147 p188 (Apr 1993)

New England Historic Genealogical Society, "Vital Records of Rhode, Island, 1636-1850" 2002 http://www.newenglandancestors.org/

Newark, New Jersey, City Directories

Newark, Tim. *Camouflage.* Imperial War Museum, London, 2007. Reproduction of two paintings licensed from the IWM. Licenses as noted in the captions.

Notes from Carole Joiner

Notes from Daniel Clinton Wilcox

Notes from Harold Robinson

Notes from Harry Hammond Wilcox, Jr.

Notes from Lou Jean Rehn

Notes from Lynn Gay Wilcox

Notes from Mark Richner

Notes from Michael Anthony Catrambone

Osborne, Martha Scott. *Wilcox/Wilcoxson Families of New England,* Heritage Books, Inc 1990.

Patton (Davidson), Alfreda. *David Kramm His Ancestors and Descendants.* IAD Printing Services, York, Pennsylvania, 1978.

Peri, Don. *Working with Walt: Interviews with Disney Artists.* 2008.

"Precautionary Camouflage," U.S.Government printing office, 1943.

Reit, Seymour. *Masquerade: The Amazing Camouflage Deceptions of World War II.* New York, 1978.

"The Rhode Island Historical Cemeteries Transcription Project Index" http://www.rootsweb.com/~rigenweb/cemetery/

Rhode Island Historical Society. "Early Records of the Town of Portsmouth," Providence, RI, 1901.

Richner, Mark E. and Brian R. Mathias, "Tracking the Fate of Private John Richner, a Pennsylvania Volunteer in the Civil War." *The Journal of the Lycoming County Historical Society,* 44:1-2, 2008.

Robinson, Caroline E. "The Hazard Family of Rhode Island, 1635-1894." Boston: Printed for the author, 1895.

Savage, James. "A Genealogical Dictionary of the First Settlers of New England" by James Savage. Pub. Boston, 1860-1862; v4

Sexton, John L., Jr. *History of Tioga County, Pennsylvania.* New York, 1883.

Sims, Lydel, "Assignment Memphis" transcribed from the original clipping from the *Memphis Commercial Appeal,* July 21, 1977.

Sloane, Eric. *Camouflage Simplified,* New York, 1942.

Stanley, Roy M. II. *To Fool a Glass Eye: Camouflage versus Photoreconnaissance in World War II.* Washington, D.C., 1998.

The Topeka *Daily State Journal.* Topeka, Kansas.

Tice, Joyce M. Tri-counties Genealogy & History, joycetice.com

Tioga Eagle Newspaper, Wellsboro, Pennsylvania.

Torrey, Clarence A. "New England Marriages Prior To 1700" As found on NEHGS CD-ROM, Boston, 2001

Torrey, Clarence A. "Stephen Gates of Hingham, Lancaster and Cambridge, Mass, and Some of his Descendants." *Genealogies of Connecticut Families from the New England Historical and Genalogical Register.* Reprinted for Clearfield Company Inc. by Genealogical Publishing Co. Inc. Baltimore, Maryland 1998, 2006.

United States Patent Office, filing for Patent number 740,962.

Van Auken, Robin, ed.. *Sunday Grit: A Newspaper Legacy,* published by the Williamsport Sun-Gazzett, 2008.. Photographs reprinted with permission of the author.

West Franklin Cemetery in Bradford County, Pennsylvania

Wheeler, Richard Anson, born 1817. *History of the town of Stonington, county of New London, CT, from its first settlement in 1649 to 1900,* with a genealogical register of Stonnington , Mystic, Conn., 1966

Wilbour, Benjamin Frankiln. *Little Compton Families,* Little Compton Historical Society, Little Compton, Rhode Island 1967

Wilcox Cemetery on North Tyner Road, Chenango County, New York

Wilcox/Willcox Family File in the Genealogy Room in the Norwich Public Library, Norwich, New York. Notes for Hopson Wilcox

Wilcox/Willcox Family File in the Genealogy Room in the Norwich Public Library, Norwich, New York. Notes on the Ancestry of Henry H. Wilcox, Jr., 1954. Facts about Edward Wilcox and son, Stephen being copied from Wm. Richard Cutter's *Genealogical and Family History of Central New York,* Vol. III, Pages 1436-6: most of the balance from various issues of the Magazine of Genealogy and Family History entitled "Your Ancestors," published by Harry Johnston, of Buffalo, who has compiled a "Genealogy of Edward Wilcox of Rhode Island."

Wilcox, Harry H. Sr., family history notebooks.

Wilcox, Harry H. Sr. original art works are all privately held and are reprinted with permission.

Wilcox, Harry H. Jr., family history notebooks and research.

Wilcox, Harry H. Jr. original art works are all privately held and reprinted with permission.

Wilcox, Harry H. Jr, "Histology of the Skin and Hair of the Adult Chincilla." *The Anatomical Record,* 108:3, November 1950.

Wilcox, Harry H. Jr., "Pelvic Musculature of the Loon, Gavia Immer." Doctoral dissertation University of Michigan, Ann Arbor, 1947.

Wildwood Cemetery, Williamsport, PA

Will of Job Willcox of Oxford, Chenango Co. New York, 1808: (NY-9-F-118) from the notes from Meredith Alair, Jr.

Williamsport High School Yearbook, 1935. James V. Brown Library.

Williamsport, Pennsylvania City Directories

Index

Note: Women are indexed under their maiden names as well as their married names. Names shown in parentheses are future married names.

www.ingramcontent.com/pod-product-compliance
Lightning Source LLC
Chambersburg PA
CBHW072131170526
45158CB00004BA/1325